THE UWI PRESS BIOGRAPHY SERIES

Douglas Hall, *Editor*

The University of the West Indies Press invites the submission of work to be considered for publication in this biography series. We recognize the need to record the lives and achievements of people of the Caribbean, but we would not exclude biographical accounts of expatriates who have lived and worked long and hard with us to our mutual advantage.

The series will not be limited to accounts of those who, by whatever means, have achieved wide acclaim or notoriety. Far more numerous than the famous are the many individuals who, by stern and skillful performance in the fields, the workshops, the marketplaces, and in the service of their compatriots have contibuted much but remain unrecognized. This series is also for accounts of them, and is dedicated to the solid contributions of the unsung.

1 A Man Divided: Michael Garfield Smith
Jamaican Poet and Anthropologist 1921–1993
DOUGLAS HALL

2 Law, Justice and Empire
The Colonial Career of John Gorrie 1829–1892
BRIDGET M. BRERETON

3 White Rebel
The Life and Times of T.T. Lewis
GARY LEWIS

4 Bechu
'Bound Coolie' Radical in British Guiana, 1894–1901
CLEM SEECHARAN

5 Demerara Doctor
Confessions and Reminiscences of a Self-taught Physician
GEORGE GIGLIOLI

BECHU

'Bound Coolie' Radical in British Guiana 1894–1901

Clem Seecharan

*Introductory Essay
by
Basdeo Mangru*

THE UNIVERSITY OF THE WEST INDIES PRESS
Barbados • Jamaica • Trinidad and Tobago

The University of the West Indies Press
1A Aqueduct Flats Mona
Kingston 7 Jamaica WI

©1999 by Clem Seecharan
All rights reserved. Published 1999
Printed in Canada
ISBN 976-640-071-7

03   02   01   00   99   5   4   3   2   1

CATALOGUING IN PUBLICATION DATA

Seecharan, Clem.
 Bechu: 'bound coolie' radical in British Guiana,
1894-1901 / Clem Seecharan

 p. cm. – (The UWI Press Biography Series)
 Includes bibliographical references.
 ISBN: 976-640-071-7
 1. Bechu. 2. Indentured servants – Guyana – Biography.
 3. East Indians – Guyana – Biography. 4 East Indians –
 Guyana – History 5. Guyana – Biography.
 F2391.E2S44   1999   988.1   dc 20

Set in Adobe Garamond, 10.5/14.25
Book and cover design by Alan Ross

Cover illustration: "Mogul", Rex Dixon 1999, Indian ink and crayon on paper.
From the collection of Dr Patricia Mohammed.

In memory of Daddy
(1927–1997)

CONTENTS

Preface ix

PART 1: INTRODUCTORY ESSAY
BECHU: THE VOICE OF CONSCIENCE
1

PART 2: SECTION A
BECHU: THE INDEFATIGABLE GADFLY
13

CHAPTER ONE
Forces which Shaped a Bengali Radical: the Indian Context
17

CHAPTER TWO
The Guianese Environment in the Early 1890s
and the Promptings of Bechu's Radicalism
24

CHAPTER THREE
Bechu's Letters in the Context of the Guianese Environment:
Bechu under Indentureship, 1894–1897
33

CHAPTER FOUR
Bechu's Letters in the Context of the Guianese Environment:
Bechu in Freedom, 1897–1901 – Bechu vs the Plantocracy
48

CHAPTER FIVE
Bechu and the Destitute 'Coolies':
the Achievement of Ghurib Das
61

CHAPTER SIX
Bechu vs his 'Protectors'
67

Contents

CHAPTER SEVEN
The Queen vs Bechu: the Libel Case, 1898–1899
73

NOTES TO SECTION A
81

PART 2: SECTION B
BECHU: HIS LETTERS AND THEIR CONTEXT
97

CHAPTER ONE
The Emergence of a 'Bound Coolie' Radical:
Bechu, the Shootings at Plantation Non Pareil, and 'Langton'
98

CHAPTER TWO
Bechu and the Norman Commission, February 1897
119

CHAPTER THREE
Bechu and his Critics: Personal Attacks
132

CHAPTER FOUR
Unmasking the Plantocracy:
Bechu, Indentureship and 'King Sugar'
152

CHAPTER FIVE
Bechu, the Salvation Army and Derelict 'Coolies' in Georgetown,
with Special Reference to the Work of Ghurib Das
257

CHAPTER SIX
Bechu and his Challenge to Colonial Authorities
288

Bibliography   306
Index   309

PREFACE

In 1995 I introduced a course, "The Indian Experience in the Caribbean", at the University of North London, where we have the most comprehensive undergraduate programme in Caribbean Studies in Britain. It was the first time a course exclusively on Indians in the Caribbean was offered in this country. This came as a surprise to my students, but I recalled that up to ten years ago, when I taught at the University of Guyana, and even later when I was at the University of Warwick, I personally lacked the confidence to introduce such a course because of the paucity of scholarly material. The Indian Caribbean experience was still marginal to Caribbean historiography.

It is to the credit of scholars such as Frank Birbalsingh, Bridget Brereton, Kusha Haraksingh, the late Chandra Jayawardena, K.O. Laurence, Walton Look Lai, Basdeo Mangru, Brian Moore, Ralph Premdas, Marianne Ramesar, Brinsley Samaroo, Verene Shepherd, Kelvin Singh, Steven Vertovec, and Donald Wood that they have published what now constitutes a body of solid scholarship on Indians in the Caribbean. Mangru, whose introductory essay appears in this book, has been a prolific contributor since the early 1980s. His work has been a pillar of scholarship and a beacon to me. The following four doctoral theses from the 1970s – pathfinders in Indian Caribbean historiography – also profoundly shaped my perspective:

(i) Lesley M. Potter, "Internal migration and resettlement of East Indians in Guyana, 1870–1920", PhD Thesis, McGill University, 1975;

(ii) Gerad Tikasingh, "The establishment of the Indians in Trinidad, 1870–1900", PhD Thesis, University of the West Indies, St Augustine, Trinidad, 1976;

(iii) Dale Bisnauth, "The East Indian immigrant society in British Guiana, 1891–1930", PhD Thesis, University of the West Indies, Mona, Jamaica, 1977;

(iv) Tyran Ramnarine, "The growth of the East Indian community in British Guiana, 1880–1920", DPhil Thesis, University of Sussex, 1977.

I hope that these could soon be revised and published; Brij Lal's pioneering work on Fiji, *Girmitiyas: The Origins of the Fiji Indians* (1983), which remains the best account of the origins of most Indians in the Caribbean, merits republication. Arnold Thomas' recently completed monograph on Indians in St Vincent also should be published.

I am indebted to Tyran Ramnarine, whose celebration of Bechu, the articulate 'bound coolie' radical in British Guiana, fired my imagination as I read his thesis at the UWI Library (St Augustine) in 1981. Bechu stayed with me. In 1995, I introduced him to my class in a tentative way, aware of my limited knowledge of the man. However, he quickly claimed the imagination of my students. Although I was gathering fragments, groping towards an estimate of this extraordinary indentured labourer, the lacuna was evident. This book is an effort to assess the man's unique contribution as an advocate of the Indian people's grievances in British Guiana 100 years ago, especially after he had appeared before the West India Royal Commission (the Norman Commission), on 1 February 1897. His combative letters to the press are assessed and reproduced in conjunction with a range of documentary evidence of their context, in order to comprehend Bechu and his times. I hope these documents inspire others to further research.

I wish to thank Professor Alistair Ross, the former Director of Research in the Humanities Faculty at the University of North London, and my colleagues on the History subcommittee, for their unfailing generosity in providing money and a sabbatical for me to research and write this book. I must also thank my friends and mentors, Professor Denis Judd and Dr Kathryn Castle, whose generosity of spirit and example have inspired my work. Helen Nelson has done an excellent job in preparing this book for publication. Sam Horne helped in a multitude of ways. My wife, Chris, is a constant inspiration.

Finally, to my friends and colleagues, Rita Christian, Jonathan Moore and Andrew Wright, 'Cheers!', for the good times away from this project.

Clem Seecharan
Caribbean Studies
University of North London
1 April 1997

PART 1: INTRODUCTORY ESSAY

BECHU: THE VOICE OF CONSCIENCE

BASDEO MANGRU

The plantation, with its rigorous discipline, authoritarian management and radical polarization of its population, has been the locus of much of the 160-year-old history of the Indians in the Caribbean. It was a history "rooted in blood and brutality",[1] for the plantation system was designed primarily to humiliate and subjugate workers to the will of the planters and to create a sense of helplessness and dependence similar to slavery. This history was punctuated by accommodation and resistance in the form of strikes, riots, beating of subordinate managerial staff and such inwardly directed aggression as suicide, maiming and deliberately creating ulcers in order to remain in hospital. The riots were largely spontaneous and unorganized as no indigenous leader emerged from the ranks of these exploited workers to articulate their grievances. It was not until the close of the nineteenth century that the spirited Bechu defied the authorities by consistently attacking the iniquities of the indenture system. This essay analyses primarily the memorandum and testimony of this redoubtable fighter before the 1897 West India Royal Commission appointed to investigate the threatened extinction of the sugar industry in the Caribbean.

Indian immigrant workers introduced into the Caribbean in the indenture period (1838–1917) were recruited largely from the north-western provinces and Oudh (modern Uttar Pradesh) in north India and from the Madras Presidency in south India. Unlike other immigrant groups imported after emancipation to supplement the unmalleable ranks of the labour force, Indian workers landed in British Guiana under a host of disabilities. For the first time in their lives many had ventured beyond the confines of their villages and the voyage must have been quite traumatic. Besides, they were the only immigrant group required to carry 'passes' to establish their identity, which made them vulnerable to bullying by creole[2] policemen. Although many possessed usable skills, they were generally labelled illiterate and deemed physically incapable of strenuous exertion under rigorous conditions. Their extreme poverty, alien origin and ignorance of the English language, a prerequisite to any form of political activity, placed them at a grave disadvantage at magistrate's courts. Consequently, they had a tendency to overact their case and embellish their ignorance with falsehood, for which they were invariably branded "congenital liars".[3] They were also largely unfamiliar with the soil, climate and type of occupation which in India was governed by the demands of the seasons. The terms on which indentured Indians entered the colonial society automatically relegated them to the lowest status. The fact is that they were all categorized as unskilled, bound workers turned into semislaves. In short, both politically and socially, the status of the indentured Indian was "nil".

In contrast, political and economic power was comprehensively monopolized by a minority white elite. Their powerful, influential position stemmed from a strong lobby at Whitehall and a "curious" constitution which was neither a Crown Colony nor a representative system of government but a travesty of both.[4] Consequently, these saccharine despots used their entrenched position to pass legislation which tended to emasculate indentured workers and subordinate all interests to those of sugar. Thus as indenture developed in postemancipation British Guiana, it displayed many of the features of slavery, as Chief Justice Joseph Beaumont (1863–68) noted in his revealing book, *The New Slavery*:

> This is not a question of more or less, of this or that safeguard, of an occasional defect here, or excess there. But it is that of a monstrous, rotten system, rooted upon slavery, grown in its stale soil, emulating its worst abuses, and only the more dangerous because it presents itself under false colours, whereas slavery bore the brand of infamy upon its forehead.[5]

The dominant position of the plantocracy contrasted sharply with the powerlessness of labour. Throughout the nineteenth century, hardly any Indian leader emerged to champion the rights of the indentured workers or organize protests on an all-estate or national level. There were several reasons why Indian leadership was stymied during this period. The majority of indentured Indians belonged to the lower and middling castes and few had experience of life beyond the limited confines of their villages. The *kayashtas* (literary castes) who could provide leadership were few, largely because of a ban in 1872 on the importation of high castes, who were accused of fomenting unrest on the estates.[6] The mechanism of control under the system, the pass laws and the use of the courts to intimidate and coerce workers, all tended to stifle the emergence of indigenous leaders. The potential revolutionaries, like 'drivers' (*sirdars*), were largely co-opted into the system through lucrative jobs and influential positions. Some who were disposed to air workers' grievances only provided "lackey-leadership"[7] as their interests were closely identified with those of the planters. The frequent use of transfers and eviction notices tended to serve as a warning to those disposed to champion the interests of workers. The absence of institutional structures within the indentured community and the isolation of Indians on the estates scattered throughout the sugar belt, also deterred labour mobilization and organization for collective action. Despite these various constraints, one Bengali of mettle launched such a scathing attack on indentureship that it was tantamount to an indictment of the whole system.

Bechu, a *kurmi* (agricultural caste) from Calcutta, was the only indentured Indian to produce a memorandum and testify before the West India Royal Commission. Orphaned at an early age, Bechu received no formal education but was schooled by a Mrs Cameron, "a white lady missionary".[8] In 1894 this resolute Bengali initially enlisted for Trinidad where he was misinformed that the indenture contract was only three years. Through fortuitous circumstances he was shipped instead to British Guiana at the age of 34 and indentured to Plantation Enmore, East Coast Demerara. He claimed he preferred Trinidad and consented to embark for British Guiana only when a bill for food and other miscellaneous expenses, which he could not pay, was presented to him. Bechu described the circumstances of his recruitment: "I was in reduced circumstances, and I met a recruiter who told me he would put me in the way of making a living if I was willing to cross the sea."[9]

Indeed, the majority of colonial recruits were enlisted while they were away from their villages and virtually without any visible means of support. It was at this psychological moment that inducements too tempting to resist were held out. Once the intending emigrant was in the clutches of the recruiter through money advances, it was difficult to extricate himself. Judging from the experience of Bechu, once feeding, clothing and other expenses were incurred at the Calcutta depot, the only alternative was colonial emigration or confiscation of such prized personal possessions as *lota* (drinking vessel) and *dupatta* (shawl).

On arrival in British Guiana, Bechu was found physically unfit for strenuous manual labour, particularly cane cutting. He was, accordingly, made an assistant driver, performing such light tasks as "assisting the creole driver weighing and serving out manure and superintending picking of cane-tops".[10] On account of frequent attacks of fever through constant exposure to sun and rain, he was assigned domestic duties at the Manager's house. Here Bechu, like the domestic slave under slavery, availed himself "of every opportunity to read". He thus seemed to have acquired a remarkable knowledge of the immigration system and the plight of indentured workers on estates.

Both the memorandum and testimony of the informed Bechu provided convincing evidence of excessively long hours of field labour. He averred: "I used to go to work at 6 o'clock in the morning. Frequently we have been kept back till 7 or 8 o'clock at night; that is done to this day; the creoles return home late." Labouring for 12 hours or more in the fields, with a short break for meals, seemed to be the rule rather than the exception on most estates. Thirty years earlier the indomitable James Crosby, the longest serving Immigration Agent General (1858–80),[11] had exposed similar practices in the county of Essequibo. This meant that despite ameliorative measures incorporated into the system in the early 1870s, conditions of employment had not changed. In fact, employers were deliberately ignoring the immigration ordinances which limited field labour to seven hours. What was most alarming was that no extra remuneration, other than the stipulated minimum of one shilling or 24 cents a day, was given. Overwork and underpayment thus constituted the main bone of contention in employer-employee relationships. Consequently, resistance rather than accommodation quickly asserted itself on the sugar estates.

It was customary for employers during periods of depression to reduce wages arbitrarily. Official sources often emphasized that workers willingly accepted the reduction because of the critical state of the industry. In the absence of leaders articulating the workers' viewpoint, it is difficult to refute the planters' arguments. But Bechu's testimony, emphasizing that workers often "tamely submitted to the reductions for fear of being buck-shotted", effectively demolished official assertions. Indeed, coercion and intimidation were part and parcel of the strategy of control, and it is only when the workers' position was stated, which was rare indeed, that a true picture could be gleaned.

Bechu's memorandum alluded to another control mechanism – task work – whose impact on the indentured workforce had hitherto not been fully explored. The task, the amount of work determined by the planters following slave emancipation, was measured by what a stalwart African labourer could perform in the allotted time of seven and a half hours. When Indians arrived, the scale was applied to them without taking into consideration that these workers were generally unskilled and that task work was alien to them. Although task work was optional, it was made compulsory on many estates as a means of controlling and punishing recalcitrant workers. According to Bechu, workers "are forced to accept it, and the terms fixed by employers are so hard that it is often the case that a task cannot be completed in less than two days, thus making it 'impossible' for any indentured coolie to earn a shilling *per diem*".[12] Consequently, the majority of indentured workers found it extremely difficult to complete the stipulated five tasks per week which meant a fine or imprisonment or both. Whether the indentured worker was imprisoned depended upon his "behaviour", but certainly his wages would be stopped.

Task work thus endowed employers with a powerful weapon through which they could coerce workers by both lengthening and undervaluing the task. The mandatory nature of task work on estates also showed scant regard by employers for the immigration ordinances. The reluctance of Immigration Agents to investigate and institute prosecutions for such violations enabled employers to ignore the laws at will. Task work also provided employers with a powerful instrument of prosecution to ensure compliance, as evidenced by Bechu: "If a man says he cannot earn a shilling a day, and lays his complaint before the deputy manager, the deputy manager tells the driver to give this man task work, and if he does not finish it, summon him."[13]

Bechu provided considerable insight into the role of drivers on estates. Prone to authoritarianism and perceived as petty tyrants, drivers were utilized by estate management to ensure docility and to extract the maximum amount of work from the labourer. Drivers allocated the tasks, provided lighter work for favourites and punished recalcitrant workers by assigning them weaker partners on stiff, clayey soil. The immigrants' complaints against the arbitrary action of the driver often fell on deaf ears as the overseer depended exclusively on his report for the payment of wages. Workers were often reluctant to retaliate against wage reductions "from fear of these drivers, who keep indentured coolies so under subjection by abuses and threats, that 'outspoken' complaints of that nature are rare". Bechu underlined the power and authority of the estate driver:

> Taking into consideration what occurred at Non Pareil recently, the coolies are really frightened to make any complaints against their employers. The coolies on Plantation Enmore are afraid of being abused by their drivers, and sometimes struck by them. Of course these drivers have a certain number of their own men, who are always on their side, and the coolies are afraid that the drivers will bring trumped-up charges against them if they were to complain.[14]

The influence of estate drivers extended beyond the confines of the cane field. Through their privileged position they were permitted to establish shops, selling commodities consumed by the Indian community. Newly imported Indians invariably fell into the driver's clutches as they were compelled to patronize his shop. The practice of paying wages in a lump sum permitted the driver to deduct arbitrarily money owed by workers for consumer goods supplied on credit. Undoubtedly, the planters were aware of the exploitative tentacles of the driver but preferred not to interfere, for the system was an effective way of maintaining the rigour on estates without earning the resentment of the labour force.

Bechu's incisive memorandum not only confirmed the findings of the Royal Commission of 1870 regarding the abuse of power by drivers, but emphasized the nature and extent of their exploitative practices on estates. The Venn Commission, appointed in 1948 to report on the organization of the sugar industry, also condemned the driver system and advocated the incorporation of a new breed of estate drivers, "educationally capable of controlling and instructing the workforce". Belatedly, it suggested that the title be changed to 'headman' as the term 'driver' was "anachronous and misleading, being attributable to the literal driving, whip in hand, of the slaves by their forerunners".[15] Today, drivers on the Guyanese estates still enjoy privilege and influence but tend to be more sympathetic to the workers; however, the odious title persists.

In the course of his evidence, the astute Bechu exposed the spineless protection provided on his plantation, Enmore, by the Immigration Department through its district agents:

> The Immigration Agent comes round once a month, he is only there for about an hour, and during that time all the coolies are in the field. People who are concerned in family quarrels are simply brought before him by the driver, and he listens to their complaints.[16]

This disclosure was tantamount to an abrogation of the duties of the Immigration Department which stood *in loco parentis* to the indentured community. The brief stay and monthly visit of the Immigration Agent implied that the officer had virtually abandoned his investigative role, which was crucial in documenting planter coercion and neglect. Additionally, Bechu claimed that the officer rarely visited the Enmore estate hospital, and had never gone to the "nigger yard" to inspect dwellings or the state of the drainage system. Neither would he offer advice to newly imported immigrants, listen to industrial grievances or prosecute employers for infractions of the law. In fact, Bechu accused the agent of "curry-favour" with the Manager of Enmore, so much so, that he "succeeded in getting his daughter employment in his house as governess".[17] As in so many instances, this was another case of authority upholding authority.

Ever since the death of Crosby, officers in the Immigration Department seemed afraid or reluctant to prosecute the interests of indentured workers, confining themselves merely to record keeping and routine matters. Gone were the days when the fearless, dedicated Crosby would enter estates, examine paylists, check sanitary conditions in the hospital, listen to complaints and prosecute employers for breaches of the law. The immigrants, too, would approach him with confidence that their grievances would be heard and a speedy redress obtained. Thus, by the late 1890s, indentured workers increasingly began to rely on self-liberating activities for survival.

In his informative memorandum, Bechu raised a very sensitive issue in the immigration camp – "Immoral Relations of Overseers and Managers, in some cases, with Coolie Women". He argued that it was "an open secret that coolie women are in the keeping of overseers". He substantiated his allegation with hard facts:

> I am in a position to state that a fellow shipmate of mine, a Punjabi, was at one time making overtures to a woman with a view to matrimony, but he was deterred from doing so, as he came to hear that she had got in tow with an overseer, who eventually gave her the money to purchase her freedom. I don't recollect the name of the overseer, but the name of the woman is Leloo, and she is at present residing at Pln 'Lusignan', East Coast [Demerara]. This is another ground for discontent and sometimes leads to riots, yet Immigration Agents close their eyes to the matter.[18]

Illicit sexual relations between Indian women and European overseers and managers, and the paucity of women which prevailed in all the recipient sugar colonies, were issues which the 1870 Royal Commission examined in considerable detail. During its tour of the various estates, the Commission cited several cases of cohabitation by overseers and Indian women which not only discredited the whole immigration system but constituted a "secret source of disaffection and disturbances" on estates. The Commission observed:

> The withdrawal of even a single woman from the coolie dwellings to the overseer's lodge is regarded with jealous eyes by her fellow-countrymen; and when it is remembered that any female above childhood is already the actual wife or partner of one of them, it is evident that no surer way could be found of sowing the seeds of discord and riot.[19]

Yet despite threats of fines, nonallotment of new recruits and removal of existing workers from estates, employers generally failed to take ameliorative action. The riots at Non Pareil on the East Coast Demerara in 1896, is a case in point. A confidential report to the Colonial Office disclosed that Acting Manager, Gerad Van Nooten, was cohabiting with an Indian woman, Jamni. The relationship infuriated her husband, Jungali, and others in the indentured community, resulting in a violent clash and the death of five indentured Indians including Jungali. What was alarming was that both the manager and the attorney not only condoned the relationship, which they regarded as private, but attempted to exonerate Van Nooten.[20]

From the second decade of the twentieth century sexual immorality and the degraded position of Indian women in the importing sugar colonies became the flashpoint of Indian politics. The notion that Indian women were leading immoral lives stirred the Indian nation which set great store by the chastity of its womenfolk. The issue galvanized Indian nationalists into a massive anti-indenture campaign which culminated in its demise in 1917.

Among the main contentions of African leaders in British Guiana in the last quarter of the nineteenth century were that there was a superabundance of labour on the estates, that immigration had made the cost of living unwarrantably high and that it had served its purpose and should be discontinued. The planters vehemently refuted these arguments and consistently voiced the need for state-aided immigration to resuscitate the sugar industry. Bechu's memorandum provided new insight into this debatable issue. He was convinced that the 100,000 Indians in the colony would supply adequately the labour needs of the 64 functioning estates. However, he emphasized that the planters were reluctant to employ reindentured workers, preferring instead to repatriate time-expired immigrants and introduce "half-starved unacclimatized men" to replace them. By all accounts, this was not sound economic policy since raw recruits had to be acclimatized at considerable expense. Besides, they were subject to attacks of malaria which was endemic in the colony. Bechu's memorandum provided the hidden reason – reindentured men "know the 'ropes' and will hardly allow themselves to be cheated out of their rights, whereas a newly arrived simpleton, in his blissful ignorance, will have to grin and take what is given to him".[21] Employers were so engrossed with labour manipulation and control that they were even prepared to evict seasoned hands from their ranges to accommodate the new arrivals.[22] Consequently, they continued to flood the labour market, although the available evidence showed an oversupply of labour and an insufficiency of work.

Bechu: The Voice of Conscience

Bechu consistently exposed the planters' tyranny and neglect in the local press. His letter in *The Daily Chronicle*, highlighting the tragic case of Bhagri, commenced thus: "So few instances of 'man's inhumanity to man' on our sugar estates find their way to your columns that I beg you will, in the interests of justice, give publicity to the case I am about to relate which occurred recently on a plantation on the East Coast, not 12 miles away from this centre of civilization [Georgetown]."[23] Bechu charged that Bhagri, who landed from the immigrant vessel *Avoca* in 1894, was indentured to Plantation Cove and John, an estate on the East Coast Demerara managed by the martinet, Frederick C.S. Bascom. Bhagri reported sick and sought treatment at the estate hospital. The sicknurse "hunted him out" on the grounds that he was not sick. The next day he was examined by the Government Medical Officer and admitted to the hospital. The following morning the sicknurse, acting on the orders of Bascom and without the knowledge of the doctor, discharged the patient and sent him back to the fields. Bechu's letter concluded on a rather sombre note: "That, however, was the last occasion the estate authorities could prosecute the poor fellow, for happily death came to his rescue and released him from the grip of his oppressors."[24] Consequently, Bechu called for a "strict enquiry" to investigate the circumstances leading to the death of Bhagri.

Bechu's damning accusation was reminiscent of those of William Des Voeux, a Stipendiary Magistrate in British Guiana in the 1860s, which produced a high-powered inquiry into the workings of the indenture system. In 1869, Des Voeux had accused medical officers of "cruel neglect of duty and unworthy truckling to the planting interests", and the planters of "cruelty, falsehood and perversion of justice".[25] He charged, additionally, that estate managers unilaterally discharged patients from the hospital during convalescence and forced them into the fields. His various accusations ruffled the feathers of the "higher class of the inhabitants" who considered the allegations libellous.[26]

Bechu's exposure also infuriated the Colonial Office and the planting interests, as it constituted a grave indictment of the indenture system. A Colonial Office minute read: "I believe Bechu story is a lie." Another official penned: "He is a very clever high caste man and makes points: but not to be believed."[27] Consequently, the planters and colonial officers determined that he be censured as his *exposé* could produce an unstable employer-employee relationship. Bechu was charged with writing and publishing "a certain defamatory libel" impeaching the conduct of Bascom to deprive him of "his good name and reputation, and bring him into public contempt".[28] Indicted for libel, Bechu was tried twice, but he was acquitted after two inconclusive verdicts (see Chapter Seven).

Not only did the planting interests conduct a campaign of vilification against Bechu, but it seemed that they wanted to silence him as well, for he had become the fly in the ointment. Although Bechu was a *kurmi*, he was accorded high caste status, for the prevailing notion was that only high caste people fomented unrest in the indentured community. His caste elevation was thus a subtle attempt to deport him without arousing criticism at Whitehall and in the India Office. In fact, a precedent had already been created a decade earlier when the *Daily Chronicle* gleefully reported:

> The Immigration Agent General's action with reference to a Brahmin connected with the Reliance disturbance is much applauded. The Immigration Agent General has heard that this person was persuading the coolies not to return to the estate, whereupon he was shipped to India sans caste, sans money, sans everything. Bravo Mr Alexander.[29]

One of the problems in studying the experiences of unlettered people is that they have left few accounts of life on the plantations, while in the documentary sources their perspective is often distorted. As such, information filtering through the Colonial Office from British Guiana and other sugar colonies tended to give the impression that indentured workers were happy and contented with their employment and that nothing was inherently wrong with the system. It was only when disturbances occurred, or the system was condemned by influential colonial officers, that the Colonial Office would assume its trusteeship role and question the effectiveness and adequacy of protective colonial legislation. Although Bechu's various allegations did not produce an official enquiry, they did stir concern locally and at the Colonial Office. Barely two years in the colony, the unflinching Bechu seemed to have an encyclopaedic knowledge of the iniquities of the indenture system which suggested that he was a voracious reader. While his observations were confined to estates on the East Coast Demerara, such conditions seemed to prevail throughout the sugar belt where workers were seen merely as animated machines.

Bechu's criticism and sustained attacks are invaluable in studying the experiences of indentured workers. He not only articulated the powerlessness of labour, but buttressed the allegations of exploitation and brutality made by Beaumont, Des Voeux and Crosby in the 1860s. Such charges effectively demolished the planters' arguments of care and protection. In such a planter dominated society, any official, much less an indentured worker, who championed the rights of immigrants or criticized the workings of the indenture system was bound to incur the odium of this powerful elite: Bechu's vigorous and sustained criticisms could lead to the demise of Indian indentureship, a situation which the planting interests were not prepared to tolerate.

NOTES

1. See C.B. Jagan, "Keynote address", *The East Indian Diaspora*, T. Depoo (ed), (New York: 1993), 13.
2. The term refers to those of African descent born in British Guiana (Guiana).
3. For details of the disabilities of immigrants at court, see Basdeo Mangru, *Benevolent Neutrality: Indian Government Policy and Labour Migration to British Guiana, 1854–1884* (London: Hansib 1987), 158–62.
4. For an analysis of the working of this constitution, see Cecil Clementi, *A Constitutional History of British Guiana* (London: Macmillan 1937).
5. Joseph Beaumont, *The New Slavery: An Account of the Indians and Chinese Immigrants in British Guiana* (London: W. Ridgway 1871), 14.
6. See CO 111/395 Scott to Kimberley, no. 27, 26 February 1873.
7. See Hugh Tinker, *A New System of Slavery: The Export of Indian Labour Overseas, 1830–1920* (London: Oxford University Press 1974), 226.
8. PP 1898, L, [C. 8657], 75.
9. Ibid, 76.
10. Ibid, 75.
11. For details of the colonial career of this redoubtable fighter, see Basdeo Mangru, "James Crosby: hero, protector, friend of Indians in Guyana", *Indo-Caribbean Review*, Volume 1, No.1 (1994), 29–65.
12. PP 1898, L, [C 8657], 131.
13. Ibid, 75.
14. Ibid. The Non Pareil episode is discussed later.
15. *Report of a Commission of Enquiry into the Sugar Industry of British Guiana*, (J.A. Venn, chairman), Col No. 249, (London: HMSO 1949), 11–13.
16. PP 1898, L, [C 8657], 75.
17. Ibid, 131.
18. Ibid.
19. PP 1871, XX, [393], 86–87.
20. See CO 111/488 Cavendish Boyle to Joseph Chamberlain, no. 353, 11 November 1896; CO 111/489 Hemming to Chamberlain, 26 November 1896.
21. PP 1898, L, [C 8657], 131.
22. See Gov W. Young to M. Hicks Beach, no. 185, 29 July 1879.
23. *The Daily Chronicle*, 13 September 1898.
24. Ibid.
25. Great Britain. Colonial Office. Murdoch to Rogers, 9 February 1870. NAG (National Archives, Guyana).
26. Gov John Scott to Earl Granville, no. 67, 31 May 1870. NAG.

27. See CO 111/516 Colonial Office (Minute), 7 June 1899.
28. *The Daily Chronicle*, 1 November 1898.
29. *The Daily Chronicle*, 3 August 1889.

PART 2: SECTION A

BECHU: THE INDEFATIGABLE GADFLY

CLEM SEECHARAN

> ... only one East Indian in the whole nineteenth century appeared as a potential leader [in British Guiana]. He was unique in that he was not of the local East Indian middle class, and he championed the cause of the downtrodden sugar worker. His name was Bechu, a Bengali who came to the colony as an indentured immigrant. He became the first East Indian to address a Royal Commission [in February 1897]. Not surprisingly he did not obtain his early education in British Guiana. He was educated in India by a missionary. His public criticisms, in the newspapers, of the sugar planters and his defence of the labourers brought him into conflict with the planting authorities (Ramnarine 1977: 233).

Until Alan Adamson, the economic historian, discovered Bechu in the early 1960s,[1] this extraordinary champion of Indian sugar plantation workers in British Guiana between 1896 and 1901, had eluded local Indian compilers of histories of Indians in the colony. Neither Peter Ruhomon nor Dwarka Nath, whose books were published in 1947 and 1950 respectively,[2] mentioned him. Yet, no indentured labourer in the Caribbean was equipped to challenge colonial society in the manner Bechu did. He was a man of amazing intellect, sardonic wit and biting subtlety of exposition, with solid principles, often to the point of inflexibility; his fearlessness and consistency of purpose were exemplary.

Bechu scrutinized the attitudes of the plantocracy and various colonial authorities, especially the Immigration Agent General and his district

Immigration Agents – the designated 'protectors' of Indians – in numerous letters to the liberal newspaper, *The Daily Chronicle*. He exposed one injustice or another, unveiling their complacency and complicity and their frequently specious rationalizations. In his first letter to *The Daily Chronicle*, on 1 November 1896, following the fatal shooting of five and the wounding of 59 Indian workers at Plantation Non Pareil on 13 October, he apprehended the Indian condition succinctly:

> In this colony . . . an agreement appears to be binding on one side only, for we constantly see coolies being brought up for 'neglecting to attend work', for 'not completing the task', and for such trivial breaches of contract, but not in a single instance have I seen a 'protector' [an Immigration Agent] charge an employer for not fulfilling his part of the contract towards an indentured immigrant. Is this fair play?

Bechu's forthrightness was even more evident when he was invited to appear before the West India Royal Commission in 1897, the first Indian in the Caribbean to be so honoured. Although still a 'bound coolie', an indentured labourer at Plantation Enmore, East Coast Demerara, he deprecated the conduct of estate authorities as well as the Immigration Agent in his district. In his memorandum to the Commission, he underlined the inviolability of the principle that justice must always be seen to be done. He objected to one glaring transgression on his estate, implicating his protector:

> Besides taking no interest in the coolies, whose protector he is supposed to be, he is on such friendly terms with the Manager as to have succeeded in getting his daughter employment in his house as governess. How is it possible, under the circumstance, to receive justice at his hands?[3]

The Manager of Enmore, G.W. Bethune, remarked that Bechu had assumed "a defiant mood" since his first letter was published, but he left the assault on Bechu's new role as a radical critic to H.J. Gladwin, Bechu's protector. Gladwin wrote promptly to the Immigration Agent General:

> He shows his gratitude for the excessive kindness with which he has been treated, by these silly effusions of which the point lies not so much in the statements themselves, as in their intention. I doubt if any other Manager would have been so kind to Bechu as Mr Bethune has been and the man's ingratitude is the more conspicuous.[4]

Bechu was becoming a potent symbol, the embodiment of a rebellious spirit. His articulation and dramatization of the 'coolie's' plight on the plantations, before the Commission, inspired quickly such a severe critical focus on the plantocracy and its allies, that the Governor, Sir Augustus Hemming, promptly acceded to Bechu's request to commute his indentureship, in February 1897. The Manager of Enmore, understandably, concurred with this measure: Bechu's radicalism collided with the sugar estates' notion of the docile, malleable 'coolie', although the latter, especially after the 1870s, was essentially fictive.

But Bechu could not be coaxed into silence. Indeed now, as a resident of Georgetown, he could easily walk to the office of *The Daily Chronicle* with his letters; he did not need postage stamps. Between March 1897 and February or March 1901, when he left British Guiana, his provocative letters were a fount of embryonic democracy, in a society where the franchise was severely restricted and the planters' power to shape policy was still considerable. Bechu's letters, often, were a catalyst for debates on the central issues of his day. He was unflappable to threats from the goliaths of privilege and unmindful of his personal security. He was incorruptible and tended to be uncompromising in his pursuit of what he saw as a principle or the truth. Like all pioneers of protest, architects of a new vision, he was not averse to varnishing the truth to dramatize his case; to challenge certainties; to evoke guilt and trouble placid minds.

Bechu's letters addressed the Indian condition in British Guiana from diverse angles: the need to suspend, if not end, indentureship and the merits of re-indenture; the condition of Indians on the estates, especially their wages; the immorality of overseers and the exploitative conduct of the drivers; the limitations of state-sponsored Indian settlements; the prospects of rice cultivation and the futility of sugar monoculture; the partisanship of the protector and the "sugar-coated" government; the despair of destitute Indians in Georgetown; their relationship with Africans. As an unusual "admirer", "a planter of 20 years", observed of Bechu in December 1897: "Most will admit his talent at wielding a pen is far above the ordinary class." Even Sydney Olivier at the Colonial Office, who had encountered him in Georgetown during the Commission's hearings in February 1897, recognized that Bechu was "a very clever high caste man".[5]

The Manager of Plantation Cove and John, however, had no such bouquets for Bechu. As Mangru observes earlier, he brought a libel suit against him because in a letter in *The Daily Chronicle* on 13 September 1898, Bechu allegedly blamed him for the death of a 'bound coolie' who, he claimed, was refused medical attention at the estate's hospital. The protracted case, which was eventually dismissed, won Bechu the admiration of his compatriots, including

Joseph Ruhomon, the colony's first Indian intellectual. To the plantocracy and the colonial authorities, however, he was a gadfly.

In 1900, Bechu came to the defence of an English missionary in British Guiana, the radical nonconformist, Rev H.J. Shirley, who quickly became another gadfly of the plantocracy and their allies. In what one could today characterize as Shirley's "theology of liberation", Bechu had detected a kindred spirit.[6] Between 1896 and 1901, Bechu was irrefutably the most strident custodian of Indian rights in the colony. Who was this man? What ingredients went into the making of his radical temperament?

CHAPTER ONE

Forces which Shaped a Bengali Radical: the Indian Context

Bechu's antecedents are somewhat obscure. Even the colonial authorities found it difficult to unravel the essential truth about this unique 'bound coolie', and Bechu seemed to have cultivated a certain mystique about his origins, apparently revelling in games with those who sought to discover his past in India, mockingly sowing unhelpful frivolities. As early as January 1897, in answer to a planter's query about his identity, he had mischievously appropriated the obnoxious notion of the non-European as the "missing link" between man and ape. He wrote that he was "a queer looking specimen of – it is believed – the human race . . . because when I was (not many years ago) exhibited in the Calcutta 'Zoo', most people, naturalists included, were ready to swear, for true, I was the 'Missing Link'." The planter had enquired further whether Bechu was, indeed, "a real, live, indentured coolie", and he had responded sarcastically: ". . . I am a real, live, animal, and what is more surprising, I am allowed to go about unchained."[7]

Later, in July 1899, even the Immigration Agent General was in a quandary as he scrambled to locate Bechu's Indian background. The Governor of British Guiana, Sir Walter Sendall, informed the Colonial Office that they had failed "to ascertain under what circumstances the man was allowed to pass himself off before the recruiting agents in India". He explained that Bechu had "enlisted under an assumed name, and such particulars as he has stated with reference to his past history have been found on enquiry to be wholly fictitious". This conclusion, however, was based on an old inquiry which the agent in Calcutta, Robert Mitchell, had undertaken following a request by the Immigration Agent General, on 23 December 1896,[8] after Bechu's initial letters to *The Daily Chronicle*. A new line of inquiry informed by some basic information which Bechu had given under oath to the West India Royal Commission, on 1 February 1897,[9] could at least have verified much of substance. Nevertheless, there was merit in the observation that he travelled to the colony under an assumed name and probably concealed his real antecedents in order to be enlisted as an indentured labourer. His real story would have given grounds for suspicion of his motives and disqualified him immediately.

Bechu told Sir Henry Norman, the Chairman of the West India Royal Commission, that he was a Bengali, born in Calcutta around 1860. He repeated this to another member of the Commission, Sir David Barbour. He added that he was orphaned at an early age and was brought up and educated by a "white missionary lady", Miss Cameron, of the Scottish Presbyterian Mission in Calcutta. Bechu remained with her until her death, around 1876, when he was 16. For about 18 years after this he worked with several British "gentlemen" in India, including a Mr Gayford, a missionary, and a Dr Eteson, a brigade surgeon, who was familiar to Sir David Barbour. Bechu said that he had also worked for a Dr Sinclair of Burma and had been to Rangoon and Mandalay. He admitted that he had never done any fieldwork, and claimed that he decided to become an indentured labourer because he was "in reduced circumstances" and a recruiter had persuaded him that he would earn a living if he was "willing to cross the sea".

He crossed the sea in the ship, *Sheila*, and landed in British Guiana on 20 December 1894. Nothing more is known of Bechu's Indian background, but even this sparse account suggests something of the forces which helped shape the rebellious spirit of this unlikely indentured labourer. It is significant that Bechu was an orphan and that his formative years were moulded by a Scottish woman in the context of the Presbyterian Mission. He would not have had the security and the socialization into the certainties of Indian society provided by the joint family, which V.S. Naipaul aptly describes as an institution which "protects and imprisons". Consequently, the constraints fed by responsibilities to the family, and the inhibitions on the spirit engendered by the minutiae of Indian rituals and the consuming demands of festivals and life cycle events, were outside of Bechu's experience. He would have been at the margins of Bengali society, but this peripheral position, in the urban milieu of Calcutta, was not necessarily a disadvantage. It would have been easier for him to be an individual – a rare privilege in Indian society. The pressure to conform, to travel the well-beaten path, would have been substantially less.

Bechu's life was embedded in Christian principles; his letters were frequently laced with Biblical references. Although he claimed to be *kurmi*, an agricultural caste, he was not a Hindu. Indeed, his faith was profoundly shaped by the theology as well as the practical, benevolent work pursued by various Christian denominations in Calcutta. The single-mindedness, so characteristic of Christian missionaries in the Tropics, was probably absorbed by Bechu. His early literacy in English equipped him to read a wide range of literature which was probably available at the Mission. As he remarked to Sir Henry Norman: "I have not been at school, [but] I have tried to avail myself of every opportunity to read and improve my time." After he left the Mission, he continued to work with Europeans of the professional class, so that books were probably always available to him. As his letters reveal, he was an omnivorous reader and digester of even minute details; and in British Guiana, as an indentured, a domestic in the Deputy Manager's house at Plantation Enmore, Bechu never stopped reading: "Even my present employer, Mr Nicholson, has given me permission to read his books whenever I have the time to do so." The Manager of Enmore did indeed confirm that Bechu had access to the reading room in the overseers' house.[10]

It is ironic, but true, that Bechu's Christian principles probably enabled him to be a better Indian in the modern India of the late nineteenth century. He was a product of the British-Indian intellectual encounter, which was most advanced in Calcutta. Bechu was evidently proud of his Bengali heritage. Often, in British Guiana, he would remind his readers of his Bengali origins – a rare feature among indentureds in the Caribbean. In February 1897, when one of his critics quoted an especially disparaging piece from Macaulay, denigrating the Bengali's character,[11] Bechu quickly countered that Bengal had made significant strides since Macaulay's time; it was reshaping itself.[12] Bechu was an exemplification of this – the fruit of an enlightened facet of the colonial encounter. He was shaped by the amalgam of European rationalism and its diverse, critical intellectual tradition, in a creative reconstruction of a positive notion of ancient India. This was what was regenerating a supine, ossified India, giving it self-belief and the confidence to criticize and rebuild itself.

Bechu's Bengali heritage focused on Calcutta, his birthplace. Until 1912 it was the capital of India. It was here that an impressive Anglo-Indian intellectual tradition reflected in the scholarship of some distinguished men – Jones,

Prinsep, Colebrooke, Halhed, Wilkins, Hunter, H.H. Wilson, among others – had flowered since the late eighteenth century in the Asiatic Society of Bengal. In the early years of the nineteenth century, this tradition of research and critical scrutiny began to seep into and reshape Bengal through the College of Fort William and the Bengal Renaissance.[13] The first modern Indian, with the gift of self-analysis and intellectual curiosity in, and magnanimity for, other peoples, was Ram Mohan Roy (1772–1833). A Bengali, his erudition was steeped in this capacious critical vision, a synthesis of European scholarship and notions of a Hinduism confident to renew itself, to deposit some of its abominable excrescences, such as *sati* or the immolation of widows.[14] As D.P. Singhal observes of this refreshing intellectual freedom of Ram Mohan Roy's Bengal, the forerunner of Bechu's Bengal:

> The new spirit of humanism and rationalism stimulated Indian thought and literature enormously. No longer was Indian writing appended to theology, mythology, and scholasticism. No gods and goddesses descended from heaven and played a part in human life. Man now occupied the foremost place, steering his course of life without divine help ... Soon new ideas began to fill old patterns and Indian writers and thinkers were inspired not only by the renewed spirit of humanism but also by the French revolutionary spirit of liberty and equality.[15]

What is of greatest significance to our understanding of the forces which shaped Bechu was the rise in Bengal, by the 1870s–1880s, of an intellectual tradition which fed on the openness, imagination, and the synthesis initiated by Ram Mohan Roy. In the Bengali, Keshab Chandra Sen (1838–84),[16] this tradition of religious reform and social reform bore rich rewards, which seeped into the consciousness of the educated elite, lifting the minds of western-educated men from the agony of self-doubt and inferiority to a questioning, rebellious plane. Without this, India, for so many centuries under foreign rule – Muslim then British – could not have evolved the rudiments of a national purpose, and never have engendered the resurgence of self-criticism and renewal, to build self-confidence to energize itself to challenge British rule.

Another Bengali, Bankim Chandra Chatterjee (1838–94), the first accomplished novelist of the Bengali language and composer of the great patriotic anthem, *Bande Mataram*, was regenerating the Bengali language, adopting the novel as the instrument of Bengali self-examination; he was moulding a new, sharper, more assertive Bengali sensibility.[17] We cannot say whether Bechu read Keshab Chandra Sen or Bankim Chandra Chatterjee, but the publication of the latter's masterpiece of Bengali prose, the anticolonial novel, *Anandamath*, in 1882, would have stirred the patriotic pulse of every literate Bengali. Moreover, the termination of Bankim's services as an official in the colonial administration, a few days after the novel appeared, would have lifted the stature of this work as a symbol of resistance to alien rule and as an epitome of the embryonic quest for self-assertion. This ambivalence to the British tradition was strongest in Bengal; the rebellious spirit became a Bengali trait of the 1880s and 1890s. Bengal was the pulse of the new India.

Rabindranath Tagore (1860–1941), the great Bengali writer and Nobel laureate, was an upper class contemporary of Bechu in Calcutta. He has charted the source of the Bengali ambivalence to the British:

> I was impressed by . . . [the] liberal humanity in the character of the English and thus I was led to set them on the pedestal of my highest respect. This generosity in their national character had not yet been vitiated by imperialist pride . . . During my boyhood days the attitude of the cultured and educated section of Bengal, nurtured on English learning, was charged with a feeling of revolt against . . . [the] rigid regulations of [Hindu] society . . . In place of these set codes of conduct we accepted the ideal of 'civilization' as represented by the British term. In our own family this change of spirit was welcomed for the sake of its sheer rational and moral force and its influence was felt in every sphere of our life . . . Then came the parting of ways, accompanied with a painful feeling of disillusion, when I began increasingly to discover how easily those who accepted the highest truths of civilization disowned them with impunity whenever questions of national self-interest were involved.[18]

Although Bechu was an orphan, he would not have been insulated from this pattern of responses. Indeed, because his life was so enmeshed in, and conditioned by, the superciliousness of many Europeans in India, his skein of emotions was probably taut; his ambivalence was deeper, more magnified; this shaped an even more rebellious spirit.[19] In 1893, the year before Bechu went to British Guiana, this spirit was transported to the West by another of Bechu's great Bengali contemporaries, Swami Vivekananda (1863–1902). His oratory and erudition at the World's Parliament of Religion, in Chicago, enthralled America and ignited a curiosity in the New India. The reverberations were uplifting to all Indians, even the 'coolies' in British Guiana.

Tapan Raychaudhuri has written on Vivekananda's towering role in the regeneration of Hinduism and the young Bengali's appeal in the West. Although he was an advocate of a synthesis between East and West, he would not countenance it if Indian national dignity were vitiated. Vivekananda still recognized a simple "us"/"them" dichotomy between the two worlds, but he gave credit to the West, as Raychaudhuri argues, as "an admirable manifestation of *rajas*, manly vigour". He contrasted this with *tamas*, in which India was mired, "pure inertia and all that is brutish in man".[20]

Jawaharlal Nehru has located Vivekananda's rebellious spirit in the context of his Bengali environment. He underlines his "increasing stress on reason" and his "passionate belief in the freedom of the mind". Vivekananda believed that religion should not be exempt from the scrutiny of reason; indeed, "it is better that mankind should become atheist by following reason", he contended, "than blindly believe in two hundred million gods . . ." Nehru regards this radical outlook as a reaction to the "evils of authority" in India – a reference to unreconstructed Hinduism with its corrosive dogmas.[21]

This passion for reform, to lift what was seen as a mountainous lethargy, also had secular implications. It accelerated as the educated elite with the credentials for admission into the colonial bureaucracy expanded. Here, the indigenous elite was precluded from reaching the summit of their professions by a rigorous aristocracy of skin. Raychaudhuri elaborates:

> The monopoly of ultimate power and the highest status by the ruling race and the consequent exclusion from the same of the entire indigenous population were built into the colonial experience. The white man was the boss. The colour of his skin was the symbol of authority . . . The Indian official could never really hope to reach the highest rungs in the bureaucracy. The perceived arrogance of one's official superiors was a fact of daily experience to men highly regarded in Indian society . . . Anxiety and a sense of inadequacy were inevitable products of a relationship so structured.[22]

In late nineteenth-century Bengal, where the British intellectual tradition had its deepest roots, "a galaxy of brilliant Hindus" had emerged. Here, the anxiety was greatest. Respect for the universal British achievement was intertwined with a severe angst, a self-doubt and a stubborn inferiority complex. This was exacerbated by racial discrimination and imperial arrogance. However, it was this perceptibly superior intellectual tradition which had enabled many Indians to recover and appreciate areas of high achievement in ancient India – art, music, sculpture, writing, etc. Recognition by the ruling race, and the greater antiquity of the Indian achievement, enhanced it. This was the source of self-belief and the incipient political culture.[23] This was the environment which shaped Bechu.

By the 1890s, the annual conferences of the Indian National Congress which was founded in 1885, were an established feature on the political landscape.

Among the foremost leaders of the movement which was still seen essentially as a reformist one – to reform rather than eradicate British rule – was Surendranath Banerjea (1848–1926), a distinguished Bengali, who had been admitted to the Indian Civil Service but was dismissed on a minor charge. Frustration had driven him into politics; in 1876 he had founded the Indian Association of Calcutta, a nationalist organization.[24]

By 1894, therefore, when Bechu left Calcutta, bound for British Guiana, we can safely say that he carried some solid Christian principles, rooted in the notion of justice for all, irrespective of race or creed. He would also have carried the ambivalence towards the British, and the rebellious temperament, already established among his educated, articulate Bengali contemporaries, the *bhadralok*. Like Vivekananda, his temper was shaped by reason and animated by a passion for freedom.[25]

There is no evidence that Bechu belonged to the intellectual circle of Calcutta. His Christianity, humble origins and lack of formal education would have precluded his being a part of the middle-class, intellectual elite with its reformist, but essentially elitist, outlook. His learning, acquired through reading, and his work experience, gave him a radical perspective, but kept him close to his roots. Though influenced by the *bhadralok*, he was not of it. He was unequivocally for the underdog.

CHAPTER TWO

The Guianese Environment in the Early 1890s and the Promptings of Bechu's Radicalism

It is difficult to accept that mere "reduced circumstances" drove Bechu into indentureship at the relatively late age of 34, in 1894. As a resident of Calcutta, with an inquisitive mind, he would have been aware of the continuing exit of 'bound coolies' to the sugar colonies. The vessels had been sailing from that port since the 1830s; the depots for the various colonies were located there; colonies of destitute returnees, who had failed to readjust to their villages in Bihar and Uttar Pradesh, had settled there.[26] Bechu had never worked in a field; he could have had no illusion about indentureship and the character of plantation labour.

It is not possible to say whether he was ever married, whether he had left a wife or any children in India. However, in British Guiana, as he wrote in January 1897, when he was 36 years old, he had "no wife, children, or any other 'encumbrance'".[27] His bachelorhood and his passion for justice for his compatriots enabled him to be the rebel in a society where power was comprehensively stacked against the indentureds. Not encumbered by responsibilities to a family, he had the space to be less circumspect, to be bold, to dare to challenge the authorities even while a 'bound coolie'. His fortitude was also evident after his indenture was terminated in February 1897. Bechu did not see the need to hide behind a pseudonym – a practice which correspondents to the press at the time rarely deviated from. Indeed, sometimes, he gave his address as 14 Water Street, Georgetown, possibly his place of employment. The premises of

A. Rohomon and Co, one of the oldest Indian businesses in the city, founded in 1893, were located there.[28] Bechu did not have to depend on the planters, or their business allies, or the government for a living. This job with an independent Indian employer, who had apparently offered to pay his commutation fees, suggests that the Rohomon family approved of his role as a champion of their poor, illiterate compatriots.

As a Bengali Christian in a sea of Hindus and Muslims primarily from eastern Uttar Pradesh and western Bihar, he was a marginal man. This was not a disadvantage. His peripheral position, as in India, enabled him to step aside emotionally from the pathos and pettiness as well as the immobilizing duties of Indian village life. Apparently, he had few personal friends. It would seem as if maintaining a distance enabled him to deal dispassionately with matters of concern to Indians. Bechu belonged, totally, to neither the world of the white authorities nor that of his Indian compatriots, but, intellectually, he comprehended both.[29] His independence, utter fearlessness, and single-mindedness fed his rebellious Bengali temperament.[30] A single man, in his late thirties, among the Indians in British Guiana, would have been a rarity; but it underlined his devotion to the broader, higher purpose.

There were many forces in British Guiana in the 1890s which were conducive to the sustaining of Bechu's rebellious spirit. The hitherto unassailable dominance of the plantocracy was being challenged by the gold and diamond industries, in the interior of the colony. Gold production rose from a paltry 406 ounces around 1884 to 12,880 ounces in 1886–88, then climbed impressively to 126,000 ounces in the 1890s. These new enterprises were controlled primarily by local merchants and professionals, many of whom were of Portuguese extraction or were light coloured people. There was a major divergence in the perspectives of these new entrepreneurs from those of the plantocracy, in at least one crucial area – access to Crown lands. Draconian measures, designed to prevent Crown lands from being "alienated" to small farmers, had been in existence because planters dominated the legislature. To change the Crown Land Ordinance it was imperative to reform the Constitution, to diminish the plantocracy's capacity to shape legislation. Portuguese prospectors and merchants were able to unite with middle-class blacks and coloureds in a campaign for constitutional reform. The latter felt alienated in a society where the sugar planters' welfare was deemed to be coterminous with the national good. Partial success was manifested in the mild reform of the Constitution in 1891. Though symbolic, this signalled the initiation of incremental land reform, which from 1898, facilitated extensive land ownership among small cultivators, amongst whom Indians were prominent.[31]

This atmosphere of political activism did percolate to a thin stratum of middle class Indians in Georgetown – shapers of the road away from the 'coolie' shame. In 1892 the first Indian organization in the Caribbean, the East Indian Institute, was founded. Its principal architects were W. Hewley Wharton, the founder and secretary; James Wharton, his brother, who later became a solicitor; Thomas Flood, a successful Indian businessman in Georgetown; and Veerasawmy Mudaliar, the Chief Interpreter at the Immigration Department, of Tamil stock. The most memorable of the Institute's accomplishments was the sending of a congratulatory address to Dadabhai Naoroji, the first Indian MP in Britain, who was elected in July 1892. It was a brave, imaginative initiative, but the indifference to intellectual and political endeavours was so pronounced that the organization had virtually collapsed by mid 1893, when W. Hewley Wharton left the colony to study medicine at the University of Edinburgh, the first Indian in the Caribbean to go to university. However, this tentative, embryonic effort conveyed to a few successful Indians the possibility that they could begin to take some responsibility for their welfare in the colony; that they could shape a new identity, away from the sugar plantations. A symbolic, psycho-logical hurdle had been shifted when Bechu arrived in British Guiana on 20 December 1894.[32]

A few days before Bechu's arrival, C.K. Jardine, the proprietor of the liberal newspaper, *The Daily Chronicle*, had published Joseph Ruhomon's ground-breaking speech of 4 October 1894, to the Indians in Georgetown: *India; The Progress of Her People at Home and Abroad* . . . This pamphlet was the first extended piece written by an Indian in the Caribbean to be published – another milestone on the weary road away from the 'coolie' stigma. Like Bechu's Bengali contemporaries, Joseph Ruhomon expressed pride in the greatness of ancient India, and he claimed this enviable legacy for all Indians in British Guiana. He also acknowledged African intellectual progress in the New World while deprecating the dismal record of Indians in the Caribbean in this sphere. This deceptively slim work is, in short, an exhortation by the first Indian intellectual in the colony, to his Indian compatriots, to emulate African scholastic efforts, and to claim, celebrate, and be invigorated by the ancient heritage of India, in order to erase the negative self-image rooted in bonded labour.[33]

Joseph Ruhomon wanted Indians in British Guiana to cultivate the intellect, to organize themselves for their own advancement. Bechu's Bengali contemporaries' vision had crossed the seas. Ruhomon wrote:

The Guianese Environment in the Early 1890s and the Promptings of Bechu's Radicalism

> Are you enthusiastic patriots for your country [British Guiana] or lovers of your ancestral home [India], and do you take a real, genuine interest in your people? Then I am sure you will do all that you possibly can by tongue, by pen, on the platform and through *the printing press*, by exhortation and by practical, tangible help, to promote and advance their interests in this colony of British Guiana where our people are so little cared for and their interests so sadly neglected . . . you are personally responsible for your own lives . . . you have the glorious gift of intellect – cultivate it . . . [emphasis added].[34]

Whether Bechu did read the pamphlet is impossible to determine, but its bold, assertive spirit would have struck a responsive chord in him. Neither is it possible to ascertain if Bechu saw the review by *The Argosy* of Ruhomon's pamphlet, on 29 December 1894, nine days after he had landed at Georgetown. This pro-planter newspaper was not inclined to be magnanimous to 'coolies' or other "tropical peoples". Its sentiments were usually congruent with the general perceptions by the ruling races of non-European peoples. In Bengal or in British Guiana, the following response would have stiffened Bechu's rebellious spirit and fortified his resolve:

> In an absolutely free country like the British Empire, a Hindoo or a Negro has equal opportunity with the Anglo-Saxon to rise to eminence, granted he has the same capacity for taking pains; but it is in this sternly necessary qualification that the hundreds of millions of the tropical and subtropical races are defective. Here and there in the present day, just as it was in the past centuries, springs up a commanding genius whose exceptional career only throws into deeper shade the utterly blank and purposeless lives of the teeming millions . . . Instead of overflowing with gratitude to the nation which has served them so well, the liberated, elevated and enlightened sons of Africa and India seem to be possessed with a feeling of truly ludicrous jealousy of the national superiority which has endowed them with such priceless benefaction.[35]

Imperial arrogance permeated all layers of the ruling class. The denigration of the 'coolie' was an instinct. Henry Kirke, a Scotsman, was for many years a magistrate in the colony; he had to adjudicate in many cases brought by planters against indentured labourers. Writing in the late 1890s, he gave an illuminating example of the perspective he took into his court:

> The houses of the magistrates and Immigration Agents are constantly besieged by coolies with petty complaints, which have to be investigated, and which, in 99 cases out of 100, are purely imaginary, or grossly exaggerated. With oriental imagery and metaphor, the coolie magnifies his wrongs until they seem almost

unbearable by any one man, but which, when touched by the spear of truthful investigation, melt away like the baseless fabric of a dream.[36]

Bechu encountered this way of seeing frequently, as his letters began to bite into the complacency of the ruling elite, after 1896. This perception of the 'coolie' was heightened as Indians on the estates started to resist more fervently, with the decline of sugar prices in 1895–96. The planters resorted to subterfuge to tide them over bleak times: prices had plummeted from around $107 (Guiana) per ton in 1883 to around $69 per ton in 1884–85; in the early 1890s, prices fluctuated between $65 and $69 per ton; a further decline had started in 1894, reaching around $49 per ton in 1895–96 and around $48 in 1897.[37] Wages were reduced indirectly by increasing the size of tasks; nonresident workers, from neighbouring villages, found it difficult to get work, as the estates relied more on their indentured labourers. The [Sugar] Planters' Association and the Royal Agricultural and Commercial Society, the principal planters' organizations, admitted to the West India Royal Commission of 1897 that the wages of free labour had been slashed by 20 to 25 percent between 1884 and 1897. As K.O. Laurence observes, this trend had antagonized the workers: "In British Guiana these developments were accompanied by 36 strikes in 24 months in 1895–1897. A number of strikes revealed on investigation that wages were unfairly and in at least one case illegally low."[38]

But, even before the 1890s, a culture of resistance had taken root on Guianese plantations. As noted earlier, the docile, malleable 'coolie' persona was more imaginary than real, certainly after the 1870s. As Look Lai observes: "Minor work stoppages, often accompanied by assaults on plantation officials, as well as acts of incendiarism on cane fields and plantation property, occurred regularly, with some periods more intense than others."[39] Indeed, between July and August 1873, there were 14 strikes; between 1886 and 1889 over 100 strikes accompanied weak sugar prices – with 42 in 1888 alone and "riotous disturbances" on several estates: Non Pareil, Enmore, Mon Repos, Turkeyen, Hope, Versailles, Farm, and Met-en-Meer Zorg. The following year there was a disturbance at De Kinderen.[40]

Such was the environment in which Bechu worked between the end of 1894 and early 1897, during his indentureship. What incensed him most, as his letters revealed often, was the inclination of the Immigration Agent General and his district representatives, the Immigration Agents – "my 'protectors'" as he sarcastically addressed them – to assess the grievances of 'coolies' under the same cloud of stereotypes as the planters.

The Guianese Environment in the Early 1890s and the Promptings of Bechu's Radicalism

In 1895, a disturbance at Plantation Success, on the island of Leguan, encapsulated the relationship of mutual distrust prevailing between the Indian worker and his protectors. The abysmal economic conditions on the estate led to the reduction of the wages of resident workers, while nonresident workers were severely underemployed. Discontent simmered. The Immigration Agent, however, did not bother to consider this central issue. Instead, he was seduced by the authorities' shift of focus onto an alleged plot, "a conspiracy" to murder the manager and the overseers of the estate. The Immigration Agent General reported that it was "instigated" by a shopkeeper and a discharged foreman. Several Indian workers were arrested for alleged threats to the authorities, made in the cane fields. Many of their compatriots followed the police and tried, unsuccessfully, to free them. They then tried to see the Magistrate and the Immigration Agent who they "violently assaulted".

The Immigration Agent General elaborated:

> The Magistrate had one arm broken; and the Immigration Agent was so severely beaten that for some weeks his life was despaired of. The immigrants then proceeded to the estate and attacked the Manager's house . . . They assailed the house with bricks and other missiles and endeavoured to break in, and it is only by means of fire arms, used with very great forbearance and moderation, that the immigrants were at last driven off . . . [41]

This was desperate behaviour by a people who could not trust their protector. When, eventually, the Immigration Agent investigated the problem of wages – the basic grievance from the beginning – he concluded that "the rate of wages, which was the ostensible cause of the outbreak, afforded no real ground of complaint . . . there was a settled determination on the part of the people to create a disturbance." The Immigration Agent General had acknowledged that there was genuine economic grievance on the estates, in 1894–95, caused by a reduction in the wage rates and a decrease in the amount of work available, especially for unindentured immigrants in the villages. Indeed, his conclusion was that: "It is not, therefore, surprising that there should have been more strikes than normal . . ."[42] However, the old assumptions of the 'coolie's' ineradicable mendacity and greed, in conjunction with his volatility and combustible temperament fed by the agitator, obtruded, rendering the Immigration Agent's capacity to defend the interests of his wards nugatory. Among planters, Immigration Agents, Magistrates and others of the ruling elite, it was axiomatic that the 'coolie' was not a rational being, therefore his grievances could not be genuine; they were, in Magistrate Henry Kirke's evocative phrase, like "the baseless fabric of a dream".[43]

By 1891, in an Indian population of 108,484 in British Guiana, 72,816 or about two-thirds resided on sugar estates. By 1901, the year Bechu left the colony, 72,692 Indians or about 55 percent still resided on plantations, but their nonestate population had risen to 57,649. However, there was chronic land hunger even for those Indians away from the estates, until the Crown Land Ordinances of 1898 and 1903 relaxed the terms of land acquisition. Alan Adamson assesses the condition of African villagers and Indian sugar workers in the late nineteenth century, before the land reforms of the late 1890s: "The tax system fleeced both in the same inequitable way; land policy made it equally difficult for either to escape the shadow of the sugar cane; and they both suffered from the racial and class prejudice of the Magistrates . . . monoculture and oligarchy made the development of either group impossible."[44]

Table 1: Indentured Free Indian Immigrants in British Guiana, 1881–1901 Estate Residents

Year	Adults (Ind)	Adults (Unind)	Children	Total Estate Residents	Non-estate Residents	Total (In colony)
1881	22,752	26,979	12,500	62,231	25,757	87,988
1891	16,710	38,356	17,750	72,816	35,668	108,484
1901	14,609	39,565	18,518	72,692	57,649	130,341

Source: Walton Look Lai, *Indentured Labour, Caribbean Sugar: Chinese and Indian Migrants to the British West Indies, 1838–1918* (Baltimore: The Johns Hopkins University Press 1993), 283.

The difficult land question, among Indian workers, was articulated with forthright clarity by Hon N. Darnell Davis, the Comptroller of Customs, to the West India Royal Commission on 30 January 1897, two days before Bechu was examined. Davis, a man of considerable erudition, was a member of the local legislature by virtue of his official position, but he was extraordinary among colonial administrators of the late nineteenth century: he was not afraid of the plantocracy; he was not afraid to let his side down; often, he empathized with the African and Indian underdog. The following exchange between him and Sir Henry Norman, the Chairman of the Commission, requires no elaboration:

Norman: Have you had the opportunity . . . of comparing their position [the Africans] with that of people in other West Indian colonies?

The Guianese Environment in the Early 1890s and the Promptings of Bechu's Radicalism

Davis: ... the black population here have not had the same opportunity of geting hold of small lots of land ... the Crown Lands Regulations have no doubt stopped the way, not only for black people, but for coolies who would become peasant proprietors.

Norman: The law has prevented it?

Davis: Yes, sir ... The Crown Lands Regulations ... were originally framed to keep the people on the sugar estates, or at all events, to keep them from settling the lands of the colony ...

Norman: ... are there any laws which operate against the settlement of land?

Davis: The existing regulations – which are liberal as compared with previous ones, which prevented settlement ... are such as block the way of the colonization of the colony. Fees and charges are such as it is practically impossible for the coolie with his average savings – the coolie who returns to India – to become a proprietor of Crown lands. I have looked up statements of the savings of coolies who have returned to India, and I find the average savings are less than will pay the cost of the smallest quantity of Crown land that would be sold under the present regulations; therefore the coolie would not only not be able to buy that small quantity of land, but he would have nothing to put into the land, or to support himself, until the land becomes productive.[45]

Then, commenting on the obscurantist Crown Land Ordinance, before the mild reform of 1890, Darnell Davis observed that between 1838 and 1890, while it operated, 32,345 repatriated Indians took £500,000 out of British Guiana, while £300,000 was spent on sending them back. Meanwhile, only 22 land grants were allocated; none to Indians or Chinese. Bechu followed the proceedings of the Commission closely; he seemed to have read its findings as well as its record of evidence and memoranda thoroughly.[46] He would have been impressed with Darnell Davis' courage and magnanimity.

In April 1898, *The Daily Chronicle* remarked that the new Crown Land Ordinance, which reduced the upset price of land from $1 to 15 cents per acre was "only one step removed from giving the land away". (Up to 1885, land could not be obtained in lots of less than 100 acres, at an upset price of $10 per acre.) It then explained the orchestrated policy of nondevelopment in the colony since Emancipation:

It was clearly not in the interest of the old planters to encourage any settlement upon the land. When labour was scarce it was necessary to conserve it as much as possible, and prevent the dispersion of the people all over the colony. Hence these prohibitive land laws, the lack of railway communication, the concentration of population in overcrowded villages, and the general poverty of the mass of the inhabitants. This, we say, was all necessary in the interests of the sugar industry, and the proprietors who lived as West Indian nabobs at home.[47]

The Daily Chronicle was right, but it had omitted a crucial area of nondevelopment – drainage and irrigation. The cheap land was almost useless without this. As with the African farmers after Emancipation, so with the new Indian rice growers in the 1890s – the plantocracy were vehemently opposed to the empoldering of the land, on the spurious premise that it was not the responsibility of the state to develop private property. Many construed that this was utterly dishonest, as the state's contribution to the importation of indentured labour amounted to a subsidy to sugar estates, to private property.[48]

The British Guiana plantocratic milieu was, by the late 1890s, combustible indeed. Bechu, shaped by his marginal position in late nineteenth century Bengali society, found this environment ideal to his temperament: his rebellious spirit was kindled quickly, on Plantation Enmore, where he was a 'bound coolie' between 20 December 1894 and 26 February 1897.

CHAPTER THREE

Bechu's Letters in the Context of the Guianese Environment: Bechu under Indentureship, 1894–1897

Plantation Enmore, about 12 miles from Georgetown, on the East Coast Demerara, belonged to the firm of Hogg, Curtis, and Campbell. The estate was required to pay no indenture fee for Bechu, as he was deemed unfit for manual labour. Bechu told the Norman Commission that he had worked for three days as a cane cutter, but he could not manage and was made an "assistant driver". His task involved "weighing and serving out manure and superintending picking of cane tops". Bechu said that he had worked from 6 am to 6 pm, often until 7 or 8 pm – days of 12 or 13 hours were not unusual. He received the statutory wage of one shilling per day, but after nine months, because of continual fever when exposed to rain, he was relieved of work in the cane field and made a domestic in the residence of the Deputy Manager of Enmore, a Mr Nicholson.

Bechu, as noted above, was allowed by Nicholson to read his books; he also had access to the newspapers. So he had first-hand knowledge of working conditions in the sugar cane fields, and was also ideally located to scrutinize the manners, mores, and attitudes of the Manager, overseers, and drivers. He inhabited the strategic world between the 'coolies' and the white authorities. He was observing, in his phrase, "learning the ropes" – a kind of apprenticeship for his critical eye. Between December 1894 and 30 October 1896, he seemed to have been anonymous; his name does not appear anywhere in the newspapers. He elaborated later:

> I have been full two years in this colony, and have been *as quiet as a mouse*, so much so, that not even my protector [the Immigration Agent] could have been aware of any existence, but when I saw that the lives of *four* [in fact, five] of my countrymen were sacrificed for nothing, and that about ten times that number [59] had been injured for life, I considered it my duty as a more enlightened one of their class to explain to the public through the press, the real cause of the disturbance, that prompt steps may be taken to prevent a recurrence . . .[49]

So the shooting of Indian workers on 13 October 1896 at Plantation Non Pareil, a few miles from Enmore, precipitated Bechu's first letter to the press, to the liberal paper, *The Daily Chronicle*. As the Non Pareil event was so seminal in Bechu's career as a correspondent, an assessment will be made of his letter of 22 December 1896 where he elaborated on it.

Bechu stated that in early October 1896, indentured labourers on Non Pareil complained of the severity of their required tasks, which precluded their earning the statutory wage of one shilling per day for seven hours' work. He added that because the estate authorities gave them no satisfaction, they had marched to Georgetown on 12 October to express their grievances to the Immigration Agent General, A.H. Alexander – an established practice. The latter told them that he would instruct the Immigration Agent of the District, H.J. Gladwin, to investigate their complaint about wages. Moreover, he assured them that no punishment would be meted out to them for their action.

Bechu said that the next day, 13 October, Gladwin and the County Inspector of Police, Captain de Rinzy, with 17 armed policemen, were at the estate where, reluctantly, about 300 'coolies' appeared, having been summoned to have their case for better wages adjudicated by their protector, Gladwin. Before the investigation commenced, four Indian workers were arrested by the police, who were armed with a warrant. Gerad Van Nooten, the Manager of Non Pareil, had alleged that these men had been conspiring to kill him. Bechu deemed this charge "groundless" because when these presumably "dangerous characters" were subsequently brought before the magistrate, they were "simply bound over to keep the peace" and transferred to another plantation. He reflected, sarcastically:

> Fancy men who only absent themselves from duty for a day being imprisoned for a month, and men found guilty of such a serious charge being set at large to, perhaps, do the same thing on the estates to which they had been transferred!![50]

Bechu argued that the workers felt betrayed by their protector and, understandably, sought to free their four compatriots from police custody. They had challenged the police that if the four were guilty, they were all guilty; they demanded to be arrested as well. The police deemed this "rioting" and Captain de Rinzy ordered that shots be fired over their heads. The shooting "exasperated" them, and being "unarmed", they resorted to hurling bricks and bottles at the police, who opened fire with buckshots: five 'coolies', including one of the 'ringleaders', Jungali, were killed; 59 were injured. Two coroners ruled that the police were "properly justified in opening fire". Bechu, however, concluded that the root of the troubles was the arbitrary increasing of tasks for indentured labourers which precluded many from earning the statutory minimum wage. He was forthright: if the planters, despite hard times, could not honour the terms of the contract, they should "liberate those who wish to be liberated".

Bechu's synopsis was substantially accurate. In January 1897, the Attorney General of British Guiana, H.A. Bovell, minuted that the police "acted indiscreetly . . . in lodging a charge of conspiracy before a Justice of Peace on insufficient grounds", in order to procure a warrant to arrest the workers; so did they in executing it, "at the time and under the circumstances . . . the arrests were made". He concurred with the Immigration Agent General that Immigration Agent Gladwin should have objected to the arrest of the four men who "in response to his invitation had come to him along with other labourers for the purpose of their complaints being investigated".[51] The Immigration Agent General had argued most perceptively and decisively thus:

> Mr Gladwin should . . . have protested against his enquiry being interrupted and against any arrests being made at the time, as the absence of four of the immigrants who apparently were regarded by the Manager as ringleaders, would prevent a full statement being obtained in regard to the complaints of the immigrants, and would also lead the immigrants to believe that they had been induced to assemble for other purposes than an enquiry into their complaints.[52]

Alexander concluded on a definitive note: "To my mind the arrest of the immigrants when they had assembled quietly and peaceably to meet the Immigration Agent had a most mischievous effect on the people, and I consider that those concerned in bringing about and effecting the arrests incurred a very great responsibility."[53] The Governor, Sir Augustus Hemming, concurred with the Attorney General and the Immigration Agent General, while indicting Harry Garnett, the Attorney of Non Pareil, for not delaying the execution of the warrant until Immigration Agent Gladwin had completed his investigation.[54] Indeed, Alexander, the Immigration Agent General, had apparently "strongly urged" Garnett to do so.

What Bechu did not state and what the authorities did not raise, until the coroners' inquests were concluded was, as Alexander minuted in January 1897, that Manager Van Nooten who caused the men to be arrested for allegedly conspiring to kill him was, indeed, "living with" a 'coolie' woman, Jamni, on the estate. He had admitted it to some "responsible persons", but the new Manager, Ebbels, and Harry Garnett, the Attorney, had refused an inquiry into the matter and were "endeavouring to screen" Van Nooten.[55] Quintin Hogg, one of the owners of Non Pareil, was equally obdurate: he did not expect his Manager "to play the spy on the lives of the white men on the estate"; he concurred with Garnett that Van Nooten's "alleged relations" with Jamni were "a purely private matter".[56]

In fact, it would appear that Jamni was, as Basdeo Mangru argues, the wife of Jungali, one of the arrested ringleaders who were killed on 13 October 1896. Van Nooten's conduct had "infuriated" him and other Indians on the estate, thus poisoning their relationship with management.[57] This had been exacerbated by the arbitrary slashing of the wages of the indentureds. It is significant that only four of the five ringleaders were arrested: Anjore, Boodhai, Reoti, and Jungali. The principal organizer, Gooljar, at whose house Gladwin stated that according to Van Nooten "extensive meetings" were held to plot "an extensive strike or riot", was not arrested. As the solicitor for the relatives of the deceased observed, Gooljar was "called up by Inspector de Rinzy and told amidst the crowd of coolies to go away . . ."[58] This suggests that Gooljar, an articulate, "returned" immigrant, was most likely to expose the seamy antecedents of Van Nooten's rage; it was, therefore, prudent to flatter him by exempting him from prosecution, in short, to bribe him in order to neutralize him.

Van Nooten's principal aim in concocting a conspiracy was to get Jungali out of his way, to secure his removal from the estate. The Immigration Agent had not even "enquired into any complaint about the . . . conspiracy". He added: "No one informed me of a plot . . . Gooljar was the spokesman. Five men were suspected – four men and Gooljar. [He] was not called out along with the others – he was cautioned and put on his good behaviour . . ."[59] The government lacked the conviction to pursue the matter, and confronted with Quintin Hogg's intransigence, dropped it.

Van Nooten seemed to have been the conspirator. Indeed, the workers were reportedly in a most conciliatory mood, although they were incensed by the arbitrary cutting of wages – an illegal act against indentured labourers, as Bechu argued and the acting Governor corroborated: "Instructions already given were

... repeated to the Immigration Agent General to inform all estate authorities that the government could not allow any reduction of wages below the statutory wage."[60] Van Nooten conceded that on 10 October, three days before the shootings, Gooljar and about 200 'coolies' had gone to his home seeking a compromise. Gooljar had complained: "We cannot live on the wages we are getting, our stomachs are not being filled." Van Nooten explained that although the wages were lower than before, the industry was "in a very bad way"; he could not raise them. Gooljar then enquired whether management could procure rice for them at the wholesale price; he had also requested that they be granted land on the estate to grow provisions. Van Nooten replied that if "the people got farms and the sugar industry got up again we would have no labourers as they would work for themselves," and that government regulations precluded the former request.[61] The Manager was obsessed with removing the ringleaders; he was not in a conciliatory mood. In pursuit of the former, peaceful protestors were shot. As the lawyer for the Immigration Department, Patrick Dargan, concluded: "If the arrest of the four men had not taken place or had been done judiciously the unfortunate occurrence by which many lives were lost and a great many men wounded, would not have occurred."[62]

Two inquests were conducted on the shootings. Both exonerated the authorities. J.P. Thorne, the stipendiary Magistrate, concluded that two of the five deceased, Jungali and Kandhai, died from "buckshot wounds inflicted by the police who in self-defence, and in the execution of their duty, fired on a riotous assembly of ... coolies." With regard to the death of Chinahoo, who died in the estate's hospital, he reported that he also died from a buckshot but, strangely, Thorne concluded: "how such gunshot wound was received there is no evidence to show".[63] The inquest on Mohabir and Rogy, who died in the Georgetown Hospital, also concluded that the police acted "lawfully" and "in self-defence".

It was routine in this colonial society that the authority of Europeans should not be seen to be challenged, that no European should let the side down. The overriding assumption was that the 'coolie' was mendacious, irrational, and excitable. Justice, therefore, could not even be seen to be done. This was what impelled Bechu to write to the press while still an indentured labourer; moreover, to articulate the grievances of his compatriots before the Norman Commission in February 1897. Possibly cognisant of Van Nooten's conduct at Non Pareil, Bechu asserted in his memorandum to the Commission that "it is an open secret that coolie women are in the keeping of overseers" and that "gross immorality exists on most of the estates."[63]

The closing of ranks among the ruling class was evident in the findings of the arbitrator into the wage rates at Non Pareil, after the shootings. These rates had already declined by 20 percent since 1894, and were reduced further at the beginning of October 1896;[64] this had precipitated the dispute. Yet the arbitrator concluded that punt loaders and cane cutters could still earn the statutory wage; only the weeders were not paid sufficiently. The Immigration Agent General, the workers' protector, concurred.[65] However, Patrick Dargan, the liberal lawyer, countered that this was not an accurate assessment based on the evidence. He explained: "It appeared from the evidence of all the immigrants examined and who spoke as to their wages that they could not earn one shilling a day for seven hours" – the minimum wage stipulated under the indenture contract. Dargan observed, poignantly, that Munroe, the arbitrator, was a planter, the Manager of Windsor Forest, and that he had recently reduced the wages of punt loaders on his estate by 10 percent.[66]

This ruling had so incensed Bechu that in his first letter to *The Daily Chronicle*, on 1 November 1896, he had reproduced a substantial portion of his indenture contract in order to emphasize that the statutory wage was *not* negotiable – that able-bodied men must be paid not less than one shilling (24 cents) per day; women and men under 16 must be paid not less than eight pence (16 cents) per day. If they were paid by task, Bechu reminded his readers, they may be paid more, but not less than the stipulated wages for time work.

Alluding to the reduction of wages at Non Pareil, Bechu said that nine shillings per week for punt loading was an inadequate wage for a difficult job undertaken from 6 am to 8 or 9 pm daily. He then drew attention to his protector who he considered a friend of the plantocracy: he could not recall an instance when a protector brought charges against a planter for breach of contract. From the beginning, Bechu's letters spared no sacred cows: he observed, with biting irony, that "our exemplary clergy" refused to accept any cuts in salary but the "indentured heathens" must accept cuts with a smile.

A trickle of letters from Indians had appeared in the press from the 1880s. Bechu's avalanche of letters to *The Daily Chronicle* was to stimulate many more to write, normally in complimentary, corroborative terms, of their articulate, brave compatriot. J.R. Wharton, a local-born Indian, a leading light in the defunct East Indian Institute, supported "this bold East Indian", asserting that the terms of indentureship tended to become "a dead letter", as was demonstrated at Non Pareil on the wages issue. The immigrant was invariably ignorant of the terms of his contract and was treated "arbitrarily" by some planters. Wharton, like Bechu, felt that with 100,000 Indians in the colony,

Table 2: Convictions of Employers and Immigrants under the Immigration Ordinance, 1874–1875

Year	Number of convictions of employers against immigrants	Number of convictions of immigrants for offences against employers
1874	59	10,336
1875	13	7,223
1876	44	5,648
1877	13	2,770
1878	18	2,074
1879	4	1,993
1880	2	2,612
1881	10	2,544
1882	6	2,875
1883	4	2,360
1884	4	1,939
1885	6	1,548
1886	9	1,552
1887	4	1,667
1888	1	2,045
1889	1	1,698
1890	3	2,079
1891	2	2,395
1892	1	2,034
1893	1	2,239
1894	2	2,855
1895	1	2,598
TOTAL	**208**	**65,084**

Source: 'Langton' [W. Alleyne Ireland], "The History of the East Indian Immigrant", *The Argosy*, 12 December 1896.

indentureship should be suspended for at least five years; there were too many destitute Indians. He blamed the government for sanctioning more indentureds at a time of depression, and advocated the award of land grants to time-expired

Indians in lieu of return passages, with a subsidiary grant of about £5 to establish homesteads.[67]

Since Bechu's first letter of 1 November 1896, he had been silent for over a month because he claimed to have "promised a gentleman, who had been exceedingly kind to me, and for whom I have the highest respect, not to appear in print again, at least for the present . . ."[68] It is almost certain that Bechu's employer, the Assistant Manager of Enmore, must have tried to restrain him because he had written so forthrightly against the planters. In 58 years of Indian indentureship in the colony, no 'bound coolie' had ever done so. Bechu could have circumvented the restraint; like most correspondents at the time he could have used a pseudonym. Instead, he always signed his name, stating his menial status with a flourish – "Indentured Immigrant, *Sheila*, 1894, Pln Enmore". He obviously enjoyed his role as a radical advocate of his people, writing from within the jaws of the system.

In December 1896, Bechu broke his silence, to rebut a proplanter writer, 'Langton' (W. Alleyne Ireland), the subeditor of the conservative weekly, *The Argosy*, who had severe misgivings about the core of Bechu's letter of 1 November.[69] He repeated that the statutory wage of one shilling for seven hours' work was not negotiable, and revealed that Van Nooten had admitted that the reduction in wages at Non Pareil was "very much more than 10 percent" in the past year. Bechu contended that men, with drivers at their backs, worked for ten hours and still could not earn the statutory minimum.[70]

'Langton' said that Bechu's allegation that punt loaders earned a wage of nine shillings ($2.16) per week or 36 cents per day, in a six-day week, from 6 am to 9 pm, was a misrepresentation. He quoted 45 cents per day as a more accurate wage for punt loaders but conceded that "hitches" resulted in the delay of punts; this led to longer hours in the field.[71] Bechu countered that it was no fault of the workers that often punts were not available, which meant they had to stay at work for up to 15 hours. Therefore, providing the worker had been at work for seven hours, he should be paid "proportionately for every extra hour of work", under the terms of his contract of indenture.[72]

Bechu had argued that 'coolies' were persecuted by planters for a range of trivial offences but he was unaware of "a single instance" of the protector prosecuting an employer for offences against immigrants.[73] 'Langton' had sought to discredit this, noting that between 1874 and 1895, 624 complaints were made by immigrants against employers, and 208 were convicted.[74] What he did not say was that during the same period, 65,084 immigrants were convicted for offences against employers! In fact, between 1890 and 1895, only ten employers were convicted – one each in 1892, 1893, and 1895; during this period 14,200 immigrants were convicted (see Table 2, which is excerpted from figures prepared by 'Langton'). Bechu was not exaggerating.

Finally, Bechu disagreed with 'Langton' that the terms of the contract were "fully explained" to the immigrants by the Immigration Agents after they were allocated to their respective sugar estates. He observed: "This was never done when the batch I belonged to arrived [in December 1894], and it has not been done in the case of any other batch since." He underlined his point with direct reference to his protector, the Immigration Agent on the East Coast Demerara: ". . . although I am nearly two years on this estate neither I nor any of my shipmates have had the honour of appearing before Mr Gladwin."[75] Bechu never missed a chance to mischievously remind his readers that his elusive protector was not aware of his existence, cleverly locating him within the universe of the planters and their allies.

'Langton' responded to Bechu, focusing on his point that workers should be paid proportionately for every additional hour they were "in attendance" beyond the statutory seven hours. He observed that the indentured labour had not made a contract "to be paid for 'being in attendance' but for 'labouring'". 'Langton' concluded that if the employer did not give the 'coolie' the chance to earn one shilling in seven hours, "he has the remedy of the law".[76]

What 'Langton', as an advocate of the planters' position, could not appreciate was that the authorities at Non Pareil had reduced the rate of wages, unilaterally, below the statutory minimum. Besides, he would not acknowledge that the insidious practice of increasing tasks to cope with the depression, was tantamount to a cut in wages. Moreover, power was so comprehensively stacked against the 'coolie' that it was inconceivable that he could get his employer prosecuted without the aid of his protector; and, as Bechu argued continually, the latter could not be relied on.

In his rejoinder, Bechu remarked that he had "effectively . . . silenced" 'Langton' with regard to his assertion that Immigration Agents visited estates to explain the terms of the contract to new immigrants. He then recommended the appointment of an "independent" official to inspect the pay lists on estates and report to the government whether indentured Indians were receiving the statutory minimum wage – another indictment of the Immigration Agents.[77]

Bechu's next encounter with 'Langton' (W. Alleyne Ireland) was on 1 February 1897, when they were both examined by the Norman Commission. Indeed, Ireland's evidence was essentially a rebuttal of Bechu's scathing criticism of many aspects of the indenture system. He denied Bechu's allegation before the

Commission that the authorities did not inspect the hospitals and the ranges on the estates; and in response to Bechu's complaint that the creole gang rarely got home before 7 pm or 8 pm although they started work at 6 am, he stated that "there are no indentured immigrants in the creole gang, because the gang consists of young children."[78] Bechu quickly countered that the latter fact was "sufficient reason why the gang should be dismissed early". He elaborated: "the poor little mites will themselves bear out, that in all weathers, they are rarely brought home before seven o'clock at night although they start work at 6 am."[79]

Bechu had told the Norman Commission that there was insufficient work in British Guiana to warrant the continuation of indentureship – that enough labour was available locally. This had elicited from Ireland the most revealing statement on the *raison d'etre* for indentureship:

> The supply of labour has no bearing upon the sugar industry, the whole origin of immigration hinges upon this point. You may have work and plenty of it for a black man and a coloured man, and they will not do it. In planting cane, if you leave certain agricultural work over, your crop is ruined, therefore it is absolutely necessary that you should have bound labour that you can command.[80]

In other words, the sugar industry, bred on slavery and bound labour, largely insulated from market mechanisms in the supply of labour with the attendant need for flexibility on the part of the employer, would not countenance the termination of its authoritarian control of its core labour force.

Bechu was already a gadfly for the plantocracy and their allies. In fact, the editor of *The Argosy*, James Thomson, a part-proprietor of a sugar plantation, had told the Norman Commission that the "only discontent" he was aware of among 'coolies' was expressed by "a learned pundit on the East Coast", an unmistakable reference to Bechu. Thomson added that he could not understand why the man was sent to the colony, as he would have been a "troublesome man" in any place.[81]

Bechu thrived on his growing notoriety. He responded quickly, underlining his status and ethnic identity: "Indentured Bengali Immigrant, *Sheila*, 1894", writing from Plantation Enmore. It was characteristic of Bechu that after he had fired his big guns at the ruling elite, with effect, he would remind his readers of his humble position. In response to James Thomson, he said that he "grieved" because "a gentleman . . . in [his] position should have condescended to malign a poor, penniless and harmless wretch like me . . ." However, this affected humility often had its sting: Bechu added that he was not surprised that Thomson had "trodden on a weak worm like me", because a short while before, as proprietor of *The Argosy*, he had taken "advantage of his position and shamefully insulted a highly respected, but defenceless Minister".[82]

Bechu then sought the sympathy of his employers at Plantation Enmore, stating that he was certain they would vouch for his good character, although he was "fighting stoutly" for his "dumb-driven countrymen". He was mistaken. The Manager of his estate, G.W. Bethune, wrote to Sydney Olivier, Secretary of the Norman Commission, on 15 February 1897, to deny "the gist" of Bechu's evidence. He pointed out that Enmore had one of the largest schools, and that it was there that "'the little mites' spend their hours"; besides, Indians were allocated plots for provision and rice and free pasturage for their cattle.[83] Bechu did not respond to Bethune, but it was accepted that child labour was an established feature of sugar cane culture.

Bechu was making an impact. In early February 1897, another planter, using the pseudonym, 'West Coast',[84] observed that Bechu's letters were "becoming too frequent and . . . monotonous"; he seemed to be "the only poor, down-trodden" Indian in British Guiana; his grievances were "imaginary". 'West Coast' asserted that Bechu's submission with regard to the working hours of the creole gang, even if true for Enmore, could not be seen as representative of the whole colony. But the crux of this planter's rebuttal of Bechu was enmeshed in a body of racial assumptions common among the ruling elite.

'West Coast' doubted his credibility because Indians would "never speak the whole truth . . . so long as they can possibly evade doing so", and he deprecated Bechu's self-pitying epithets in his letter of 4 February 1897 – evidence that he still "possesses the low, cringing and abject habit common to his nationality". He felt that Bechu's "good education and ready pen" could be better utilized. Bechu did not refute this planter's racial slurs, but he accused him of cowardice, of lacking "a spark of manliness", for not using his real name. That, in Bechu's eyes, was a greater weakness than his own supposed mendacity.[85]

Bechu's correspondence stimulated letters from several Indians on their condition in the colony. His performance before the Norman Commission also heightened his stature. Special acclamation came from 'East Indian Descendant', a regular correspondent from New Amsterdam. 'East Indian Descendant' was, in fact, Joseph Ruhomon, the first Indian intellectual in British Guiana. He saw Bechu as "the redoubtable, invincible . . . champion of his race" and applauded his "fearless and straightforward" way of articulating his people's case.[86]

Bechu had, indeed, answered young Ruhomon's exhortation of late 1894 superbly, that Indians should use the "printing press", among other channels, to advance their interests which were "so sadly neglected".⁸⁷ Ruhomon's estimate of the man, therefore, carried in it the idea of his fulfilling a mission:

> Bechu is undoubtedly a man of integrity and sound, honest principles, and not one to recklessly sacrifice them for fear of offending those in whose employ he has been thrown by the irony of fate . . . This well-informed and intelligent Bengali has thoroughly grasped the facts of the case, and naturally so from his position on the estate, and the reasons he is clever enough to summon for his use; and from what I know, I do not think . . . he in any way overstates the case in speaking of the present system of drudgery imposed on our East Indian immigrants on the plantations . . . ⁸⁸

Joseph Ruhomon had been so incensed by the planter's ('West Coast's') racist attack on Bechu that he responded quickly, noting that no race had a monopoly on "the popular art of lying". One should not simply take a labourer from the cane fields as representative of the whole Indian race, nor could one be justified in seeing the "English barbarian" from the East End of London as representative of the English nation. Besides, Ruhomon contended, if Indians on the plantations "cringed before their white employer", it was because they were forced into "a miserable existence . . . under the most trying circumstances". He deprecated 'West Coast's' calumny on Bechu's nationality as "a most libellous reflection on the East Indian race", adding that he showed "a profound and most lamentable ignorance of our national traits and characteristics of which we are so justly proud".⁸⁹

As his pseudonym suggests, Ruhomon was born in British Guiana of Indian parents and, like J.R. Wharton (another of Bechu's supporters), was among the first generation of educated Indians in the colony. But Ruhomon, as was so evident in his 1894 pamphlet, took great pride in his Indian antecedents – an instrument for retrieving his people's dignity from the shame of the 'coolie' universe. By February 1897, his self-esteem and rising self-confidence – a beacon for his compatriots – had not diminished:

> Bechu . . . is eminently qualified to answer the charges made against him by . . . ['West Coast'] . . . I have not the slightest need to take up the cudgels on his behalf . . . But as the honour of the entire Indian race in the colony, or rather, in the whole habitable globe is involved in the false, malicious, and sweeping indictment by 'West Coast', I would be wanting in my duty as a member of the race if I did not attempt to vindicate its fair name and reputation which have been so unwarrantably and grossly assailed.⁹⁰

Bechu's Letters in the Context of the Guianese Environment: Bechu under Indentureship

The rebellious spirit of Bechu and Joseph Ruhomon was contagious. That it was percolating to a visible minority is reflected in a letter which appeared in the same issue of *The Daily Chronicle* as Ruhomon's letter cited above. It was written by Ramsawmy, a resident of Georgetown, a man of Tamil stock who had gone as a 'bound coolie' to the colony in 1885. He was challenging a reputable minister of the Anglican church, Canon Josa, who had sought to discredit Bechu's assertion that the creole gang, comprising young children, worked very late in the cane fields. Ramsawmy was appalled at Canon Josa's claim that these children were "well cared for and most happy". He wished that the education authorities and the Children's Protection Society could see the reverend gentleman's remarks, concluding forthrightly that "it is because he gets his salary and collection without exertion and in the cool" that he could have no sympathy for the children. Some "cringing coolies" were already by the 1890s refusing to live on their knees!

These early Indian defenders were probably emboldened by the flippancy with which disparaging Eurocentric notions of 'coolie' character were paraded in colonial society. Another of Bechu's critics, 'Civis Mundi', an Englishman, was not impressed with Ruhomon's efforts to establish the "nobility of his own race". Moreover, like 'West Coast', he relied on what he saw as defects in the Bengali character, in his attempt to rebut Bechu. Reminding his readers that Bechu was a Bengali, he quoted Macaulay's assertions that the Bengali was feeble and effeminate, lacking "courage, independence, and veracity". Deceit was endemic in him.[91]

Bechu challenged 'Civis Mundi', also, to reveal his identity, if he had "the pluck of an Englishman", while diminishing his evident pride in his Englishness – "by mere accident he was born on English soil." He felt that Macaulay would have been "ashamed" of his remarks if he were alive, as Bengalis had made "remarkable" strides in their "social, moral, and religious condition".[92]

'Civis Mundi's' rejoinder to Bechu appeared in *The Daily Chronicle* of 16 February 1897, which, as will be seen shortly, was the day Bechu wrote to the Immigration Agent General seeking commutation of his indentureship. This critic observed that Bechu was fond of attacking those who claimed the "privilege of anonymity", but that he did not have "'the greater freedom and less responsibility' of an overseer's domestic servant". It is necessary to repeat that it was unusual for correspondents to use their names, underlining the apprehension of many in this oligarchical, plantocratic environment. In this context, therefore, Bechu's persistence in challenging the powerful assumes a heroic dimension.

In mid February 1897, Joseph Ruhomon returned to Bechu's defence, as he deemed Macaulay's infamous pronouncement on Bengali character[93] a mere "opinion" – "only a medium between knowledge and ignorance". It certainly was "not history or absolute fast", because frequently he "allowed his expressions to take rise from a highly exuberant and prolific imagination". Macaulay's characterization of the Bengali bore no resemblance to Ruhomon's, and in what may be interpreted largely as a tribute to Bechu's role as a gadfly in British Guiana, Ruhomon concluded:

> . . . for subtlety of intellect, for strength of purpose, for bravery under trying circumstances and for true nobility of character, to use Macaulay's own words, 'no class of human beings can bear comparison with them' . . . If two or three Bengalis have been found answering to Macaulay's description of them, I have no hesitation in saying Bechu is a most exceptional one, and he deserves to be looked upon as a distinct credit to his own race.[94]

Earlier, in December 1896, John Russell, a friend of the sugar planters, writing from Perseverance, Essequibo, appropriately enough to *The Argosy*, to remonstrate with the "gifted" Bechu, considered his letters an "extremely ill-timed attack on the planters and the immigration system". He was, of course, alluding to the depression in sugar prices and the planters' determination to secure more indentured labourers, on the eve of the visit of the Norman Commission. Russell's letter encapsulated all the venom which the irrepressible 'bound coolie' radical attracted from the authorities.

He wondered how Bechu was able to delude the agent in India, posing as an agricultural labourer while being so "accomplished" in the English language. Russell then called up the familiar racist assumptions of the Anglo-Indian, to diminish Bechu's work. He attributed his uncompromising expositions to youth – Bechu was, in fact, 36 – and to a "peculiar lack of tact and discretion" manifest among Bengali aspirants to the upper echelons of the Indian Civil Service, which "so effectively disqualified" them. Russell then sought to demolish the letters: they had the "specious open-palmed ingenuity of the practised 'bazar-baboo'"; they could only impress the "superficial" reader.

Russell tried to excite the passions of Africans ("sons of the soil") against Bechu, arguing that the 'coolie' was "peculiarly and individually" protected, almost pampered, in the colony. The indentureship system was an "almost perfect system of protection". Bechu's "misplaced compassion" for his compatriots was actuated by what Russell termed "the fiery effusions of the professional agitator urged to extremes in his hunger for notoriety". He concluded with a plea for Bechu to mend his "agitating" ways, for it was "injudicious to open and maintain any attack calculated to engender ill-feeling between employer and employed", especially at a time of depression in the sugar industry. Russell's letter may be seen as the planter's enraged call for Bechu's silence.[95]

On 16 February 1897, Bechu forwarded a petition to the Immigration Agent General,[96] requesting the termination of his indentureship by the payment of commutation fees. He gave three reasons for his action: (i) that the head overseer at Enmore, who had become Deputy Manager (Bechu was a domestic in his predecessor's home), informed him that he would be sent back to the fields; (ii) that he could not work in the fields because of his irregular heartbeat; (iii) that an Indian merchant in Georgetown had offered him a job. The Immigration Agent General stated that he had received confirmation from the merchant, possibly A. Rohoman of 14 Water Street, that he would pay the commutation fee and provide Bechu with employment.

The authorities at Plantation Enmore, to whom Bechu apparently had promised a cessation in letters to the press, were probably using the threat of transfer to the field to extract silence from him after he had reneged on his promise (to stop his letter writing). They must, therefore, have been buoyed by his request for commutation; they raised no objection; and the Immigration Agent General moved with unusual despatch to grant Bechu's request. He observed that as Bechu had been deemed unfit for work in the field, the estate had paid no indenture fee for him, consequently, no commutation fee was payable by Bechu. On 24 February 1897, just a week after his petition, his indentureship was terminated; on 26 February, he received his Certificate of Exemption from labour. The next day Bechu wrote to the Immigration Agent General:

> Respected Sir,
> Permit me to tender my very best thanks to you for the prompt measures you have taken to obtain for me my freedom and that too 'without money and without price'. I shall ever remember this act of kindness of yours with the deepest gratitude more especially as I feel myself undeserving of such a concession.[97]

Bechu was invariably courteous, sometimes excessively so, but he could not be silenced; he was an incorruptible man. In fact, his freedom made him an even more strident advocate of his people. In Georgetown, where he moved to in March 1897, he had immediate access to his forum, *The Daily Chronicle*; as noted earlier, he could hand in his letters, he did not require postage stamps.

CHAPTER FOUR

Bechu's Letters in the Context of the Guianese Environment: Bechu in Freedom, 1897–1901

Bechu vs the Plantocracy

Between March 1897 and February or March 1901, when Bechu left the colony, no issue agitated him and exercised his combative energies as much as the question of Indian indentureship and options for Indians in British Guiana, away from the sugar plantations. He was an implacable foe of the system. He was emphatic to the Norman Commission in February 1897: "I consider there is not sufficient work, I do not see the necessity for bringing any more [indentureds]."

It is noteworthy that the proplanter legislature had, between 1895 and 1898, increased the contribution from general revenue towards immigration costs from one-third to two-thirds. British Guiana was, in fact, subsidizing the sugar planters; this was an indirect bounty no different from that received by German and French beet sugar producers. However, the Commission, in late 1897, in response to the planters' request for more indentured labourers, came closer to Bechu's position. They observed that "with the possibility of having . . . to send back to India large numbers of coolies, at a cost which the colony could not meet, there are strong objections to bringing fresh immigrants from India."

They elaborated: " . . . it seems unwise, having regard to the particular circumstances of British Guiana, to bring any more until there is some prospect of the revival of the sugar industry." The Commission did not recommend the imposition of countervailing duties against bounty-fed European beet sugar.

While conceding the "vital importance" to the colony of sugar, the Commission advocated crop diversification, while pointing to the need for improved communications to the interior to promote agricultural settlements and expand mining and forestry. In a strident note in favour of the termination of the draconian Crown Lands Regulations, they warned: " . . . if the sugar industry is maintained the government must be careful not to allow its influence to retard the settlement and opening up of new lands, which have hitherto been left inaccessible and undeveloped, partly owing to the interest of the colony having hitherto been entirely concentrated on sugar."

This was the context in which the planters mounted a sustained campaign to get more indentured labourers. In November 1897, in spite of the depression and the Commission's recommendation, a solid proplanter, proimmigration advocate admonished Bechu for wanting to terminate the system. He felt that the colony could accommodate many more Indian indentureds, possibly 50,000 or more; this would enable planters to bring more land under sugar. This correspondent was arguing that the whole cost of immigration should be covered from general revenue: the whole colony would benefit from a thriving sugar industry. At the end of their five-year term of indentureship, Indians could be allocated empoldered land free of charge.[98]

The retention, at all times, of a body of bonded labour was at the core of the planters' strategy to weather the low sugar prices. Bechu, however, saw this as a design to "glut" the labour market. He argued: "in the present depressed condition of the colony, immigration should be suspended at once."[99] Predictably, the proimmigration advocates quickly countered that deprived of immigrants, "the colony is ruined in a very short time".[100]

Bechu's continual articulation of his opposition to Indian indentureship inspired a vigorous debate on this central question at the end of the nineteenth century. Another proplanter correspondent, 'Well-Wisher', was at variance with Bechu, arguing that the importation of 8,000 to 10,000 Indian indentureds, "free", for the sugar estates, would generate the recovery of the sugar industry. The planters' access to "reliable, resident labour", in short 'bound coolies', was crucial. But 'Well Wisher' betrayed his darker motives when he suggested apprehension of the growing tendency of Indians to settle in villages, cultivating rice and seeking independence, "the exodus . . . from the estates". He bemoaned the fact that the "manufacture of sugar in some districts will have to be postponed until the rice crop is reaped."[101]

Bechu rejected the argument in favour of more immigrants for sugar, recalling that since 1891, 5,000 'coolies' per year had been brought to the colony with no perceptible benefit to the people. He observed that during this period 21 shiploads of Indians, seasoned agricultural labourers, were repatriated – "an ugly fact". Bechu was certain that if half the money "squandered" in charting ships for this exercise had been offered to these people to remain in British Guiana, it would have enhanced possibilities for a settled population and the development of the colony.[102]

On the question of the fledgling rice industry, Bechu remarked that the Indians' effort had been hampered because "the (sugar) planters and a few traders whose business it was to furnish the estates with supplies were opposed to the scheme". He could see no prospect for the development of rice if countervailing duties were imposed on beet sugar imported into the UK: a revived sugar industry in British Guiana would be antagonized by a buoyant rice culture – a potential magnet for its Indian labour. Bechu was confident that free Indians would no longer accept "starvation wages" on the sugar estates[103] if they could grow rice and provisions; during the slack season, indentured and unindentured workers could not earn more than 6 pence (12 cents) per day, half the statutory minimum wage.[104]

It is, therefore, somewhat strange that Bechu became a consistent advocate of reindenture, in order to stem repatriation to India. In reply to a suggestion by a member of the 1897 Commission that a bounty could encourage reindenture, he had disagreed: "If they were made to reindenture themselves they would not accept, but if they got half the amount in cash and half in land, it might induce them to start rice cultivation."[105] However, by early 1898, he submitted that even if 10 percent of potential returnees were dissuaded from doing so, by reindenturing, that was desirable: the colony must retain the labour it had; he was immovably against new recruits from India.[106]

The planters and their allies, however, saw no merit in reindenture. They preferred the more malleable novices, those who "did not know the ropes". It is interesting that even when proplanter correspondents expressed support for land settlements and the rising rice culture, they were uncompromising in their demand for more indentured labourers. As 'Old Timer' wrote in January 1898:

> The sugar estates require . . . reliable resident labour, without which they cannot be carried on successfully . . . At the end of five years they would be free to go and

work where they liked. As the free coolies have now made a successful start to grow rice they will prefer not to attach themselves too closely to the estates, but will want to give most of their time to their rice patches, in fact, to be their own masters to go and come as they like . . . If immigration ceases it means the beginning of the end for the sugar industry.[107]

Bechu penetrated the ruse of the plantocracy. He noted that the acreage under cane in British Guiana had contracted, from 76,101 in 1892 to 66,236 in 1897; the demand for labour was necessarily reduced; and the statutory wage was not given to workers in the "slack season". Like his compatriot, Joseph Ruhomon, Bechu was always solicitous of the welfare of African Guyanese, observing that: "the suffering Negro and creole labourers" were made to subsidize immigration "through the taxation of foodstuffs and other commodities . . . to flood the labour market . . . to keep down wages at starvation point."[108] Indeed, as noted earlier, between 1 April 1895 and 31 March 1898, the period of greatest depression, two-thirds of immigration costs, instead of the usual one-third, were met from general revenue. This had led Bechu to support the government's proposals for reindenture – the award of $25 for three years and $50 for five years. His contention was that reindenture "not only saves the costly expense of bringing immigrants all the way from Calcutta, but provides against the loss of acclimatizing and training them to work".[109] But the complacency endured in some quarters.

In early 1898, the prominent planter and legislator, R.G. Duncan, remarked that there was no alternative on the horizon to remotely threaten sugar. It was the "legitimate" industry of British Guiana:[110] no sacrifice was too great for Moloch. This old certainty was, however, challenged by a correspondent who asserted that the "death knell of sugar as the mainstay of the colony" had sounded; "one hundred years of unprogressive, oligarchical rule" had provided a harvest of gloom. It was time for radical change: a larger population; reclamation of the land; and the introduction of new industries to give hope to the poor.[111]

Yet the capacity of the plantocracy to bend even some of its more obdurate critics to its saccharine obsession was astounding. *The Daily Chronicle*, which had been, like Bechu, committed to a more diverse culture beyond sugar, lost its resolve. It is interesting to observe the paper's vacillation. In February 1898, it deprecated the obstinacy of those besotted with sugar, "Little Demeraraites", while extolling the potential for a "Greater British Guiana", beyond the beaten track of coastal sugar plantations. *The Chronicle* elaborated:

There are those of little faith who cannot foresee any prospect for the colony than that of a sugar-growing province. We do not quarrel with them, but let them see to it that they refrain from exerting their influence to prevent or delay the realization of the hopes of more sanguine men.[112]

By May 1898, the Planters' Association, having failed to persuade the Norman Commission and the British Government of the wisdom of imposing countervailing duties on beet sugar, had identified a central role for indentured labour in the planters' strategy for survival.[113] Although they had to reassume coverage of two-thirds of the immigration costs from April 1898, they appealed to the Governor, Sir Walter Sendall, to raise their quota for indentured labourers from 2,400 to 3,600 for the 1898–99 season.[114] The Governor concurred but, amazingly, *The Daily Chronicle* also quickly lent its voice to the chorus of support for more 'coolies'.[115] The paper posited that a "reservoir" of Indian labour was of benefit not only to sugar, but to every other undertaking. It then proceeded to make the planters' case for them:

> If British Guiana is to go forward, then it must have labour and a great part of that labour must be indentured . . . If needs be, let the Imperial Government bear one-third of the cost, the Colonial Government another, and if the Indian Government must be permitted to insist upon the return passage, let the Imperial Government assume that liability for a term of years.[116]

Bechu was not impressed with *The Chronicle's volte-face*. He remarked that if the paper had sought to remedy the defects of the immigration system with the same passion it was now calling for more indentureds, many more immigrants would have been procured for the colony. Bechu challenged the Planters' Association to improve the lot of the 'coolies' they already had before importing more. The escalating colony of destitutes was a severe indictment of the system.[117] He again censured the Immigration Agents for ignoring the fact that, often, the statutory wage could not be earned, and the planters for not treating Indians as "rational beings" amenable to persuasion. He was especially appalled by the aptly named drivers, Indian foremen, frequently "tyrannical" men who manifested no "sacred or honourable" ties to their compatriots. Bechu appealed to the planters to take the initiative, to shed their "Shylock-like" passion for profits.[118] He wanted them to be magnanimous:

> (The planters) must really strive to enter into the feelings of the labourers they have on the spot who they should endeavour to conciliate; and whatever differences there may be in social standing or enlightenment between the employer and

employee, if there were a common ground upon which they could stand it would conciliate the weaker party. The stronger *ought* to be the first to come forward and invite co-operation.[119]

Bechu's commitment to his 'bound coolie' compatriots was unwavering. Yet between February and October 1899, he was publicly silent. A planter had brought a libel charge against him for a letter he wrote in September 1898 (see Chapter Seven); apparently, during the prolonged trial, he could not write to the press, even under a pseudonym – a common practice. However, the wide-ranging debate initiated by Bechu on the Indian condition remained prominent in the newspapers.

In early 1899, *The Chronicle* was still marching to the planters' drum, but it slanted its argument in broader terms. The paper was looking to Indians for the "formation of new agricultural enterprises and the . . . establishment of a peasantry". Besides, it was to the Indians' advantage to settle in British Guiana, where they were already "thriving" and would soon be able to exert influence in public life. *The Chronicle* saw Indian immigration as the motor of development: "If no limits were set on the number of immigrants the colony is permitted to introduce annually – if, in other words, the application of the planters for labourers were granted to the full – a strong impulse would soon be given in the direction of development and progress."[120]

Shortly afterwards, the paper lent further support to the planters' case by advocating the abolition of the return passage entitlement which had underpinned the system for its duration and which the paper erroneously asserted the 'coolies' "do not require . . . and do not ask for".[121] This would have enabled the planters to reduce their cost of production. *The Chronicle* did not say that although Indians had to pay a portion of their return passage, by 1895, 2,071 returned to India in that year; 2,059 in 1896; 1,529 in 1897; 1,238 in 1898; and 1,145 in 1899.[122] It was Bechu's argument that people were taxed to bring indentured labourers to the colony, while the haemorrhaging of seasoned workers proceeded unabated in the absence of a viable land settlement policy.

In March 1899, on learning that the Colonial Office had approved a quota of 5,000 Indian indentureds for 1899–1900 (4,961 were actually landed), *The Chronicle* advanced a thesis on indentureship which was congruent with that of the plantocracy:

> . . . for the time that our condition is so closely bound up with sugar, as long as the native labour prefers to remain unemployed rather than accept what he regards as an inadequate wage, the planters must be allowed to look elsewhere for their

labour supply; and any act of the Colonial Office or the local government which interferes with that right would be against the interests of the country.

However, it was inclined to temper its strong prosugar thesis by identifying the Indian as the instrument of future development: by his "frugal and thrifty" attitudes and deep sense of familial responsibility, he would supply "the initiative needed to beneficially occupy a portion . . . of the vast cultivable territory" of British Guiana.[123]

Bechu was unable to reverse this new-found obsession with indentured labour, but in July 1899, two correspondents to the paper challenged this thesis, arguing that if the government had a policy of preparing drained and irrigated land for time-expired Indians, in lieu of return passages, the loss of "valuable labour" to India would not have been perpetuated. Sugar must "not arrogate to itself the supreme control of all below it".[124]

The Corentyne Coast, in Berbice, was a place with a salubrious climate, drier, windswept, and less malarious. The time-expired Indians were especially enamoured of this section of the coast, but, even here, agricultural effort was hazardous without a comprehensive system of drainage and irrigation. In November 1897, Bechu had argued that the current Land Regulations, designed to cripple peasant initiative, should be abolished. He believed that Indians were equipped to advance rice culture in British Guiana if they were given small loans in lieu of return passages, to acquire lands of their own choice, rather than wasting money on abandoned estates, such as Huis't Dieren, Whim, and Helena, which were "poisoned by free application of manure".[125] Bechu was certain that at least the domestic consumption of rice could be met by Indian cultivators in the colony, but the government was so obsessed with sugar that it was "prop[ping] up a tottering industry which eventually *must* fall", but would not help small farmers. Bechu was deeply disturbed by the persistence of sugar monoculture:

> How is it that certain sections of our community – the Governor and the Government Secretary included – cannot be convinced that Providence never intended that British Guiana should always remain a sugar-growing colony? It has times without number been brought to the notice of these good people that the undeveloped lands of the colony are amongst the richest existing in any part of the tropics, and yet they religiously cling to the idea that there is nothing but sugar for this magnificent colony of ours![126]

Even the conservative, proplanter *Argosy* had, in February 1898, appreciated some of the problems of the fledgling rice industry. It recognized that Indian growers had made rapid progress, noted the hazards encountered on lands which were not drained and irrigated; acknowledged that small farmers could not afford to empolder these lands, but, significantly, did not recommend government help as a recompense for the inordinate assistance, tantamount to subsidies, which sugar had received.[127]

Yet the planters' sense of being wronged was unassuageable; indeed, it was heightened by the Norman Commission which had observed that the plantocracy had been committed to the stagnation of the peasantry. This was no longer tenable: the small farmer must be encouraged. The Commission asserted:

> The settlement of the labourer on the land has not, as a rule, been viewed with favour in the past by the persons interested in sugar estates. What suited them best was a large supply of labourers, entirely dependent on being able to find work on the estates, and, consequently, subject to their control and willing to work at low rates of wages. But it seems to us that no reform affords so good a prospect for the permanent welfare in the future of the West Indies as the settlement of the labouring population on the land as small peasant proprietors . . .

Indeed, the far-reaching land reforms of 1898 and 1903 stemmed appreciably from this unequivocal signal from this august body. However, rumours of 'King Sugar's' death were highly exaggerated. Amalgamation of estates, technological innovation, subsidized 'bound coolie' labour, were all instrumental in its survival. The greatest casualty of its revival was the retention of the old mantra that the rise of an African and Indian peasantry in the colony was detrimental to the long-term interests of sugar; the notion that the latter were congruent with the national interest endured.

The Argosy, by early 1899, had become an advocate of the settlement of time-expired Indians on empoldered lands, even arguing that they be given "special consideration". Charges for land reclamation, however, could not be made on general revenue,[128] a view endorsed by the liberal *Chronicle*. The plantocratic perspective was resilient: vast areas of leased land already empoldered were held, but not used, on the sugar estates; subsidy to immigration and fiscal concessions were still available for the "legitimate" industry; support for rice, however, should not be expected from the state.

By early 1900, with some recovery in the price of sugar, the planters were again becoming sensitive about their nonresident workers. Although some estates afforded these workers access to small plots to grow rice, they were often quickly deprived of this facility when conditions improved. A classic example of this was Anna Regina, in Essequibo, where in late 1898 Indian rice growers were forced to relinquish their plots during a period of amalgamation. *The Daily Chronicle* observed of the case: "One of the principal activities that the authorities have in view, in dispossessing the free coolie immigrants of their rice farms on the estate, is to secure an adequate supply of labour, the coolies having devoted their whole time and attention to the cultivation of their farms."[129]

By February 1900, the planters' demands for indentured labourers had become so strident that *The Chronicle*, once again, became a severe critic of the immigration system. It noted that although 198,000 'coolies' had been taken to British Guiana, the current Indian population was only 114,500. As Bechu argued consistently, lack of commitment to the long-term interests of Indians drove far too many seasoned workers back to India. *The Chronicle* virtually proceeded to restate its indictment of the system:

> The artificial conditions that have been established [under indentureship] make the planters entirely independent of the ordinary laws which regulate the amount to be paid to the labourer. Improved prices for sugar have no effect upon the scale of remuneration allowed either to indentured or unindentured immigrants. At present well-equipped sugar estates under capable management are yielding handsome returns, in proof of which we need but point to the general tendency to increase the area under cultivation. But the lot of the labourer has not been improved, by the smallest extent in consequence of the increased profits that sugar is now earning . . . Until some better provision is made for the retention of the coolie in the colony the introduction of immigrants in such quantities as demanded by the planters would be an imprudent and unprofitable undertaking.[130]

This stung the planters. E.C. Luard, the Manager of Plantation LBI and prominent advocate of the plantocracy, quickly challenged the paper to state what wage was adequate to attract the necessary labour from local sources, thus obviating the need for indentureds.[131] *The Chronicle* showed no remorse: "There is something seriously wrong with the colony's economic condition when notwithstanding that we have thousands of unemployed labourers in our midst, we still continue to introduce an indentured supply [sic] of cheap labour from outside sources."[132]

In June 1900, Bechu again deplored the repatriation of good workers to India and warned that it was futile to offer them unempoldered lands in lieu of return passages, as was the case at the failed settlements at Huis't Dieren, Helena, and Whim: "no sane immigrant with any spunk in him would be so foolish as to forego his claim to a back passage for a solitary [unreclaimed] acre, as it would be tantamount to Esau's selling his birthright for a mess of pottage."[133]

Bechu's Letters in the Context of the Guianese Environment: Bechu in Freedom

Bechu's ally, Joseph Ruhomon, endorsed this completely, elaborating on the limitations of the Whim settlement, on the Corentyne, where Indian farmers were precluded from growing rice and provisions simultaneously, because of a lack of imagination in the distribution of holdings. It would have been perfectly possible for all farmers to have access to clay lands as well as sand reefs. This, Ruhomon contended, was "absolutely necessary" for an "independent and permanent living".[134] The problem, of course, was that the ruling class could not conceive of British Guiana being anything but a sugar colony. It was, therefore, imperative not to facilitate activities which could undermine the labour supply to the sugar plantations.

Bechu's impact on his compatriots was already evident. In August 1900, Thomas Drepaul, a creole Indian rice farmer from Cromarty, Corentyne, underlined the centrality of drainage *and* irrigation for the sustenance of a vibrant peasantry. He dramatized the hazards of agriculture, away from the empoldered sugar estates. Drepaul elaborated:

> I have a wife, six children, and an aged mother to support. The last two or three years we have suffered much: work not to be had sufficient for me to support such a family. I planted rice with others aback here at the beginning of the year. Last month and the month before we cut it, but there was so much water the heads of the rice fell in it, and I find it sour and very little of it good to eat. Last year [1899] we did not get one grain [because of the drought]; the year before little – the water was too much. A good crop, however, may be got at the end of this year if the water in [the] savannah holds out. If it goes away before the rice is ripe it will be a loss again. We cannot grow rice here unless we are sure of water . . . If we get water whenever we want it, we can get two crops of rice in one year, and live well and be able to pay for the water. I have been sending money for my family in India, but for two years I have not been able; the times are too hard.[135]

The times were no easier for African workers, many of whom refused to work for the generally poor wages on the sugar estates. They, understandably, were inclined to blame 'coolies' for their ills, for "taking the bread out of their mouths". Bechu always empathized with Africans, arguing that they subsidized immigration to further undermine their condition in the colony; the system should be suspended until local labour could get remunerative employment.

It is a measure of the incomprehension between various interests that the proplanter *Argosy* could argue otherwise. It was convinced that Africans should be and were, indeed, generally grateful that the 'coolie' has made his life better! There was room for more indentured labourers in British Guiana:

The coolie saved the situation, and enabled our strong-hearted predecessors to keep their estates alive; and gradually after the terrible years of the 40s and 50s, the estates began to flourish, and out of their returns the whole community... began to reap the advantages that accrue from wealth. So far from the coolie being the natural enemy of the black labourers as mischiefmakers would make out, – there is not now a thinking black man in the colony who is not ready to admit that through the sugar estates, cultivated largely by coolie labourers, he is blessed with a liberal education system, a splendid postal system, an easy means of communication, thorough police protection, and all the advantages of a civilized country. The tendency of the government should be – and the Governor freely acknowledges that he is so inclined – to increase rather than decrease the yearly indents, for the colony is craving for population... The citizen who opposes immigration is an enemy of the State... [136]

This plantocratic definition was at variance with what one may consider the creole or African perception of the role of 'coolie' labour in 1890s British Guiana. In early 1897, the popular African leader, Dr J.M. Rohlehr, a Berbician, submitted a memorandum to the Norman Commission in which he advanced several crucial arguments against Indian immigration.[137] He stated that 'coolie' labour undermined the bargaining position of African labour, which could not be sustained on the paltry wages on sugar estates. He explained: "The black labourer has to house himself and family, pay his medical adviser, contribute to the support of his church, school his children, and clothe himself decently. The coolie is supplied with a house, doctor and medicine, schooling for his children, and he has a protector in the immigration depot. It is plain that the black labourer must require more to keep him than the coolie..."

Dr Rohlehr added that the overall cost of Indian indentureship, including the payment of back passages, rendered it anything but cheap. He was categorical: "I am convinced that it is unnecessary to continue to import more coolies." If a fraction of the funds expended on 'coolie' labour were paid to creole labourers, "there would be an abundant supply of black labour on the sugar estates."

The gist of Dr Rohlehr's argument was repeated by a creole correspondent to *The Daily Chronicle* in January 1901, shortly before Bechu left the colony. He stated that the immigration system had four "fatal defects": (i) it was, in fact, an "emigration" system, facilitating the continual haemorrhaging of labour to India; (ii) it tended to "pauperize" the colony, as time-expired Indians repatriated considerable money and jewellery, having "stinted themselves of the necessaries of life"; both labour and capital drained way; (iii) the general taxpayer was penalized to sustain a system for the benefit of one industry – sugar; this was tantamount to a bounty, "more detrimental . . . and less excusable than the continental bounty"; (iv) the "native labourer" (African) had to subsidize the importation of foreign labour "to work for wages on which . . . [he] cannot live". This creole writer, alluding to the abstemious living of many Indians, concluded: "The native labour cannot live on a gallon of rice a week, nor can he clothe himself with a yard of cotton. Thus he is punished by being made to contribute one-third of the cost of introduction of his important competitor."[138]

It was within the fertile interstices of these perceptions of 'coolie' labour that the later, more demonstrative racism among Africans and Indians in British Guiana was rooted. Recalling his boyhood in the early years of this century, one African Guyanese wrote: "I often heard men grumbling about the Indian coolies who were brought over to work on the plantations for the sake of cheap labour."[139] This impression had become an aspect of African lore in Guyana; it had led Walter Rodney, in the late 1970s, to assess the enduring consequences, among Africans, of Indian indentureship:

> This kind of socialization indicates the deeply ingrained nature of the Creole characterization of Indians as persons who undermined the quest of Africans for employment at decent wages. Another closely related aspect of the image of Indians in creole African eyes was that they were pampered planter protégés, who were given housing and medical facilities . . . Oral interviews of blacks born in the 1890s have demonstrated their deep-rooted feeling that planters discriminated in favour of Indians. From this standpoint, it was but a short step to direct racial animosity.[140]

Bechu did not see Indians as the "pampered protégés" of the planters, but he appreciated the implications of continued indentured immigration. In late 1900–early 1901, on the eve of his departure from the colony, he discussed the cost of the immigration system in light of the welfare of all local labour, African and Indian. He observed that in 1899–1900, "the exorbitant sum" of $355,439.90 was expended on 4,959 indentured labourers, while $100,079.74 was consumed by return passages, for a total expenditure of $455,519.64. A persistent advocate of reindenture, Bechu felt that seasoned workers could have been procured "on the spot for less than half that amount".[141]

Bechu was always sensitive to the feelings of Africans in British Guiana. This was evident in November 1900 when he challenged a proimmigration correspondent, Francis G. Harvey, who deemed the cost of indentureship "paltry" compared with the benefits of the sugar industry.[142] Bechu recommended Barbadians as agricultural labourers in the colony, and suggested a cheaper, long-term alternative, as Dr Rohlehr had done in 1897. Bechu wrote:

> ... I am at a loss to understand what that gentleman terms 'cheap labour'. Our imported labour may be viewed as cheap in one sense, seeing that the men on arrival are paid 6 pence *per diem* instead of the statutory wage, but if Mr Harvey will just take the trouble to figure out the charges in connection with the recruiting and transportation of our immigrants, the cost of their clothing and supplies on the voyage, and the cost of medical services, he will find that it would be far cheaper in the long run to offer a higher wage and secure all our agricultural labour locally.[143]

As if to dramatize the plight of local African labourers and underline the absurdity of the immigration system, Bechu, in his penultimate letter, in January 1901, reproduced an advertisement from a New York newspaper requesting labour for Hawaiian sugar plantations. He saw this as "a splendid opportunity" for the "sturdy black labouring population" in the colony to obtain "steady employment and liberal wages".[144]

Writing from Tuschen, West Coast Demerara, on 4 February 1901, as he was "about to say farewell to this colony", he again manifested concern for the welfare of local labour. In what may be seen as a final note of gratitude to the editor of *The Daily Chronicle*, he acknowledged his recent efforts "to lighten the burden of the taxpayers by strongly protesting against the introduction of more immigrants so long as we have such a large unemployed labouring population in the colony".[145]

Bechu never gave credence to the popular notion of the "laziness of the Negro"; he deftly observed that inadequate wages under what he termed "another form of slavery", indentureship, were driving Indians as well away from the sugar plantations, in some cases, in despair, to the dereliction of menial jobbing and begging in the streets of Georgetown. This bleak aspect of the Indian condition, especially jarring to Bechu, a resident of the capital since March 1897, epitomized Indian indentureship at its worst.

He used the destitute Indians in Georgetown to indict the whole system; but he was magnanimous to the Salvation Army for providing food and shelter for many of the jobbers, at a nominal cost. Bechu, as noted earlier, was a Christian, but his faith was not focused merely on saving souls. It was rooted in the idea that the ministry of Christ must embrace the underdog, providing hope and dignity to lives stunted by what he saw as the greed of the powerful, such as the plantocracy in British Guiana.

CHAPTER FIVE

Bechu and the Destitute 'Coolies': the Achievement of Ghurib Das

In June 1897, Bechu had expressed support for some of the leaders of the Salvation Army who were tried and convicted for disturbing the peace with their tambourines and their drumming. This gave him the opportunity to indict the old, established Christian denominations for seeking easy options, preaching to the converted and eschewing the vineyard of the damned. Bechu saw them as allies of the privileged.[146] In the Salvation Army and its charismatic leader from mid 1897, Alexander Alexander (Ghurib Das), he found a kindred spirit – the irrepressible servant of the broken reeds of indentureship, the 'coolie' jobbers.

In October 1897, *The Argosy* applauded the exceptional achievement of the Salvation Army among Indian derelicts in Georgetown, precisely the feature of its mission which had appealed to Bechu. The paper observed:

> [At the Salvation Army Coolie Shelter] many otherwise homeless coolies, waifs and strays about town find a cheap bed and a cheap supper, with a degree of order and cleanliness quite unobtainable for them in any other quarter. It is quite in accordance with the principles of the Armymen to associate their evangelical work with practical efforts for the bettering of the condition of the poor . . .[147]

The principal architect of this admirable effort was Alexander Alexander,[148] a Scotsman who went to British Guiana in 1883 and worked for many years as an overseer at Plantation Aurora, in Essequibo. He had joined the Salvation Army in 1886, in Scotland, while on a brief holiday. So Alexander had first-hand knowledge of Indians on sugar estates; he also had the commitment, fed by his religious convictions, to do something to improve their lives. On his visits to Georgetown he had been appalled by the destitution of Indian jobbers and felt impelled to help. He left his job on the estate, moved to Georgetown, and dedicated his life, within the Salvation Army, to salvaging some self-respect for Indian jobbers and derelicts. This compassionate man even assumed a Hindu name, Ghurib Das, "the poor servant", adopted Indian dress (kurta, dhoti, turban), learnt Hindustani, the colloquial Hindi, and walked barefooted most of the time. He had remade himself, shedding the white overseer's persona – a source of apprehension among Indians. *The Argosy* explained his rationale:

> He early learned that coolies had no respect for one who pretended to be a teacher and who did not exercise a considerable amount of self-denial. No consecrated man with the Hindus may eat flesh, so Captain Alexander [Ghurib Das] has been a vegetarian for years . . . Shortly after adopting the coolie dress . . . [he] sent a copy of the photograph home [to Scotland]. The only comment his sister made upon it . . . was 'I hope you did not send one to any other body.'[149]

She was obviously not proud that he had gone 'native'. He was often called 'Coolie' Alexander: that represented arrival; acceptance. The work could go on.

Already, by late 1897, he had established two shelters for Indian jobbers in Georgetown, offering them three meals a day at a cost of 8 cents per day, and night shelter at one cent. This amounted to a cost of 54 cents for seven days; Sundays were catered for free. By late 1898, he had opened a home for poor Indian children and orphans; the school which he founded for them was also located here.[150]

By mid 1898, Bechu had recognized Ghurib Das' admirable work. He was advocating the establishment of a government-sponsored "industrial farm", preferably under Ghurib Das, who he acknowledged "is so much liked by the coolies that he could get them to cheerfully work under him in any capacity . . ."[151] Bechu's suggestion was probably prompted by the plight of some "debilitated" ones, who were, as one correspondent observed, "known to eat the garbage off the streets".[152]

Like Bechu, Ghurib Das was not afraid to blame the plantocracy for the growing colony of jobbers and derelicts in the capital. In 1897–98 alone, 766 Indians had deserted the sugar estates. If the planters would initiate a "farm scheme" to enable estate workers to improve their condition during the "slack" period, advised Ghurib Das, there would be a contraction of deserters – the source of the destitutes and jobbers in Georgetown.[153] He repeated his admonition a few days later, in August 1898, urging the estate authorities to make better provisions for their workers in the "slack" season. He noted that most jobbers did not earn more than 6 cents per day and elaborated: "why they prefer this half-starved life, in many cases, is the harsh and inhuman, unsympathetic way they are treated by many of their more fortunate brethren, the 'drivers', hence the great percent of deserters from estates . . ."[154] The drivers or foremen were the instruments of Managers and overseers – all were implicated.

Ghurib Das' criticism of the planters soon evoked a sharp response from Norman Bascom, a planter, the brother of the Manager of Plantation Cove and John, East Coast Demerara. He castigated him and the Salvation Army, "an ostensibly religious organization", for aiding and abetting deserters, offering them a "royal road", by providing cheap food and lodging. They ought to demand from 'coolies' their certificate of exemption from labour, before they were allowed access to their facilities.[155] Three days after Bascom's letter was published, Bechu's controversial letter appeared in *The Chronicle*; it was the subject of the libel action which the Manager of Cove and John brought against him (see Chapter Seven).[156] This effectively removed Bechu from the debate on 'coolie' destitutes for several months; the tentacles of sugar fed into every pore of Guianese life; but Ghurib Das' work on behalf of the poor was undiminished.

In September 1898, he complained to the Georgetown Town Council of the "grave" need for a few water closets for the destitutes, and deprecated the tendency for street urchins to pelt them as they were forced to defecate in the open. Ghurib Das again indicted the planters for the growing colony of jobbers in the city – 766 warrants were issued for indentureds who had deserted the sugar estates in 1897–98; 670 men and 96 women.[157] Like Bechu, he argued that while the planters' "incessant cry" was for "more immigrants", a "shipload" of seasoned labourers, "much superior to the unacclimatized $65 ones", was being squandered in the capital. They were both also contemptuous of the "foot-kissing" demanded by drivers and "admired by many Managers and overseers". Ghurib Das concluded:

> Every man is not a Bechu who can air his grievance in the public newspaper when his hands get blistered, nor is everyone blessed with health and strength to earn his 10 shillings a week . . . many are born weak and continually need some counsel and help. If a little timely counsel and humanly help among the immigrants on the estates were included in the Managers' memorandum, there would be fewer homeless inhabitants in the streets of Georgetown.[158]

In February 1899, he again encouraged the planters to allocate indentured Indians plots of land on the estates to grow crops for home use. This, he believed, would stem desertion while inculcating a sense of belonging to the estate, changing their perception of the environment[159] – a view wholly endorsed by *The Chronicle*.[160] The planting fraternity, however, opted for a hard measure, the use of the police to apprehend deserters in Georgetown. About a week after Ghurib Das' letter, the police raided 129 "coolie jobbers and loafers", detaining them at the Immigration Depot; 38 were identified as deserters and were returned to the estates whence they had fled.[161]

What the plantocracy could not comprehend was that desertion had, indeed, become an instrument of protest; it was one dimension of the immigrant's culture of resistance, given the general perception that his protector's role was gravely compromised. The records are replete with reports of 'bound coolies', especially recent arrivals, fleeing estates, beating a path to the forests, impelled by the notion that they could find an overland route to Calcutta!ature[162]

In February 1900, a planter from the East Coast Demerara called on the authorities to issue licences to 'coolie porters and jobbers' in Georgetown in order to eradicate the epidemic of desertions.[163] Ghurib Das endorsed the call because he thought this would terminate the "inhuman" raids on Indian jobbers at all hours of the night, noting that, often, bona fide time-expired jobbers could not locate their certificate of exemption from labour, thus suffering the indignity of arrest. He also recommended a statutory wage rate for Indian jobbers, and police protectors to ensure that they were not defrauded.[164]

The Georgetown Town Council, obviously at the planters' behest, quickly enforced a by-law requiring "coolie jobbers" to be licensed, and they started to prosecute defaulters.[165] Bechu intervened, suggesting that the Magistrate should not imprison defaulters, as their labour in jail was "unproductive". He felt that convicted deserters should be returned to the estates to do the work for which they were brought to the colony.[166] The magistrate responded to Bechu, noting that he did not have the authority to return deserters to the estates. Meanwhile, all "coolie jobbers" were under intense scrutiny. Many bona fide time-expired ones, who could not afford the licence fee of one shilling, were prosecuted. On 2 March 1900, for instance, 12 such jobbers were fined one dollar each or seven days' imprisonment.[167]

This had so incensed Bechu that he deplored the imposition of a fee on jobbers engaged in earning "an honest living". He observed, in his unfailingly clinical manner, that because "they scorned the idea of being a nuisance to the public", of being "professional beggars", they were subject to a punitive measure: the reward for effort was jail.[168] Another correspondent also deprecated the practice, a severe imposition, as jobbers had to scour "every corner of the city in order to get a job for a cent or a penny, which only serves for a meal or half-a-meal". He explained the rationale for this "highly improper" fee, another example of the planters having their own way: "The main object of the planters in having recourse to this measure and molesting the lives of the jobbers is that indentured immigrants abscond from the estates. Is it judicious to punish all the coolie jobbers for the sake of one or two indentured immigrants?"[169]

Ghurib Das soon had grave reservations about the licence fee, declaring that it was an act of racial discrimination: " . . . poor 'Sammy' [Indian jobbers] . . . [are] always hauled before the Magistrate, while others can be seen picking many of the choice jobs." Jobbers from other racial groups were not required to have a licence.[170] Indian indentureship cast a long shadow.

Like Bechu, nothing could cripple the spirit of Ghurib Das. In August 1900, he was seen cycling on the Essequibo Coast, attired in his Indian outfit, collecting funds for victims of the famine in India. His appeal underlined the "necessity of self-denial and pity" – qualities which he had in abundance.[171]

Ghurib Das' devotion to the poor Indians yielded much in a short time. In October 1900, a little over three years since he started his work, *War Cry*, the organ of the Salvation Army, reported that the Indian paupers in the Alms House in Georgetown, had declined from about 400 to 110; their three shelters were providing accommodation for 250 every night, while receipts from the sale of cheap food averaged about $240 per week.[172]

The Jamaica Times captured the essence of the man – his purity of motives and magnanimity of spirit – having encountered him in September 1900, in Jamaica, where he had gone to raise funds to help others to promote similar work:

> . . . the Captain [Ghurib Das] has not hesitated to enter fully into the East Indian life, and to get in touch with their lives by adopting their costume, and like themselves going barefooted. A man thoroughly in earnest in his aim at sacrificing self in the service of man, and a shrewd man he is, as emphatic as General Booth [Tucker, founder of the Salvation Army] . . . against any form of charity that tends to pauperize or demoralize the recipients, and he thoroughly shares the General's view that all that is done to better a man's body must aim at a change in that man's nature.[173]

It is hardly surprising, therefore, that Bechu should have identified him so inextricably with the welfare of his destitute compatriots. That, however, did not spare Ghurib Das from the ire of Bechu's pen. In November 1900, he had tried to refute Bechu's allegation that often on estates, the wages bargained for by

African as well as Indian labourers were not honoured when the task was completed: he had encountered no such case during his twelve years on sugar estates.[174] Bechu retorted that Ghurib Das was "sticking up for the planters" because he had "an eye to business", alleging that shortly before he went to Jamaica, "he succeeded in collecting a pretty decent sum from them for the Salvation Army."[175] Ghurib Das admitted that he had received "handsome donations" from the planters to help with his school for Indian children as well as his home for overseers who were experiencing dire times. He added: "the planters appreciate this part of my work."[176]

It is noteworthy that, in refuting Bechu's allegations, Ghurib Das had advised him to "try a little practice in elevating and encouraging the masses".[177] He was a practical, pragmatic man engaged in a demanding business to alleviate the lives of destitute Indians; he had to compromise, although he never lost his high ideals. Bechu, on the other hand, was the inveterate critic, the uncompromising watchdog of Indian interests. They were men of different temperament, trying in their own way to lift the Indian in British Guiana beyond the poverty and self-deprecation of the 'coolie' universe.

CHAPTER SIX

Bechu vs his 'Protectors'

Walter Rodney has conferred historical recognition on Bechu's wide-ranging critique of indentureship in the colony:

> Bechu . . . astonished planters and colonial officials with vigorous and sustained attacks on the abuses of indentureship . . . His denunciations included substantial allegations of immoral exploitation of Indian females by overseers, instances of the callous turning away of time-expired immigrants from estate hospitals, active discouragement of those seeking repatriation, and numerous examples of planters breaking the labour code by their treatment of indentured labourers. Bechu's exposures sometimes led to remedial action such as the dismissal of offending overseers, but he also became the target of a campaign of vilification carried out by planters and by important sectors of the colonial administration. This redoubtable fighter was twice tried on one charge of libel after accusing Plantation Enmore's [in fact, Cove and John's] Manager of causing the death of an immigrant by turning him away from the estate hospital when he was desperately in need of treatment.[178]

In short, Bechu's central task was to expose anyone who he considered to be infringing the rights of his inarticulate compatriots. It does not detract from his resolute, unimpeachable campaign of exposition to repeat that he was a bachelor in British Guiana – no family or extended family, the claims of which overwhelmed most Indians and stifled social responsibility, encumbered Bechu's rebellious spirit. There were, indeed, no sacred cows in his universe of protest.

In his memorandum to the Norman Commission, Bechu castigated Managers and overseers, asserting that "gross immorality exists in [sic] most of the estates". He gave a specific example, the case of a Punjabi, a shipmate of his, who wished to marry an Indian woman, Leloo, on Plantation Lusignan. He was "deterred" from doing so after he learnt that she was having an affair with an overseer who later paid for her indentureship to be commuted. Bechu identified this as another source of discontent, leading sometimes to riots – possibly an allusion to Non Pareil – "yet Immigration Agents close their eyes to the matter".[179]

In July 1898, he drew attention to the case of one, Purdaree, an indentured man on Plantation Ogle, who was charged with assaulting an overseer for stopping his wages. Bechu remarked that the latter practice was "indefensible", and it often induced 'coolies' to vent their frustration, violently, on drivers and overseers. This, he contended, led one to feel that "those who had been appointed to protect the immigrants", the Immigration Agents, "do not take the slightest trouble to see to their interests".[180]

Bechu argued that though, in principle, the 'coolie' could seek redress of his grievance by complaining to a Magistrate, it was virtually impossible for him to comprehend and utilize the complex system. It was, therefore, the duty of the Immigration Agents "to enquire into and remedy" such cases of dissatisfaction. Bechu concluded on a maxim which encapsulated the man's passion for justice: "The Immigration Agent should be easily approachable to the meanest coolie; but he should be unapproachable to the lordliest employer."[181]

His vigilance enabled him to detect, quickly, possibilities for collusion or suggestions of compromise between colonial officials with the authority to adjudicate in Indian affairs on the estates, and the powerful plantocracy. In July 1898, *The Daily Chronicle* had noted tersely, unobtrusively, that "Mr Magistrate Gall has removed from Haslington House to Plantation Enmore."[182] Bechu grasped the implications of this seemingly inconsequential item immediately. He pointed out that Mr F.A. Gall was the acting Stipendiary Magistrate of the Mahaica Judicial District, and that he had moved to a house "adjoining the residence of the Manager of Plantation Enmore". Bechu thought it imperative that justice had to be seen to be done. He asked:

> However high-minded that official [Gall] may be, is it right . . . that he should be living in close proximity to the Manager of the estate, when he is constantly required to take cognisance of the complaints of immigrants and to determine their wages? When a Magistrate can live on a plantation and be on friendly terms with the Manager and exchange his hospitalities who, permit me to ask, is to protect the *indentured* man?[183]

Bechu vs his 'Protectors'

Bechu's unremitting vigilance in all matters affecting his "dumb-driven" compatriots led the Immigration Agent on the Essequibo Coast, Henry W. Taylor, to an agitated denunciation of him: a "dangerous demagogue" whose allegations were "monstrous".[184] In May 1897, Bechu had written to *The Daily Chronicle* on behalf of an indentured labourer, Surjudass, whose wife, allegedly, had been seduced by an overseer; when the man reported this to the Immigration Agent, apparently he received no help.[185] Taylor asserted that Bechu's allegations were an "unprovoked attack" on him; the complaint of Surjudass was "utterly without foundation"; and he demanded that Bechu mind his own business: "I . . . warn him that any such interference with the people in my district will only result adversely on them, so that if he really has the interest of his fellow countrymen at heart, he will leave me to protect their interests . . ."[186] Bechu had no doubts that officials like Henry Taylor were already compromised: "Surjudass, *like most coolies*, has apparently learnt from dear bought experience that it is useless seeking the assistance of his protector, *for such officials are virtually the protectors of the planters.*"[187]

In November 1897, Bechu extended this assessment to the immigration system as a whole. He had written to the Government Secretary requesting that the Governor make a concession by granting him a passport to travel to England to further his studies. Although the Governor had commuted his indentureship on 26 February 1897, he had to be resident in the colony for five years before he could be granted one. Bechu was informed that before such a concession could be made, he had to repay the cost of his introduction to the colony. He was not prepared to do this, although "my time is being wasted" in British Guiana. He reminded the Immigration Agent General that one of his compatriots had offered to pay his commutation fee in February 1897 and was told that that was not necessary, since the estate had paid no indenture fee for him because he was deemed unfit for fieldwork. The acting Immigration Agent General replied that the commutation fee was "quite distinct from the claim which the colony has against you for the cost of your introduction".

Bechu was enraged. He demanded of the Immigration Agent General that he be addressed as "Mr", and deprecated the basis of the ruling. He wrote caustically:

> If, as you say, the ordinance demands it, I must take steps to have that objectionable section of the ordinance repealed, as it is in my humble opinion tantamount to slavery. I can[not] but view with disregard the style in which I have been addressed. Common courtesy demands that when addressing the humblest individual it is necessary to prefix 'Mr'.[188]

The letter dated 24 November 1897 was addressed: "To Bechu".

Bechu forwarded all his correspondence on this matter to *The Chronicle*, noting that "the tendency has been to treat us British-born subjects in this British colony as common slaves". He explained:

> The immigration law of British Guiana has always seemed to me to be the most objectionable piece of legislation that ever saw the light of day. Anybody who runs his eyes over its pages will see at a glance that the framer was evidently under the thumb of the planters, who were all-powerful in the Court of Policy [the legislature] at the time it was drafted. The law – such law! – practically treats us East Indians as a race apart from all other British subjects in the colony, and places us under most irksome and oppressive restrictions.[189]

The Chronicle ran a leader on the matter, arguing that it would create "a dangerous precedent" if Bechu were allowed to leave the colony after only three years, without reimbursing the colony for his cost of introduction. This paper, for several years, provided Bechu with a forum, thereby frequently attracting the odium of the ruling elite. However, its concluding advice to him illustrates the condescension and lack of empathy which still tainted perceptions of even this articulate Indian – he was still a 'coolie':

> Bechu's heroic fulminations against what he calls 'irksome and oppressive restrictions' of the immigration law, and his insistence upon being addressed with the peculiarly English prefix of 'Mr' are more calculated to raise a smile than seriously to impress anyone who reads them. It is a pity that Bechu, Anglicized as he is, has not yet acquired the Englishman's sense of the ridiculous. It would save him many a bad *faux pas* in his little controversies.[190]

It is noteworthy that the *Report of the West India Royal Commission of 1897* also did not honour Bechu with "Mr" before his name – the only witness to be so treated. Like Joseph Ruhomon, Bechu was a pathfinder for his people. The insecurities were so severe that seemingly trivial slights cut near to the bone. A "sense of the ridiculous" could not come easily, on the hard Indian Guianese road to self-reclamation, dignity, and self-assurance. In his place, in his time, even Bechu's irony and subtlety spoke of intensity.

In July 1898, he apparently earned the contempt of the Immigration Agent General for stating that Indians at the Immigration Depot in Georgetown, awaiting return ships to Calcutta, were provided with poor food which cost 16 cents per head, per day. Bechu contrasted this with the "superior stuff" which was offered at Ghurib Das' shelters for Indians at 6 cents per head, per day. The sole beneficiary of the immigration authorities' incompetence was the contractor who supplied the poor food. This allegation was the crux of a private letter Bechu had sent to the Financial Representative of Georgetown – a legislator. Somehow, the letter was leaked. Bechu seemed apprehensive of the consequences, although he relished a fight: " . . . the immigration authorities here have somehow got scent of the letter and have not only sworn vengeance against me for bringing to notice the enormous profit the contractor makes by the transaction but have actually threatened to run me in for inciting my countrymen to rebel." He concluded on an ominous note, imputing darker motives to the authorities: "In any other country where the Union Jack floats I would treat such menace with silent contempt, but as in a colony like this, it is not difficult to trump up a charge of the nature contemplated, one cannot be *too* careful . . ."[191]

Bechu was irrepressible: he must have been fortified by the rise of a tradition of letter writing to the press by Indians in British Guiana. The cascade of letters by him and Ruhomon deepened their sense of the possible, giving them self-respect, self-confidence and courage. In July 1898, for instance, Joshua Ramphul, an Indian businessman from New Amsterdam, had criticized the employment of Madras interpreters in his town where very few immigrants were of Tamil stock.[192] Another correspondent, also, had exposed the folly of appointing Madras interpreters at the office of the Immigration Agent General in Georgetown, where most complaints were lodged by speakers of Hindustani, not Tamil.[193] Bechu responded that proficiency in colloquial Hindi should be made compulsory for Immigration Agents and overseers, within one year of their appointment. He believed that this would minimize areas of misunderstanding between the authorities and 'coolies', shaping a more harmonious industrial climate on the plantations. Bechu, as usual, was able to frame his argument with telling simplicity: "It seems passing strange that the ignorant *uneducated* coolie should be required to learn a foreign language, and that the *educated* European should save himself a little trouble to acquire the language of the people with whom he has so much to do."[194]

On 6 January 1901, shortly before Bechu left British Guiana, *The Daily Chronicle* carried a letter by him which may be seen as his epilogue on his protectors. It is a tribute to the man that this letter was as forthright and embattled as his first, to the same paper, on 1 November 1896:

> You must have 'smole a smile' when reproducing in your columns the reports of the Immigration Agents with respect to work and wages on the sugar estates in this

colony, for you must know full well what dependence to place on official reports.

Men do not gather grapes from thorns, nor do they get reforms from officials and the system that created the need of reform . . . I have no hesitation that our immigration system cannot be made clean without a new broom. It should be made impossible for employers of labour to deprive those poor people of their statutory wage.

Were the coolies happy and contented as they are represented to be, why was there the necessity of sending to Berbice an armed police force a short time back? It indeed has become a custom to despatch armed men to stop those who wish to lodge their complaint with 'Crosby' [the Immigration Agent General] when they fail to get justice on the spot.[195]

Bechu's work in exposing the plantocracy and its allies in British Guiana was not unique. In various ways the venerable Immigration Agent General from 1858 to 1880, James Crosby; Joseph Beaumont, the Chief Justice of the colony from 1863 to 1868; and G.W. Des Voeux, a Stipendiary Magistrate from 1863 to 1869, had done so at considerable cost. They had let their side down.[196] The difference with Bechu was that he was a 'bound coolie'; he was the antithesis of the docile 'coolie'; he was the quintessential rebel, close to the roots, charting and demonstrating possibilities for redefinition and reassertion through resistance. He was telling his illiterate, inarticulate compatriots that they did not have to live on their knees; that, in the words of Pascal, "the beaten track is for the beaten man." Bechu did not walk the beaten track, and he tried to make anyone who did, feel uncomfortable. He could not be ignored. That was what agonized and antagonized the ruling elite, leading to the protracted libel case against him which meandered to a withdrawal after two inconclusive trials in 1899.

CHAPTER SEVEN

The Queen vs Bechu: the Libel Case, 1898–1899

The libel charge was brought against him by F.C.S. Bascom, the Manager of Plantation Cove and John, East Coast Demerara, based on a letter by Bechu published in *The Daily Chronicle* of 13 September 1898. He spoke of a tragic incident on a plantation "not 20 miles away" from Georgetown, but he did not mention its name or the name of its Manager or any other authority on the estate. Bechu alleged that Bhagri, aged 29, an indentured labourer who had arrived in British Guiana in 1894, died because of gross neglect by the authorities on the estate: the sicknurse (dispenser) "hunted him out" from the estate's hospital, claiming that he was not ill; the following day the Government Medical Officer (GMO) examined and admitted Bhagri and he remained in hospital overnight, but the next morning the sicknurse again turned him out, "under orders from the Manager". Bhagri was sent back to work. Bechu concluded: "That, however, was the last occasion the estate authorities could prosecute the poor fellow, for happily death came to his rescue and released him from the grip of his oppressors."

In October 1898, during preliminary hearings to ascertain whether a *prima facie* case had been made out against Bechu for libelling F.C.S. Bascom, the Immigration Agent for the East Coast Demerara, F.D. Sealy, stated following an enquiry he conducted on 8 August 1898, at Plantation Cove and John, that he "formed the opinion that the estate's authorities were blameable for not insisting on Bhagri going to hospital before 5 August", the day he died. Significantly, he submitted that had he not known that Bhagri had "died at Cove and John, he should not have thought that that was the estate referred to in ... [Bechu's] letter".[197]

Both trials, in April and June 1899 respectively, were inconclusive. In October 1899, before a third trial could begin, the case was thrown out after the Crown had requested a *nolle prosequi*.[198] The plaintiff, F.C.S. Bascom,[199] had denied giving any orders to the sicknurse with regard to Bhagri, who had been released from jail on Saturday, 30 July 1898. The sicknurse, George Evans, denied ever seeing Bhagri until about two minutes before he died on Friday evening, 5 August. He had received no request for medicine from Bhagri; he never went to the hospital for medical attention. The GMO, Dr A.T. Ozzard, also denied ever seeing the man before he performed the post mortem on 6 August and ascertained that he died from acute pneumonia. The driver of Bhagri's gang, Achibar, claimed that he had spoken to him on the Saturday, Monday and Tuesday before he died, when he had urged him to go to work. He testified that Bhagri had told him that he was not sick, but he wanted to rest for a week. Achibar had said that on Thursday, the day before Bhagri died, he advised him to go to the hospital because as an indentured he was bound to be at work unless he was pronounced ill. The next day he saw Bhagri and repeated the same advice, as he did not look "bad": "he no lay down just sit down." It is obvious that if the driver did, indeed, speak to Bhagri on Saturday, Monday, Tuesday, Thursday and Friday, he was of the opinion that Bhagri was not ill and that he simply wanted to rest after being in jail for two months.

It is noteworthy that Norman Bascom, the brother of the plaintiff and overseer of the shovel gang to which Bhagri belonged, testified that he "did not hear that he was sick". Achibar, the driver, had told him that "Bhagri looked badly but he, Bhagri, said he was not ill." The consensus among the key estate authorities seemed to have been that he was not really sick, consequently medical attention was not urgently needed, if at all.

The Immigration Agent, F.D. Sealy, stated at both trials that there was no truth in Bechu's letter but, incredibly, he admitted that in conducting his enquiries at Cove and John on 8 and 13 September 1898 (the latter at the request of the Immigration Agent General, on the day Bechu's letter was published), "I took no statement from Bhagri's wives [he had two] and shipmates ... I did not think it necessary to take evidence from [his] wives and shipmates. I took evidence from [the] driver [Achibar] and overseer [Norman Bascom] ... I took evidence from estate authorities." Ironically, as Bechu would have underlined, this protector of Indians did not deem it necessary to speak to any of them in a matter of the utmost gravity. As Rajkowah, Bhagri's younger wife, revealed in court: "I never saw Chota Crosby [Sealy] on estate . . . have never seen him" – a vindication of what Bechu had asserted continually about protectors. Yet, even without the benefit of the testimonies of Bhagri's wives, Sealy had told the preliminary hearing that the "estate's authorities" were "blameable" for "not insisting on Bhagri going to hospital before the 5 August".

In court, at the trials, however, Fulloo, Bhagri's senior wife, testified that on Tuesday, 2 August, Rajkowah, the other wife, went to the sicknurse, Evans, to procure medicine for Bhagri and that he turned her away, telling her that the sick man had to be examined before any medicine could be issued. She said that the next day she and Rajkowah took Bhagri to the hospital, but Evans refused to treat him "as he has no fever". Fulloo added that "the sicknurse chucked me away"; they had to take Bhagri home unattended. She recalled that to take him to the hospital "two of us had to support him; he was very sick". They took him to the hospital again, on Friday. Evans refused to treat him; he did not even "take his pulse or temperature". Bhagri was taken home where he died on Friday evening. Alerted by his wives' screaming when they thought he had died, two of his shipmates took his body to the hospital where sicknurse Evans, strangely, "admitted" him, claiming that he died two minutes after admission. Fulloo's evidence was corroborated by Rajkowah, at the trials.

It is important to note that both wives were emphatic that at no time did Achibar, the driver, visit Bhagri; neither did Bhagri state that he wanted to rest for a few days before going back to work, as Achibar had testified. He was, indeed, sick with fever. Whether the driver did or did not visit Bhagri on several occasions is somewhat immaterial: of significance is the fact that he conveyed to the key man, the overseer, Norman Bascom, the idea that Bhagri was not really sick although he looked weak; he wanted to rest for a few days. This could have strengthened the old assumption that 'coolies' were inclined to feign illness to abscond from work. It is not possible to ascertain whether Norman Bascom or any other authority on Cove and John spoke to the sicknurse about Bhagri. Evans denied that he received any orders or instructions about the man; even if it were so, however, it is inconceivable that he would have admitted it, but his intransigence in dealing with a man who was obviously very ill, suggests the hand of a superior force.

It is clear that Bechu's letter contained several inaccuracies: (i) Bhagri was never admitted to hospital, neither, according to the Government Medical Officer, Dr Ozzard, did he ever see or admit him to the hospital; (ii) Bhagri did not go to work during the week when he died. Therefore, the major allegation by Bechu that the Manager instructed the sicknurse to discharge Bhagri could not be sustained; whether the Manager or some other authority did instruct the sicknurse not to treat or admit Bhagri cannot be ascertained.

If the Immigration Agent had carried out an impartial inquiry, if he had summoned Bhagri's wives and possibly some of his shipmates and neighbours, he might have come nearer to the truth. However, the fact that he found the authorities on the estate "blameable" for "not insisting on Bhagri going to hospital", although his inquiry was severely flawed, suggests that he probably knew more than he admitted.[200] If that were so, then his grave failure to interview any of Bhagri's relatives or friends becomes comprehensible.

Bechu was not examined at the preliminary hearings or at either of the trials, so the source of his information on Bhagri remains obscure. However, his defence counsel had argued that if there was any doubt that the "Manager" Bechu referred to in his letter was not meant to be F.C.S. Bascom, the plaintiff, then the charge of libel could not be sustained. He submitted that the defendant was, in fact, referring to Norman Bascom, the plaintiff's brother. At the preliminary hearings, W.A. Sawtell, editor of *The Daily Chronicle*, had said that before he published Bechu's letter on 13 September 1898, he had written to him to ascertain who he was referring to; Bechu had replied that he meant Norman Bascom.[201] Sealy, the Immigration Agent, had testified thus: "If I had not made enquiries I would not at once have known it [Bechu's letter] referred to Cove and John . . . Judging by [the] last part of [the] letter [the manuscript which had been altered for publication] I would say [the] writer meant Norman Bascom as Manager . . ."[202] Norman Bascom concurred: "I was writer of the letter referred to in [the] end of Bechu's letter to *The Daily Chronicle* [13 September 1898]."[203] In short, the defence had proved that F.C.S. Bascom was not being libelled even if some of the allegations in Bechu's letter were potentially libellous to Norman Bascom.

Bechu was not daunted by the difficulties engendered by the case and the heightened antagonism which he received from the plantocracy and their allies, the colonial authorities, including the Immigration Agent General and the Immigration Agents. His was a crusade to expose the endemic rottenness of plantation society; no price was too harsh to pay in his single-minded pursuit of justice for his compatriots. His fortitude and astounding continuity of purpose frustrated his enemies.

In February 1899, after he was indicted for libelling F.C.S. Bascom, Bechu refuted Norman Bascom's assertion that several of their 'coolies' on Plantation Cove and John earned well above the statutory wage during the previous month.[204] This was a red flag to the bull. Bechu quickly pounced on Norman Bascom, a regular contributor to the press on sugar matters: "The Manager of

Plantation Cove and John [F.C.S. Bascom] is exceptionally fortunate in having a brother so near at hand to blow his trumpet whenever he gets the slightest chance of doing so." He gave little credence to Norman Bascom's very short list of good earners; these, Bechu argued, must be placed in context: " . . . all who are familiar with the workings of a sugar estate are well aware that each driver has a few 'foot-kissers' whose weekly earnings exceed the limit fixed by law, but these are very, very, few indeed." He challenged Norman Bascom to submit the wage list of the shipmates of the big earners he had paraded. Bechu had no doubts that most 'bound coolies' earned less than the statutory wage of one shilling for seven hours' work.[205]

Between April and October 1899, during his libel case, he seemed to have been restrained from writing to the press, but he could not be cowed into compliance or even silence. On 27 April 1899, Bechu wrote to the Secretary of State for India, Lord Hamilton, to complain that Kally (Kali), an indentured man on F.C.S. Bascom's plantation, had been assaulted by the Chief Engineer, Daniel Spencer. Then, in a remarkable point of corroboration, he observed that F.D. Sealy, the Immigration Agent of the East Demerara District, had reported the matter, in "an office note dated 14 December 1898", to the Immigration Agent General: " . . . [I am] not at all satisfied with the treatment which the immigrants receive on Plantation Cove and John and that the action taken by the Manager of that estate clearly shows that he encourages his officials to ill-treat the immigrants." Bechu did not say how he got access to this damning piece of evidence, the "office note", but he quickly drew Lord Hamilton's attention to another fact: "this Estate, *Your Lordship* will be surprised to learn, still continues to receive fresh batches of indentured immigrants!"[206]

Bechu's report was correct. The Immigration Agent General, A.H. Alexander, had written to F.C.S. Bascom on 22 December 1898, stating that after reading the proceedings of the case of assault against Spencer, he felt that he was "not a fit person to be retained in the position which he holds on the estate". Bascom then requested that Alexander should proceed no further with the matter, as Spencer had been "a very valuable and trusted servant" at Cove and John for 15 years; he had been "severely punished" already – the Magistrate had fined him $10 or one month's imprisonment, and he was remorseful over his "hasty action". The Immigration Agent General recanted, noting that he had done so "with considerable hesitation and reluctance".[207]

In his letter to the Secretary of State for India, after his first libel trial, Bechu had noted that although the jury had retired twice, they were still unable to arrive at a verdict. He explained the problem:

> ... *Your Lordship* will scarcely wonder why when *Your Lordship* learns that several of their number are employed on sugar estates and the chief one – the *Foreman*, happened to be an overseer – a class of men who dislike me beyond measure because I have before the *West India Royal Commissioners* as well as in the daily newspapers complained of their immoral relations with female immigrants.[208]

Indeed, three of the jurors were overseers, including the foreman, C.R. Barrett, while two were engineers and one a bookkeeper, possibly employees on sugar estates also. The jury in Bechu's second trial, in June 1899, comprised two overseers, including the foreman, E.D. Cameron; three others were possibly estate employees, two panboilers and an engineer. To reach a conclusive verdict, the jury had to vote in the ratio of 10:2 or 11:1. This was not attainable given its composition.[209]

Even before the case was withdrawn in October 1899, at the request of the prosecution, the Immigration Agent General seemed to have accepted the estate's version of Bhagri's death:

> After his release from jail he was forwarded to the estate, and he appeared to be ill, suffering from fever, he was ordered to go to hospital, but he begged to be allowed to stay in his house along with his wife. This request was granted, but pneumonia supervened, and he died suddenly before he could be seen by the doctor.[210]

This was the version passed on by the Governor to the Colonial Office. The India Office also received it, and expressed Lord Hamilton's "satisfaction", in August 1899, although Bechu had suggested to him that he should "cause a strict enquiry to be made with regard to Bhagri's death". He was apprehensive of the judicial system.

Bechu was not deterred. On 10 July 1899, he had written to the Immigration Agent General, Alexander, noting that the judge at his second trial had advised him to inform him of "irregularities on sugar estates before rushing into print". Bechu stated that he wished "humbly [to] beg" the Immigration Agent General's attention to a report in *The Argosy* of a case pertaining to an overseer; he added that he was about to forward the details of the case to the Secretary of State for India.[211]

On the same day as Bechu, Immigration Agent Sealy also wrote to Alexander on the same case. He explained that J.F. Jackson, an overseer at Enmore (Bechu's old estate), had "enticed away" a young 'coolie' girl to a house he had rented at Ann's Grove, a neighbouring village. Sealy had investigated the matter and had concluded that it was "perfectly true" – "she was hidden from her parents . . . There is much talk about it in the district."[212]

Possibly apprehensive of Bechu's threat to report the case to the Secretary of State for India, on 14 July 1899 – four days after Bechu's letter – the Immigration Agent General wrote to the Manager of Enmore, G.W. Bethune, urging him to dismiss the overseer, Jackson. The next day Bethune informed Alexander that Jackson had "justly earned his dismissal".[213]

The response of Bechu's erstwhile protector, A.H. Alexander, suggests grudging recognition of Bechu's role in expediting Jackson's dismissal, and regretted that the gadfly was irrepressible. On 17 July 1899, he had minuted Governor Sendall thus: "It is, I think, a pity that the antecedents of Bechu in India cannot be ascertained."[214] Writing confidentially to the Secretary of State for the Colonies, on 19 July, the Governor also suggested the impotent rage among the ruling elite spawned by Bechu's remorseless, radical scrutiny of the colonial condition:

> The most probable explanation of his presence here is that he is a fugitive from justice. A man with his superior education and unquestionable ability is not likely to have taken up the career of an indentured labourer in the West Indies without some overpowering motive for leaving his native country.[215]

Sydney Olivier, at the Colonial Office, who as Secretary of the Norman Commission, had encountered Bechu in Georgetown in February 1897, had a different perception of the man: "This is not the first time Bechu has 'got home' on overseers or the Immigration Department, which is the real reason why they are so anxious to . . . [deem] him a criminal."[216] Earlier, he had minuted that Sir Henry Norman and Sir David Barbour of the Commission felt that Bechu "must have got into some trouble to go into indentureship".[217] Olivier, a Fabian socialist, could probably appreciate some of the man's promptings; he was more magnanimous: "Possibly Bechu is a Hindu philanthropist who indentured with a view to functioning as an amateur 'protector of immigrants'. There is much evidence for this than for his being a criminal, on his record in British Guiana."[218]

Bechu, however, had no doubts of his mission in British Guiana, and he understood why the sugar planters and the colonial officials considered him the most reprehensible 'bound coolie' to reach the colony. He indicted both in his letter to the Secretary of State for India:

> . . . it is certain that to appeal to the authorities on the spot would involve too much of personal reflection on those whose connivance has entailed a shameful reproach to the administration of justice . . . [M]y countrymen . . . like myself have had the misfortune to come to *Demerara*, the political system of which colony has

very appropriately been divined and defined by Mr Trollope . . . as 'despotism tempered by *sugar*'. To these two twin forces the immigration system is as sacred as was the old system of *slavery* in former days, and for one of my humble position to have ventured to touch it with profane hands or to have dared to unveil it, is considered on this side of the *Atlantic* to be a capital and inexpiable offence.[219]

In November 1901, a few months after Bechu had left British Guiana, *The Daily Chronicle*, which had demonstrated strength and integrity by providing Bechu with a forum in this authoritarian plantation colony, carried an incisive leader on Indian immigration and sugar.[220] It encapsulated many of the ideas which Bechu had advocated without vacillation. The paper stated that it could not concur with those who saw immigration as "an inviolate institution which no profane finger might touch"; this inflexibility was "mainly responsible for the present industrial backwardness of the colony"; sugar could not be the sole basis for the future welfare of British Guiana. Indeed, the industry had many features which were incompatible with its development: even when prices were good and profits "handsome", the purchasing power of the people did not improve because the dividends went to "gentlemen who for the most part reside in Great Britain and contribute nothing to the revenues of the colony". The labourers on the estates were not beneficiaries; this labour had to be imported, and the repatriation of some of it entailed a further drain on savings. *The Chronicle* concluded:

> Our objective is to secure that this purely artificial status of the local sugar industry shall be placed upon a sounder and more natural footing. The profits accruing from the cultivation of the soil should not be allowed to drain so copiously into other countries. In effect, the resident population ought to benefit more from the sugar industry than it does at present. The question as to whether the prosperity of sugar in the colony benefits all classes requires to be put beyond dispute. To this end it is necessary . . . that immigration be conducted on more statesmanlike lines, involving not only its judicious limitation and if possible its ultimate abolition, but also a settlement of the immigrants in the colony as their terms expire . . .[221]

In 1917, the last indentured labourers from India arrived in British Guiana; in April 1920, all indentures were cancelled, and by then many Indians had settled on the land, while an Indian middle class of rice cultivators, cattle herders, businessmen and professionals had already emerged and was expanding. Yet the question of the role of sugar and who benefits from sugar, has remained central to the debate on the development of Guyana throughout the century: sugar has been at the core of its political culture. One hundred years since Bechu wrote his first letter to *The Chronicle*, in 1896, many of the principles he enunciated remain relevant to Guyanese sugar workers; his incorruptibility and fortitude, also, are his legacy to all Guyanese.

I have been unable to ascertain what became of this 'bound coolie' radical after he left the colony around February 1901. I hope that this incomplete story induces others to ask further questions about his work in British Guiana and to try to locate him thereafter.

NOTES

1. Alan Adamson pointed to Bechu's unique role as a defender of Indian rights, noting his appearance before the Norman Commission of 1897:

    The ... [Indian immigrant] was isolated from the rest of British Guiana society by his language and culture and by the rigour of the labour laws. He was normally illiterate, and he had no experienced leaders to whom he might look for protection. When he expressed himself, it was through direct, spontaneous action – the inchoate 'riots' and 'disturbances' which shook the sugar coast from the 1860s on. The only piece of direct verbal evidence of his feeling in the nineteenth century is the testimony of Bechu, an exceptionally articulate immigrant who appeared before the West India Royal Commission of 1897. Judged by what he had to say, the common lot of the immigrant was to be overworked, underpaid, robbed, and beatened by drivers, overseers, and managers alike. Certainly the system he described deserved Chief Justice Beaumont's earlier appellation, the New Slavery (Adamson, *Sugar Without Slaves: the Political Economy of British Guiana, 1838–1904*. New Haven: Yale University Press 1972, 265). Other references to Bechu are on pp. 152–53, 156. Adamson's book is based on his PhD thesis of 1964.

2. Peter Ruhomon, *Centenary History of the East Indians in British Guiana, 1838–1938* (Georgetown: The Daily Chronicle Ltd 1947); Dwarka Nath, *A History of Indians in British Guiana* (London: Nelson 1950).

3. *Report of the West India Royal Commission, 1897* (H.W. Norman, chairman) (London: HMSO 1897), Appendix C. – Part II, British Guiana, section 158.

4. CO 111/513 Sendall to Chamberlain, no. 182, 6 July 1899, encl.

5. Olivier had minuted: "He is a very clever high caste man and makes points sometimes: but not to be believed uncorroborated." (CO 111/516 Offices, India, 7 June 1899), minute, 8 June 1899. This was in response to a minute of the same day, on Bechu's libel case, by one of his colleagues: "I believe Bechu's story is a lie but I suppose we must ask the Governor for a report . . ." – ibid.

6. See Bechu's letter in *The Daily Chronicle*, 29 December 1900. A radical Congregational Minister in New Amsterdam between 1900 and 1903, Rev Shirley was constantly accused by the ruling elite of inciting the people. In December 1900, he had responded:

    The people have enough to incite them . . . When men have to work for 12 hours at throwing sugar as thick and heavy as clay for just over a penny an hour, and dig three rods of trench a foot deep for which sometimes they get nothing at all, if the overseer does not pass their work through a shower of rain washing into it after its being dug . . . is that not calculated to embitter man? (*The Daily Chronicle*, 16 December 1900.)

7. *The Daily Chronicle*, 12 January 1897. In response to the planter's suggestion that he was better educated than most, Bechu continued in the same vein: "I don't know about being *far better educated*, but the *little* I know is due to my having taken advantage of my opportunities when young. If it is possible to educate monkeys why should not the '*connecting link*' between man and him be taught as well?" (Emphases in the original.)

8. The Immigration Agent General said that he was impelled to ascertain Bechu's Indian antecedents because he believed that "a man of apparently fair English education would not have come to this colony as a common labourer unless there had been some good cause or necessity for leaving India . . ." (CO 111/513 Sendall to Chamberlain, no. 182, 6 July 1899, encl).

9. I have relied primarily on Bechu's evidence to the Norman Commission for his background in India. See *Report of the West India Royal Commission* [1897], Appendix C. – Part II, British Guiana, section 98.

10. G.W. Bethune, the Manager of Enmore, was responding to the publication of Bechu's first letter: "I am told he has adopted a defiant mood since the publication of the letter, which of course he has seen, having access to the Reading Room in the Overseers' house" (CO 111/513 Sendall to Chamberlain, no.182, 6 July 1899, encl).

11. *The Daily Chronicle*, 12 February 1897.

12. *The Daily Chronicle*, 15 February 1897.

13. David Kopf, in a work of outstanding scholarship, has assessed the contribution of early British orientalists and the Asiatic Society of Bengal to the rise of the Bengali intelligentsia and the reshaping of the Hindu perspective, in Calcutta. In this process, he argues, the College of Fort William played a seminal role:

It was the College of Fort William that made printing and publishing in the classical and vernacular tongues possible in India on a large scale. This development was stimulated by its ever-increasing need for authentic publications and was possible because it possessed the requisite financial resources. Within its first decade of operation, Fort William had created an array of peripheral and satellite institutions that fostered an atmosphere conducive to the expansion of the communicative arts.

Kopf elaborates on the significance of the rise of a vernacular press:

There is . . . one crucial difference between the objectives of early Orientalists and those of the College of Fort William. Whereas Jones and Wilkins translated the Sanskrit classics into English for European readers, the college – perhaps unwittingly – encouraged translations into the Indian vernaculars, thereby creating a body of printed material which would eventually break the intellectual monopoly of the Brahmans (Kopf, *British Orientalism and the Bengal Renaissance: The Dynamics of Indian Modernization, 1773–1835*. Berkeley: University of California Press 1969, 114–15).

14. D.P. Singhal has explained the sources of Ram Mohan Roy's own capacious vision, the pivot of the Bengal renaissance:

He was a scholar of Sanskrit, Hebrew, Greek, Persian, English, and Arabic. A devout Hindu inspired by the vedantic philosophy, he was also deeply influenced by Sufism and was an admirer of Christianity and Western thought . . . He was perhaps the first earnest modern scholar of comparative religion. Making a clear distinction between Western virtues and Western failings, he defended Hinduism against the attacks of missionaries as stoutly as he challenged the orthodoxy to abandon its ritualistic conventions. He kept in close touch with Oriental research and interpreted the ancient Indian texts in the light of Western doctrines and ideas. Consequently he became an uncompromising and vehement opponent of idolatry and of all rituals connected with it . . . He accepted the humanism of European thought . . . he set India on a course of cultural reformation, which gradually gathered momentum and support, and eventually made it possible for modern India to emerge (Singhal, *Indian and World Civilization*, Vol. II. London: Sidgwick and Jackson 1972 [1969], 280–81).

15. Ibid, 282–83.
16. Jawaharlal Nehru has traced the path of Keshab Chandra Sen's radicalism on social and religious issues:

The real impact of the West came to India in the nineteenth century through technical changes and their dynamic consequences. In the realm of ideas also there was shock and change, a widening of the horizon which had so long been confined within a narrow shell. The first reaction, limited to the small English educated class, was one of admiration and acceptance of almost everything western. Repelled by some of the social customs and practices of Hinduism, many Hindus were attracted towards Christianity, and some notable conversions took place in Bengal. An attempt was therefore made by Raja Ram Mohan Roy to adapt Hinduism to this new environment and he started the Brahmo Samaj on a more or less rationalist and social reform basis. His successor, Keshab Chandra Sen, give it a more Christian outlook. The Brahmo Samaj influenced the rising middle classes of Bengal but as a religious faith it remained confined to few, among whom, however, were some outstanding persons and families (Nehru, *The Discovery of India*. New Delhi: Oxford University Press 1981 [1946], 335).

17. Leonard A. Gordon has summarized Bankim Chandra Chatterjee's contribution to the Bengal renaissance. He writes:

. . . he encouraged . . . the use of historical knowledge and traditions as tools for instruction and exhortation toward future goals. He was aware that history might be a crucial weapon in the battle for social and political advancement in Bengal. Certain myths and misunderstandings had to be criticized through a new reconstruction of the past . . . he thought that Bengalis could go beyond their limitations and play a crucial role in the regeneration of India. He stands at the junction between the old effeminate image of the Bengali and a new image of strength and accomplishment (Gordon, *Bengal: The Nationalist Movement, 1876–1940*. New York: Columbia University Press 1974, 80–81).

For an excellent study of Bankim Chandra [Bankimchandra Chattopadhyay], see Tapan Raychaudhuri, *Europe Reconsidered: Perceptions of the West in Nineteenth Century Bengal* (Delhi: Oxford University Press 1988), 103–218.

18. Quoted in Nehru, 321–22.
19. Like many Indians, however, Bechu's rebellious role in colonial society did not vitiate his loyalty to the Empire and the Queen Empress. In September 1898, shortly after the letter which earned him a charge of libel was published, he wrote to denounce a planter

who having "failed to get a countervailing duty put on bounty-fed sugar", was advocating the union of the West Indies with the United States. Bechu was contemptuous of this:

> True, as you say in this morning's leader, that 'where communities of white men have the management of their own affairs . . . what are known as subject races obtain treatment which is far from generous and often not even just,' yet notwithstanding the fact that the lot of us East Indians in this colony is not all that it might be, I am perfectly safe in saying that we as a people are content to remain under the Union Jack rather than fall prey to the Golden Eagle, to see stars and possibly stand a chance of being 'beaten with many stripes' (*The Daily Chronicle*, 24 September 1898). (The leader Bechu refers to is from the previous day's issue.)

20. Raychaudhuri, *Europe Reconsidered*, 315.
21. Nehru, *The Discovery of India*, 187–88.
22. Raychaudhuri, *Europe Reconsidered*, 333–34.
23. See my *India and the Shaping of the Indo-Guyanese Imagination, 1890s–1920s* (Leeds: Peepal Tree Books 1993), 9–17.
24. Leonard A. Gordon examines two events which shaped Banerjea's political temperament:

    > Banerjea went to England in the late 1860s to prepare for the ICS [Indian Civil Service] examination. Within a short time he was faced with two serious crises. The first was a dispute about his age which would determine his eligibility for the examination. He survived this predicament . . . proving that he was a year younger than officials said he was. As a result, he began to see his own battles as an Indian cause, tied in with the fate of all his countrymen. The second crisis led to his dismissal from the ICS for what many thought inconsequential errors. This ouster closed a number of other career avenues, such as the bar. He was reduced, Indian friends told him, to death in life. But Banerjea transformed his dismissal into a life-long cause, in which he sought to enlist all his countrymen (Gordon, *Bengal: The Nationalist Movement*, 29).

25. Nehru observes that Vivekananda was a passionate advocate of abhay (fearlessness and strength); he repudiated mysticism and superstition which he considered weakening. Vivekananda argued: "If there is a sin in the world it is weakness; avoid all weakness, weakness is sin, weakness is death . . . anything that makes you weak physically, intellectually and spiritually, reject as poison, there is no life in it, it cannot be true. Truth is strengthening" (Quoted in Nehru, *The Discovery of India*, 338–39).
26. See CO 114/172, Report of the Immigration Agent General, 1919, for excerpts from the letters of some repatriated immigrants who were stranded in Calcutta. Their experiences were no different from those of their compatriots in the 1890s.
27. *The Daily Chronicle*, 12 January 1897.
28. See, for example, Bechu's letters in *The Daily Chronicle*, 7 February 1899; 9 February 1899, while he was on a libel charge.
29. There is no evidence that Bechu had a personal relationship with any of the successful Indians in British Guiana in the 1890s – people such as businessmen Thomas Flood and Gool Mohumad Khan; Veerasawmy Mudaliar, the former Chief Interpreter of the Immigration Department; Joseph Ruhomon, the writer and thinker; E.A. Luckhoo, the first Indian solicitor in the colony; F.E. Jaundoo, Chief Interpreter and first captain of the Asiatic Cricket Club; J.R. Wharton; and W. Hewley Wharton, the first Indian doctor in the Caribbean. Indeed, when Dr Wharton returned to British Guiana in December 1899, after graduating from Edinburgh, Bechu was not among the

"prominent East Indian residents" who signed the address of welcome to him (*The Daily Chronicle*, 30 December 1899; *The Argosy*, 30 December 1899).

30. See, for instance, his letters in *The Daily Chronicle*, 4, 15 February 1897, where he signs his name with a flourish, heightened by the fact that the latter was in response to a letter deprecating the Bengali character: "Bechu (Indentured Bengali [sic] Immigrant *Sheila*, 1894)."

31. For comprehensive studies of the changing Crown Land Ordinances from the 1890s and the consequences for Indian landholders, see Michael Moohr, "Patterns of change in an export economy: British Guiana, 1830–1914", PhD Thesis, University of Cambridge (1970), 113–15; his "The discovery of gold and the development of peasant industries in Guyana, 1884–1914: A study in the political economy of change", *Caribbean Studies*, Vol 15, No. 2 (1975); and Lesley Potter, "The post-indenture experience of East Indians in Guyana, 1873–1921", in *East Indians in the Caribbean: Colonialism and the Struggle for Identity*, Bridget Brereton and Winston Dookeran (eds), (Millwood, NY: Kraus International Publications 1982).

32. In October 1892, after the election of Dadabhai Naoroji, the first Indian MP in Britain, the British Guiana East Indian Institute, in its letter of congratulations, observed: ". . . we . . . hope that the example which you have so nobly set will be fruitful in actuating others of our ancient race to follow; and thereby rid themselves and countrymen of the political oblivion in which they have been presumed hitherto to be sunk" (*The Daily Chronicle*, 7 October 1892).

33. See my introduction to Joseph Ruhomon's *India . . . : The Centenary Edition, 1894–1994* (forthcoming), for the significance of this pamphlet.

34. Joseph Ruhomon, *India; The Progress of her People at Home and Abroad, and how Those in British Guiana may Improve Themselves* (Georgetown: C.K. Jardine 1894), 28-29.

35. The paper concluded: "Mr Ruhomon and other ambitious and deserving 'brothers of the sun-kissed face' [a sarcastic reference to Ruhomon's Aryanism] should regard the British as their dearest friends, and look to the source of their racial elevation as the surest quarter in which to find what is best and safest for guidance and emulation" (*The Argosy*, 29 December 1894).

36. Henry Kirke, *Twenty-Five Years in British Guiana* (London: Sampson Low, Marston and Co 1898), 341.

37. Walter Rodney, *A History of the Guyanese Working People, 1881–1905* (Baltimore: The Johns Hopkins University Press 1981), 225.

38. K.O. Laurence adds:

It appears . . . that in 1895–96 the effective wage was again reduced in British Guiana, and to a smaller extent and less generally in Trinidad. The labour market was well enough stocked to give the planters the upper hand and the indentured immigrant was being used deliberately to depress wages, while the acreage cultivated in cane was decreasing" (Laurence, *A Question of Labour: Indentured Immigration into Trinidad and British Guiana, 1875–1917*. Kingston, Jamaica: Ian Randle Publishers 1994, 305).

39. Walton Look Lai, *Indentured Labour, Caribbean Sugar: Chinese and Indian Migrants to the British West Indies, 1838–1918* (Baltimore: The Johns Hopkins University Press 1993), 145.

40. Laurence, *A Question of Labour* . . . , 486.
41. CO 114/64 Report of the Immigration Agent General 1894–1895.
42. Ibid.
43. In 1896–97, for instance, the 'protector' of Indians admitted that because of "the continued depression" in the sugar industry, wages on the estates had to be reduced, "in some cases from 20 to 25 percent", and he applauded the Indian workers for their "admirable" response, having recognized the "gravity" of the situation. Inadequate wages in 1895–96, however, had led to at least 25 strikes, and the same authority had concluded: "The special enquiries held at different times when strikes occurred, resulted in most instances, in the establishment of the fact that the rates of wages were fair, and such as to admit of industrious immigrants earning more than the statutory minimum" (CO 114/68; CO 114/74, Reports of the Immigration Agent General, 1895–96 and 1896–97).
44. Adamson, *Sugar Without Slaves*, 265–66.
45. *Report of the West India Royal Commission* Appendix C. – Part II, British Guiana, section 87.
46. See Bechu's letters to *The Daily Chronicle*, 3, 4 February 1897 where he referred to the evidence of W. Alleyne Ireland ['Langton'] and James Thomson respectively. In the latter case, he spoke of reading "the whole of the evidence" given before the fourth sitting of the Commission.
47. Leader, *The Daily Chronicle*, 22 April 1898.
48. In December 1900, the radical Congregational minister in New Amsterdam, Rev H.J. Shirley, repudiated the pertinacious official dogma that the empoldering of the healthy Corentyne Coast was beyond the colony's financial capacity:

    Why is immigration continued? We hear again and again that nobody has suggested the ways and means for the Corentyne water scheme. That is a paltry subterfuge. If they wish they could find the means. The abolition of the unnecessary immigration expenditure would be one of the items towards it, and others could be the disestablishment of the churches and the reduction of the Civil Service vote. These three items would, in time, pay off a loan for the Corentyne water scheme (*The Daily Chronicle*, 16 December 1900).

49. *The Daily Chronicle*, 22 December 1896.
50. Ibid.
51. CO 111/492 Hemming to Chamberlain, no. 3, 2 January 1897, encl.
52. CO 111/489 Hemming to Chamberlain, no. 389, 8 December 1896.
53. Ibid.
54. See note 51.
55. CO 111/492 Hemming to Chamberlain, confidential, 6 January 1897 encl. Governor Hemming wrote that he considered the conduct of Ebbels and Garnett "very reprehensible".
56. CO 111/500 (Individuals – Quintin Hogg), 1 February 1897.
57. CO 111/489 Hemming to Chamberlain, 26 November 1896.
58. CO 111/489 Hemming to Chamberlain, no. 389, 8 December 1896, encl.
59. CO 111/488 Cavendish Boyle to Chamberlain, no. 353, 11 November 1896, encl.
60. Ibid (covering letter).

Notes

61. See note 59.
62. *The Argosy*, 21 November 1896.
63. See note 3.
64. Rodney, *A History of the Guyanese Working People*, 36. The following notice, signed by the attorney of Non Pareil, was circulated on the estate on the eve of the troubles:

> TO THE
> MECHANICS & LABOURERS
> ON THE ESTATE
>
> Owing to the exceedingly LOW price of SUGAR, the lowest that has ever been known, it is ABSOLUTELY IMPOSSIBLE for us to pay the Old Rate of Wages and Carry the Estate on; I am aware that even the Old Rates were a reduced rate, but under the circumstances there is nothing for it but to still further reduce all round. It is a hard thing to ask, but if the Labourers and Mechanics will cheerfully accept the Reduction there is just a hope for the Estate and nothing more. If they refuse we must close up, and that almost at once. Should Prices rise to a paying level I need hardly say that I will give back what has been cut off.
>
> September 1896, HARRY GARNETT

(Quoted in ibid, 50).

65. See note 59.
66. Ibid.
67. *The Daily Chronicle*, 5 November 1896.
68. *The Daily Chronicle*, 9 December 1896.
69. *The Argosy*, 5 December 1896.
70. See note 68.
71. *The Daily Chronicle*, 12 December 1896.
72. *The Daily Chronicle*, 15 December 1896.
73. *The Daily Chronicle*, 1 November 1896.
74. See note 69.
75. See note 68.
76. See note 71.
77. See note 72.
78. *Report of the West India Royal Commission* Appendix C. – Part II, British Guiana, section 99.
79. *The Daily Chronicle*, 3 February 1897.
80. See note 78.
81. *Report of the West India Royal Commission* Appendix C. – Part II, British Guiana, section 92.
82. *The Daily Chronicle*, 4 February 1897.
83. Bethune had remarked:

> ... it has been pointed out to me that the Bengali immigrant, Bechu, in his evidence before the Royal Commissioners, made special allusion to the Enmore estate as the one on which the Creole gang is daily employed in the fields from 12 to 13 hours, and I take an early opportunity of asserting that such an allegation is absolutely unfounded (*Report of the West India Royal Commission* Appendix C. – Part II, British Guiana, section 159).

84. *The Daily Chronicle*, 6 February 1897.
85. *The Daily Chronicle*, 9 February 1897.
86. Ibid.
87. See note 34.
88. See note 85.
89. *The Daily Chronicle*, 10 February 1897.
90. Ibid.
91. *The Daily Chronicle*, 12 February 1897.
92. *The Daily Chronicle*, 15 February 1897.
93. David Kopf argues that Macaulay's and Trevelyan's ethnocentrism fed a rebellious spirit among the Bengali intelligentsia in Calcutta. Although it undermined the syncretic, more tolerant, vision of the Orientalists, it fortified the Bengali resolve for reform and regeneration of Hindu culture, the precursor of Indian nationalism. He writes:

> ... Victorian Englishmen like Macaulay expressed a certain offensive crudeness which in retrospect reflected the values they espoused. Some of the adjectives used by Houghton [*The Victorian Frame of Mind*, 1957] to describe this class of Englishmen should indicate something of their personalities: obstinate, rigid, arrogant, dogmatic, and self-righteous. Macaulay's style of behaviour and writing was apparently so obnoxious that even his warmest admirers today must surely wince from embarrassment by his complete lack of tact or sensitivity for the feelings of the very people whom he wished to reach ... If Anglicists such as Trevelyan and Macaulay believed that they were writing the obituary for Hindu cultural customs and civilization as they had succeeded in doing for the Orientalist movement, they proved to be poor prophets. Trevelyan's Hindu 'corpse' began to stir in the 1830s, started kicking in the 1840s, became more aggressive in the 1850s, and emerged as belligerently defiant in the 1860s. Though the British Orientalist movement died during the Bentinck administration [1828–1835], its primary legacy of a reconstituted Hindu cultural tradition lived on in the self-image of the Bengali intelligentsia (Kopf, *British Orientalism*, 247, 272).

94. *The Daily Chronicle*, 17 February 1897.
95. *The Argosy*, 19 December 1896.
96. CO 111/513 Sendall to Chamberlain, no. 182, 6 July 1899, encl.
97. Ibid.
98. *The Daily Chronicle*, 30 November 1897.
99. *The Daily Chronicle*, 1 December 1897.
100. *The Daily Chronicle*, 7 December 1897.
101. *The Daily Chronicle*, 31 December 1897.
102. *The Daily Chronicle*, 5 January 1898. On 30 January 1897, two days before Bechu was examined by the Norman Commission, Hon A.H. Alexander, the Immigration Agent General, gave evidence. The following exchange with Sir Henry Norman illustrates the extent to which Bechu's protector's stance on Indian indentureship diverged from his own:

Norman:: As I understand your statement while the cultivation on estates has decreased the number of immigrants on estates has increased?

Alexander: That is so.

Norman: And besides that, the number of immigrants not residing on estates has also increased. The natural inference from that is, that there is an abundant supply of labour for any reasonable purposes required?

Alexander:	In the colony somewhere.
Norman:	And yet no doubt there are persons in the colony who would go on importing immigrants if the sugar industry does not collapse?
Alexander:	It is necessary they should do so, because at certain times it is impossible to get the labour you require; it is there but it is not available when you want it . . .
Norman:	Then whatever amount of labour you have here, and if you induce a much larger proportion of immigrants to remain here than remain at present, you still would have to get indentured immigrants in order to have a reliable supply?
Alexander:	I think so, sir, if you keep up estates in the same condition as they are at present, you would have to possess on each estate an indentured gang.
Norman::	Even though indentured coolies were perhaps double, you would still want an increase?
Alexander:	I always think so . . .
Norman:	Do you think it is worth while to give inducement to persuade a larger number of coolies to stay here than at present remains?
Alexander:	I do not think it would make a difference . . .
Sir David Barbour:	It is very expensive to import immigrants?
Alexander:	No one would think of doing it if he could avoid it.
Barbour:	There is a sufficient supply of labour in the colony if it could be made available?
Alexander:	Quite so.

Report of the West India Royal Commission Appendix C. – Part II, British Guiana, section 88.

103. Acting Judge A.H. [Henry] Kirke was asked by Sir Henry Norman whether "coolies and Negroes" were "generally well fed and nourished". He replied: "I think so. A certain number of coolies get anaemic. They do not take enough nourishment, but it is their own fault, I think . . ." Norman suggested it might be from "want of means". Kirke responded: "I do not think so." Ibid, section 89.

104. The Government Secretary, Cavendish Boyle, informed the Norman Commission that the reduction of wages for fieldwork, between 1891 and 1897, was about 25 percent; and he said the workers had "behaved very well under the trying circumstances". The situation was exacerbated by the telescoping of the whole harvest around the October grinding season: "The result has been a long and trying 'slack time', during which estates have difficulty in finding work for the people, involving some hardship and a great deal of discontent." Ibid, section 137.

105. Ibid, section 98.
106. *The Daily Chronicle*, 5 January 1898.
107. *The Daily Chronicle*, 4 January 1898.
108. *The Daily Chronicle*, 16 January 1898.
109. Ibid.
110. *The Daily Chronicle*, 12 February 1898.
111. *The Daily Chronicle*, 25 February 1898.
112. Leader, *The Daily Chronicle*, 13 February 1898.
113. On 15 February 1898, Henry K. Davson, whose family owned the Blairmont Estate in Berbice, British Guiana, informed the Secretary of State for the Colonies that the withdrawal of 'coolies' from sugar estates because of rice cultivation, cattle rearing, railway works, huckstering, etc, had escalated the cost of labour by 20 percent. This

"scarcity", he asserted, was "aggravated" during the harvest season. The next day he wrote to Edward Wingfield, the Permanent Undersecretary of State for the Colonies, underlining the centrality of Indian indentured labourers:

> The letter has been prompted by my intense anxiety on the subject of immigration to British Guiana. Grants-in-aid, the abolition of bounties or failing them, countervailing duties, important as they are, occupy a secondary place (as far as that colony is concerned) to a continuance of immigration. Without the requisite labour we are powerless (CO 111/509 [Individuals – Henry K. Davson], 15 February 1898).

114. CO 111/504 Sendall to Chamberlain, no. 206, 23 June 1898, encl. It is noteworthy that H.E. Murray, a member of the delegation of the Planters' Association which met Governor Sendall on 4 May 1898, claimed that although he had increased wages by 25 percent, he still faced a scarcity of labour on the Corentyne: ". . . there was little to choose between the free coolie and the free black labourer from the point of view of reliability and willingness to work."
115. In 1897–1898, an avalanche of letters from the plantocracy, clamouring for more 'coolies', descended on the Colonial Office. Among the prominent correspondents were Quintin Hogg (West India Committee), Charles Parker (West India Association of Liverpool), and W. Middleton Campbell – absentee planters with sugar plantations in British Guiana. See CO 111/498 (Offices – Miscellaneous [Quintin Hogg]), 9 January 1897; CO 111/498 (Offices – Miscellaneous [Charles S. Parker]), 15 December 1897; CO 111/509 (Individuals – W. Middleton Campbell), 6 August 1898.
116. Leader, *The Daily Chronicle*, 12 July 1898.
117. *The Daily Chronicle*, 13 July 1898.
118. *The Daily Chronicle*, 27 August 1898. Bechu had asked:

> Is it any wonder . . . that a coolie who has worked out his five years, tries his luck on some other estate, or else comes to town to swell our army of jobbers, preferring to 'fill his belly with the husks that the swine do not eat' to a life of slavery in a colony which boasts of being a Christian colony?"

119. *The Daily Chronicle*, 30 August 1898.
120. Leader, *The Daily Chronicle*, 21 January 1899.
121. *The Daily Chronicle*, 26 January 1899.
122. Dwarka Nath states that prior to 1 September 1895 the entire cost of repatriation was covered from the immigration fund. Male immigrants introduced between 1 September 1895 and 31 October 1898 were required to pay a quarter of the return passage, while women paid one-sixth. From 1 November 1898, new male immigrants had to contribute a half; women paid one-third. D. Nath, *A History of Indians in Guyana* (London: The Author 1970 [1950]), 159, 222.
123. Leader, *The Daily Chronicle*, 28 March 1899.
124. *The Daily Chronicle*, 14, 28 July 1899.
125. *The Daily Chronicle*, 2 November 1897.
126. *The Daily Chronicle*, 24 November 1897.
127. Leader, *The Argosy*, 5 February 1898. The paper concluded on a predictably unimaginative note: "The longer the problem of how best to employ the coastlands is

regarded, the clearer will it appear that the one cultivation for which they are suited is sugar, 'the natural and legitimate industry' of the colony, to quote the words of the Secretary of State . . ." *The Argosy* had no doubts that sugar must always be "king": " . . . the whole fabric of the community may be said to rest upon sugar . . . To talk of saving the colony by substituting some other cultivation for that of sugar is mere foolishness . . ." (*The Argosy*, leader, 2 April 1898).

128. *The Argosy* argued thus:

> It is very hard for a number of small settlers on a large block of land to combine satisfactorily amongst themselves to maintain a drainage scheme for the whole block; and unless the whole block is included the scheme is practically useless. The government alone can render the working of such a scheme possible: but on no account should it be done at government expense. The settlers should be made clearly to understand what the cost of the scheme would be; and how much would fall to be paid towards it by every holder . . . before the government should undertake the scheme (*The Argosy*, leader, 21 January 1899). See also its leader of 27 May 1899.

129. *The Daily Chronicle*, 13 December 1898.
130. Leader, *The Daily Chronicle*, 28 February 1900.
131. *The Daily Chronicle*, 3 March 1900.
132. Leader, *The Daily Chronicle*, 4 March 1900.
133. *The Daily Chronicle*, 12 June 1900.
134. *The Daily Chronicle*, 16 June 1900.
135. *The Daily Chronicle*, 10 August 1900.
136. Leader, *The Argosy*, 3 March 1900.
137. *Report of the West India Royal Commission* Appendix C. – Part II, British Guiana, section 170.
138. *The Daily Chronicle*, 25 January 1901.
139. Rollo Ahmed [Caleb Buller], *I Rise: The Life Story of a Negro* (London, 1937), quoted in Rodney, *A History of the Guyanese*, 181.
140. Ibid, 181.
141. *The Daily Chronicle*, 25 October 1900.
142. *The Daily Chronicle*, 6 November 1900.
143. *The Daily Chronicle*, 9 November 1900.
144. *The Daily Chronicle*, 6 January 1901.
145. *The Daily Chronicle*, 5 February 1901.
146. *The Daily Chronicle*, 11, 13, 17 June 1897.
147. *The Argosy*, 30 October 1897.
148. This biographical sketch of Alexander (Ghurib Das) is based on J.R.B., "Regenerating the coolies: Ghurib Das and his work", *The Argosy*, 2 March 1901.
149. Ibid.
150. Ibid.
151. *The Daily Chronicle*, 3 August 1898. Bechu was not persuaded by the editor of this paper's proimmigration stance:

> You are constantly telling us, sir, that one of our surest needs in this colony, which has such enormous natural resources, is free East Indian labour, and yet you seem to shut your eyes to the fact that there is at the present time in this city more than a shipload of unemployed labourers of that

class who are knocking about the streets without the slightest effort being made to utilize their services.

152. *The Daily Chronicle*, 4 August 1898.
153. *The Daily Chronicle*, 16 August 1898. Ghurib Das elaborated, alluding to the oppressive character of the planters' regime:

> Your Industrial Farm Scheme will work well when you get General Booth [founder of the Salvation Army] to take it over, and get it superintended by those whose God is not the Almighty dollar . . . The class and quality of labourers to deal with require assistance to start any scheme for their benefit, but they are simple and easily managed with a little tact and patience.

154. *The Daily Chronicle*, 23 August 1898.
155. *The Argosy*, 10 September 1898.
156. *The Daily Chronicle*, 13 September 1898.
157. CO 114/78, Report of the Immigration Agent General 1897–98: ". . . the number of warrants does not represent individual desertions, as in some cases there are several warrants against the same immigrant for repeated desertions."
158. *The Daily Chronicle*, 1 September 1898.
159. *The Daily Chronicle*, 16 February 1899.
160. Leader, *The Daily Chronicle*, 17 February 1899. The paper commented:

> . . . [Ghurib Das] urges . . . that the planters should encourage the unindentured coolies to take up their residence on the estates by giving them small grants of land – half an acre each would be sufficient – for the purpose of cultivating products for their own consumption. A gift of this description would give the coolie a certain home interest in his surroundings and would enable him to tide over 'the slack season' . . . That such terms would be readily accepted by the coolies themselves, there can be no doubt. The offer of land seems to possess a special attraction for the East Indian, who invariably makes an industrious farmer . . . There are many coolies now in the city who would only too willingly return to the estates if the inducements offered them were at all sufficient.

161. *The Argosy*, 25 February 1899. These periodic raids by the police had been going on since about 1883.
162. The following case from the island of Leguan, in May 1900, is a poignant, if bizarre, tale of the overpowering instinct to be free:

> . . . a coolie lad, a cow-minder at Uniform, whilst walking through the high grass in search of cattle, was surprised by two cooliemen hiding under a clump of paragrass. He was frightened, as the men scarcely had any clothes on, and reported the fact to the man in charge of the estate. Several other coolies with dogs turned out and found the men to be two of 14 newly indentured coolies who, four days previously, ran away from Plantation Success. Later in the day five more were seen walking along the drift mud in the Clonbrook koker trench. Seven more were found aback of Enterprise under a large Oronoque tree, where they had camped with their blankets, etc. They presented a wretched appearance, and were all desperately hungry. Several constables conveyed them back to the estate. The men said they were in search of a way to Calcutta, and alleged that the cause of their running away was that the driver beat them in the field and the *Sahib* [overseer] would not believe their complaints (*The Daily Chronicle*, 29 May 1900). For similar stories of elusive quests of "the road to India overland", see *The Daily Chronicle*, 10 January 1900 and 19 July 1900.

163. *The Daily Chronicle*, 20 February 1900. Another East Coast planter's experience with his deserters spoke of despair, but it does not lack humour:

> I have some deserters on this estate who periodically are arrested in town, taken before the District Magistrate, convicted of desertion, and who then serve out their punishment, return to the estate in [the] charge of the police, and then immediately run away again. I wait a short time, have my deserters identified and arrested in town, and the same comedy is re-enacted. Passing by the market [in Georgetown] on the way to the Ferry or Suddie stelling I often see one or other of my deserters (*The Daily Chronicle*, 23 February 1900).

164. *The Daily Chronicle*, 21 February 1900.
165. *The Daily Chronicle*, 3 February 1900.
166. *The Daily Chronicle*, 2 February 1900.
167. See note 165.
168. *The Daily Chronicle*, 6 March 1900.
169. *The Daily Chronicle*, 10 March 1900.
170. *The Daily Chronicle*, 30 March 1900.
171. *The Daily Chronicle*, 4 August 1900.
172. *The Daily Chronicle*, 10 October 1900.
173. Ibid.
174. *The Daily Chronicle*, 10 November 1900.
175. *The Daily Chronicle*, 11 November 1900.
176. *The Argosy*, 2 March 1901.
177. See note 174.
178. Rodney, *A History of the Guyanese*, 155–56.
179. *Report of the West India Royal Commission* Appendix C. – Part II, British Guiana, section 158.
180. *The Daily Chronicle*, 23 July 1898.
181. Ibid.
182. *The Daily Chronicle*, 7 July 1898.
183. *The Daily Chronicle*, 8 July 1898.
184. *The Argosy*, 15 May 1897. Taylor's letter was dated 11 May 1897; it had an angry, hysterical feel: "As such attacks [Bechu's] are calculated to interfere with me in my official capacity and hamper me in the discharge of my duties, I must claim some sort of protection." The editor of *The Argosy*, however, did not view Bechu's allegations with the same severity: "As Mr Taylor signs his letter and seems anxious to have it published, we insert it; but in our opinion he is only breaking a fly upon the wheel."
185. The issue of *The Daily Chronicle* in which this letter appeared is missing from the files of the Newspaper Library (Colindale).
186. See note 184.
187. This quote from the missing letter is reproduced in Taylor's letter (see note 184).
188. *The Daily Chronicle*, 30 November 1897.
189. Ibid.
190. Ibid (leader).
191. *The Daily Chronicle*, 1 July 1898.
192. *The Daily Chronicle*, 22 July 1898.

193. *The Daily Chronicle*, 26 July 1898. This correspondent, 'Perseus', observed:

> I should like to point out ... the serious anomaly existing in the office ... where not a few of the so-called interpreters, who know comparatively little of the Hindustani language, are supposed to attend to the coolies, who not unfrequently [sic] have important statements to make, and serious complaints to lodge in which their vital interests are involved. Surely there is a considerable amount of slackness and want of efficiency in the Immigration Service of this colony that call for a good deal of attention on the part of the government.

194. *The Daily Chronicle*, 28 July 1898.
195. Bechu was probably referring to Plantation Blairmont, West Bank Berbice, where in May 1900 workers had gone on strike over wages and had attacked a symbol of their oppression – a driver. He had to be kept at the police station "for safety". Other drivers and overseers sought refuge in the Manager's house. *The Daily Chronicle*, (9 May 1900) carried the following caption on the incident:

> SERIOUS STRIKE ON PLN BLAIRMONT
> POLICE INTERVENTION NEEDED
> WORK ENTIRELY SUSPENDED

However, it must not be assumed that Indian workers were docile victims as the stereotype often suggested. In September 1900, on this same estate, *The Daily Chronicle*, reported:

> Blairmont was again thrown into a flutter today when eight coolies attacked the head overseer, Mr Symes, aback and belaboured him with sticks. It appears that about 60 or 70 new coolies struck work on Monday on the ground that they ought to receive higher wages than old coolies who had cattle and were thus able to work for the price.

A culture of resistance had, indeed, taken root (6 September 1900).

196. See Basdeo Mangru, "James 'Papa' Crosby: protector of indentured Indians, 1858–1880" in his *Indenture and Abolition: Sacrifice and Survival on The Guyanese Sugar Plantations* (Toronto: Tsar 1993), 17–42; and his "The Hincks-Beaumont imbroglio: partisan politics in British Guiana in the 1860s", *Boletin de Estudios Latinoamericanos y del Caribe*, No. 43 (1987): 99–114.
197. See *The Daily Chronicle*, 6, 25 October 1898.
198. See *The Daily Chronicle*, 11, 12, 13 April 1899 for coverage of the first trial.
199. I have relied almost exclusively on the court report of the second trial – Regina vs Bechu – in June 1899, for the following discussion of the case (CO 111/513 Sendall to Chamberlain, no. 182, 6 July 1899, encl.)
200. *The Daily Chronicle*, 6 October 1898.
201. Ibid.
202. See note 199.
203. Ibid.
204. *The Daily Chronicle*, 5 February 1899. Norman Bascom's quotation of the earnings of a few of his workers who had earned above the statutory minimum in January 1899, had struck a discordant note in Ghurib Das. He countered:

Notes

If wages on the estates were as Mr Bascom would have us believe I wonder who is responsible for our overcrowded streets with coolies in Georgetown whose average earnings are, I believe, not over 10 cents *per diem*. While the estates may boast of still being . . . the mainstay of the colony, they must not forget that without 'Sammy' [Indians] their estates would be worth hundreds instead of thousands. 'Sammy' is worthy of more honour, with all his faults, than generally falls to his lot, and often his weakness is taken advantage of (*The Daily Chronicle*, 7 February 1899).

205. Ibid (Bechu's and Ghurib Das' letters were published in the same issue).
206. CO 111/516 (Offices – India), 7 June 1899. Bechu had signed this letter "E. Bechu"; this mysterious "E" remains intriguing.
207. See note 199.
208. See note 206.
209. See note 199.
210. Ibid.
211. CO 111/513 Sendall to Chamberlain, no. 205, 19 July 1899, encl.
212. Ibid.
213. Ibid.
214. Ibid.
215. CO 111/513 Sendall to Chamberlain, confidential, 19 July 1899.
216. See note 211 (Minute [Sydney Olivier], 4 August 1899).
217. See note 206 (Minute [Sydney Olivier], 8 June 1899).
218. See note 215 (Minute [Sydney Olivier], 4 August 1899).
219. See note 206.
220. Leader, *The Daily Chronicle*, 3 November 1901.
221. Ibid.

PART 2: SECTION B

BECHU: HIS LETTERS AND THEIR CONTEXT

COMPILED AND EDITED BY CLEM SEECHARAN

CHAPTER ONE

The Emergence of a 'Bound Coolie' Radical: Bechu, the Shootings at Plantation Non Pareil and 'Langton'

Bechu's first letter to the press appears on 1 November 1896, two weeks after five Indian workers are shot and 59 wounded at Plantation Non Pareil, a neighbouring estate to Enmore, where Bechu is indentured. He attributes the fatal incident to the unilateral slashing of wages by the planters, an illegal act; but he also indicts the protectors of Indians, the Immigration Agents, for dereliction of duty.

Bechu (Indentured Immigrant, Sheila, 1894) to the Editor,
The Daily Chronicle (Pln Enmore, 30 October 1896):

Sir, Will you kindly permit me, through the medium of your widely circulated paper, to say a few words with regard to the official investigation which has been made concerning the rate of wages paid to the indentured labourers on Plantation Nonpareil [sic]?

Being a *coolie* myself, and an *indentured* one in the bargain, I have up to now refrained from saying anything in the matter, but as I see it mentioned in last Saturday's issue of *The Argosy* that the referees after due enquiries are satisfied that the wages paid for punt loading and cane cutting is [sic] ample, and that the price for weeding is only a trifle below the usual rate, I am curious to know on what they have based their decision.

Prior to registering myself for service in this colony, I, in common with the rest of my countrymen, had to sign an agreement which is printed in three different languages and which reads as follows:

(1) *Period of Service:* Five years from date of allotment.

(2) *Nature of Labour:* Work in connection with the cultivation of the soil or the manufacture of the produce of any plantation.

(3) *Number of days on which the immigrant is required to labour in each week:* Every day except Sundays and authorized holidays.

(4) *Number of hours in each day during which emigrant is required to labour without extra remuneration:* Seven hours in the field or ten hours in the factory buildings.

(5) *Monthly or daily wages or task work rates*: Able-bodied males of and above 16 years of age shall be paid one shilling, equivalent to ten annas and a half for each day's work. Adult males not able-bodied or minors of and above ten years and under 16, or female adults or minors of and above ten years of age shall be paid 8 pence, equivalent to 7 annas for each day's work *and when performing extra work shall be paid in proportion for every extra hour of work.* Wages earned will be paid weekly, but if the emigrant is required to work by task instead of by time, the same wage shall be paid as to unindentured labourers on the same or other neighbouring plantations, *and such wages may be more, but shall not be less than the minimum wage payable for time work.*

(6) *Condition as to return passage*: The emigrant, on completing a continuous residence of ten years in British Guiana and holding or becoming entitled to a certificate of exemption from labour, shall with family, if any, should they not be under indenture, or if under indenture should commutation money have been paid to their employer, be provided with a free return passage back to Calcutta. After completing a continuous residence of five years and holding or becoming entitled to a certificate of exemption from labour the emigrant may return to India at his own cost. Blankets and warm clothing are supplied *gratis* on leaving India, but not for the return voyage.

(7) *Other conditions:* Rations shall be provided for the emigrant and family, if any, by the employer for three calender months following the date of allotment according to the scale sanctioned by the Government of British Guiana, at a cost of 4 pence, equivalent to 3 annas and a half daily for each adult above 16 years of age,

half rations to minors of ten and under 16 at half the cost, and to each infant under ten years one-third of a ration free of cost. A suitable dwelling shall be assigned to the emigrant and family, if any, free of rent and shall be kept in good repair by the employer; medicines, comforts, medical attendance, hospital accommodation and appropriate diet shall be provided free of cost.

It will be observed from paragraphs four and five of the above that every male immigrant above 16 years of age is entitled to a rate of wage of not less than one shilling per day and every female and every male under 16 years of age is similarly entitled to a wage of not less than 8 [eight] pence per day, for seven hours in the field and ten hours in the factory, and that when performing extra work they shall be paid in proportion for every extra hour of work.

Immigrants required to work by task instead of by time shall receive the same wage that is paid to unindentured labourers on the same or other neighbouring plantations, or to indentured labourers on the neighbouring plantations and such wage *may be more, but shall not be less than the minimum wage payable for time work*.

Now, on the face of the above, let me appeal to you, to say whether 9 shillings per week is adequate payment for punt loaders who have to work from 6 am to 8 or 9 pm daily; and is not an indentured immigrant justified in appealing to his protector when any attempt is made on the part of his employer to fix terms which prevent him from earning at least one shilling a day *for a day of seven hours?*

In this colony, however, an agreement appears to be binding on one side only, for we constantly see coolies being brought up for 'neglecting to attend work', for 'not completing their task', and for many such trivial breaches of contract, but in not a single instance have I seen a protector charge an employer for not fulfilling his part of the contract towards an indentured immigrant. Is this fair play?

I am well aware that this is a hard time for not only planters, but for every individual in this colony who depends upon trade or labour to earn a livelihood, but when our exemplary clergy think it hard to part with a single cent out of their stipulated salaries, how can it be expected that indentured heathens will do so cheerfully? Verily 'unto every one that hath shall be given and he shall have abundantly, but unto him that hath not shall be taken away even that which he hath'.

Thank you, Sir, in anticipation for granting me this little space.

The Daily Chronicle, **1 November 1896**

One of Bechu's compatriots, an Indian born in the colony, applauds his boldness in defending the indentured Indian, for whom the contract of indentureship is marked more by its contravention than its application.

J.R. Wharton (Georgetown) to the Editor, *The Daily Chronicle:*

Sir, I was pleased to read Bechu's letter in your issue of Sunday last anent the wages paid to East Indian immigrants on the estates of this colony and more particularly as the circumstances which caused this bold East Indian, although an indentured immigrant, to place the case of the coolie (as he is commonly called) in this colony in its proper light before the public, at a time when some practical steps should be taken to alleviate the sufferings and hardships of the poor coolie in this colony, and I think he deserves some credit.

I am not acquainted with the author of the letter, but I know there are many who, along with me, agree with the writer in everything he has expressed. As regards the stipulations contained in the contract entered into between the immigrant and the Emigration Agent in Calcutta, prior to the former's embarkation for these shores, as Bechu reproduces them for the information of the public, I have nothing to say except that these particular conditions become a dead letter no sooner than they have been agreed upon. It is all very well for the authorities to refer the question of wages to persons who are themselves personally interested in such matters and it is no surprise that their decision should be pronounced in a manner more favourable to the planters than the unfortunate labourers. It is only too obvious and requires no comment that this finding of the arbitrators is in contradistinction to the contract which the immigrants are made to sign, because we see that the conditions and liabilities imposed upon the employer were not carried out at Non Pareil. Yet we find men – members of the planting community – giving it as their opinion that the rate of wages paid to the labourers of Non Pareil was fair! But this is by the way. I do not wish to pose as a champion of the coolie labourer. What I would like to draw the attention of the public to is the arbitrary manner in which he is treated in this colony. Apart from the anomalous conditions under which he is introduced here, and these are never made known to him before he sets sail for this colony, Bechu being evidently a solitary exception, the immigrant comes here like a blind man, [and] submits to his employers as willingly as one could desire. But if this were all, things would be very pleasant. Unfortunately there are some, I shouldn't say all, employers who whether from a natural habit to tyrannize or from ignorance of the terms of the contract, overdo things to the prejudice of the immigrant which go so frequently to render most unpleasant results, sometimes culminating in a trial before the Supreme Courts.

Recently, and for sometime past, the fact has forced itself upon us that the labour market is glutted, and we see, day by day, sugar plantations being thrown out of cultivation and abandoned, yet the annual importation of East Indian immigrants to this colony continues in numbers as before, and the government, of course, pays the piper which the poor taxpayers tacitly contribute to. What good is there in plunging the colony year after year into heavy liability when it is so clearly demonstrated that no corresponding benefit is derived by the government?

I think the time has arrived when, with an East Indian population of over 100,000 in this colony, immigration should be stopped, and the government would only be acting in the best interests of its future welfare were it, say, for the next five years to cease importing immigrants. Hundreds of coolies are seen knocking about with no employment, and we invariably see large numbers of them drafted into that government institution, the prison, at every criminal assize, from want of work. With all their faults the planters, I think, cannot be so much blamed as the government in sanctioning the importation of thousands of coolies annually when they are fully aware of the depressed state of affairs in the sugar industry here.

Latterly, I see the government has been offering to the time-expired East Indian immigrants plots of Crown land to settle down upon, thereby obviating the expenditure of something like £18 for each adult for return passages, but this inducement, as it is called, is abortive, without something more tangible accompanying it like, say, a sum of £5 being given to every immigrant who takes a piece of land and settles down, with which sum he will be enabled to start operations and see his way to forming a homestead for himself, and by this means the government would save a large sum of money in the shape of back passages, but at present no one unless he had some means of his own would care to accept the offer of the government.

The Daily Chronicle, **5 November 1896**

The Emergence of a 'Bound Coolie' Radical: Bechu, the Shootings . . .

'Langton' (W. Alleyne Ireland) makes the planter's case in the aftermath of the Non Pareil shootings.

. . . Not a little of the evil repute of British Guiana in the matter of treatment of immigrants (I am speaking now of 20 years ago) was due to the extreme apathy of the inhabitants of the colony as to hostile statements made about them. This indifference or laziness still exists and is even now doing the colony great harm. An example comes very aptly to hand in connection with the subject of this article. In *The Daily Chronicle* of November 1st, this year, appeared a letter written by an indentured immigrant [Bechu] in which certain statements were made and certain questions asked which should certainly have been dealt with by some member of the planting body. To us here it is not of much importance what is said of us on the spot, but these statements go forth to the world and are quoted as facts sooner or later. As the matters referred to in the letter I am about to quote bear directly on the subject of my article, I propose to deal with them.

As to the recent dispute as to wages on Pln Non Pareil the letter says:

> The referees after due enquiries are satisfied that the wages paid for punt loading and cane cutting is ample and that the price for weeding is only a trifle below the usual rate, I am curious to know on what they have based their decision.

Surely someone might have taken enough interest in the matter to have answered the enquiry.

I am able to inform the writer of the letter that the referees came to their decisions from actual inspection of each kind of work. This form of investigation is the one always pursued in cases of a similar nature.

One paragraph of the letter is of special interest as it contains the expression of opinion as to the price paid for punt loading. The passage runs:

> Now on the face of the above (the indenture contract) let me appeal to you, to say whether 9 shillings per week is adequate payment for punt loaders who have to work from 6 am to 9 pm daily, and is not an indentured immigrant justified in appealing to his protector when any attempt is made on the part of his employer to fix terms which prevent him from earning at least one shilling a day for a day of seven hours?

In this passage the labour contract is referred to and I may therefore quote it. It is Paragraph 4 of the contract, and is as follows:

Number of hours in each day during which emigrant is required to labour, *without extra remuneration*: seven hours in the field or ten hours in the factory buildings' [emphasis added].

This means seven hours actual labour.

By experiment I find that two average men can load a punt of canes under ordinary circumstances in 45 minutes, without any pressing or extraordinary exertion.

This at 10 cents a punt would give 90 cents to be divided between two men for a day's work.

It is true that punts are not always ready and that there are hitches of one sort and another, but this is amply made up for by the fact that a man can earn 45 cents in a day under favourable circumstances. I am assured that punt loading is the most popular work on estates amongst the indentured men and this would hardly be the case if there were any serious drawbacks to earning good money as a rule.

Towards the end of the letter the writer says:

In this colony, however, an agreement appears to be binding on one side only, for we constantly see coolies brought up for 'neglecting to attend work', for 'not completing their task', and for such trivial breaches of contract, but in not a single instance have I seen a protector charge an employer for not fulfilling his part of the contract towards an indentured immigrant. Is this fair play?

For the general principle of a coolie getting redress for grievances against an employer, I refer the writer to Section 213 of Ordinance 18 of 1891. That there have been prosecutions of employers by immigrants is proved by the Annual Reports of the Immigration Agent General. During the last 22 years, 1874–95, the number of such cases has been as follows:

Number of complaints laid by immigrants against employers 624; Withdrawn 67; Struck out 106; Dismissed (either for want of prosecution or on the merits of the case) 243; Convicted 208.

As to the writer referring to 'neglecting to attend work' and 'failing to complete a task' as trivial breaches of contract, everyone who knows anything about organization must realize that such breaches of contract are subversive of all discipline and are apt to become epidemic.

On November 5th last, another letter appeared in *The Daily Chronicle* [J.R. Wharton's], which was also passed over in silence by those whose duty it was to point out the errors and absurdities in it.

This writer makes two statements which are absolutely at variance with the facts of the case under consideration. He says:

> As regards the stipulations contained in the contract entered into between the immigrant and the Emigration Agent in Calcutta, prior to the former's embarkation for these shores, as Bechu (the writer of the letter referred to above) reproduces them for the information of the public I have nothing to say except that these conditions become a dead letter no sooner than they have been agreed on.

And further on:

> Apart from the anomalous conditions under which he (the indentured immigrant) is introduced here, and these are never made known to him before he sets sail for this colony, Bechu being evidently a solitary exception, the immigrant comes here, and like a blind man submits to his employers as willingly as one could desire.

Statements like the above should not have been allowed to pass unchallenged. If the writer of the letter refers to Section 55 of Ordinance 18 (25) of 1891, he will see that it is specially provided that any contract made in India between a labourer and an Emigration Agent of this colony is valid and enforceable against either the colony or the employer as the case may be. As to the reading of the contract to the immigrants before they leave India, I quote from a minute description of the system of recruiting in India published in *The Argosy* of September 26th, 1896, page 5, column 2:

> Those (emigrants) who pass (the medical examination) are then taken before a Magistrate in small batches of 15 or 20 at a time, and he explains the terms of contract which in addition, however, are endorsed on the registration papers in three different languages.

Further, the terms of contract are fully explained to the immigrants after their allotment here by the Immigration Agents who visit the estates first after the new coolies are settled.

As to the immigrants submitting like blind men to their employers as willingly as one could desire, the Annual Reports of the Immigration Agent General show that between 1874 and 1895, 65,084 indentured immigrants were convicted of breaches of the labour contract.

Towards the close of his letter, the writer says:

> Hundreds of coolies are seen knocking about with no employment, and we invariably see larger numbers of them drafted into that government institution, the prison, at every criminal assize, for want of work.

Careful enquiry has furnished me with no single case of a man who has been imprisoned for 'want of work'.

'Langton' [W. Alleyne Ireland], "The History of the East Indian immigrant", *The Argosy*, 5 December 1896

Bechu responds to 'Langton', with the submission that many indentured labourers do not receive the statutory minimum wage of one shilling [24 cents] for seven hours' work, and that task work is arbitrarily imposed on workers.

Bechu (Pln Enmore) to the Editor, *The Daily Chronicle*:

Sir, More than a month having elapsed since my letter, anent the rate of wages paid to indentured East Indian immigrants appeared in your columns, and seeing that no one has replied to the queries that were put in it, I made up my mind to let the matter drop, especially as I had promised a gentleman, who has been exceedingly kind to me, and for whom I have the highest respect not to appear in print again, at least not for the present, but as in last Saturday's issue of *The Argosy*, 'Langton', who is treating *us* to a very interesting, and to *me* instructive 'History of the Indian Immigrant' in this colony, has challenged the statements made by me, I feel justified in breaking my word, and therefore beg you will give me a chance of defending myself, because what he says is likely to travel quite as far and wide as he apprehends my previous statements have done, and those who do not see my contradiction may be led to accept what he tells us, as Gospel truths.

Before refuting his statements, however, I mean to place his replies and my queries side by side, so that you and your numerous readers may be able to judge for yourselves whether it is time that I should retire.

'Langton' is evidently the planters' friend, I seek impartial judgment.

Wages on Pln Non Pareil

Query (1)	Reply (1)
The referees after due enquiries are satisfied that the wages paid for cane cutting is ample, and that the price for weeding is only a trifle below the usual rate.	The referees came to their decision from actual inspection of each kind of work.
I am curious to know on what they have based their decision?	This form of investigation is the one always pursued in cases of similar nature.

Now, this answer simply begs my question. Of course, the referees rode down to the spot, and as a matter of form, walked through the fields, but what I wish to know is whether they inspected the *Order Book of the estate, and took the trouble to see what rate of wage was paid last year, and for the previous four years *for the same kind of work and in the very same fields?* In the Coroner's Court, Mr Van Nooten [Manager of Non Pareil] himself admitted that the rates had been reduced very much more than ten percent during the past year.

Although an employer may be at liberty to pay free labourers as little, or as much as he pleases, I maintain that he has no right whatsoever to fix terms which will prevent an indentured man from earning at least one shilling in seven hours. There are lots of indentured men who work by time and have drivers at their backs all day long who cannot and do not earn that amount in ten hours. As regards the form of investigation which Langton informs us is the one always pursued in cases of similar nature, I am curious to know the authority for it. I was given to understand that *no task labour* could be imposed on an *indentured labourer* unless he preferred it to time work and even then no tasks could be given unless the sub-Immigration Agent had inspected it, and was satisfied that it was not severe and could ordinarily be performed in seven hours. I think I am safe in adding that the Protector of Immigrants in Trinidad if no one else, will fully bear me out in this statement.

* Mr Munroe, who I presume, is the Manager of an estate, should know the existence of such a book.

The Indentured Contract

Query (2)

Now on the face of the above let me appeal to you and say whether nine shillings per week is adequate payment for puntloaders who have to work from 6 am to 9 pm daily, and is not an indentured immigrant justified in appealing to his protector when any attempt is made on the part of his employer to fix terms which prevent him from earning at least one shilling a day for a day of seven hours?

Reply (2)

This means seven hours actual labour.

By experiment I find that two average men can load a punt of canes under ordinary circumstances in 45 minutes without any pressing or extraordinary exertion.

This at 10 cents a punt would give 90 cents to be divided between two men for a day's work.

It is true that punts are not always ready and that there are hitches of one sort or another but this is amply made up for, by the fact that a man can earn 45 cents in a day under favourable circumstances. I am assured that punt loading is the most popular work on estates amongst the indentured men, and this would hardly be the case if there were any serious drawbacks to earning good money as a rule.

Perfectly true, but whose fault is it, if two average men do not load the required number of punts to entitle them to their shilling after seven hours? Why should they be made to remain 15 hours, and sometimes longer, in the open – in the boiling sun and in the pelting rain? Is it not because the punt overseer does not, or, rather, cannot, at all times, supply empty punts as soon as a trip is ready?

Surely 'the labourer is worthy of his hire'. If therefore an indentured labourer can prove that he has been in attendance for over seven hours, why is not he, under the terms of his contract paid proportionately for every additional hour?

I am glad to learn that under Section 55 of Ordinance 18 (25) of 1891, it is specially provided that any contract made in India between a labourer and an Emigration Agent of this colony is valid and enforceable against either the colony or the employer as the case may be.

The reason why the Non Pareil punt loaders felt dissatisfied was because they were restricted to a certain number of punts when they knew full well that were the number of punt loaders reduced they could, certainly 'without any pressing or extraordinary exertion' be in a position to give *seven hours and more* actual labour.

It is not difficult to explain why punt loading, in spite of its long hours, is most popular, for a cursory glance at the several pay lists will show that no other gang on an estate can earn as many shillings at the end of the week as that gang though the other gangs have to give fully nine hours *continuous labour.*

Redress for Grievances

Query (3)

In this colony, however, an agreement appears to be binding on one side only, for we constantly see coolies brought up for neglecting to attend work, for not completing their tasks and for such trivial breaches of contract, but in not a single instance have I seen a protector charge an employer for not fulfilling his part of the contract towards an indentured immigrant.

Is this fair play?

Reply (3)

For the general principle of a coolie getting redress for grievances against an employer I refer the writer to Section 213 of Ordinance 18 of 1891. That there have been prosecutions of employers by immigrants is proved by the Annual Reports of the Immigration Agent General during the last 22 years, 1874–1895. The number of such cases has been as follows:- Number of complaints laid by immigrants against employers 624, withdrawn 67, struck out 106, dismissed for want of prosecution or on the merits of the case 243, convicted 208.

Fancy a coolie, and an indentured one in the bargain, who is struggling to keep body and soul together, being referred to Ordinances, Annual Reports, and standard publications on immigration!!! I doubt if during the remaining time of my indenture I shall have a chance of seeing the outer covers of those publications, leave alone reading the contents. It is very comforting, however, to know that there have been *prosecutions* of employers by immigrants in the past, the present generation instead of growing wiser prefer to be like 'dumb-driven cattle.' In annual reports the East Indian immigrant is invariably held up as '*industrious and peace-loving*', so it is only when his wages are interfered with that he rebels. He is blissfully ignorant of Section 55 of Ordinance 18 (25) of 1891 and his protector takes good care to see that he does not take advantage of it.

With regard to the attack made on Mr Wharton, I shall remain perfectly silent, because I feel sure that that gentleman needs no champion. I have no hesitation, however, in giving a flat denial to the statement that the 'terms of a contract are fully explained to the immigrants after their allotment here by the Immigration Agent who visits the estate first after the new coolies are settled'. This was never done when the batch I belonged to arrived, and it has not been done in the case of any other batch since. Indeed, although I am nearly two years on this estate neither I nor any of my shipmates have had the honour of appearing before Mr Gladwin [the Immigration Agent] . . .

The Daily Chronicle, 9 December 1896

'Langton' rebuts Bechu's interpretation of key clauses of the indentureship contract. He states that Bechu is seeking "notoriety, not information".

Langton [W. Alleyne Ireland] to the Editor, *The Daily Chronicle:*

Sir, I have neither the time nor the inclination to enter into a lengthy controversy with Bechu as to the correctness of the facts contained in my article on 'The History of the East Indian Immigrant'; but as some of the statements made by Bechu might lead persons ignorant of the matter to adopt views inconsistent with the true facts, I beg you will insert the following observations in your valuable columns:

(1) Bechu refers to the fact that wages are lower this year than during the previous four years. This is a mere *ignoratio elenchi*. The point to be decided by the referees at Non Pareil was not whether the wages paid for punt loading and other work were more or less than the wages paid for the same class of work at some other time; but, whether an ordinary labourer could or could not earn one shilling by seven hours' labour at the price paid at the time the dispute arose. The referees decided that the price for punt loading was fair, viewed from the standpoint of their enquiry.

(2) Bechu says: 'I was given to understand that no task labour could be imposed on an indentured labourer unless he preferred it to time work.'
I cannot of course throw any doubt upon what Bechu has been given to understand; but I give here the words of the labour contract, bearing on the point of task labour. This contract [is] signed by every coolie who comes here under indenture and the terms of contract are printed in three dialects. 'But if the emigrant be required to work by task instead of by

time, the same wage shall be paid as to unindentured labourers on the same or other neighbouring plantations or to indentured labourers on the neighbouring plantations, and such wage may be more, but shall not be less than the minimum wage payable for time work.' By this clause the planter can put any indentured labourer to task work without consulting the labourer's inclination in the matter, the only condition being that he must pay a sufficient wage.

(3) Bechu says: 'If therefore an indentured labourer can prove that he has been in attendance for over seven hours, why is not he, under the terms of his contract, paid proportionately for every additional hour?' The reason is obvious. The indentured labourer has not made a contract to be paid for 'being in attendance' but for 'labouring'.

If a coolie can show that his employer has not given him a chance of earning one shilling by seven hours' labour, he has the remedy of the law – a remedy that everyone else in the colony has to have recourse to in cases of breach of contract.

(4) Bechu says 'Fancy a coolie, and an indentured one in the bargain, who is struggling to keep body and soul together, being referred to Ordinances, Annual Reports, and standard publications on immigration!!!' Further on he continues, 'in annual reports the East Indian immigrant is invariably held up as "industrious and peace-loving".'

These two passages taken together are very amusing. In the first Bechu derides the notion of a coolie being referred to annual reports and marks his sense of the extreme foolishness of such a reference by three notes of exclamation. Ten lines further on Bechu himself quotes from the annual reports and gives his quotation the attribute of invariability; thus creating a strong impression in the mind of his readers that he has consulted these annual reports frequently.

I certainly seem to have been in fault when I referred Bechu to the works in which he could get information. I had expected that anyone capable of writing an intelligent letter, such as Bechu wrote in November, would have been glad to have pointed out to him the source of information used by his critic – I was evidently mistaken – notoriety, not information, seems to be what Bechu is in search of . . .

The Daily Chronicle, 12 December 1896

Bechu still contends that the minimum wage is not being met. This must be rectified in order to prevent a "repetition" of the Non Pareil disaster.

Bechu (Pln Enmore) to the Editor, *The Daily Chronicle:*

Sir, I have perused 'Langton's' latest production which appeared in last Saturday's issue of your paper, and I think it only natural that he, after making certain misstatements with regard to the wages paid to indentured immigrants should persist in sticking to them, but as you have been so indulgent as to give publicity to both our letters it remains for you and your numerous readers to decide which of our statements is to be depended upon. Since 'the proof of the pudding is in the eating of it,' so the correctness of my statement can easily be proved, if before a repetition of the Non Pareil incident takes place, an independent official is deputed to visit the several estates to inspect the pay lists and report to government whether the indentured coolies *are* or *are not* receiving their shilling *per diem*, and if not why not.

With regard to the two passages which 'Langton' quotes in paragraph 4 of his letter, I must confess that they do look extremely funny when placed side by side. Considering how amused I felt at his referring me to books and publications which it is impossible for me in my present position to get hold of, I ought to have explained that I derived my information from the newspapers in which reviews on *all* Annual Reports from time to time appear. Indeed most of my knowledge I pick up from newspapers which I usually beg or borrow from someone, so there is no occasion for 'Langton' to get alarmed if I am fishing for 'notoriety' because I shall never, like him, be able to pose, before the public, as an historian.

By the way, have you noticed with what assurance 'Langton' made that statement about sub-Immigration Agents visiting estates before the arrival of new coolies and explaining to them the terms of their agreement, and how effectually I have silenced him on that point?

The Daily Chronicle, 15 December 1896

The Emergence of a 'Bound Coolie' Radical: Bechu, the Shootings . . .

On the eve of the Royal Commission Bechu reproduces a long article from an English newspaper to advance his case that the colony must move beyond sugar and its obsession with Indian indentured labourers.

Bechu (Pln Enmore) to the Editor, *The Daily Chronicle*:

Sir, I beg to forward for your perusal the accompanying able article on the 'West Indies and the Sugar Trade', which is printed at page 5 of *The Standard*, dated the 14th December last, and which you may not have spotted out yet owing to the pile of papers that came in by the last mail. It deserves to be reproduced in your columns, if for no other reason, to, at least, 'show up' those cute customers, who have been endeavouring to make capital out of the 'Non Pareil riot' by trying to hoax the Home Authorities into the belief, that unless immediate steps are taken to check the bounty-fed competition of continental beet sugar, a large number of the best cane plantations in this colony will go out of cultivation, and that riots on a much more serious scale than those which have already occurred in Demerara are likely to take place. These self-interested parties who took such pains to inform the British public of the *formidable riot* amongst the Indian coolies whose wages the planters were *compelled* to reduce, very conveniently, *omitted* to mention that the coolies referred to, are under *indenture* and that *there can be no reductions in the case of indentured coolies, who are under a stringent contract, which the government has to enforce.*

To make their case look more absurd these wiseacres in one and the same breath press for a continuance of immigration, as if the 100,000 ill-paid coolies already in the colony are not more than enough to meet the requirements of the 64 estates now under cultivation!!

The West Indies and the Sugar Trade
(From a Correspondent to *The Standard*.)
(Enclosure to the above)

That the government intends to send a Commission to the West Indies to enquire into the economic condition of those colonies is a hopeful sign that a part of the Empire which has hitherto been much neglected is about to receive its due need of attention. Until the Commission is appointed, and we are acquainted with the exact terms of its reference, it would be premature to discuss the probable outcome of the measure; but it is a clear inference, from existing facts, that no Commission is likely to be of lasting benefit to the West Indies which is solely empowered to collect information and to report upon the state of the cane sugar industry. It is doubtful whether even if the continental bounty system could be abolished, the West Indies could long continue to rival other cane growing areas in the production of sugar; and it is reasonably certain that if they are again to win a prominent commercial place in our imperial system, their rich resources in soil and climate must be turned into account in the development of new enterprises. As there is no immediate prospect of the abolition of bounties, the Commission is likely to find that the only real service it can perform is to devise measures whereby the population of the colonies can be helped over the present crisis, and their energies directed into new channels. The future of the West Indies is not inseparably bound up with the fate of the cane sugar industry, though it is generally and erroneously assumed that, if the cultivation of the cane comes to an end final ruin will fall upon them. They are in their present plight because to employ a colloquialism, they have put 'all their eggs into one basket', and the only sure and permanent relief that can be afforded them is to help them to provide other baskets for other products. If the Commission is to take broad views and cover wide ground, if it is to concern itself with the general development of these colonies, and not merely with the prolongation of the sugar industry, and a perpetuation of the economic and social system that depends upon the prosperity of the planter, its existence will be justified. If otherwise, one may be doubtful of its utility, unless, of course, the beet-sugar-producing countries of Europe quickly consent to abandon their present means of fostering cultivation and manufacture. Is there any sign of such an abandonment? If there is, it is so difficult to discern, that it is of scant practical value for men of business. This, at least, is the view of the planters, who again, as at intervals for many years past, urge the Imperial Government to redress the balance against them by imposing a countervailing duty upon imported beet sugar. They would not do that – for government after government has declined to accede to their request – if they had not lost hope that the Powers of Europe will suffer themselves to be persuaded that bounties are not only iniquitous from the standpoint of the economist, but also unjust and injurious to the taxpayer from whose pockets they are drawn. The planters in our colonies recognize facts as to the extent of disbelieving that bounties will cease in the near future, and that France, Germany and Austria can be induced by Great Britain to put an end to them. There are in that case, but two courses open, either to impose a countervailing duty in the interests of the planters – a proposal we will not discuss because it is outside the range of practical politics – or to take steps to provide for the population which will be thrown out of employment should the planters find themselves, in the last resort, compelled to stop their factories and let their cane fields relapse into bush.

Where the proposed Commission can do inestimable service is in ascertaining for Mr Chamberlain what may best be done to enable the people of the West Indies to fend for themselves, should the avenue of employment now afforded by the sugar estates be gradually narrowed until it closes altogether. The word 'gradually' is used, not without good reason. Though it may be admitted that, with sugar at its present price, it is impossible for all but the best managed estates – those conducted with the highest scientific skill and fitted with the finest machinery – to continue working at a profit it does not follow that there will be any sudden and general collapse of the industry throughout those parts of the West Indies and Guiana where it predominates. This is an opinion which we believe will be shared by those who have knowledge of the local circumstances, and are not parties to the campaign of exaggerated agitation which has recently been renewed in England and in the Western Tropics. The cessation of cultivation, should it occur, will be gradual. Estates will drop out season by season and in twos and threes. The weakest will go first – that is to say, those whose owners have not sufficient capital to hold on until there is a turn in the market, or who are working on soil which is becoming exhausted. The diminution in the area of cultivation and, therefore, in the scope for employment will however, if present prices continue much longer, be serious enough to tax the ingenuity of the Local Governments and of the Colonial Office. The Commission, therefore, should set to work promptly and make periodical reports, so that the Imperial Government may map out its line of policy in view of local emergencies. That there will be rioting on a large scale, Negro revolts against the whites, massacre and pillage and various other terrible evils as the alarmists have foretold, there is no reason to believe. The reasons for this confidence are manifold. The Negro population of the British West Indies as a whole and the coolies of Guiana and Trinidad are accustomed to settled government. They are a peaceful, law-abiding, orderly and – by men of strong character and tact – easily governed people. To those who make it their business to know them and understand them – men whose services the Colonial Office can command by the score – they may be led and guided without social danger. The Negro in particular is but a child of unusual growth and though like big children everywhere, he can be a little unruly at times, he obeys invariably a superior will, and submits to mastership with a good grace.

In each of the colonies again there is a considerable proportion of the population which is not dependent for its livelihood upon the continuance of the sugar industry. In Guiana there are the goldfields now employing several thousands of sturdy blacks, and promising to use up all the spare labour which that colony, if not all the British West Indies, can yield; in Trinidad there are the cocoa and coffee plantations, the asphaltic deposits, and the carrying trade with Venezuela; in Dominica and the Virgin Islands where the sugar industry has almost entirely disappeared of recent years, there are various minor resources, which in the aggregate keep the population; and the same may be said of the Windward Islands. In Jamaica, once the premier sugar-producing country in the world, there is a large coffee-growing industry, and an important trade in tropical fruits with America. As for Barbados, the production there is mostly entirely confined to sugar, and as the population is of great density and astonishing fecundity the problem presents special difficulties. For many years emigration has been an imperative necessity for Barbados, for this is the only island that has not wide reserves of primeval land. It supplied thousands of labourers for the Panama Canal, and its muscular and intelligent, if somewhat self-assertive, Negroes form a notable element in every West Indian colony. The government is already fostering further emigration from the island, and even should the worst happen, and the estates pass out of cultivation, the soil is so fruitful and the Negro wants so little besides plantain and saltfish, that a large population will be able easily to maintain themselves. Taking then a broad view of the West Indies as a whole, the dependence of their people upon sugar is not so absolute as at first sight appears to be the case. The transition from dependence on one product to many has, with the exception of Barbados, not only begun, but sufficiently far advanced to warrant the belief that, if needs must, entire independence of the sugar industry will be successfully achieved. If all the planters say about the prospects of their industry under existing fiscal conditions be true, it is an independence such as this that must be prepared for by the Imperial Government, by the various West Indian Governments, and by the people of those colonies. The transition stage will, no doubt, be fruitful in anxieties to governments and to peoples; it will bring severe hardships to those who have capital invested in the sugar industry and to those traders whose business it is to furnish the estates with 'supplies', but these people, or their forerunners, particularly in the preabolition days, and before the equalization of sugar duties by Lord John Russell, made huge fortunes; and there is no way that can be seen (unless the Commission can discover one), short of a countervailing duty in their sole interest by which they can escape the ordinary, or extraordinary, risks of commercial enterprise.

If the sugar industry is allowed to become extinct, are the West Indies, it will be asked, to relapse into bush? Which is to be the home of Negroes, who will themselves fall back into semisavagery? Is that to be the issue of, in some cases, over three centuries of British rule? Are groups of the loveliest islands in the world, set amidst seas in which Englishmen of other days helped so materially to win our maritime supremacy, to be abandoned by the white man and left to a population of blacks and half-breeds? To all of these questions a negative answer can justly be given. It does not follow that because the sugar industry has failed – assuming that it will fail, which yet remains to be proved by the logic of facts – there will be no room for English capital, brains and energy. The openings there are more abundant than in many of our more recent tropical possessions, where the climate is not nearly so good, and where there are Arab Confederacies to be broken up by force of arms and at enormous expense, or native wars to be fought. If it is profitable for the Empire to build a railway to Uganda, surely it is equally advantageous to spend money in like, or in other ways, upon these 'undeveloped estates'. The simple truth is that – always excepting Barbados – the sugar industry only touches the fringe of the West Indian colonies. Behind that fringe lie mountain, valley, and plateau, capable of supporting a population infinitely larger than that which now huddles on the coastline of the islands and of Guiana, and is crying aloud for capital. The work of the future is the peopling of those magnificent and fertile regions, whose richness and beauty are as primeval today as they were in the fifteenth century, when nomadic Caribs were their only inhabitants. The task of the government is to distribute the population over these areas as it is freed from labour on the sugar estates, and to encourage the flow of British capital and enterprise.

No fear need be entertained that the Negro and the coolie will not be able to get a subsistence. If they do not succeed, we have no scruple in saying that they deserve to starve. As for the indentured coolies in Guiana and Trinidad, they are under contract guaranteed by the government, and if the planters cannot find work for them, and they will not take up land or accept other compensation, they have a right to a return passage to India, at the expense of the colonies, which means ultimately, at the cost of the Imperial Government. There need be no difficulty with them. Should any arise, it will be because the Imperial Government has been so anxious to assist the planter that it has allowed the colonial taxpayers to pay one-third (? half) of the cost of immigration for his benefit. If he has not been given bounties, he has at least been subsidized in the form of cheap labour, for the Negro has through the taxation of foodstuffs and other commodities, been compelled for years to pay for one-third of the cost of introduction and maintenance of a system which has flooded the sugar estates with imported labour to compete with him. It is necessary to remind the public of these facts, when the planters hint at coolie risings in consequence of the reduction of wages. There can be no reduction in the case of indentured coolies, for the coolies are under a stringent contract which the government has to enforce, and, if the planters fail, make good in one form or another.

This scepticism as to any coolie rising on a large scale is expressed with a full knowledge of the facts of the *emeute* in Demerara recently, so far as they have been disclosed in the inquiry under the Immigration Ordinance. The loss of life in this affair has been wrongfully cited as an example of what will soon happen unless the Imperial Government comes to the aid of the planters. Such fears are exaggerated if not groundless; but should they be realized, any coolie violence will have to be repressed, until the East Indian is convinced that the government will deal honestly with him according to his bond, whatever the planter may or may not be able to do. If the planters really thought that their industry was coming to an end, and that there would be coolie risings they would not in Guiana import coolies now at the rate of about 2,500* a year. This is largely a question of tactful government and of finance. In any case it is not to be apprehended that there will be any insuperable difficulty with the coolies should every cane field have to be abandoned. It will be one of the duties of the Commission to ascertain how they may best be retained in larger numbers in the colonies which now possess them, and be utilized for the development of untouched resources. In Guiana and in Trinidad they will make excellent farming squatters, and in the former country many such will be needed to supply the goldfields with ground provisions, for those fields will, it is hoped, in course of time be the mecca of the Negro labourer throughout the West Indian Islands.

* Ever so much more. The number of immigrants introduced during the four previous seasons was as follows:

1892	5,004
1893	4,451
1894	5,569
1895	6,051

[*Note inserted by Bechu]

The Daily Chronicle, 7 January 1897

CHAPTER TWO

Bechu and the Norman Commission, February 1897

Memorandum by Bechu to the West India Royal Commission, 1897.

Wages

Although indentured coolies are, according to the letter of the law, entitled to one shilling *per diem*, and women and children to 8 and 4 pence respectively, for seven hours, without extra exertion, they do not as a matter of fact earn that wage unless they serve for nine or ten hours, and *not even then*. One witness is reported to have stated that, in consequence of the depression in the sugar trade the coolies 'in most cases accepted his reductions, realizing that estates were in difficulties on account of low prices'; but instead of saying, '*accepted the reductions*', he ought to have said *tamely submitted* to the reductions from fear of being buckshotted, as some of their countrymen in Pln Non Pareil were because they claimed their rights. Again, the Hon the Immigration Agent-General is reported to have said that 'considering the large number of immigrants under indenture, he did not think there were many complaints about the amount of wages, but that there were more complaints against indentured immigrants for neglecting work'; but I know for a positive fact that from fear of their drivers, who keep indentured coolies so under subjection by abuses and threats, that *outspoken* complaints of that nature are rare. It is well known, however, that complaints against indentured immigrants are more numerous, and that is simply because drivers and overseers, to show off their *brief authority*, bring them up for the most trivial faults.

Tasks

Although it is *optional* for indentured immigrants to take *task work* they are *forced* to accept it, and the terms fixed by employers are so hard that it is often the case that a task cannot be completed in less than two days, thus making it *impossible* for an indentured coolie from earning a shilling *per diem*. I should feel deeply grateful if the *Order Book*, which is kept up in all estates, is referred to; it will only *then* be seen how during the past five years the rate, for the same nature of work, for which a man was paid one shilling when the Immigration Act of 1891 came into force, has now to be performed for 6 pence.

Under Section 18 of the Immigration Ordinance it is the duty of the Immigration Agent to give advice to coolies, conduct investigations, institute prosecutions, and to assist the Magistrate in the estimate of wages; but the officer in charge of the district to which I belong [H.J. Gladwin], beyond visiting the estate once a month for a little over an hour, taking down a few 'averages' of the earnings of the stronger men, and listening to a few family quarrels, does little else. Only a couple months back I had occasion to deny a statement which was made in *The Argosy*, to the effect that this officer most religiously explains to all newly arrived immigrants the terms of their contract, and that denial had the effect of bringing him to a sense of his duty when the last three shipments arrived. He seldom visits the hospital, and, as long as I have been on Pln Enmore has never on one occasion been to the 'nigger yards' or inspected any of the coolie dwellings. Besides taking no interest in the coolies, whose protector he is supposed to be, he is on such friendly terms with the Manager as to have succeeded in getting his daughter employment in his house as governess. How is it possible, under the circumstance, to receive justice at his hands?

Continuance of Immigration

Considering the accounts which have from time to time been sent to the English press, to the effect that social order in this colony will be at considerable peril unless a bounty is given to the planters, it is difficult to understand how more East Indian immigrants are wanted at the present time. There are now 100,000 coolies in this colony, and surely that number ought to more than suffice for the 64 estates under cultivation? 5,000 out of these immigrants will be eligible to return to India, but only 2,000 out of that number will, it is believed, be sent. Instead of retaining as many of them by offering them money in lieu of back passage, they are to be returned and a lot of half-starved unacclimatized men brought in their places. It is very doubtful if these time-expired men, even if they are offered a bounty as an inducement to remain will accept the offer, and even if they do so, the planters would be reluctant to have that class of re-indentured men, since they know the 'ropes' and will hardly allow themselves to be cheated out of their rights, whereas a newly arrived simpleton, in his blissful ignorance, will have to grin and take what is given him.

Immoral Relations of Overseers and Managers, in Some Cases, with Coolie Women

The Hon Darnell Davis, in the course of his evidence, pointed out that there is a paucity of women (East Indian) and suggested that the sexes be equalized, but is it possible that coolies will lawfully take unto themselves wives when such gross immorality exists in most of the estates, notwithstanding what the Royal Commissioners of 1871 had to say in the matter, and although the very same matter has on several occasions since been brought to the notice of all estate Managers by the Immigration Department, still it is an open secret that coolie women are in the keeping of overseers. I am in a position to state that a fellow shipmate of mine, a Punjabi, was at one time making overtures to a woman with a view to matrimony, but he was deterred from doing so, as he came to hear that she had got in tow with an overseer, who eventually gave her the money to purchase her freedom. I don't recollect the name of the overseer, but the name of the woman is Leloo, and she is at present residing at Pln Lusignan, East Coast. This is another ground for discontent and sometimes leads to riots, yet Immigration Agents close their eyes to the matter.

There is not the slightest doubt that if the suggestions made by the Hon Darnell Davis in his evidence, with regard to more women being brought to the colony to equalize the sexes, [were implemented] a great deal of both immorality and discontent among the emigrants would be avoided, and their people would be far more willing to settle in the country.

BECHU
Indentured Immigrant,
Pln Enmore, East Coast [Demerara]

Report of the West India Royal Commission, 1897 [H.W. Norman, chairman], (London: HMSO, 1897), Appendix C. – Part II, British Guiana, section 158.

Bechu before The West India Royal Commission, 1 February 1897.

[Paragraph]

1923 *Norman:* (Chairman, Sir Henry Norman) What is your name?
Bechu: Bechu
1924 *Norman:* What caste?
Bechu: Koormi [Kurmi].
1925 *Norman:* What part of India did you come from?
Bechu: Calcutta.
1926 *Norman:* Are you a native of Calcutta?
Bechu: I am a Bengali.
1927 *Norman:* Are you an indentured coolie?
Bechu: I have been an indentured coolie two years and one month.
1928 *Norman:* Have you been employed on an estate?
Bechu: Plantation Enmore.
1929 *Norman:* Are you employed there now?
Bechu: Yes, sir.
1930 *Norman:* Are you working in the fields?
Bechu: I am working as a domestic with the Deputy Manager.
1931 *Norman:* Have you ever worked in the field?
Bechu: The first three days I was put to cane cutting, and when I could not manage that they gave me work as an assistant driver.
1932 *Norman:* You were educated at some government school?
Bechu: No, sir, I have not been educated in any government school, I was brought up by a white missionary lady.
1933 *Norman:* She must have educated you?
Bechu: I mean I have not been at school, I have tried to avail myself of every opportunity to read and improve my time. Even my present employer, Mr Nicholson, has given me permission to read his books whenever I have the time to do so.
1934 *Norman:* What made you come here?
Bechu: I was first going to Trinidad; but after detaining me at his depot for about a week the recruiter told me there were no ships for Trinidad, and that he could send me here. I objected, since he had promised to send me to Trinidad. I said I did not care about coming here where the indenture would be for five years; he showed me the Trinidad contract form, in which it was stated that the indenture for Trinidad was only for three years. As he had gone to some expense in feeding me for a few days, and would not allow me to leave until I had paid him for those few days, I consented to come here.
1935 *Norman:* Is the agent in Calcutta the same for Trinidad and Demerara?

Bechu and the Norman Commission, February 1897

	Bechu:	No, sir, he made me over to another man.
1936	*Norman:*	When you went to this recruiter, did you live under his charge or go to the Immigration Agent?
	Bechu:	No, sir. I was with the recruiter, from there I was taken to Alipore, and registered there by a registration officer.
1937	*Norman:*	And it was decided that you were to come here?
	Bechu:	Yes, I was 13 days in the British Guiana Immigration Depot.
1938	*Norman:*	And then you came here?
	Bechu:	Yes, I have been here two years and a month [since December 1894].
1939	*Norman:*	And all this time you have been doing domestic service?
	Bechu:	For nine months I was in the field, assisting the creole driver weighing and serving out manure, and superintending picking of cane tops, etc.
1940	*Norman:*	After that nine months?
	Bechu:	When it was found that I was constantly getting fever by exposure to rain, the head overseer, with the consent of the Manager, brought me to serve in his house.
1941	*Norman:*	While you were in the field, you got a shilling a day?
	Bechu:	Yes, sir, except for the first three days.
1942	*Norman:*	How many hours were you employed?
	Bechu:	I used to go to work at 6 o'clock in the morning, and come back at 6 o'clock in the evening. Frequently we have been kept back till 7 or 8 o'clock at night; that is done to this day; the creoles return home late.
1943	*Norman:*	There is some time given for meals?
	Bechu:	About an hour or half-an-hour, it all depends upon the number of fields to be manured, watered, or the number of punts of cane tops to be loaded.
1944	*Norman:*	According to your account you were kept 11 or 12 hours?
	Bechu:	Yes, sir, that is a fact.
1945	*Norman:*	Could you not go back?
	Bechu:	If I left as an indentured immigrant I would have been prosecuted.
1946	*Norman:*	Is that the estate on which you now are?
	Bechu:	Yes, sir; Plantation Enmore.
1947	*Norman:*	You always got your shilling?
	Bechu:	Yes, sir.
1948	*Norman:*	You say that is generally the case, they kept more than seven hours.
	Bechu:	To this day.
1949	*Norman:*	You say the coolies tamely submit to this, for fear of buckshot?
	Bechu:	Taking into consideration what occurred at Non Pareil recently, the coolies are really frightened to make any complaints

against their employers. The coolies on Plantation Enmore are afraid of being abused by their drivers, and sometimes struck by them. Of course these drivers have a certain number of their own men, who are always on their side, and the coolies are afraid that the drivers will bring trumped-up charges against them if they were to complain.

1950 *Norman:* Do not they complain? Did you never make complaints?

Bechu: As regards myself, I never had occasion to make complaints; I always receive my just dues.

1951 *Norman:* But you are made to work longer than you ought to do?

Bechu: Considering the estate authorities made a concession in my case I thought it would be unreasonable for me to complain.

1952 *Norman:* With regard to task work, I think you were here when evidence was given that task work was optional?

Bechu: I have always been under that impression, but one correspondent to *The Argosy* tried to deny that statement. It was denied in the public prints, but the Immigration Agent General in his evidence bore out my statement that task work was optional.

1953 *Norman:* But you seem to say it is not optional?

Bechu: It is forced on them. If a man says he cannot earn a shilling a day, and lays his complaint before the Deputy Manager, the Deputy Manager tells the driver to give this man task work, and if he does not finish it, summon him.

1954 *Norman:* Is there not plenty of opportunity of complaining to the Immigration Agent when he comes round?

Bechu: The Immigration Agent comes round once a month, he is only there for about an hour, and during that time all the coolies are in the field. People who are concerned in family quarrels are simply brought before him by the driver, and he listens to their complaints.

1955 *Norman:* You seem to have written to *The Argosy*?

Bechu: No, sir, I never wrote on immigration matters.

1956 *Norman:* You had occasion to deny a statement?

Bechu: Yes, sir, I denied it in *The Chronicle*.

1957 *Norman:* You say the Immigration Agent does not inspect coolie dwellings. Are they not kept in good order?

Bechu: No, sir, he never troubles himself to look at them to see whether the drainage is in perfect order.

1958 *Norman:* Or the hospitals?

Bechu: The hospitals too.

1959 *Norman:* Do you mean to say he never visits the hospitals?

Bechu: Very rarely.

1960 *Norman:* How do you know?

Bechu: Because I live near it, and I am always on the dam. I can see when

Bechu and the Norman Commission, February 1897

		he comes and goes.
1961	*Norman:*	You do not think any immigrants are wanted at the present time?
	Bechu:	I consider there is not sufficient work, I do not see the necessity for bringing in any more.
1962	*Norman:*	You think if a bounty was offered to immigrants to remain here instead of going back they would not accept?
	Bechu:	If they were made to reindenture themselves they would not accept, but if they got half the amount in cash and half in land, it might induce them to start rice cultivation.
1963	*Norman:*	In point of fact, do you think large numbers would remain?
	Bechu:	No, sir, there are at present 5,000 coolies who are eligible to return to India.
1964	*Norman:*	Do you suppose they will return?
	Bechu:	I know for a fact that people are constantly making applications to the authorities, and they do not get a chance to go. Only last year there was a man who on three occasions made application to go to India; he was refused, and on the last occasion he came to me and begged me to write a letter to the Immigration Agent General. I wrote a petition in the name of this man and said he had deposited 25 dollars which was the amount he had saved during 12 or 15 years. I asked if after these 25 dollars were expended were they going to feed the man; the Immigration Agent General under those circumstances allowed him to return.
1965	*Norman:*	Do you know thousands of coolies do remain?
	Bechu:	Those who have no families in India prefer to stay, but if they have families they prefer to return; if they have got no one to go to they consider this is their home, and consequently stay here.
1965a	*Norman:*	You have made charges about immoral relations, we do not consider it is our business to investigate cases of that kind, but what you say will be sent before the government for such inquiries as they think proper.
	Bechu:	I thank you, sir.
1966	*Sir David Barbour:*	You say you are a native of Calcutta, and that you were born there?
	Bechu:	Yes, sir.
1967	*Barbour:*	How did you come to be brought up by a missionary lady?
	Bechu:	I lost my parents when I was young, sir, and she took charge of me.
1968	*Barbour:*	Can you recollect the name of that lady?
	Bechu:	Miss Cameron, sir.
1969	*Barbour:*	Where did she live?
	Bechu:	She lived near the Presbyterian mission.
1970	*Barbour:*	How long after that did you remain in Calcutta?
	Bechu:	I remained up to the time of her death.

1971	Barbour:	And what did you do then?
	Bechu:	I have worked with other gentlemen since.
1972	Barbour:	How many years were you with other gentlemen?
	Bechu:	About 18 years.
1973	Barbour:	Then you were about 36 years old when you left India?
	Bechu:	Yes, sir.
1974	Barbour:	What were the names of the other gentlemen you were with?
	Bechu:	Mr Gayford, a missionary.
1975	Barbour:	And who else?
	Bechu:	Dr Eteson, brigade surgeon; you remember him, sir.
1976	Barbour:	I do. And after that?
	Bechu:	There are so many gentlemen.
1977	Barbour:	Who was the last gentleman?
	Bechu:	Dr Sinclair of Burmah.
1978	Barbour:	Did you go to Burmah?
	Bechu:	Oh, yes, sir. I have been to Rangoon and Mandalay.
1979	Barbour:	How did you happen to come here?
	Bechu:	I was in reduced circumstances, and I met a recruiter who told me he would put me in a way of getting a living if I was willing to cross the sea.
1980	Barbour:	You never had done any fieldwork?
	Bechu:	No, sir.
1981	Barbour:	You say you sent a petition to the Immigration Agent about a man who did not get a passage?
	Bechu:	Yes, sir.
1982	Barbour:	What was his name?
	Bechu:	Sukee, sir.
1983	Barbour:	This man had applied on several occasions before?
	Bechu:	So he told me.
1984	Barbour:	You cannot say from your own knowledge?
	Bechu:	No, I cannot, but the sicknurse, I understand, gave him leave on more than one occasion to come to town for that purpose.

Report of the West India Royal Commission [1897], Appendix C. – Part II, British Guiana, section 98

Bechu responds to the evidence of his old critic, W. Alleyne Ireland ('Langton'), subeditor of the proplanter newspaper, *The Argosy*, before the West India Royal Commission on 1 February 1897; the section reproduced below this letter is Ireland's rebuttal of several key points made by Bechu earlier that day to the Commission. W. Alleyne Ireland was the author of *Demerariana: Essays, Historical, Critical and Descriptive*. Bechu is referring to his "The history of the East Indian immigrant", a 28-page essay published on 1 September 1897. This essay appeared originally as a six-part series, under his pseudonym 'Langton', in *The Argosy* of the following dates: 7, 14, 21 October, 5, 12, 19 December 1896. See *The Daily Chronicle*, 31 August, 2 October 1897.

Bechu (Indentured Immigrant, *Sheila*, 1894) to the Editor,
The Daily Chronicle, Pln Enmore, 2 February 1897:

Sir, In the course of his evidence before the Royal Commissioners, the able author of the 'Exhaustive History of East Indian Immigrants' [W. Alleyne Ireland ('Langton')] has, notwithstanding my having already cornered him on one or two occasions, challenged a statement made by me to the effect that the creole gang is being kept back very late. It does not signify in the least if there are *few* or *many* indentured coolies in that gang or not, the very fact of its being 'composed of very young children' is in itself sufficient reason why the gang should be dismissed early, nevertheless it is a *positive* and *undeniable* fact, which the poor little mites will themselves bear out, that in *all* weathers, they are rarely brought home before 7 o'clock at night although they start work at 6 am.

I am no grumbler, and would be the last person in the world to stir up ill-feeling when it does not exist, but tackling an apparent evil deserves, if it does not command, success.

The Daily Chronicle, 3 February 1897

[Paragraph]
2001 *Chairman:* What is your opinion with regard to indentured coolies?
(W. Alleyne Ireland): I have been listening with great interest to the evidence of the witness who has just spoken [Bechu]. The coolies arrive on the estate and very shortly afterwards the Immigration Agent visits the estate. There is a muster of coolies in the estate's yard; the terms of indenture and contract are explained to them; they are allotted houses and the men are introduced to the work. For three months after the time they go on to the estate they are fed at the expense of the estate, which also provides them with employment. After a time when they get accomplished, they repay the exact

amount. In regard to there being no inspection of homes or hospitals, the dwelling-houses have to be inspected by a government inspector. The medical inspector has to visit each cottage and signify his approval of its situation and ventilation before the coolies can be put in at all. With regard to the remark about the creole gang being kept back very late, as a matter of fact there are no indentured immigrants in the creole gang, because the gang consists of young children. In reference to complaints, and what was said about no coolie being able to make complaints against the Managers, I can give you the exact number of complaints which have been made during a series of years. The number of convictions of employers for offences against immigrants is 208 since 1874, that is, 208 employers since 1874 have been convicted of offences against immigrants on the complaint of the immigrant, so that shows that a large number have complained and do complain . . .

2006 *Chairman:* What is your opinion with regard to increasing the supply of coolies when there is in the colony at the present time an excess of labour?

Alleyne: The supply of labour has no bearing upon the sugar industry, the whole origin of immigration hinges upon this point. You may have work and plenty of it for a black man and a coloured man, and they will not do it. In planting cane if you leave certain agricultural work over, your crop is ruined, therefore it is absolutely necessary that you should have bound labour that you can command. Black people will not work, my experience of them is exasperating beyond description . . . It is impossible to depend upon black labour.

2007 *Chairman:* Is it within your knowledge that task work has been given to indentured coolies that could not fairly be done in seven hours?

Alleyne: I have heard of it and a good deal has been written in the press by the last witness [Bechu], but my own experience is that I have never known of such a case . . .

2008 *Chairman:* You have heard that wages have been reduced?

Alleyne: Yes.

2009 *Chairman:* Have they not received their shilling?

Alleyne: No, the position is this: when sugar was paying, the planter, who is never really at heart a mean man, would give them an opportunity of earning 2 shillings or more instead of the one shilling which was the legal wage; now the stress and strain has come he has had to cut down until he is within his legal right, it has been cut down to the legal minimum.

Chairman: That is only as regards task work?

Alleyne: No, and day work too, there will always be a large number of coolies who do not earn one shilling a day.

Bechu (Indentured *Bengali* Immigrant, *Sheila*, 1894) to the Editor,
The Daily Chronicle, Pln Enmore, 3 February 1897:

Sir, When I addressed you yesterday, I had not an opportunity of reading the whole of the evidence which was given before the Royal Commissioners, at their fourth sitting, and I was grieved, on perusing it right through today, to see that a gentleman in Mr James Thomson's [editor, *The Argosy*] position should have condescended to malign a poor, penniless, and harmless wretch like me in the way he has done before such an august body. His evidence against me reminds me very forcibly of some lines I learnt many years ago, which run as follows:

> He who steals my purse, steals trash
> 'Twas mine, 'tis his, and has been slave to thousands,
> But he who filches from me my *good name*
> *Robs* me of that which *not enriches* him and leaves *me* poor indeed.

Although I have been fighting stoutly on behalf of my dumb-driven countrymen, and have consequently been *compelled* to bring a lot of *injustice* to light, yet I feel confident if my employers, and my immediate employers more specifically, were asked to testify to my character and conduct during the two years I have served under them, they would *never* speak ill of me. Considering how Mr Thomson, not long ago, as proprietor of a newspaper, took mean advantage of his position and shamefully insulted a highly respected, but defenceless Minister, I am not surprised at his having trodden on a weak worm like me.

The Daily Chronicle, 4 February 1897

James Thomson, a Scotsman who had been in British Guiana for 36 years, was the part-proprietor of a sugar plantation. His newspaper, *The Argosy*, was virtually the organ of the plantocracy. He, like Bechu, appeared before the West India Royal Commission in February 1897. After the fatal shooting of Indian workers at Plantation Non Pareil in October 1896, Bechu would have found the following response by Thomson to Sir David Barbour especially repellent:

Sir David Barbour: Do you know if there is any discontent amongst coolies?
James Thomson: The only discontent I hear expressed, is by a learned pundit on the East Coast [Demerara], [Bechu], I do not know how he came to be shipped here at all. He would be a troublesome man in any place.
Barbour: You know of no general discontent?
Thomson: No.

Report of the West India Royal Commission [1897], Appendix C. – Part II, section 92

The Daily Chronicle, 2 February 1897, reported Thomson's allusion to Bechu, with another interesting slant on his identity:

> Asked if he thought there was any discontent amongst the coolies, he [Thomson] said the only discontent expressed was by a learned Punjaub [sic] on the East Coast [Bechu]. How he came to the colony, witness did not know, but he would be a troublesome gentleman [sic] anywhere.

Both Thomson and *The Daily Chronicle* were wrong: Bechu told the Commission that he was a Bengali of the Koormi caste. He was definitely not a Punjabi or a pundit (Brahmin).

Bechu's employer, G.W. Bethune, the Manager of Plantation Enmore, wrote to Sydney Olivier, Secretary of the Commission, on 15 February 1897, to "deny the gist" of Bechu's evidence. He stated:

> *Sir*, I have the honour to state, for the information of the West India Royal Commissioners, that since the departure from Demerara of the Royal Commission it has been pointed out to me that the Bengali immigrant Bechu, in his evidence before the Royal Commissioners, made special allusion to the Enmore estate as the one on which the creole gang is daily employed in the fields from 12 to 13 hours, and I take an early opportunity of asserting that such an allegation is absolutely unfounded.
>
> There is on this property one of the largest schools for the children of the East India [sic] immigrants, and it is in this institution that 'the little mites' spend their hours.
>
> The proprietor of this important property, with a cultivated area of over 2,000 acres, naturally takes a deep interest in the welfare of the labourers on his land, and for many years past he has been the main

support of a church on the estate, and whilst paying the resident minister an annual stipend for special services, he is also a liberal contributor to the salary of a resident Hindi catechist.

The immigrants on this property have the privilege of free pasturage for cattle, and are allowed to cultivate plots of land with provisions, and rice is now being grown by them in the abandoned canals.

In my capacity, therefore, as agent of this property, I must emphatically deny the gist of the above-mentioned immigrant's report to the West India Royal Commissioners, as to the neglect of the East Indian immigrants on the sugar estates in this colony.

Report of the West India Royal Commission [1897], Appendix C. – Part II, section 159

Bethune was responding to Bechu's evidence before the Commission on his experience at Plantation Enmore:

Chairman: How many hours were you employed?
Bechu: I used to go to work at 6 o'clock in the morning, and come back at 6 o'clock in the evening. Frequently we have been kept back till 7 or 8 o'clock at night; that is done to this day; the creoles [children born in the colony] return home late . . .
Chairman: According to your account you were kept 11 or 12 hours?
Bechu: Yes, sir, that is a fact . . .
Chairman: You say that is generally the case, they kept more than seven hours?
Bechu: To this day.
Chairman: You say the coolies tamely submit to this, for fear of buckshot?
Bechu: Taking into consideration what occurred at Non Pareil recently, the coolies are really frightened to make any complaints against their employers. The coolies on Plantation Enmore are afraid of being abused by their drivers, and sometimes struck by them. Of course these drivers have a certain number of their own men, who are always on their side, and the coolies are afraid that the drivers will bring trumped-up charges against them if they were to complain.

Report of the West India Royal Commission [1897], Appendix C. – Part II, section 159

CHAPTER THREE

Bechu and his Critics: Personal Attacks

Another planter challenges Bechu's veracity, but maligns all Indians:

'West Coast' to the Editor, *The Daily Chronicle:*

Sir, It seems to me Bechu's letters are now becoming too frequent and, consequently, monotonous.

Both in his evidence before the Royal Commissioners, and in the letters which he has written from time to time to the newspapers, Bechu has amply borne out the fact so well known by those long resident amongst that class of people, that

(1) An East Indian will never speak the whole truth, and nothing but the truth so long as he can possibly evade doing so, and
(2) That the East Indian looks on the white man as one of the most easily gulled mortals on earth.

I rather like Mr Bechu's style in his last letter – 'a poor penniless and harmless wretch . . . a weak worm like me' – that sounds so much like the East Indian I have met in my daily routine round a sugar estate, who, when he wants anything out of me, will lay his head at my feet and repeat in Hindustani the English of which is: 'You are my father and mother, I left all else in India, here you are the only one I have to look to'; so Bechu still possesses the low, cringing and abject habit common to his nationality, although some one [sic] in his evidence before the Commissioners said that long residence in the colony made a 'man' of an East Indian.

Does Bechu imagine anyone will seriously believe the creole gang goes to work at 6 am and ceases work at 7 pm? If Bechu in all his letters refers to 'Enmore', the only estate on which he can possibly have gained his information, let him say 'on Enmore the creoles go to work, etc, etc', don't be vague and endeavour to make the public believe it is the ordinary rule on all estates. Mr Bechu is undoubtedly possessed of a good education and ready pen which might be put to a better purpose; at present he seems to be the only poor down-trodden East Indian in the colony who has a grievance and that only imaginary.

The Daily Chronicle, 6 February 1897

Bechu responds to 'West Coast'; he accuses him of cowardice.

Bechu (Indentured Immigrant, *Sheila*, 1894) to the Editor,
***The Daily Chronicle*:**

Sir, Granting that your correspondent 'West Coast', whose letter appeared in last Saturday's issue of your paper is, as he wishes all your readers to believe, every inch a *gentleman* and I a *born liar*, is it fair for him to attack me under a *nom de plume*?

> I care not from what land he came
> Or where his youth was nursed
> If yes he answers when I ask
> Has he a true man's heart?

It strikes me that *he has not*, for if he had even a spark of *manliness* in him he would most assuredly have given his full name and address and not *hit* me, as it were, in the dark. None but a *coward* and an *assassin* could do so.

The Daily Chronicle, 9 February 1897

Bechu's compatriot, Joseph Ruhomon (1873–1942), comes to his defence. The latter was the first Indian intellectual in British Guiana, the author of *India; The Progress of her People at Home and Abroad, and how Those in British Guiana may Improve Themselves*, published in December 1894.

'East Indian Descendant' (New Amsterdam) [Joseph Ruhomon] to the Editor, *The Daily Chronicle*:

Sir, I am following with a good deal of interest your excellent reports of the proceedings of the Royal Sugar Commission. Much of the evidence that has already been given by gentlemen qualified to speak on the different aspects of the sugar question, is decidedly important, and the Commissioners will evidently go away with a more or less correct impression of the present condition of our staple industry, with its most important bearings on the colony and its prospects. But you will please allow me to state, Sir, anent the evidence given by one or two of the witnesses, it was robbed of a certain amount of absolute veracity when they referred to the East Indian immigrants employed on sugar estates, as being cared for, and working under an easy and reasonable system of labour which makes them comparatively happy and contented, and quite reconciled to all the changing circumstances incidental to the fluctuations of the sugar industry. It was fortunate for his, or I should say, our unhappy dumb-driven brethren (for I too am an East Indian descendant) that the redoubtable, invincible Bechu, one of the champions of his race in British Guiana, was one of those summoned to give evidence – a wise and commendable action on the part of the Commissioners – and I heartily congratulate him on the fearless and straightforward manner he put the real facts of the case before that important assembly. Bechu is undoubtedly a man of integrity and sound, honest principles, and not one to recklessly sacrifice them for fear of offending those in whose employ he has been thrown by the irony of fate. He is evidently largely dowered with 'the hate of hate, the scorn of scorn' as may be seen from his views expressed so lucidly in the newspapers, an action on his part which has been so wrongfully attributed to his desire for notoriety. This well-informed and intelligent Bengali has thoroughly grasped the facts of the case, and naturally so from his position on the estate, and the means he is clever enough to summon for his use; and from what I know, I do not think Sir, he in any way overstates the case in speaking of the present system of drudgery imposed on our East Indian Immigrants on the plantations in the colony. The planters, and the planters' friends, to serve their own interests, may put it in any way they like, but as a matter of absolute fact which is indisputable, these poor, down-trodden people are far from being treated with that leniency and just consideration which they so greatly deserve. If Mr James Thomson [editor, *The Argosy*] was himself in the position of one of these wretched people, he might have a different statement to make.

It is to be hoped, Sir, that the important revelations made by Bechu before the Royal Commissioners will in due course be submitted to our government for their consideration, and that firm and effective practical measures will be taken to render the conditions of labour on our sugar plantations less burdensome and considerably easier than those which obtain at present to the severe discomfort of so many of our East Indian brethren who have come from over the seas for occupations so servile and results so absurdly unprofitable.

The Daily Chronicle, 9 February 1897

The same compatriot [Joseph Ruhomon] returns to Bechu's defence; he rebuts 'West Coast's' racist attack of Bechu. He is proud to be a vindicator of the "East Indian race".

'East Indian Descendant' (New Amsterdam) [Joseph Ruhomon] to the Editor, *The Daily Chronicle*:

Sir, I again have to crave space in your paper in order to say a few words in reply to certain remarks made in your issue of Saturday last, by someone subscribing himself 'West Coast' in a letter headed 'Bechu, Indian Immigrant, *Sheila*, 1894'.

Bechu, Sir, is eminently qualified to answer the charges made against him by this sarcastically disposed writer, and as he alone is peculiarly in the right position to do so, I have not the slightest need to take up the cudgels on his behalf, so far as he is personally concerned in the matter. But as the honour of the entire East Indian race in the colony, or rather, in the whole habitable globe is involved in the false, malicious and sweeping indictment made by 'West Coast', I would be wanting in my duty as a member of the race if I did not attempt to vindicate its fair fame and reputation which have been so unwarrantably and grossly assailed.

In the first place, what does 'West Coast' mean by the assertion, 'An East Indian will never speak the whole truth, and nothing but the truth so long as he can possibly evade doing so?' May it not be that he himself is not speaking the whole truth, and nothing but the truth, by making such a statement that cannot stand the light of truth, and bear out the experience of countless numbers? Are other nationalities considerably more truthful and infinitely less wanting in honest veracity than the East Indian? Poor lying East Indian! Always speaking gigantic untruths when you can possibly evade telling the truth!! You are the most despicable rascal abroad!!! I do not know of what well-favoured, truthful nationality 'West Coast' happens to be (his letter, though, savours highly of the white 'pork-knocking planter'), but he evidently thinks that the King David's declaration 'all men are liars' refers exclusively to the East Indians, and that all others are peculiarly exempted by a special decree from on high. He has yet to learn however, that poor Sammy [the Indian] is not a greater rascal in the popular art of lying than the red man, the black man, or even the white man, more especially in this colony, where the latter has so much more to gain than anyone else less fortunately situated in life.

'West Coast' also refers to what he calls 'the low, cringing and abject habit common to his (Bechu's) nationality'. This, Sir, is a most libellous reflection on the East Indian race and the writer displays a profound and most lamentable ignorance of our national traits and characteristics of which we are so justly proud. It is not the poor indentured immigrants on our sugar estates whom 'West Coast' ought to accept as a criterion by which to judge the race in general. If they bow and cringe before their white employer, and assume a thoroughly respectful attitude which 'West Coast' has construed to mean an 'abject' and 'low' habit common among them, it is because the white man is indeed their 'father and mother' in this colony in the sense that he is absolutely depended upon for their means of eking out what is a miserable existence to them, carried under the most trying circumstances. If 'West Coast' is so parsimonious in his habits as to mockingly sneer at the abject East Indian grovelling at his feet for some pecuniary favour, at least he might reserve his reflections for his own enjoyment, rather than publish them to the world for it does him no credit and only betrays his own 'low', 'mean', 'abject' habits, to which no doubt he is well accustomed.

To estimate the East Indian at his right value, Sir, 'West Coast' must study him as he is at his best. For take him all in all, the East Indian when brought under civilizing influences and bathed in the light of culture and education, is undoubtedly one of the most perfect creatures in God's earth. No more is 'West Coast' therefore justified in picking up an immigrant from the cane field and saying 'here, this is a splendid type of what all East Indians in general are', than I would be in pointing to the average 'English Barbarian' in the East End of London, as a perfect model of what the English people in general are.

As 'West Coast' is obviously one who is largely possessed of that obnoxious race prejudice which cannot do anyone the slightest particle of good, I shall conclude by quoting for his benefit the following words from Oliver Goldsmith:

> Let a man's birth be ever so high, his station ever so exalted, or his fortune ever so large, yet if he is not free from national and other prejudices, I should make bold to tell him, that he had a low and vulgar mind, and had no just claim to the character of a gentleman.

The Daily Chronicle, 10 February 1897

Another of Bechu's critics resorts to racism, depreciating his Bengali background.

'Civis Mundi' to the Editor, *The Daily Chronicle*:

Sir, It is not surprising that 'An East Indian Descendant' [Joseph Ruhomon] should be so convinced of the general nobility of his own race (by the way, which is it? For India contains about as many races as Europe), but it certainly is a little amusing that he should expect other people to share his conviction. Let me commend to his careful perusal Macaulay's summing up of the Bengali character in the essay on Warren Hastings, and after he has read it perhaps he will not be so scandalized at the poor opinion held by Europeans of his countrymen's *morale*. The passage is as follows:

The physical organization of the Bengali is feeble even to effeminacy. He lives in a constant vapour bath. His pursuits are sedentary, his limbs delicate, his movements languid. During many ages he has been trampled upon by men of bolder and more hardy breeds. Courage, independence, veracity, are qualities to which his constitution and his situation are equally unfavourable. His mind bears a singular analogy to his body. It is weak even to helplessness for purposes of manly resistance; but its suppleness and its tact move the children of sterner climates to admiration not unmingled with contempt. All those arts which are the natural defence of the weak are more familiar to this subtle race than to the Ioanian of the time of Juvenal, or to the Jew of the dark ages. What the horn is to the buffalo, what the paw is to the tiger, what the sting is to the bee, what beauty, according to the old Greek song, is to woman, deceit is to the Bengali. Large promises, smooth excuses, elaborate tissues of circumstantial falsehood, chicanery, perjury, forgery, are the weapons, offensive and defensive, of the people of the Lower Ganges [Bengal].

Bechu is a Bengali.

The Daily Chronicle, 12 February 1897

Bechu responds to 'Civis Mundi'.

Bechu (Indentured Bengali Immigrant, *Sheila*, 1894),
Pln Enmore, to the Editor, *The Daily Chronicle*:

'CURSED BE HE WHO MOVES MY BONES'

Sir, The above, as you know, is Shakespeare's epitaph, but 'Civis Mundi', who has tried to disturb Macaulay's ashes by quoting a passage, which that great man, had he been living today, would positively have been ashamed of, richly deserves something more salutory than a curse, for having in this enlightened age reproduced such a libel.

Considering what a remarkable change for good has been made in the social, moral, and religious condition of the people of Bengal, since Macaulay shook off his mortal coil, it is a *lie* to say that the Bengalis of the present day are as black as their ancestors have been painted. 'Civis Mundi' might as well have quoted English History to show what the Britons were like at the time of the Druids.

'Civis Mundi's' only boast appears to be that because by mere accident he was born on English soil, he is heir to all the good qualities of an Englishman. Poor boast that! How much better it would have been had he endeavoured to prove the truth of Longfellow's beautiful lines, that:

> Lives of great men all remind us
> *We* can make our lives sublime
> And departing leave behind us
> Footprints on the sands of time.

No, no, 'Civis Mundi' has adopted a great *nom de plume* but would that he had as great a soul. The next time he writes, he should if he has the pluck of an Englishman give his name to his letter.

The Daily Chronicle, 15 February 1897

'Civis Mundi's' rejoinder to Bechu:

Sir, Bechu is fond of 'jumping upon' those of his critics who avail themselves of the privilege of anonymity, but he should remember that we do not all enjoy 'the greater freedom and less responsibility' of an overseer's domestic servant. Moreover, my identity is not of the least importance. I merely reproduced a passage from Macaulay, for which obviously I have no responsibility whatever. That passage was written about half a century ago, and Bechu would have us believe that in that short space of time the Bengali character has changed as completely as the British in 18 or 19 centuries. Can the Ethiopian change his skin, or the leopard his spots? Not, methinks, in the course of 50 years.

The Daily Chronicle, 16 February 1897

'East Indian Descendant' [Joseph Ruhomon] again praises Bechu as he challenges Macaulay's "opinions" of the Bengali character:

'East Indian Descendant' (New Amsterdam) to the Editor, *The Daily Chronicle*:

Sir, In your issue of Friday last, someone signing himself 'Civis Mundi' in a letter headed 'East Indian Characteristics', erroneously thought I was referring exclusively to the Bengali race, whereas, if he knew English and carefully studied my last letter, he would have seen that I was referring to the East Indian race *in general* and not to any special branch of it.

The writer evidently thinking I am a Bengali, for what reason I know not, recommended for my careful perusal Macaulay's opinions of the Bengali's character in his essay on Warren Hastings, and on these opinions he bases his own estimation of the character of Bechu who happens to be a Bengali. It practically comes to this, Sir, not having any definite opinions of his own, he has dragged in Macaulay into the matter, a weakness on his part.

I for one, Sir, do not attach much value to the opinion expressed by anyone, and I take it for what it is worth. Whatever Macaulay has said is his own opinion and is not representative of the opinions of others. A man is at perfect liberty to say whatever he likes, but whatever he says must not be regarded as coming authoritatively from him. Opinion is only a medium between knowledge and ignorance, and it is not history or absolute fact. Macaulay, I undoubtedly admit, was a great and learned man, but he, too, often allowed his expressions to take rise from a highly exuberant and prolific imagination.

From my own knowledge, I can say the Bengali is not what Macaulay represents him to be. He is just as honest and truthful as any other nationality. I further say this, for subtlety of intellect, for strength of purpose, for bravery under trying circumstances, for shrewdness in business and for true nobility of character, to use Macaulay's own words, 'no class of human beings can bear comparison with them.'

If, Sir, two or three Bengalis have been found answering to Macaulay's description of them, I have no hesitation in saying Bechu is a most exceptional one, and he deserves to be looked upon as a distinct credit to his own race.

The Daily Chronicle, 17 February 1897

Bechu and his Critics: Personal Attacks

Bechu is making an impact; he antagonizes a friend of the plantocracy who deprecates his "puny criticism". Familiar Anglo-Indian prejudices permeate the letter.

John Russell (Perseverance, Essequibo) to the Editor, *The Argosy*:

Sir, Only the absence of any reply (except 'Langton's') to the letters of Bechu in your daily contemporary [*The Daily Chronicle*], by others more interested in the assertions and charges therein contained [the sugar planters], constrains me, with much diffidence, to venture into public print.

It is not my object to join issue with your contemporary's gifted correspondent, but I consider it quite time that someone should at least remonstrate with him regarding his extremely ill-timed attack on the planters and the immigration system.

Not knowing Bechu, his career in India, or the circumstances that induced him to represent himself as an agricultural labourer so successfully as to elude even the vigilance of our lynx-eyed veteran Agent in India, and, without enquiring how so accomplished a linguist in the 'sarkar tongue' [English] should have been reduced to such an expedient, I can only conclude that his offence is that of youth, or that peculiar lack of tact and discretion which has so effectually disqualified the Bengali 'competition wallah' for the higher grades of the Indian Civil Service.

His case is stated with the specious open-palmed ingenuity of the practised 'bazar baboo', calculated to impress the superficial reader of the press, ignoring as he does the existence of a powerful and far-reaching department of the government, subject not only to the detailed supervision of the Governor, but to the criticism of the Secretary of State and a jealous and ever watchful Indian Government.

Has Bechu, in his youth, zeal and inexperience, any conception of the vast machinery employed to safeguard the interests of the coolie in this colony?

Is he not aware how it is a source of bitterness to both Europeans and the 'sons of the soil' [Africans] that the coolie is peculiarly and invidiously protected, even to the extent of that bugbear to modern lawmakers, special legislation?

I must, however, strongly deprecate the spirit in which Bechu's letters have been received by some members of the planting community. There exists throughout a moderation and respectful hesitancy entirely foreign to the fiery effusions of the professional agitator urged to extremes in his hunger for notoriety. The many indiscretions are to my mind merely the outcome of inexperience and youth, aroused by misplaced compassion for the financial grievances of less gifted compatriots, under the influence of popular excitement, the result of incidents which culminated in a deplorable contretemps justified, however, by searching Magisterial and Executive Inquiries [the Non Pareil shootings].

Besides, allowance must be made for a certain amount of bitterness engendered by the false position in which the writer finds himself. I feel sure, taking Bechu to be the intelligent man suggested by his ably composed letters, that he will take my mild criticism in the spirit actuating this letter; and I am sure also, that the more temperate majority of his readers will not only sympathize with him in his present circumstances, but will offer him every facility to acquaint himself with the almost perfect system of protection accorded to the East Indian immigrants during their service under indenture.

At this time when the sugar estate proprietors are making a brave stand, almost in the nature of a forlorn hope, against a combination of adverse circumstances beyond conception when the laws regarding wages were being framed, and even the coolies themselves are generously recognizing the serious aspect of affairs, it is surely injudicious to open and maintain any attack calculated to engender ill-feeling between employer and employed, so I would advise Bechu to revert to his promise made to his 'gentleman friend' and refrain from further agitating any vexed question regarding which subsequent better acquaintance and experience generally will no doubt tend to modify his views.

Bechu, on the other hand, should not be surprised that planters or others should not have joined issue with him in public print, the fact being that the community is inured to periodical outbursts by some 'two previous' newcomers in the shape of a Magistrate or other official, who, in the exuberance of indignant confidence born of overweening self-conceit ignores the fact that the system of immigration in this colony has been built up and perfected by able, just, and experienced officials, and has weathered the full blast of combined attacks resulting in searching inquiries, and that it is now quite impervious to any puny criticism founded on isolated incidents and individual interests.

The Argosy, 19 December 1896

Bechu is incensed by John Russell's condescending, personal attack of him; he elaborates on the Non Pareil shootings of October 1896 in his rebuttal, underlining his role as an "enlightened" articulator of his people's grievances.

Bechu (Indentured Immigrant, *Sheila*, 1894),
Pln Enmore, to the Editor, *The Daily Chronicle*:

Sir, Although there is much to take exception to, in Mr John Russell's letter, which appeared last Saturday in the columns of your contemporary [*The Argosy*], I shall pass them over, because, as he has been frank enough to admit that he does not know me, my 'career in India, or the circumstances that induced me to represent myself as an agricultural labourer so successfully', he can be pardoned for jumping at such absurd and irritable conclusions. If he really wishes to be enlightened on these points, I shall be happy for his edification to appear before the nearest Magistrate or JP, who will take down my sworn deposition and forward it to him on his paying the usual fee chargeable for such documents, else, if he considers me a suspicious character he has *only* to wire Scotland Yard for a detective who will soon find out my previous history and no doubt give him an interesting and most sensational account, as to how I managed 'to elude *even* the vigilance of the lynx-eyed veteran Agent in India'.

Mr Russell, like 'Langton' [W. Alleyne Ireland], next accuses me of 'hungering for notoriety'. Now, Sir, if such was really my end and aim, don't you think it would have been a more sensible, and far wiser policy, on my part to have taken the tip from the lord of that 'unjust steward', that St Mark tells us of, in his Gospel, and make to *myself* 'friends of the mammons of unrighteousness; that when I fail, they may receive me into everlasting *habitations*', or to be more correct, should I say *plantations*? Since I have not adopted that course, it is plain therefore that I have no such mercenary motive in view.

Indeed, I have been full two years in this colony [since December 1894], and have been *as quiet as a mouse*, so much so, that even my protector [the Immigration Agent] could not have been aware of my existence, but when I saw that the lives of *four* of my countrymen were sacrificed for nothing, and that about *ten* times that number had been injured for life, I considered it my duty as a more enlightened one of their class to explain to the public through the Press, the real cause of the disturbance, that prompt steps may be taken to prevent a recurrence of the deplorable *contretemps*, as Mr Russell styles it. Where the justification comes in, however, I fail to see because briefly stated the story is as follows:

On a certain day in October [1896], three gangs of indentured coolies belonging to Pln Non Pareil [sic], after complaining to the estate authorities that the work imposed on them would not permit them to earn their shilling *per diem* in seven hours, and receiving no satisfaction started off to town [Georgetown], without leave, to consult the Immigration Agent General. (This, 'Langton' informs us, is one important privilege secured by Ordinance 7 of 1873). On their arrival at the depot, 'Big Crosby' [the IAG] saw the men and directed them to return to the estate, and said that he would instruct the sub-Immigration Agent to visit the spot and enquire into the matter. After a little hesitation, the men on being promised by the Hon Mr Alexander [the IAG] that they would not be punished for having proceeded to town to make their complaint to him, came back to the estate and went to their respective *logies*. On the arrival of Mr Gladwin [the Immigration Agent of the district] and Captain de Rinzy with 17 armed policemen, the coolies were invited to come before their protector. At first, they did not enter appearance, but when later on a boy was despatched to tell them that Mr Gladwin was waiting to decide their case, about three hundred coolies, *unarmed* turned out. When they had all seated themselves and proceedings were about to be commenced, Captain de Rinzy called out four or five men present, against whom warrants had been taken out at the eleventh hour, and placed under arrest for conspiring to take Mr Van Nooten's [Manager of Non Pareil] life, a groundless charge evidently, because when these *dangerous characters* were placed before the Magistrate they were simply bound over to keep the peace for short periods, and ordered to be handed over to the immigration authorities for transfer to other estates. (Fancy men who only absent themselves from duty for a day being imprisoned for a month, and men found guilty of such a serious charge being set at large to, perhaps, do the same thing on the estates to which they had been transferred!!) Of course, when the rest of the coolies who were ignorant of the charge for which their *matties* [colleagues] were arrested, and bearing in mind that 'Big Crosby' had assured them that not one of their number would be punished for having gone to town, followed the Police in a body and told them to arrest the whole lot of them, and not only four men, since they were all equally guilty. This Captain de Rinzy looked upon as 'rioting', and ordered his men to fire over the heads of the coolies to frighten them away, but instead of having the desired effect, only exasperated the coolies all the more, and seeing they were *unarmed* they defended themselves with bricks and bottles and whatever else came in their way. This the coroners, after a most searching inquiry, looked upon as if the whole proceedings were premeditated, and found that the police were perfectly justified in opening fire. Of course, if the coroners are supposed to be infallible we must bow to their findings, but while doing so there is no reason why steps should not be taken to avoid a repetition of such a sad affair.

We are all alive to the fact that these are hard times, but if the planters are unable to keep to the terms of their contract, let them liberate those who wish to be liberated – set free – and then there will be no occasion for dissatisfaction even if the men cannot earn 6 pence *per diem*.

The Daily Chronicle, 22 December 1896

The planters and colonial authorities in British Guiana are exasperated by the remorseless critique of colonial society sustained by Bechu. Possibly, in an attempt to silence this 'bound coolie' radical, the Immigration Agent General, A.H. Alexander, intervened and terminated his indentureship in February 1897. Bechu's critique of the plantocracy even while an indentured, had fed curiosity and apprehension of this enigma.

'Planter' to the Editor, *The Daily Chronicle*:

Sir, Who is Bechu? Is he really an indentured immigrant, if so what was his cost to Enmore; does he do any fieldwork, if so how do his earnings compare with his contract? Where does he obtain files of the English daily papers, and when time to read them? If Bechu is a real live indentured coolie it strikes me that he has had the Agent in Calcutta on toast; he is far better educated than most of us are, at all events in some respects, but what the dickens has he come here for? The kindest thing that could be done for him would be to ship him back to India where his talents might be more appreciated.

The Daily Chronicle, 9 January 1897

Bechu's response to 'Planter' is laced with sarcasm; he is evidently enjoying himself:

Bechu to the Editor, *The Daily Chronicle*:

Sir, I am sorry to encroach on your valuable space again, but as no one is in a better position than myself, to answer 'Planter's' queries, you will perhaps allow me to give him all the information he seeks.

Why 'Planter' should take such a deep interest in me, 'passeth knowledge' but in the hope that he will manage to scrape up enough coin to buy up my time and pay my passage back to India, I gladly furnish him with the undermentioned particulars, *free*! *gratis*!! and *for nothing*!!! I am, Sir, etc,

BECHU, Indentured Immigrant, *Sheila*, 1894
Pln Enmore, EC, 11th January 1897

'Planter's' Questions	Bechu's Answers
Who is Bechu?	A queer looking specimen of – it is believed – the human race, (but evidently of the rarest description) because when I was (not many years ago) exhibited in the Calcutta 'Zoo', most people, naturalists included, were ready to swear, for true, that *I* was *the* 'Missing Link,' but since there was no Darwin to declare me to be *the Simon pure*, I unfortunately lost my chance of making a fortune. What would that eminent professor not have given, to have had, just one *wee* glimpse of me before he departed from these earthly scenes of his labours?
Is he really an indentured immigrant?	Really, indeed, and unfortunately so.
What was his cost to Enmore?	*Nil.* The colony I understand bore the entire cost of my introduction.
Does he do any fieldwork?	No, I am a domestic *animal*, but my bosses are gentlemen, and don't treat me as if I were:

Bechu and his Critics: Personal Attacks

'Planter's' Questions *continued*	Bechu's Answers *continued*
	'A little better than their dog A little dearer than their horse.'
How does his earnings compare with his contract?	Favourably. I get my just and lawful due, viz: one shilling *per diem*. (This circumstance does not, however, prevent me from crying for *justice* on behalf of *my dumb-driven* brethren, who, at times, being unable to plead their cause foolishly take the law into their own hands.)
Where does he obtain files of English daily papers, and when time to read them?	(1) *Vide Daily Chronicle* of 14th Dec last [in fact, 15], as to how I manage to get a squint at newspapers. (It is to be hoped 'Planter' has missed no copies from his files.) (2) Those who have a desire to improve themselves always make the time to do so, besides, why should *I* not have plenty of time to read, seeing I am an indentured immigrant, and am bound, by law, to serve only *seven hours* out of the 24.
If Bechu is a real live indentured coolie, it strikes me that he has had the Agent in Calcutta on toast.	It is a positive fact that I am a *real, live, animal*, and what is more surprising, I am allowed to go *unchained*. For a reply to the latter part of this question, I beg to refer 'Planter' to the veteran Agent in India, who doubtless, will be better able to answer it than I.
He is far better educated than most of us are, at all events, in some respects.	I don't know about being *far better educated*, but the *little* I know is due to my having taken advantage of my opportunities when young. If it is possible to educate monkeys why should not the *'connecting link'* between man and him be taught as well? If 'Planter' is death on education he should lose no time to shut up schools and do away with Education Commissions, else, in course of time, he will find 'too much *educated* coolymans' in this colony, it strikes me.

BECHU – 'BOUND COOLIE' RADICAL

'Planter's' Questions *continued*	Bechu's Answers *continued*
What the dickens has he come here for?	For the same reason 'Planter', and all other colonists have come, viz to *earn* my living.
The kindest thing that could be done for him would be to ship him back to India, where his talents might be more appreciated.	If I could get the chance of getting back to India now, I dare say *after all I have seen in this colony*, I could be of more service there, to my brethren, than I ever will be here, – If 'Planter' has more money than brains, and would be so kind as to buy up my time, and pay my *passage back to Calcutta, I promise faithfully to return by the next mail, and he may depend upon it, that, till my dying day, I shall, without fail, pray for his *health, wealth, long life*, and *prosperity*.

*Having no wife, children, or any other 'encumbrance', my passage will not cost very much, after all.

The Daily Chronicle, 12 January 1897

The Immigration Agent General, A.H. Alexander, to the Governor of British Guiana, Sir Walter Sendall, 1 July 1899 – 'A short history of Bechu'.

The following is a short history of Bechu, who came here as an immigrant in the ship *Sheila* on the 20th December 1894.

> On arrival he was indentured to Pln Enmore at 'no fee', in consequence of his being apparently physically unfit for manual labour.
>
> When received on Pln Enmore, the Manager, in consideration of his inability to do ordinary estate's labour, gave him special employment, first with the creole gang as Assistant Supervisor, at 24 cents a day, and afterwards, when found unfit for that, he was taken on as a domestic servant in the overseers' house.
>
> In October 1896, Bechu commenced writing letters to the newspapers, in connection with which the Immigration Agent of the District wrote as follows:

He shows his gratitude for the excessive kindness with which he has been treated, by these silly effusions of which the point lies not so much in the statements themselves, as in their intention. I doubt if any other Manager would have been as kind to Bechu as Mr Bethune has been and the man's ingratitude is the more conspicuous.

Respecting the publication of Bechu's first letter in *The Daily Chronicle* [1 November 1896], Mr Bethune made the following remark: 'I am told he has adopted a defiant mood since the publication of the letter which of course he has seen, having access to the Reading Room in the Overseers' House'.

On the 16th February 1897, Bechu sent in a petition to me to be allowed to pay commutation money for the remaining period of his indenture, giving as his reasons for this application, (a) That the Head Overseer, who had become Deputy Manager, had informed him 'for reasons unexplained', that he must go to the field to work: (b) That he was unfit for fieldwork on account of irregular heart action: and (c) That he had been offered an appointment in Georgetown by an East Indian merchant [possibly Abdool Rohoman].

The merchant referred to wrote to me stating that he was prepared to pay commutation money for Bechu, and to give him employment.

As Bechu had been allotted at 'no fee', no commutation money was payable, and consequently on the 24th February 1897, I determined [terminated] his indenture and he received a Certificate of Exemption from Labour on the 26th February 1897. On the next day he wrote the following letter thanking me:

Respected Sir,
Permit me to tender my very best thanks to you for the prompt measures you have taken to obtain for me my freedom and that too 'without money and without price'. I shall ever remember this act of kindness of yours with the deepest gratitude, more especially as I feel myself undeserving of such a concession.

Believing that a man of apparently fair English education would not have come to this colony as a common labourer unless there had been some good cause or necessity for his leaving India, I wrote to our Agent at Calcutta, on 23rd December 1896, asking him to endeavour to obtain some particulars of Bechu's history. Mr Mitchell, however, could not obtain any information in regard to him, from which it must be inferred that not only did he emigrate under an assumed name, but that on arrival here he gave an incorrect account of his antecedents.

CO 111/513, Sendall to Chamberlain, no. 182, 6 July 1899, encl

---

On 19 July 1899, Governor Sendall writes to the Secretary of State for the colonies on the elusive antecedents of Bechu, suggesting that he is a "a fugitive from justice".

Sir, Referring to my despatch no. 205 of even date with this [following a letter from Bechu alleging 'immoral relations' between an overseer and an Indian woman], and the remarks made by Mr Alexander as to the antecedents in India of the immigrant Bechu, we have already endeavoured, without success, to ascertain under what circumstances this man was allowed to pass himself off before the recruiting agents in India.

He enlisted under an assumed name, and such particulars as he has stated with reference to his past history have been found on enquiry to be wholly fictitious.

He was totally unfitted for work on the estates and was on that account released from his indentures very soon after his arrival.

The most probable explanation of his presence here is that he is a fugitive from justice. A man with his superior education and unquestionable ability is not likely to have taken up the career of an indentured labourer in the West Indies without some overpowering motive for leaving his native country.

CO 111/513, Sendall to Chamberlain, confidential, 19 July 1899

Sydney Olivier who, as Secretary of the West India Royal Commission, had encountered Bechu in British Guiana in February 1897, was much more sympathetic in his assessment of Bechu, as the following Colonial Office minutes reveal:

CO minute: It is, I think, a pity that the antecedents of Bechu in India can not be ascertained.

CO minute (S.O. [Sydney Olivier]): Why? because he has 'got home' on the overseer in this case ... This is not the first time Bechu has 'got home' on overseers or the Immigration Department, which is the real reason why they are so anxious to [brand?] him a criminal.

CO 111/513, Sendall to Chamberlain, no. 205, 19 July 1899, Minutes, 4 August 1899

CO minute (S.O. [Sydney Olivier]): ... Mr Alexander's observation herein referred to was not, it seems to me, very opportune. Possibly Bechu is a Hindu philanthropist who indentured with a view to functioning as an amateur 'protector of immigrants'. There is much evidence for this than for his being a criminal, on his record in British Guiana.

CO 111/513, Sendall to Chamberlain, confidential, 19 July 1899, Minutes, 4 August 1899

CHAPTER FOUR

Unmasking the Plantocracy: Bechu, Indentureship and 'King Sugar'

Bechu explains his role in exposing the "evils" of the indentureship system in British Guiana, thus earning the calumny of the privileged. He writes to the Secretary of State for India:

To The Right Honourable
    LORD GEORGE FRANCIS HAMILTON MP
    Her Majesty's Principal Secretary of State for INDIA.
    St James' Park,
    SW LONDON
    ENGLAND

Dated Georgetown Demerara, the 27th April 1899.

Mr Lord,

(1)   It being the highest as well as the most dearly cherished privilege of every British-born subject without regard to class, creed, or colour to approach Her Most gracious Majesty the QUEEN-EMPRESS when it is certain that to appeal to the Authorities on the spot would involve too much of

personal reflection on those whose connivance has entailed a shameful reproach to the administration of justice, permit me though only an indentured immigrant, who came to this colony in the Ship *Sheila* in 1894, to address YOUR LORDSHIP on a matter which affects the welfare of a large number of my countrymen who like myself have had the misfortune to come to DEMERARA, the political system of which colony has very appropriately been divined and defined by Mr Trollope under a happy inspiration as 'despotism tempered by sugar'. To these two twin forces the immigration system is as sacred as was the old system of SLAVERY in former days, and for one in my humble position to have ventured to touch it with profane hands or to have dared to unveil it is considered on this side of the ATLANTIC to be a capital and inexpiable offence.

(2) As an indentured immigrant I have YOUR LORDSHIP, during the past four years & four months of my sojourn in British Guiana had extensive and exceptional opportunities afforded me of observing from 'behind the scenes' the actual workings of the system of immigration which led me long ago to apprehend its evils and impelled me to offer myself as a witness before the WEST INDIA ROYAL COMMISSIONERS who, YOUR LORDSHIP may perhaps have noticed, have recorded my evidence at pages 73, 74 and 131, of Appendix C Volume II of their REPORT.

(3) I know, YOUR LORDSHIP, that the IMPERIAL GOVERNMENT have for HUMANITARIAN reasons and in the LABOURERS' interests imposed an extra cost upon BRITISH GUIANA towards the importation of East Indian immigrants into this colony but, with all the precautions that have been taken for the protection of us strangers in this STRANGE LAND, I regret exceedingly to inform YOUR LORDSHIP that our lot here is not as happy as some interested parties would have YOUR LORDSHIP believe.

(4) As an instance may I beg to invite YOUR LORDSHIP's kind perusal to a case which I gave publicity to in the DEMERARA *DAILY CHRONICLE* dated the 13th September 1898, and for which I stand indicted on a charge of libelling Mr F.C.S. Bascom, the Manager of Plantation Cove and John, a sugar estate on the East Sea Coast of BRITISH GUIANA. This

case came off for hearing at the session of January 1899 and again at the April sessions, but as YOUR LORDSHIP will observe from *The Daily Chronicle* report, although the JURY retired twice, on neither occasion were they able to arrive at a verdict, and YOUR LORDSHIP will scarcely wonder why when YOUR LORDSHIP learns that several of their number are employed on sugar estates and the chief one – the FOREMAN, happened to be an overseer – a class of men who dislike me beyond measure because I have before the WEST INDIA ROYAL COMMISSIONERS as well as in the daily newspapers complained of their immoral relations with female immigrants.

(5) Having said this much I humbly and respectfully beg to leave the matter entirely in YOUR LORDSHIP's hands, feeling confident that YOUR LORDSHIP will cause a strict enquiry to be made with regard to BHAGRI's death.

(6) In conclusion I beg to inform YOUR LORDSHIP that since the institution of these proceedings against me an indentured immigrant named KALLY was assaulted by Mr Daniel Spencer, the Engineer of Plantation Cove and John, and it is a positive fact that Mr Sealy, the Immigration Agent for the district in reporting the matter to the IAG stated in an office note dated the 14th December 1898 that he was 'not at all satisfied with the treatment which the immigrants receive on Plantation Cove and John and that the action taken by the Manager of that estate clearly shows that he encourages his officials to ill-treat the immigrants'.

And this estate YOUR LORDSHIP will be surprised to learn still continues to receive fresh batches of indentured immigrants!

Apologizing for taking up so much of YOUR LORDSHIP's time.

I am, etc.
(Sd) E. Bechu

CO 111/516, Offices (India), 7 June 1899

Bechu is implacable in his opposition to the continuation of Indian indentureship. He argues that the sole beneficiaries of the system are the sugar planters, and that all forms of free labour, by Africans and Indians, are stifled by the coercive mechanisms built into indentureship.

Bechu (Georgetown) to the Editor, *The Daily Chronicle*:

Sir, Addison tells us that: 'The most abject *flatterers* degenerate into the greatest tyrants,' and such was my sentiment when I read in this morning's issue of your paper [*DC*, 30 March 1897] the letter of your correspondent, who wrote under the strange *nom de plume*, 'An Admirer of Bechu's Talent'! Poor me! How I wish I had *but one* talent that I might employ it for the benefit of my fellow creatures.

Is this correspondent aware that there are 59 estates now under cultivation, and that the total number of beds in these estates amounts to 3,271 only? At the present rate of a cent an opening for cane cutting, or even at the old rate of a shilling an opening, does he think there is sufficient inducement to bring more immigrants from India? How does he expect the 69,474 unfortunates who are at present residing on those estates to subsist? Does he want to glut our labour market with 50,000 more coolies in order that they may come here and *thrive* on the smell of a burnt oil rag?

It is my decided opinion that in the present depressed condition of the colony, immigration should be suspended at once, and I am very hopeful that when the question of bringing the 2,500 fresh shipments of coolies the planters have requisitioned for the ensuing year comes to be discussed in the Combined Court, the people's representatives who are perfectly aware how we are circumstanced, will fight tooth and nail against the proposal.

The Daily Chronicle, 1 December 1897

Bechu was responding to the solid proplanter, proimmigration letter of his 'admirer', whose stance epitomises that of the plantocracy even during the depression of the late 1890s: give everything to sugar – for the presumed good of all.

'An Admirer of Bechu's Talent' to the Editor, *The Daily Chronicle*:

... I would venture to say that the sudden collapse of the staple industry – which will happen if the sugar estates do not receive help speedily – would mean ruin to one and all in the meantime, and would cost the Imperial Government millions, as we have the land to grow sugar and rice. Instead of stopping migration as Bechu hints at, does he not think that by increasing immigration eight or tenfold for a few years, it would be the means of placing the sugar industry in a position to compete with continental countries. To put the lands here to the useful purpose they are adapted for, let the sugar estates have all the immigrants they may require, indentured for five years free of charge; then the colony should give them, when their times have expired, land free and properly drained. If that were done the East Indians would become a prosperous middle class in the colony. I hope Bechu will give this matter careful thought, and let me know if he thinks 50,000 or more of his countrymen could not better themselves in this colony by getting the land free after five years' indenture.

The Daily Chronicle, 30 November 1897

Bechu's reservations about his planter-'admirer' seem justified, as the latter proposes support for Bechu's declared interest in wanting to leave British Guiana to study in England. His 'admirer' seems too anxious to be rid of him.

'An Admirer of Bechu's Talent' to the Editor, *The Daily Chronicle*:

Mr Bechu's reply to my letter is very much milder than I anticipated. Most will admit his talent at wielding his pen is far above the ordinary class. It would be a pity if such talent was curtailed for the want of a few dollars. Do you think it would be possible to raise sufficient in the colony for this purpose? Mr Bechu would be able to repay the government the expense it has been put to in bringing him from India. I for one shall willingly subscribe my mite, and I believe a great many more will do so, if you undertake the collection.

Although his attacks on the planting body and the government have been severe, let him see how generous British subjects can be for the advancement of ambition even though he is of East Indian descent. I have had dealings with his countrymen for over 30 years, and well know their worth; there is quite sufficient time if the *Sheila* only arrives by the middle of January, to allow Mr Bechu his wish of going to London by that vessel to attain the one talent he desires that he might employ for the benefit of his fellow countrymen. Although the 59 estates can only number 3,271 beds now (I take his own figures), by allowing them [the planters] immigration free, the beds would soon amount to ten times that number. I unhesitatingly say, stop immigration altogether, and the colony is ruined in a very short time, and not only the immigrants now here, but all others may have to try and *thrive* on the smell of a burnt oil rag; but increase immigration, and we shall all have at all events, sugar, rice and coconut oil to live on.

I was a planter for 20 years, and I can assure Mr Bechu he has not received his information correctly about the price of cane cutting at old rates; his quotation of a cent an opening being the present price, must be a misquotation. I frankly admit my inability to quote authors with Mr Bechu, so I am done with him; you shall however hear from me if a subscription list is opened for his benefit.

[We cannot undertake the collection of subscriptions. Bechu has his own methods, and he does not see why he should pay. – Ed DC]

The Daily Chronicle, 7 December 1897

Bechu rejects his 'admirer's' generosity; the fact that he has been "a planter for 20 years" seems especially repellent to Bechu.

Bechu (Georgetown) to the Editor, *The Daily Chronicle*:

Sir, Your footnote to the letter of 'a planter for 20 years', which appeared in this morning's issue of your paper, is entirely endorsed by me. The only reply I have to give with regard to his magnanimous offer is: 'Thy money perish with thee.' I am very thankful to your correspondent for drawing my attention to two glaring mistakes which appeared in my last letter. My notes are so disconnected that instead of writing 67,208.5 acres under cultivation, I wrote 3,271 beds. Since your correspondent professes to have been 'a planter for twenty years', he should have known that the price I quoted for cane cutting was intended for a *bed* and not for an opening. At any rate, he has taken a precious long time to discover the errors.

The Daily Chronicle, 8 December 1897

'Well-Wisher', also, like Bechu's 'admirer', advocates more immigration from India, "free" to the sugar estates. This, he contends, would redound to the benefit of both the sugar planters and the immigrants. Unlike Bechu, he thinks reindenture is an unworkable proposition: free Indians want to grow rice, to be independent of sugar estates.

'Well-Wisher' to the Editor, *The Daily Chronicle*:

Sir, Mr Bechu is somewhat of my opinion about the countervailing duties, but we are at variance with each other on some other matters; would the introduction from the congested districts of India *free* to the sugar estates here of eight to ten thousand immigrants a year, for five years, not be the means of turning the deficit to an overplus on the colony's revenue?

I maintain the sugar estates can be carried on, and cultivation very considerably improved and increased to the requirements . . . as there is to be found anywhere, *were they assured of reliable resident labour*. Profits might be small, but the industry would be continued. I also maintain it would not saddle the Home Government *with a farthing expenditure*. Most of the time-expired immigrants are now engaged in growing rice, and look happy and contented. At present the exodus of immigrants from estates, as their time expires, looking out for land to grow rice, build their huts, and be independent, are very numerous. In fact, by the end of next year, the manufacture of sugar in some districts will have to be postponed until the rice crop is reaped. In the county of Berbice . . . had the sugar crop been what it was expected to be at the beginning of this year, January would not have seen it finished. I hear that one estate will take to the end of January next and the crop is considerably under what was expected. Mr Bechu and some of our representatives would support a measure that would damn the colony . . . [he] must know his countrymen's intentions and inclinations better than I do. I live amongst them, although not a planter, and have asked many if they would reindenture. The indolent say 'yes', but the industrious, and especially those with families, say most emphatically 'no, they must grow rice, and were they to go to reap their crops and watch the estates' work, they would have to pay $10 and costs, or go 30 days to gaol. Then their rice would be lost to them'.

I have given the matter considerable thought, and the only lasting remedy I can think of is the introduction of immigrants and opening up the country. The immigrants themselves say they can grow a better crop of rice here than they can in India; a great many of them who have paid for their return passages the $5 have, I believe, withdrawn it . . . The present tendency seems to be to make this colony their home, but to be free and independent.

The Daily Chronicle, 31 December 1897

Bechu remains opposed to immigration while few incentives are offered to "trained agriculturalists" to remain in British Guiana. Every effort, even re-indenture, should be made to induce Indians to remain in the colony; but he is apprehensive of the prospects for rice if countervailing duties are imposed on European beet sugar, and the fortunes of cane sugar are revived.

Bechu (Georgetown) to the Editor, *The Daily Chronicle*:

Sir, At this the commencement of another year, I don't like the idea of having to say hard things about anyone, but it really does seem to me that your correspondent 'Well-Wisher' deserves such things. For who would at this critical time, when our cane sugar industry is, so to speak, hanging from a slender thread, and when the estimates for the ensuing financial year are being prepared on extremely careful and economical lines, be so foolish as to suggest that the sugar estates be given eight to ten thousand immigrants a year for the next five years, free of cost, or in other words at the expense of the taxpayers. Since 1891 this colony has been importing coolies at the rate of five thousand a year, and what advantages has it derived? Absolutely none. It is nevertheless an ugly fact that during the same period it has gone to the enormous cost of sending away 21 shiploads of men with some little means, after they had become useful labourers and got accustomed to the country. Had half that amount which had been squandered in chartering vessels to carry back these trained agriculturalists to the land of their birth been offered them in hard cash as an inducement to remain, we would long ere now have had the basis of a population which would have rendered the development of this colony sure and certain.

If 'Well-Wisher' will look up the files of the *Royal Gazette* and *Colonist* he will see that the cultivation of rice was started in this colony so far back as 1881, and that a rice-growing company was actually formed in those days, but because the planters and a few traders whose business it was to furnish the estates with supplies were opposed to the scheme, it died a natural death, after nine days' wonder or talk – and I guess it will be so with our present venture in that direction, if a countervailing duty is imposed upon imported beet sugar.

Indeed the free coolies are too wide awake to their own interests to accept starvation wages when they can grow rice and other provisions to advantage. 'Well-Wisher' talks of certain estates having had to pay the piper last grinding season. Well I don't dispute that point, but if he will in company with a representative of your paper go through the pay lists of those very estates he will see that the majority of the labourers *unindentured* as well as *indentured* scarcely earned more than 6 pence *per diem* in the slack season.

It's not likely that the immigrants who have served out their time and who are therefore entitled to a return passage would *as a body* reindenture or forego their claims to a return passage to India, but I do maintain that even if ten percent of those about to leave these shores could be induced to remain in the country, the colony would by that means become richer in population and power of production and, however slow the progress, we would from year to year and little by little add to our small number of peasant proprietors.

How 'Well-Wisher', who although not a planter, has made the discovery that only the *indolent* are willing to [re-]indenture is a mystery to me. In India with its teeming population the recruiters cannot afford to pick and chose but just nab the first fellow they come across, and if the poor devil does not happen to be in trim to pass the doctor, he is physicked and fattened in the depot hospital till the next vessel is ready to sail. 'Well-Wisher' must remember that I have been behind the scenes and must therefore have learnt enough to teach him a wrinkle.

The Daily Chronicle, 5 January 1898

Unmasking the Plantocracy: Bechu, Indentureship and 'King Sugar'

'Well-Wisher' sees British Guiana as a potentially important colony for Indian settlers, and argues that their cultivation of rice will not be a "nine days' wonder", even if countervailing duties were imposed.

'Well-Wisher' to the Editor, *The Daily Chronicle*:

Sir, I trust you will allow me to let Mr Bechu understand, however hard he may hit, and however vituperative he may become, my back is broad and can stand all even better than the effect of water on a duck's back. The coolies imported to this colony from India from year to year have been its mainstay, and will, I hope, be so for the future. I quite agree with Mr Bechu the government has been lacking in not providing means before this of offering inducements to those immigrants who have already left the colony, but it is never too late to mend. They are doing so now and it is to be hoped by giving them land, not only 10 percent but 75 percent or more may be induced to stay.

I do not require to look up the files of any newspaper to find out when the cultivation of rice was started in this colony. Mr [William] Russell on the West Coast of Demerara tried it years before 1881, but the land selected could not be sufficiently supplied with water. In 1874 I persuaded a coolie who was with me then *and is now with me* to plant rice in unused canals, where water could be got when required from the service canal. It was a success then on a small scale. Ever since then I have encouraged rice growing, and I predict the present venture will not turn out a 'nine days' wonder or talk' but a lasting good to the colony of British Guiana.

A countervailing duty if imposed (which I very much doubt) will never give the death blow now to rice. Mr Bechu will have to explain his views more clearly, or I must be very dense, denser even than I ever considered myself. At one time he advises reindenture, then again he says: 'The free coolies are too wide awake to their own interest to accept starvation wages when they can grow rice and other provisions to advantage.' I shall be most happy to accompany you, Mr Editor, or any representative of your paper to go through the pay list of any properly worked sugar estate you may mention, and we shall see the 6 pence *per diem* doubled or more against the names of every good working able-bodied coolie even in the slackest season. Although not a sugar planter, I am morally certain that there is not a Manager but what would let us have every facility, even if Mr Bechu were to accompany us. I expect he means the idle days added to the working days.

I have already said I live amongst the coolies, and this is how I get my information. Mr Bechu must have read 'Old Timer's' letter in Tuesday's *Chronicle*. I hope if he has he will give it fair digestion. He says he has been behind the scenes and has learnt enough to teach one a wrinkle or two. I earnestly hope he will do so. I am a poor devil myself, and have also been physicked and fattened before taking a voyage, so we are both on a par. India with its teeming population should be only too ready to accept the Imperial Government's help in getting rid of 50 thousand of Mr Bechu's countrymen over here where they become prosperous and independent. Aye, even ten times that number would not starve, as they sometimes do in their own country, and would be able to physic and fatten themselves and become men to be relied on. Many thanks 'Old Timer': I am of the sixties. I hope to read your productions again. I suppose the planters are afraid of being called selfish were they to write to you as I do, but had they petitioned for immigrants instead of a countervailing duty they might have been some chance of success [sic]. Think of the boon it would confer on the immigrants.

The Daily Chronicle, 11 January 1898

'Well-Wisher' is buoyed by the support he receives from 'Old Timer', who endorses his call for the "free" importation of eight to ten thousand Indian indentured immigrants a year for five years, to assist the sugar estates. It would bring prosperity to all. He sees no merits, however, in reindenture.

'Old Timer' to the Editor, *The Daily Chronicle*:

. . . it would benefit everyone living in British Guiana, also thousands of our fellow subjects in India. Our tradesmen would get work, who have so long suffered from the want of regular employment, there would be plenty of labour for all the different industries, more money would be in circulation, and prosperity would again smile on the land, and contentment would reign in our midst . . .

Everyone realizes that what we want here most is population, without which the country cannot be opened up and developed, and the East

Indian although not exactly the class of labour we would prefer, adapts himself in time fairly well to the work required of him, and many of them who have been here for six or seven years can hold their own pretty well against the more robust Negro . . . The sugar estates require . . . reliable [resident] labour, without which they cannot be carried on successfully . . . At the end of five years they would be free to go and work where they liked.

As the free coolies have now made a successful start to grow rice they will prefer not to attach themselves too closely to the estates, but will want to give most of their time to their rice patches, in fact, to be their own masters to go and come as they like . . . I am old enough to remember the period between 1850–60, and the struggle the planters had then for labour. There can only be one opinion amongst those who knew the colony at that time, viz, but for immigration and the indomitable pluck of the planters during the period 1845 to 1855, I assert the country would now have been a barren waste from the Corentyne to the Amacura. Even during the early sixties, labour was double and in some things, three times the present rates, and sometimes could hardly be procured at any price. It was only when immigration was established on a permanent footing from India that proprietors would spend any money in new machinery, which in recent years has done so much to reduce the cost of production . . .

. . . the Mother Country has had the benefit of all these years . . . of cheap sugar at the expense of the West Indies and due to unfair competition; surely it is not too much to ask them to assist us in this our time of need, and this country can most effectively be assisted by adding to our population, which will help every one. Reindenture will be [of] no benefit to any one. The best men will not enter on a term of [re-]indenture, and if they did, it would soon be found we had a very dissatisfied lot to deal with, who would always think because they were bound advantage was being taken of them by estate authorities. No, if there is any money to spend, let it be done by bringing people here, but not under the return passage system. If immigration ceases it means the beginning of the end for the sugar industry.

The Daily Chronicle, 4 January 1898

Bechu is not persuaded. He contends that 'Negro and creole' workers are made to subsidize a system of labour which keeps wages at "starvation point". He again recommends reindenture as a means of keeping some seasoned Indians in British Guiana.

Bechu (Georgetown) to the Editor, The Daily Chronicle:

Sir, As one who professes to take an intelligent interest in the affairs of this colony, 'Well-Wisher' has ventilated his views freely enough on the labour supply question, and it now remains to be seen whether the people's representatives in the Combined Court will, in the present condition of the Colonial Exchequer, and with a diminution (from 76,101 acres in 1892 in the area to 66,236 acres in 1897) of cultivation, and therefore in the scope for employment, adopt his suggestion to introduce a system of labour that must be paid for by the suffering Negro and creole labourers, for Mr Editor do not these poor people through the taxation of foodstuffs and other commodities provide for the payment of the expenses of immigration simply to flood the labour market for no other purpose than to keep down wages at starvation point? To prove the truth of my assertion that the statutory wage is not given to indentured coolies in the slack season, I am ready to accept 'Well-Wisher's' challenge and accompany him and a representative of your paper, to say Plantations Reliance or Anna Regina, both of which being the properties of such a well-known personage as Mr Quintin Hogg, must, I take it, be regarded as properly worked sugar estates.

Indeed, I have always advised reindenture and still do so, because it not only saves the costly expense of bringing immigrants all the way from Calcutta, but provides against the loss of acclimatizing and training them to work. 'Well-Wisher' tells us that he lives amongst the coolies and yet he seems to be ignorant of the fact that there are three classes of 'free' coolies in the colony, ie, those who have served out their ten years and prefer to go to India, unless perhaps it is made worth their while to remain in this colony; those whose five years have just expired or are about to expire; and those East Indians born in the colony. The last two classes, I am sure, would be glad to accept the local government offer of $25 and [re-]indenture themselves for three years or $50 and [re-]indenture themselves for five years, but although the acting Immigration Agent General was, over a month ago, directed to ascertain what number of coolies would be willing to [re-]indenture, he has kept the matter so quiet that with the exception of one or two favoured ones nobody appears to know anything about the offer.

'Well-Wisher' ought to feel ashamed to declare that ever since 1874 he has encouraged rice growing, for his efforts in that direction have been practically *nil*. Does not his failure to have brought matters to a head only confirm my statement that because of opposition [from the planters], the company formed in 1881 died a natural death?

The Daily Chronicle, 16 January 1898

In the midst of the sugar depression, Bechu finds an ally in 'British Citizen', who advocates "minor industries", the lessening of dependence on sugar monoculture.

'British Citizen' to the Editor, *The Daily Chronicle*:

. . . [The planter] should at once begin to put other staples on their abandoned plantations. They should let, lease or sell to people who may be willing to take up the lands, and encourage them to cultivate minor industries. It is over 30 years since the price of cane sugar began to fall, and it has now almost reached its lowest ebb. It is my conviction that neither Imperial help nor countervailing duty will bring the price of sugar up to what it was 30 years, or even 20 years ago. With the success of beet growing in England and the extended cultivation of the cane in Egypt and other countries, one cannot tell to what extent overproduction may reach, the subsequent result of which will be the further lowering of prices. A mixed cultivation on West Indian plantations seems to me about the surest way to keep off the evil.

The Daily Chronicle, 8 February 1898

The Daily Chronicle joins the debate; like Bechu and 'British Citizen', they argue that enough has already been sacrificed to moloch, 'King Sugar', "the sinking ship"; they must diversify.

> Industries that don't pay on their own bottom must be dropped; and Mr Chamberlain's suggested grant will do harm instead of good if it is regarded by the West Indian planter as a dole to enable him to keep his heart up until he is once more in a position to grow canes at a large profit. That time will not come . . . There is not the slightest reason why West Indian colonists should go down with the sinking ship; but they must clearly recognize that what they have been accustomed to regard as their staple is going down. There are plenty of boats on board and with Mr Chamberlain's life line what possible reason is there that a position of safety should not be reached?

Leader, *The Daily Chronicle*, 11 February 1898

R.G. Duncan, a prominent planter and president of the Royal Agricultural and Commercial Society, responds swiftly to *The Daily Chronicle*, resurrecting many of the old arguments for sugar in British Guiana; his silence on Indian progress with rice is eloquent.

R.G. Duncan to the Editor, *The Daily Chronicle*:

> I should be pleased to know what boats there are on board as regards British Guiana. Can you or anyone in the colony indicate any industry so well suited to our soil, climate and conditions as our 'legitimate' industry sugar? Is there any reason to believe that any known agricultural product can be grown here to replace sugar? Is there any agricultural industry springing up in our midst, that by encouragement or assistance can be fostered so as to eventually replace our staple?
>
> Our 'legitimate' industry is not dead, nor if given fair play, will it die. It is the most suitable and profitable industry for the colony, having in view conditions of soil, climate, labour, etc.

The Daily Chronicle, 12 February 1898

The Daily Chronicle is not reconciled to Duncan's saccharine promptings. It counterposes to what it sees as the obstinancy of "Little Demeraraites" rooted in sugar, the broader, imaginative potential for a "Greater British Guiana" beyond the sugar plantations of the coastland.

> . . . Fortunes have been made out of this alluvial strip in the past, and we do not doubt that more will be made in the future. We do not wish to see anyone change his position who prefers to stay where he is, and we have never shared the idea that it is the duty of gentlemen who put their money into sugar to sell out and invest it in the interior of the colony. We merely wish to point out that the argument of history is in favour of a Greater British Guiana springing up, perhaps in the near future, and they will derive the benefit who may be ready to profit by it. There are those of little faith who cannot foresee any prospect for the colony than that of a sugar growing province. We do not quarrel with them, but let them see to it that they refrain from exerting their influence to prevent or delay the realization of the hopes of more sanguine men.

Leader, *The Daily Chronicle*, 13 February 1898

Another advocate of "minor industries" slates the plantocracy for their selfish warping of all colonial endeavour to a singular purpose, sugar monoculture:

'Advance' to the Editor, *The Daily Chronicle*:

> *Sir,* The planters were not statesmen; they were not men of broad and independent views; they were not as a class even colonists in the true sense of the word; they were men actuated by one idea, and that to use every effort to make their business pay, and invested with power they suborned all and every for that sole object . . . While we should . . . co-operate to save and maintain our only important industry, the mistakes of the past must be carefully avoided and neither to that nor any other industry should we again yield ourselves willing slaves. The death knell of sugar as the mainstay of this colony has sounded . . .
>
> The abolition of bounties or the imposition of countervailing duties on sugar would undoubtedly give us temporary relief . . . [but] we must by

every possible means increase our population, develop our waste lands and introduce new industries, especially industries which the poor man, with little capital, can enter into with some prospect of at least earning a living for himself and his family.

Nearly 100 years of unprogressive oligarchical rule has produced today a condition of things so startlingly pregnant with disaster to the whole colony that thoughtful men are aghast at the fearful cruelty which has been perpetuated.

The Daily Chronicle, 25 February 1898

It is noteworthy that this spate of support for "minor industries" had been preceded by Bechu's timely intervention, in November 1897, on behalf of the promising, embryonic rice culture, initiated by Indian pioneers.

Bechu (Georgetown) to the Editor, *The Daily Chronicle*:

Sir, Rice being the only industry that can immediately, or in the near future, replace the deficiency caused by the decline of sugar, it is comforting to know that it is being cultivated on a much larger scale than it has hitherto been in this colony, which is so entirely suited to its culture. But why, Mr Editor, should not it become general? The country is flat, rich, easily flooded, water is abundant and the seasons admirably adapted for its cultivation. The land can be prepared by fire and plough. The seed once sown requires little else than attention and management as regards the application of water. The crop can be cheaply reaped and prepared for the market, now that a proper rice-milling machine has been obtained. Nearly half the population of the world lives on rice. Cattle, horses, stock of all sorts thrive on paddy. Poultry fatten on the broken grain, and pigs will not refuse it although damaged. Both East Indians and Chinese thoroughly understand the culture of rice and, wonderful to relate, those whose attentions were at one time exclusively engaged in the production of sugar, are trying their hand at it with success.

Plantation Enmore [Bechu's ex-estate], I understand, has 150 acres under cultivation, Melville 250, Cane Grove 200, Clonbrook 65, Greenfield 60, Vryheid's Lust 50, Hope 35, La Bonne Intention 30, and

Success 18 acres . . . [all on the East Coast Demerara]. There is also a considerable amount cultivated in Essequibo, up the river [Berbice] opposite Ma Retraite, and at New Calcutta on the Corentyne Coast. To give a greater impetus to the industry it would be a wise policy on the part of the government to abolish the present Land Regulations and utilize the money which is needlessly being spent on the purchase of abandoned estates, the soils of which have been poisoned by the free application of manure, on making small loans to time-expired immigrants, on good security, and to creole Indian youths above the age of 15 who have no desire or intention of going to India with their parents when it is time for them to claim a return passage.

Something of this sort must be done, and done without further delay, to open up the country and make the colony prosperous again . . .

The Daily Chronicle, 2 November 1897

Bechu deprecates "sugar-coated" government; again makes his case for rice; dismisses demands for more Indian immigrants but, strangely, persists with his recommendation of reindentureship.

Bechu (Georgetown) to the Editor, *The Daily Chronicle*:

Sir, How is it that certain sections of our community – the Governor and the Government Secretary included – cannot be convinced that Providence never intended that British Guiana should always remain a sugar growing colony? It has times without number been brought to the notice of these good people that the underdeveloped lands of the colony are amongst the richest existing in any part of the tropics, and yet they religiously cling to the idea that there is nothing but sugar for this magnificent colony of ours! Might not it be truly said of them, 'None are so blind as those who will *not* see?'

When great big provinces like Bengal and Burmah [sic] depend upon rice for their prosperity, why cannot we? One-third of our population live on that grain, and allowing that, with the cost of labour here, it is doubtful whether colony-grown rice will ever be exported in competition with Indian rice, yet should not the local demand alone supply an ample field for enterprise in this direction? The government is ever ready to give all the help it possibly can to prop up a tottering [sugar] industry which eventually *must* fall, but it will not raise a finger to encourage private enterprise. No, when it comes to that it says: 'It is for the people themselves to work out their own salvation!'

What puzzles me again is how, in view of the serious reduction or collapse of the sugar industry, the planters have the face to urge for the importation of more labourers. They have scores of times warned the Imperial Government that if no heed is taken of their demand, there are likely to be coolie risings on a large scale, and His Excellency [the Governor] in his famous letter to the Chairman of the West India Commission [Sir Henry Norman] startled us by stating that 'even now it is almost impossible to avoid feeling that we are as it were sitting over a powder magazine'! Is it consistent under these circumstances to import any more immigrants?

According to the figures before me, I see that there were on the 31st March last [1897] as many as 17,847 indentured and 35,935 unindentured immigrants in the colony. In addition to that number there were 15,692 children under the age of ten years, a great majority of whom comprise what is known on sugar plantations as the 'creole gangs'. With this total of 69,474 residing on 59 estates now under cultivation, who our energetic acting Immigration Agent General unblushingly tells us *have realized the gravity of the circumstance which had rendered a reduction of some 20 to 25 percent in wages a matter of absolute necessity*, and with an approximate number of 47,296 *not* residing on estates, our labouring population, blacks, coolies, and Portuguese, rejoice to learn that instructions have been received from home to suspend East Indian immigration till the colony shall have recovered from its present pitiable condition.

If the powers that be fear that by reintroducing the reindenture system they will have every time-expired immigrant asking to be reindentured, the easiest way of getting over the difficulty would be to reindenture no one who has exceeded the age of 30, or better still indenture only creole Indians. It is a curious question what position our rulers expect this unfortunate class to occupy in the colony. They adopt the European style of dress, speak better English than their parents, and were trained to work in the fields as soon almost as they were able to crawl. For these reasons alone they should make excellent colonists, and it, indeed, is incumbent on our government to induce them to settle in this colony instead of allowing them to go to India when it is time for them to claim a return passage. But no, to please a handful of planters, they are willing to populate the colony and depopulate it again at an enormous cost. This is business!

The Daily Chronicle, 24 November 1897

Bechu's optimism on the prospects for rice cultivation in the colony is echoed by a correspondent:

'Interested' to the Editor, *The Daily Chronicle*:

There is not the slightest doubt about rice being one of the great industries of this colony in time; and at no distant date, the coolies with their rice beds and their cattle are to be the peasantry of the colony . . .

The Engelberg Huller [for rice-mills] is making very pretty rice, and when it can be supplied with properly matured paddy, the rice will bear comparison to the best imported.

The Daily Chronicle, 17 April 1898

The appetite of the plantocracy for bound labour to tide the sugar estates over the depression, remains undiminished. Indeed, it becomes the central plank of their strategy for survival. On 4 May 1898, the British Guiana Planters' Association sent a deputation to the Governor, Sir Walter Sendall, seeking an increase in the quota of indentureds, from 2,400 to 3,600 for 1898–99. R.G. Duncan was the principal advocate of the planters. He addressed the Governor:

> . . . If there is one vital and important question connected with the welfare of the colony regarding which unanimous views are held by all shades of intelligent public opinion, it is the necessity that exists for extended and continued immigration. The great want of this colony – the admitted want

– is population, and it has been abundantly and conclusively proved that only through the agency of sugar estates can new immigrants be introduced and made valuable and useful colonists. Every able-bodied immigrant introduced becomes a taxpayer and a producer. By his labours he adds to the general progress and prosperity of the colony, and in the course of time, he handsomely recoups the revenue for the cost of his introduction. It appears to me that there should be no limit to immigration except with regard to the number applied for by the employers who are anxious to obtain the services of the immigrants. And it would be wise policy on the part of the government to do everything in their power to assist, encourage and foster immigration . . . With regard to the present scarcity of labour on sugar estates, I may say that I am connected with, or interested in, sugar estates that produce about one-fifth of the entire crop of the colony, and on every one of these estates, without exception, the price of wages has gone up recently, and the want of labour has been seriously felt. Consequently the work on estates has been very much hampered and delayed. In many instances it has been considered highly desirable to increase the acreage in cultivation, and I have received instructions to that effect. But not only has the want of labour rendered this unadvisable [sic], but, at the present moment, a curtailment has to be carried out. Were the labour supply sufficient, were the rate of wages such that the sugar estates can afford to pay, I could, considerably and at once, increase the area under canes, and thereby, I consider, add to the prosperity of the colony. During the three years ending 1894/95, an annual average of 5,000 immigrants was introduced. During the three years that closed with the immigration season 1897/98, an average of 1,800 only per annum was introduced. At the present moment the indentured immigrants on the sugar estates are being considerably reduced by the termination of the indenture period of large numbers, and those being introduced do not adequately fill the place of the numbers that are getting free. At the present moment those that are being introduced are just about sufficient to balance the number that return yearly to India. You will therefore see, Your Excellency, that this question to the sugar planters is a very serious and very important one. They view with grave alarm the impossibility of obtaining the labour they require at the time they require it, and at the rates of wages they can afford to pay. Their willingness to pay two-thirds of the cost of introducing immigrants as against one-third paid during the last three years, and the fact that they have readily consented to pay one-half of the cost of return passages, must prove, without a doubt, the great need there is, at the present moment, of obtaining a further supply of labour. I am sure, Your Excellency, you will fully recognize that population is required, and that with a decreasing population or a stationary population and an industry that barely pays its way, the revenues of the government must suffer; whereas with abundant population and a staple industry that more than holds its own, the government revenues must very considerably benefit. I hope, Your Excellency, you will, in pursuance of a broad and statesmanlike policy, use your influence to assist this colony in getting the population that it so much needs, and the sugar estates in getting the labour which they so much require. The free people have many avenues of labour open to them and their conditions of life are extremely easy. It is on indentured labour that the sugar estates must rely for that steady and continuous labour which is absolutely necessary for economic and profitable working. There may be many who hold that there is abundant population here, but that population is not available when it is most required on the estates. The sugar estates, when requiring canes to be cut, sugar to be made, and numerous necessary works undertaken, are utterly unable to get labour, the free labourers having their own work to attend to. I speak from personal experience: to obtain the labour necessary the planters' work is hampered and great loss is thereby sustained. It is only by having a certain amount of labourers who will work the six days in the week that estates can be carried on in a profitable and successful manner.

CO 111/504, Sendall to Chamberlain, no. 206, 23 June 1898, encl

---

It is astounding how quickly colonial officials and other elements in the ruling class danced to the planters' tune. The Governor becomes an instant advocate of more indentured labourers, and he skilfully parades the supposed broader colonial benefits, beyond the partisan interests of sugar. Governor Sendall writes:

> There is undoubtedly a great want of population here; anything which may increase the population will greatly assist the ultimate development of the colony. It is also true, as stated by the deputation, that the indenture system is the only means hitherto devised of accustoming East Indian

immigrants to the methods of agriculture and the conditions of life in this colony, and of training them to become self-reliant and capable of maintaining themselves after the termination of their indentures. I also have reason to believe that there is greater difficulty at the present time than formerly existed in obtaining the services of free or unindentured labourers, although it is at present uncertain whether this will continue, as the term of service of the great majority of the large number of immigrants introduced in the three years ending 1894–95 will expire this year and in 1899, and the number of free labourers will be proportionately increased.

CO 111/504, Sendall to Chamberlain, no. 206, 23 June 1898

Bechu's invariable ally, *The Daily Chronicle*, soon joins the debate solidly in favour of a continuation of Indian indentureship, even suggesting a reduction of the planters' contribution. This bolsters the plantocracy's case and underlines their resilience and enduring power to define and shape the colonial condition.

> . . . we in British Guiana are all agreed as to the essential importance of immigration [Indian indentureship] to our staple industry and if Trinidad, with its conspicuous division of opinion on the subject, is to be assured of the continuance of immigration for the next two or three years, British Guiana which agrees on this matter with a unanimity unattainable upon any other subject, should receive at least equal consideration . . . *The Chronicle* has pointed out time and again, the value of the East Indian immigrant is not confined to the sugar industry. He is an important factor in the progress of the whole colony, actually and still more potentially, and without a steady stream of East Indian coolies pouring into the country, the reservoirs of labour – not for the sugar industry merely but for every other undertaking started for the development of the country's resources – will be dried up. This consideration does not apply in the case of Trinidad, where a reasonable degree of prosperity and a fair variety of resources remove the necessity for sticking out into new avenues of industrial activity. But in British Guiana, with our one industry and our abundant opportunities for creating others, the argument is of the utmost importance. If the Imperial Government desires this colony to remain what Mr Stead once

called it – England's miserable holding in the north of South America – well and good, immigration may be stopped as soon as they please. But if British Guiana is to go forward, then it must have labour and a great part of that labour must be indentured . . . [The Imperial Government] is pledged to assist the colonial sugar industry and the West Indian colonies generally and to protect them against the effects of bounty-fed competition. They will not impose countervailing duties, and for that we do not see that they are to be blamed. They have tried to mitigate or abolish the bounty evil by international action, and have just failed for the second time in ten years. It now remains for them to redeem their promise in some way. That way, in the case of British Guiana, should be to give all the assistance possible in connection with coolie immigration. If needs be, let the Imperial Government bear one-third of the cost, the Colonial Government another, and the sugar estates the remaining share, and if the Indian Government must be permitted to insist upon the return passage, let the Imperial Government assume that liability for a term of years.

Leader, *The Daily Chronicle*, 12 July 1898

Bechu responds immediately to *The Daily Chronicle*'s unequivocal support for Indian indentureship. Disconcerted though he probably is by this, he is no less strident in his opposition to immigration. [Bechu's address in this letter is that of A. Rohoman and Co, probably his Indian employer.]

Bechu (Lot 14, Water St, Georgetown) to the Editor, *The Daily Chronicle*:

Sir, When perusing your leading article this morning [12 July], concerning the continuance of East Indian immigration to this colony, it occurred to me that if you make as desperate an effort to have the defects in our present immigration scheme remedied or modified, you might succeed in getting the Government of India to relent and give Demerara, for her very importunity sake, as many more immigrants as she needs to keep her a going concern. It is eminently a case for sensible and conciliatory action on both sides.

Before the Planters' Association convenes a public meeting for the purpose you suggest, they must first learn to make the lot of the coolies already in the colony as comfortable for them as circumstances will admit. Better by far, stop the introduction of Indians altogether than to bring them this distance and then cast them adrift, as so many have been, after taking their life's blood out of them. Had it not been for the Salvation Army Shelter, and Mr Alexander's [Ghurib Das'] 'Home', hundreds of them would to this day have been knocking about the streets as they were wont to do before those institutions came into existence.

The Daily Chronicle, 13 July 1898

Bechu's opposition to immigration is not diminished by the power of his detractors. He forthrightly challenges *The Daily Chronicle*'s position, arguing that the planters have not honoured their obligations to the indentured labourers in their "Shylock-like" pursuit of profits.

Bechu (Georgetown) to the Editor, *The Daily Chronicle*:

Sir, In the concluding portion of this morning's leading article, I was truly ashamed to see you again 'harp on such a mouldered string' as we have had drummed into our ears ever since Mr Chamberlain has declined to impose a countervailing duty on sugar, viz: *Cheap and reliable labour for the planters*, and you also reproduced a somewhat lengthy article from *The Outlook* on the same subject in which the writer – an Anglo-West Indian, of course – says that 'were it not for [the] cheap labour of the East Indian coolie, West Indian sugar would long ago have gone under.' The description of labour this gentleman talks of, Sir, is cheap enough in all conscience, but I do assure you, the Demerara planter 'won't be happy till he gets it' brought down to starvation point by glutting the labour market with indentured immigrants, out of whom Shylock-like he takes the pound of flesh to make cent per cent profit, as his slave-loving predecessors used to do when sugar was king. Although the Government of India permit these useful people to come to this colony under a stringent contract to receive a *shilling* a day, for a day of *seven* hours, yet as I stated in my written evidence which is recorded at page 131, Appendix C, Volume II, of the *Report of the West India Royal Commissioners*, the unfortunate wretches do not earn that wage although they are forced to work 'by the sweat of their brow' long beyond the time fixed by law – the weekly pay lists will prove the truth of this statement, but who is there that will take the pains to verify the fact? The Immigration Agents know it full well, but so long as they receive their salaries regularly they do not seem to care a jot whether the coolie gets his statutory wage or not.

If the planters were alive to their own interests and dealt with their coolies like rational beings, they would find that they could get these intelligent and tractable people to work honestly and cheerfully for them without the supervision of tyrannical drivers – that designation suits those fellows to a 'T' – (who are chosen by the arbitrary will of managers) for whom the coolies have not the slightest respect, but to whom a stubborn and unwilling obedience is rendered, simply because the poor devils do not like the idea of being sent to jail as common criminals.

The drivers, Sir, are not bound to the coolie by any ties which he considers sacred or honourable, and as it occasionally happens disputes take place which at times amount to mutiny. Is it any wonder then that a coolie who has worked out his five years, tries his luck on some other estate, or else comes to town to swell our army of jobbers, preferring to 'fill his belly with the husks that the swine do not eat' to a life of slavery in a colony which boasts of being a Christian colony?

There are one or two points, Sir, in 'Anglo-West Indian's' article which should not be allowed to pass unchallenged, but I have already trespassed too much on your valuable space. His statement, however, that the coolie 'can claim to be sent back to Calcutta, and the government dare not say him nay', is all *gammon* for there are many to prove that they have been to the depot to register their names, but have been turned out on some pretext or another.

The Daily Chronicle, 27 **August 1898**

Bechu's fearlessness in taking on the goliaths of privilege was extraordinary; his tenacity of purpose, also, was unassailable. He finds a new way of advancing the merits of free labour:

Bechu (Georgetown) to the Editor, *The Daily Chronicle*:

Sir, It affords me very great pleasure to forward for reproduction in your widely circulated paper the accompanying paragraph concerning the late

Sir Michael McTurk . . . :

> A superior man who saw that it would be impossible to keep the freed people in a state of half-liberty, called apprenticeship. A rich and experienced planter, *he did not fear to appeal to free labour*, and the result crowned his boldness. The initiative which he took on that occasion gave him the envied title of *Knight*. Never was distinction better merited. Yet, what was not of less value in his eyes was that by it he obtained a popularity to which no European in this colony ever reached before. *Solely through that popularity he always had more labourers than he had need of.* When the planters generally were driven to expedients to procure labour, he was able, *without the least effort*, to produce in 1842, on his two contiguous plantations, *Montrose* and *Felicity, 700 hogsheads* (560,000 kilograms) of sugar. The high favour which he enjoys with the freed class proves that the African race, so maligned by prejudiced men, has at least the sufficiently rare value of wisdom [Bechu's emphases].

The above, Sir, has been culled from a little book* which was written by a Frenchman so far back as 1843, when this stick-in-the-mud colony was in its transition stage from slavery to liberty, and I think it clearly shows that if our present day planters were to 'go and do likewise' instead of begging and praying for more *indentured* labourers, without whom *they say* it is impossible for them to work their estates, they will have gained a great point. It is useless, Sir, for them to depend any longer for their prosperity upon a flow of foreign labour which costs an enormous sum annually, and may at any time be stopped.

[The planter] must really strive to enter into the feelings of the labourers they have on the spot who they should endeavour to conciliate; and whatever differences there may be in social standing or enlightenment between the employer and employee, if there were a common ground upon which each could stand, it would tend to conciliate the weaker party. The stronger *ought* to be the first to come forward and invite co-operation. To be plainer, they must 'stoop to conquer' – and if they only do that, they will prove in the stern reality of everyday life, what the famous Lily Langtry does in her favourite play, that it is possible to 'stoop with grace and conquer with a smile'!

---

*A Treatise on Slavery by M. Felix Milliroux of Paris, translated from the French by the Rev J.R.S. McFarlane of Salem Chapel, Lodge, Demerara.

The Daily Chronicle, **30 August 1898**

Unmasking the Plantocracy: Bechu, Indentureship and 'King Sugar'

Bechu, like his compatriot Joseph Ruhomon ['East Indian Descendant'], was especially mindful of the feelings of Africans in British Guiana on Indian indentureship and its ramifications. He would have empathized with some of the anti-immigration thoughts of Dr J.M. Rohlehr, a prominent African leader from Berbice, communicated to the West India Royal Commission in February 1897.

Dr J.M. Rohlehr to The West India Royal Commission, 4 February 1897, Memorandum on Labour Questions:

Gentlemen, . . . I am a native of the colony, a medical practitioner, and, by virtue of my profession, I come very much in contact with the poorer and labouring classes. Knowing that the time at your disposal is limited, I venture to submit to you my opinion on some of the subjects that engage your attention, and, though you may not have time to call me before you, yet these notes may be of some use to you.

My father being a planter, I was early taught to take an interest in all that concerned sugar making. I began my career as an overseer, and for years I was engaged on several different estates. With few exceptions, I have invariably found the black people willing labourers, and they are much more to be relied on than coolie labour. In spite of the large reduction in wages, if the people were encouraged, they could be got to work at almost any price. During my electioneering campaign for the seat of financial representative for the country of Berbice in the general election just closed [1896], I found that in all the large villages adjoining sugar estates there is a strong feeling against the planters. The complaint is that the Managers would not give the [black] people work. When the Managers are compelled, that is, when they have such work that the coolies cannot do so well, or when they are pressed for more labourers, then they give the people only two or three days' work in each week. Now, as prices are so low, two or three days' work is not sufficient to keep a working man, and so he goes from estate to estate in search of work, leaving his home on Sunday afternoon and returning on the next Sunday morning.

A good deal of black labour is lost to the estates from the want of knowledge on the part of the overseers, who are generally men that have not been sufficiently long in the colony to understand the disposition of the people. The black labourer has to house himself and family, pay his medical adviser, contribute to the support of his church, school his children, and clothe himself decently; he feeds himself much better than the coolie. The coolie is supplied with a house, doctor and medicine, schooling for his children, and he has a protector in the immigration depot. It is plain that the black labourer must require more to keep him than the coolie; moreover, one black labourer can do as much work as two or three coolies, and yet not infrequently he is given only such work as will prevent him earning any more than a coolie.

Looking at the large outlay for the importation of immigrants, the upkeep of the immigration department, medical department, dwellings, medicine, and back passage, I am convinced that it is unnecessary to continue to import more coolies. If a portion of the money spent on the items enumerated above were used in paying the black people a fair price for their labour, there would be an abundant supply of black labour on the sugar estates, for the black man prefers remaining near home than going to the goldfields. I have never found in my experience as an overseer that the black people have refused to work where the price offered them has been reasonable. Managers and overseers have grown into the habit of driving the people away when they ask for an advance on the prices offered, and of telling them that coolies will do the work; but, as a matter of fact, coolies find the task so hard that they cannot earn more than 3 or 4 shillings a week. In this particular I quite endorse Bechu's statement.

In former years an overseer served from eight to ten years before he was considered fit to manage an estate, now three to four years' service is considered sufficient to entitle an overseer to assume the management. This brings me to the question of management.

In my opinion there is a lack of careful supervision of fieldwork on the part of Managers and overseers, who are generally satisfied with riding on middle walks and side lines more than with visiting the inner parts of the fields and spending sufficient time in them to see that the work is faithfully performed. This is perhaps attributable to the fact that overseers and Managers, in some cases of only a few years' stay in the colony, are unable to stand the scorching rays of a tropical sun, and who therefore do their best to get away as fast as possible. I am of the opinion that native overseers will prove of greater value to the estates than Europeans. A few Managers realize this fact, and I will be astonished if their estates do not give a better return . . .

Report of the West India Royal Commission [1897], Appendix C.– Part II, section 170

The Daily Chronicle, however, had become such a vigorous proponent of immigration that they envisaged unlimited Indian immigration as the instrument for quickening the development impulse of British Guiana, "striking out along new and neglected avenues of industrial activity". This would have antagonized Africans in the colony.

> ... The value of the coolie to Demerara is not confined to the upkeep of the staple industry – there are other special and peculiar reasons why he should be induced to permanently settle in this colony. As *The Chronicle* has time and again pointed out, the East Indian constitutes an important factor in the progress of the country generally. We must look to them ultimately to supply the initiative which will result in the formation of new agricultural enterprises and the consequent establishment of a peasantry. His presence is necessary if the reservoirs of labour are not to become exhausted, and if the cultivated area in the colony is not to be allowed to contract. British Guiana is in this unfortunate position, that owing to causes purely physiological, which it is unnecessary now to discuss, it does not possess a naturally increasing population, so that if the colony is to go forward and expand, the deficiency must be made good by immigration. For that purpose no better material can be procured than the East Indian labourer, who is taken from a position 'always terribly near the brink of starvation', and whose life in India is chronically threatened by famine and plague. These stern conditions have perhaps inured the coolie to those habits of frugality and industry which make his sojourn in British Guiana profitable to himself and at the same time serviceable to the colony ... As a rule those coolies who have not availed themselves of the opportunities offered for returning to their native country have turned out useful and prosperous members of the community. Thus, today, we find growing up a thriving East Indian population who promise soon to possess a considerable share of the wealth of the colony, and who possess a standard of intelligence which will ultimately secure for them a rightful influence in public affairs. The creole coolies inherit the industry of their parents, have a greater spending capacity, and because of their closer acquaintance with the conditions that surround them, they are more alert to avail themselves of the facilities ... for settling on the land and earning a substantial livelihood by raising cattle and tilling the soil ... If no limit were set to the number of immigrants the colony is permitted to introduce annually

– if, in other words, the application of the planters for labourers were granted to the full – a strong impulse would soon be given in the direction of development and progress. With a large labouring population in our midst there would arise the necessity for striking out along new and neglected avenues of industrial activity – a movement which in the long run would prove of far greater benefit to the colony at large than the awkward expedient of countervailing bounty-fed beet sugar at home.

Leader, *The Daily Chronicle*, 21 January 1899

To bolster its position on 'coolie' immigration, *The Daily Chronicle* reproduces an article from *The Morning Post* (London). It advocates the abolition of return passages as well as more Indian immigration to halt the slide into extinction of sugar, while noting the progress of Indians in British Guiana as landowners and cattle rearers.

One of the last things that Lord Curzon of Kedleston did before he left for India was to promise consideration for the subject of coolie emigration from India to the British West Indies. It is thought by many in this country that there is no necessity to import native labour from India, but those who know the facts of the case are well aware that if this importation be stopped a further burden would fall on the sugar planter, who but for this addition to his labour supply might have to abandon the cultivation of the cane. Not only does the coolie make money while he is in the West Indies, but he saves money, and those who do not return to India when their time is up buy property and cattle. In British Guiana at the present time some of the largest cattle holders are time-expired coolies. They own landed property and become absorbed in the general population. In short, the great majority of them do not desire to return to their native country, and it would be a graceful act on the part of the Indian Government to consent to the abolition of passage money in future contracts with the immigrants. The coolies themselves do not require the assistance nor do they ask for it; and even at the present time they are called on to pay a portion of their passage money. But what the planters want is to be relieved of any liability in the matter at all. And, seeing that the importation of labour is a necessity, and the coolies do not care about going back, it seems only reasonable that the Indian Government should give way, and abolish this extra tax on the production of cane sugar.

The Daily Chronicle, 26 January 1899

A local correspondent agrees with *The Morning Post* that Indian labour is crucial to sugar, but rejects its call for the abolition of the return passage. He contends that the "coolieman's" progress is a personal achievement: his thrift and abstemious living enable him to save out of meagre wages. Bechu would have concurred.

'Demerarian' to the Editor, *The Daily Chronicle*:

The contributor of that article says that it is an important step to import Indian labourers, and were it not for that, a further burden would fall on the sugar planters, which would probably lead to the financial abandonment of cane. I agree with him on this and confirm his statement by repeating one of his lines, 'the importation of Indian labourers is a necessity,' not only as estate labourers, but as colonizers, agriculturalists and hearty proprietors. If the importation of coolie labour is a necessity, do you think it is right to rob them of their free return passage? 'Coolies', he says, 'not only make money, but save money in the West Indies, and in British Guiana some of the largest [cattle] holders are time-expired coolies.' I have no reason to doubt this, because all my doubts were cleared by the report of the banks . . . that the coolie depositors and deposits are materially increasing yearly, but I would like to explain how it came about . . . coolies, as a rule, belt their waists as tight as they possibly can to save a little money to buy a cow, and however small the amount may be it is deposited in the banks, and owing to the increase of their numbers annually the amount of coolie deposits in the banks must be directly proportionate. But how sad and shameful it is for planters to complain of the want of labour when they are not prepared to pay for it. I know that the weekly earnings of the strongest and most industrious coolie man don't exceed 6 shillings, and he is very fortunate if a part is not stopped. If coolies were like Europeans or were accustomed to wear clothing, the depositors would be very few. We must not be envious of a coolieman because he takes a hundred dollars of our money home; we must first know how economical he was, and what misery he must have undergone to save it. In short, we must congratulate baboo for his denial and accumulation, and endeavour to help him in his immigrant career.

The Daily Chronicle, 29 January 1899

The Daily Chronicle, on learning in March 1899 that the Secretary of State for the Colonies has approved a quota of 5,000 indentured labourers for British Guiana in 1899–1900, offers a dissertation on the centrality of Indians to the development of the colony. Their potential as settlers is emphasized: "the coolies take congenitally to agricultural pursuits." (Bechu's silence is protracted; he is immersed in the libel case against him, between April and October 1899 [see Part II, Section A, Chapter Seven].)

... There are some ... who believe that if all the money now spent in the maintenance of our extensive immigration system were used to increase the wages of the native working classes, the inducement offered would be sufficiently strong to break down that prejudice against agricultural labour which is one of the more regrettable features of our social life [*see* Dr J.M. Rohlehr's memorandum]. But the majority, whether their interests are planting or commercial, hold a different opinion; and we agree with them in the view that to prevent the collapse of the sugar industry, as well as to supply the incentive for development in new industrial directions, we require our indigenous population to be supplemented from without. It certainly does appear to be a peculiar anomaly ... that ... we should 'have to send thousands of mile for labourers, whilst the majority of the natives are sitting idle'. The British radical of the Labouchere cast considers it intolerable. He characterizes contract labour as another form of slavery, and one of his habitual questions is 'what would the British people think if the colliers of Lancashire and Lanark were superseded by foreign labourers on the sole ground that the latter could be had for lower wages?' The attitude of this type of politician proceeds from a confounding of the conditions, social and climatic, in the tropics with those in England. We do not propose, however, to enter into an apology for the immigration system. But so far as British Guiana is concerned there are special causes which make it necessary. There is, first of all, the indisputable aversion to fieldwork shown by the masses of the people. It may be due to the 'elevating' influences of education, to inherent idleness, to nature's overbountifulness, or to inadequate wages; all these reasons have from time to time been offered in explanation. At any rate, it is admitted that only through the agency of contract labour can a constant and reliable supply be obtained for agricultural purposes in this colony. Now, agriculture is fated to be the mainstay of British Guiana, and for the time being the only form it takes is sugar cultivation and manufacture. There is no other industry to take the place of sugar, a circumstance which is the greatest source of mischief to us at the present time. If we had a peasant proprietary like Jamaica, or a number of alternative industries like Trinidad, the discontinuance of immigration would be scarcely alarming, but for the time that our condition is so closely bound up with sugar, as long as the native labourer prefers to remain unemployed rather than accept what he regards as an inadequate wage, the planters must be allowed to look elsewhere for their labour supply; and any act of the Colonial Office or the local government which interferes with that right would be against the interests of the country. There is also the prospect that these large annual supplies of coolie immigrants will eventually serve to redeem the colony from the predicament into which the exclusive cultivation of the one product has brought it. We regard the permanent settlement of the coolies in the country after the term of their industrial residence has expired as one of the most important and far-reaching movements now at work in our midst. The census returns for 1841 showed that there were 343 East Indians in British Guiana; at the end of 1897 it was estimated that there were about 114,500 out of a total population of 286,484. And this number would have been much larger if the efforts now being made by the authorities to induce the immigrants to remain in the colony had been commenced years earlier. The special significance attaching to this great increase lies in the fact that the coolies take congenitally to agricultural pursuits, their highest ambition being to possess a small area of land and a few cattle. Frugal and thrifty, peaceful and uncomplaining, with deep-rooted home ties and fond of his children, the East Indian promises to do what the black population seem incapable of doing – of supplying the initiative needed to beneficially occupy a portion at least of the vast cultivable territory within the boundaries of British Guiana. As has been observed by Dr Morris [agricultural adviser to the Norman Commission of 1897], this colony, though equal in size to Austria, has an area under cultivation no larger than the county of Surrey. Those, therefore, who are honestly anxious of seeing the country develop along the surest and most abiding lines of progress and prosperity will have little hesitation in approving of the introduction, while the colony has still the resources, of the greatest number of East Indians possible. It is morally certain that the time is fast approaching when the Colonial Office will close India as a source of supply against this colony, and unless we have then a population containing the potentiality of natural increase the result must be retrogression. On the other hand, it is evident that so long as we continue to import labour, the colony is in a measure responsible for that growing population of unemployed East Indians who crowd the streets of the city [Georgetown]. It sounds a remarkable anomaly to be introducing 5,000 labourers whilst we have nearly that number living a parasitical, unproductive existence in the capital of the colony; yet we confess this class is very difficult . . . to deal with [satisfactorily]. For the most part they are the dregs of the immigrant population, disinclined or unfitted to work on the plantations, and of little value to the estates' proprietors. They prefer to earn a precarious half-a-bitt [4 cents] a day in town rather than get the steady wage and free shelter, with the hard and constant work, of the sugar plantation. Well-directed enterprise on the part of the authorities might, we think, save many of this class from degenerating into a condition of idleness and uselessness, with the prospect of being inmates of the Alms House.

Leader, *The Daily Chronicle*, 28 March 1899

The Argosy, the unabashedly proplanter weekly, sees Indian indentureship as a blessing to the whole colony – planter and 'coolie' alike; it pronounces the system as virtually flawless and prays for its continuance. (Bechu is still silent; his libel case drags on.)

But for coolie labourers, British Guiana would in all probability have been by this time a mere geographical expression, the place itself of no value and no interest to the civilized world. As it is, its sugar industry has developed, the colony has flourished, and the coolies are already not only the most important section of the labouring population, but an important and wealthy section of the middle class, promising in course of time to be the chief landed proprietors in the colony. The system has withstood all the many attacks that have been made against it, and it has always been the case that the more malicious the attack and the closer the investigation into the alleged iniquities, the more clearly the integrity of the system as between employer and employed, and its merits in general, have been brought into prominence. It may now be regarded as beyond the influence of adverse criticism, and it is not too much to hope that through a continuance of the system for several years to come the colony will develop into a far more important sugar country than it is at present, and the East Indians into a still richer and more influential section of the people.

Leader, *The Argosy*, 22 April 1899

The Daily Chronicle's contention is that neither the abolition of bounty on beet sugar nor the imposition of countervailing duties on bounty-fed beet by the British Government offers a solid future for the colony's sugar industry. Its viability must be predicated on cheap, reliable, indentured Indian labour which would reduce production costs and render cane sugar competitive. The paper is unequivocal: no "sweetheart Sammy" ['coolie'], no sugar.

A number of planters here are of opinion that the future welfare of the sugar industry depends on either the abolition of the beet bounties, or the levying of countervailing duties on bountied beet. We were never more mistaken in any matter than we are in this, as, although the beet bounties place the beet sugar manufacturer on his legs a bit, it does not give him such terrible odds against the cane sugar maker as is generally supposed. If we can export the best possible produce as to command the highest prices possible, our industry will live in spite of the presence of beet bounties, or the absence of countervailing duties, provided we can keep the cost of producing a ton of sugar to what it is now. Much more depends on the continuance of indentured East Indian immigration, than our bounties or countervailing duties, and, while shouting zealously against the bounty business, we have lost sight of this.

Years of testing have convinced us that no other labourer than the indentured coolie is so well suited for the prosecution of the industry, and that with him it lives or dies, as from him and him alone we can obtain the constant supply of labour at fair rates so necessary for the welfare of what is still our backbone, and very nearly the only industry on which we can rely.

. . . We are so accustomed to seeing the indentured coolie going regularly to work day after day that we accept his presence as a matter of course, instead of as the greatest blessing we have. [W]e would find if we tried it, almost impossible to draw a picture in our mind's eye of what the state of affairs would be if we were so unfortunate as to have East Indian immigration discontinued. Better – far better it would be for us, if the bounties on beet sugar were to be increased, than for this evil to befall us. Imagine our labour supply from India stopped and our planters dependent solely on free labour; then try to imagine the inevitable battle between labour and capital that must end in the defeat of the latter; as the free labourer with the goldfields at his back cannot be starved out. The raising of the labourers' pay can have but one effect, and that is to increase the cost of producing sugar with no accompanying rise in the market price. Our planters will then either have to close their factory doors or manufacture sugar to sell at a loss. It is obvious they will do the former. Then away goes our sugar industry – it cannot live without its sweetheart Sammy. No, the free labourer will do as a backstay, but the moment we use him as shrouds, our masts go by the board.

The Daily Chronicle, 19 May 1899

Bechu is still silent but, in July 1899, two correspondents to *The Daily Chronicle* challenge the government's ineptitude in inducing Indians to settle in British Guiana and their obsession with 'King Sugar'.

'Bona Fide' to the Editor, *The Daily Chronicle*:

. . . Mr Blair, in his lecture before the Royal Agricultural and Commercial Society, says: 'Rice can be grown in British Guiana quite as well, and perhaps more profitably than in Ceylon, and I shall not be surprised, if, in the near future, we are able to export large quantities of rice.' So we shall, if the time-expired immigrants are given land when they want it. But before the government has the lands ready for these people, many will leave the colony merely for the dilatoriness of the government in not having the lands ready for them. I observed in *The Berbice Gazette* about a week ago, that about 100 immigrants left the Corentyne to sail by the ship *Rhone*. From what I can hear, few would leave that district were they provided with suitable lands to make a livelihood. It is a great pity to lose such valuable labourers if they can be kept in the colony at all; and their readiness to take up land when offered to them, shows the tendency to make this colony their home. When will the Governor and his Advisory Council rise to the emergency? Not, I expect, until we have lost thousands who could have been secured, and thousands spent on returning them to India . . .

The Daily Chronicle, 14 July 1899

'V.V.' to the Editor, *The Daily Chronicle*:

Sir, Are you to continue as before, pushing everything on one side for sugar? Surely the sugar industry is pampered quite enough at present, to the injury of other prospective industries, without quite killing them all . . . the time has come when sugar must not arrogate to itself the supreme control of all below it. None but a fool will wish injury to the sugar industry, but they will be equally fools if they allow sugar to crush out everything else.

The Daily Chronicle, 28 July 1899

The momentum in favour of Indian immigration is relentless. In September 1899, *The Daily Chronicle* carries an article, "The Coolie in Guiana", which underlines their merits as settlers while extolling the advances made by Indian women in the colony.

Without doubt the indentured East Indian is the most important man in the colony, for on his very presence depends the future welfare of the sugar industry. He is the back-stay of the industry, and to term him the hope of Guiana would not be exaggerating.

To keep the coolie here should therefore be the aim of those in power, and a land grant, instead of a return passage, would be the surest means of making the colony attractive to him. In this way, besides being the upkeep of the sugar industry, the coolie could be used to open up the country, and to develop the rice industry. We need a class of smallholders, and as the East Indian is possessed of most of the qualities which go to make up a thrifty farmer, we might do worse than give him an opportunity to settle here for good . . .

The average coolie is very thrifty, and even before the term of his indenture has expired contrives to save, what to him amounts to an independence, and to certainly more than he would be able to do in India during his whole lifetime . . . He has no millstone round his neck in the shape of relatives to support, and if he is a married man his wife instead of being an expense to him is on the contrary a source of revenue, for she receives a fair wage, as do also his children.

The East Indian woman in Guiana is an emancipated being, and is subject to few of the terrors and none of the cruelties which attend her everyday existence in India. The fact that she receives her wages in her own hands at the pay table, gives her a feeling of independence, and renders her husband less domineering than he would be in India.

The women who come from southern India are a bad lot, and much given to be faithless to their husbands. If it were possible for those who pull the strings of immigration in India to send us only northerners, we would have fewer cases of wife murder.

The Daily Chronicle, 24 September 1899

The Corentyne Coast (Berbice) was salubrious, less malarial, with good soils. It attracted many "time-expired" Indian rice growers, cattle herders, and market gardeners; but their progress was impeded by the government's unresponsiveness to frequent assertions of the necessity for a comprehensive drainage and irrigation scheme in the district – an obduracy fed by the plantocracy's fear of minor industries, potential beacons for estate labour. Bechu's enforced silence continued, but several correspondents expressed views on the problems of Indian settlers which were compatible with his. Even the conservative *Argosy* had been able to empathize, in early 1898, although it concluded with the familiar paean to sugar:

... in the past, as at the present day, the great obstacle in the way of those who were disposed to grow some exportable produce other than sugar, was the drainage question, it being quite beyond the means of any member of the farmer class to empolder [drain and irrigate] a tract of waste land, or to maintain for any length of time the dams and trenches necessary to keep empoldered land in order. The truth by this time ought to be known and acknowledged by every observant colonist, that the front lands are not suitable for the cotter or farmer, unless he owns or leases land situated within an empoldered district, the drainage and water supply of which are kept up at the expense of the government or some man or firm in the possesion of money. A most desirable arrangement, if it could be arrived at, would be a portion of a sugar estate held in lease by farmers, who, having their drainage and water supply guaranteed, could give their time to the planting of economic products without the dread that the next wet season or high springs would flood their fields and ruin their young cultivation by either fresh or salt water ... Until a system is in vogue under which the farmer will get protection from the sea and the savannah [the flooded backlands], the higher lands on the river banks, with their natural drainage, are the most promising spots for him to select. Already the rice industry, the development of which has been characterized by unusual rapidity, is being threatened with disastrous effects from inroads of the sea or the bush water or the stagnant rain water, owing to the rice growers having selected for their farms, which, at one time empoldered and drained is now unfurnished with either dams or canals ... the most industrious rice-grower, be he black man or white man, Eastern or Western, will get disheartened and abandon the industry when he finds, as he must find on empoldered land with no water supply, that his crop, perhaps on the eve of maturity, is liable to be totally destroyed by untimely flooding, or parched to death because there is no water to irrigate it at the right time. The longer the problem of how best to employ the coastlands is regarded, the clearer will it appear that the one cultivation for which they are suited is sugar, 'the natural and legitimate industry' of the colony, to quote the words of the Secretary of State [for the colonies] ...

Leader, *The Argosy*, 5 February 1898

The planters' obsession that the success of the rice culture could be a magnet, drawing 'coolies' irretrievably from the sugar estates, is unassuageable. So even when they faintly allude to the Indian's fortitude in adapting rice to the precarious coastland of British Guiana, amidst monumental hydraulic problems, they are quick to pronounce on the inevitable futility of the effort, given their supposed incapacity for industry, self-reliance, or communal responsibility. No mention is made of the state's inviolable subsidy to 'King Sugar' through Indian indentureship, nor for the need of a fractionally compensatory aid to small farmers, by way of drainage and irrigation. *The Argosy*'s agricultural retrospect for 1897 and 1898, written by R.G. D[uncan], a prominent planter, epitomizes this stance:

> The only minor industry that has made any notable advance [in 1897] is that of rice cultivation, and this owes its progress almost entirely to the encouragement and support offered it by sugar planters. At least half the area under rice in this colony now, is situated on sugar estates . . . The rice industry has come to stay, and all the rice required for consumption in the colony will be produced locally. There is not much hope of a paying export trade, as it will be difficult to compete with the cheaper product of India, where labour is one-sixth of the cost it is in this colony . . . The growing of rice is unfortunately largely carried on under precarious conditions. Except on sugar estates, land under cultivation can seldom be irrigated during spells of drought, and crops will often be lost in consequence. In many cases no effective provision of any kind has been made for drainage, and crops will suffer from excessive flooding during heavy rains. It is difficult to convince our peasantry of the necessity of combining to execute works for the common good. They trust everything to Providence, and are slow to learn that 'heaven helps those who help themselves' . . . The dearness, scarcity and unreliableness of labour, forms a great stumbling block to any endeavours made to start a new industry, and entirely prevents the introduction of new capital. The bulk of our peasantry is not sufficiently industrious or self-reliant to start small permanent cultivations on their own account, and until the colony possesses a teeming population, I fear little improvement may be looked for, as with a kindly soil and climate, the conditions of life are extremely easy, and ambition rarely disturbs the even tenor of the peasantry's existence.

R.G. D[uncan], 'Agricultural Retrospect for 1897', *The Argosy*, 8 January 1898

Most [sugar] estates suffered during the year [1898] from an inadequate supply of labour, and in many instances where extension of cultivation was contemplated, it was found injudicious to attempt it, on account of the irregularity and uncertainty of the labour supply. For the 1898 immigration season, the government sanctioned the introduction of only 2,400 East Indian immigrants, a number quite insufficient to meet the labour requirements of estates . . . It is quite evident that in the future development of British Guiana, the East Indian will be a dominant and important factor.

The rice industry is daily attracting free resident labourers from the sugar estates, and quite 10,000 coolies are now engaged in that industry. During the coming year the indentures of around 5,000 immigrants will expire, and to maintain the labour supply necessary for the sugar estates at least 5,000 East Indian immigrants will have to be introduced annually. Even this number will not be sufficient to admit of cultivation being increased to any material extent . . . It was thought by many people that the labour requirements of this colony would be met and its resources developed by the introduction of immigrants from the more populous of the neighbouring West Indian islands, but it is now generally realized and admitted that the only hope for the colony lies in the continuance of East Indian immigration.

Minor Industries

No progress can be reported with regard to minor industries during the year . . . The rice industry has not made much progress due to the fact that the bulk of it is grown under very precarious conditions, and no suitable provisions made for irrigation or drainage . . .

It was thought by some superficial observers that if land was cheap and accessible, the question of minor industries would be solved, and an industrious peasantry established along the banks of the rivers. Land is now cheap enough, and steamers are plying along the lower reaches of the rivers, but Minor Industries make no progress. Notwithstanding what self-satisfied experts who pay flying visits to this colony [the reference is to Dr Morris, agricultural adviser to the 1897 Royal Commission, a strident advocate of diversification] may assert as to the fertility of the soil and salubrity of the climate, there are few countries less adapted to the successful prosecution of small industries than British Guiana. Great extremes of drought or rainfall are experienced, the difficulties with regard to drainage are enormous, reliable labour is unprocurable, and the clearing and tilling of land are most expensive.

Hundreds of endeavours to establish small industries have ended in failure . . . it is not the simple matter many inexperienced people seem to believe. Capital, combination, persevering industry, and special training are necessary for the prosecution of any agricultural industry in this colony.

R.G. D[uncan], 'Agricultural Summary, 1898', *The Argosy*, 31 December 1898

The plantocracy see themselves as victims, betrayed by the West India Royal Commission of 1897. The report does not endorse the imposition of countervailing duties on bounty-fed beet sugar; it advocates agricultural diversification and the creation of a West Indian peasantry; it rejects the old mantra of the paramountcy of sugar, and calls for the suspension of Indian indentureship "until there is some prospect of the revival" of sugar. That is why, from 1898 onwards, the planters carry out a virtual crusade to get more indentured 'coolies' – this becomes the backbone of their strategy for resuscitation, while denigrating minor industries. For them the old equation was inviolable: no 'coolies' = no sugar; no sugar = the death of the colony (barbarism).

SUBSTITUTION OF OTHER AND PROFITABLE AGRICULTURAL INDUSTRIES FOR THE CULTIVATION OF SUGAR CANE

It may be that no industry, or series of industries, can be introduced into the West Indies which will ever completely take the place of sugar, and certainly no such result will be attained within the space of a few years, but it is of the utmost importance that no time should be lost in making a beginning of substituting other industries for the cultivation of the sugar cane.

System of Peasant Proprietors

If the sugar estates are thrown out of cultivation, it is extremely improbable and, in fact, it may be stated to be impossible, that any industry to be conducted on large estates can ever completely take its place, we have therefore no choice but to consider how means can be found to enable the mass of the population to support themselves in other ways than as labourers on estates. If work cannot be found for the labouring population on estates, they must either migrate or support themselves by cultivating small plots of land on their own account. No large industry, other than agriculture, offers any prospect of success, except possibly the gold industry in British Guiana, and when large estates cannot be profitably worked the adoption of the system of cultivation by petty proprietors is inevitable.

The labouring population in the West Indies is mainly of Negro blood, but there is also, in some of the colonies, a strong body of East Indian immigrants, and the descendants of such immigrants. The Negro is an efficient labourer, especially when he receives good wages. He is disinclined to continuous labour, extending over a long period of time, and he is often unwilling to work if the wages offered are low, though there may be no prospect of his getting higher wages from any other employer. He is fond of display, open-handed, careless as to the future, ordinarily good humoured, but exciteable and difficult to manage, especially in large numbers, when his temper is aroused.

The East Indian immigrant, ordinarily known as the coolie, is not so strong a workman, but he is a steadier and more reliable labourer. He is economical in his habits, is fond of saving money, and will turn his hand to anything by which he can improve his position.

The cultivation of the sugar cane has been almost entirely carried on in the past on large estates, but both the Negro and the coolie like to own small patches of land by which they may make their livelihood, and take a pride in their position as landholders, though in some cases they also labour at times on the larger estates, and are generally glad to have the opportunity of earning money occasionally by working on such estates, and on the construction and maintenance of roads and other public works. The existence of a class of small proprietors among the population is a source of both economic and political strength.

The settlement of the labourer on the land has not, as a rule, been viewed with favour in the past by the persons interested in sugar estates. What suited them best was a large supply of labourers, entirely dependent on being able to find work on the estates, and, consequently, subject to their control and willing to work at low rates of wages. But it seems to us that no reform affords so good a prospect for the permanent welfare in the future of the West Indies as the settlement of the labouring population on the land as small peasant proprietors; and in many places this is the only means by which the population can in future be supported [emphasis added]. The drawbacks to the system of peasant proprietors have hitherto been their want of knowledge and care in cultivation, and the habit of what is called praedial larceny. The latter term is applied to the theft of growing crops, which is said to be very prevalent. We do not believe it will disappear until such practices are universally condemned by native public opinion, which, unfortunately, does not appear to be the case at present, and in the meantime each colony must deal with the question as may seem best. The small proprietors show some desire to improve their modes of cultivation, and we shall have some suggestions to make on this subject.

But whilst we think that the governments of the different colonies should exert themselves in the direction of facilitating the settlement of the labouring population on the land, we see no objection to the system of large estates when they can be maintained under natural economic conditions. On the contrary, we are convinced that in many places they afford the best, and, sometimes, the only profitable means of cultivating certain products, and that it is not impossible for the two systems, of large estates and peasant holdings, to exist side by side with mutual advantage.

It must be recollected that the chief outside influence with which the governments of certain colonies have to reckon are the representatives of the sugar estates, that these persons are sometimes not interested in anything but sugar, that the establishment of any other industry is often detrimental to their interests, and that under such conditions it is the special duty of Your Majesty's government to see that the welfare of the general public is not sacrificed to the interest, or supposed interests, of a small but influential minority which has special means of enforcing its wishes and bringing its claims to notice [emphasis added].

Report of the West India Royal Commission [H.W. Norman, Chairman], (London: HMSO, 1897), paragraphs 111–18

BRITISH GUIANA
System of Indian Coolie Immigration

More than a third of the inhabitants are either natives of India, imported at great cost to enable sugar cultivation to be carried on, or the descendants of such immigrants. There is no doubt that, apart from employments which require special skill, there are already sufficient coolie labourers in the colony to carry on the cane cultivation and the manufacture of sugar and rum; but as the immigrant coolie is only indentured to an estate for five years he is at liberty at the end of that term to choose his own occupation, and many leave the estates and only work intermittently on them, whilst after ten years in the colony they can claim a return passage to India. There are about 72,000 coolies residing on estates, of whom nearly 20,000 are under indentures, and 44,000 not on estates nor under indentures, altogether about 116,000 persons.

A considerable proportion now remain in the colony after the expiry of their ten years' engagements, residing either on the estates or elsewhere, but it is possible that if there were any general abandonment of sugar production the whole condition of affairs in the colony would so change that there might be a general desire among the immigrants to return to India, and this would entail a very heavy expenditure. There is an agreement of opinion that the labour of the Negro is fitful and cannot always be obtained when wanted. On this ground, the planters urge that immigration should still be maintained, so as to give them at all times reliable labour, although it is admitted that the number of immigrants to be brought in may be less than formerly.

The present is not an opportune occasion for introducing a change which may hamper the sugar industry, but with the possibility of having at no remote period to send back to India large numbers of coolies, at a cost which the colony could not meet, there are strong objections to bringing fresh immigrants from India. At any rate it seems unwise, having regard to the particular circumstances of British Guiana, to bring any more until there is some prospect of the revival of the sugar industry. Meanwhile the needs of planters might be met by transferring indentured coolies from any estates that may unfortunately go out of cultivation to other estates that are still working, and it is understood that this method is already followed [emphasis added].

Alternative Industries

The report of Dr Morris shows that whilst British Guiana now depends on sugar products for the maintenance of the colony, it is certain that under the most favourable circumstances it must be a considerable number of years before other industries could be so far extended as to give employment to the number of people now employed on sugar estates or deriving their living from the sugar industry. Indeed it is hardly possible that all the other industries in the colony, apart from gold .... could for many years to come produce a return in any way equal to that which has been obtained from sugar and rum.

It would, therefore, be most desirable in the interests of the colony to maintain the production of sugar, as well as to encourage the cultivation of all the products mentioned by Dr Morris, which have been neglected in the past. Foremost among these may be named rice, coffee, cocoa, fruits, and cocoa-nuts, whilst something may be expected from attention to the forests and from cattle raising.

Rice to the value of £180,000 was imported in 1895–96 for consumption in the colony. Rice of excellent quality is already grown in British Guiana, and every effort should be made to produce locally all that is wanted of this article. Coffee and cocoa to the value of £7,560 were also imported, though there is no reason why the coffee and cocoa consumed should not also be produced there.

Report of the West India Royal Commission [1897], **paragraphs 186–91**

Advocates of minor industries (especially rice) and 'coolie' settlements are inspired by the Royal Commission Report. One correspondent, in April 1898, reports the success in husking padi at Ho-a-Hing's rice-mill in Berbice, where the Engleberg huller is introduced; and he calls for the dissemination of scientific knowledge to rice farmers.

'M' to the Editor, *The Argosy:*

... Our rice industry should be encouraged by all means. Skilled advice and information of a useful and practical kind should be disseminated by a government Agricultural Department. We should know what are the best grains to grow, when to grow them, when to reap them, when to stack and how long; and how to avoid 'sun cracks' which cause the grain to be broken in passing through the mill.

Where would we have been as a sugar-growing colony if the best machinery and the best technical knowledge had not been obtained? The rice industry is in such a favourable position now that a little useful information disseminated would be of immense advantage.

The Argosy, 16 April 1898

Even *The Argosy* recognizes that the perennial drift, with the fluctuating fortunes of the sugar industry, is not an imaginative prospect for British Guiana. But it remains a solid advocate of Indian indentureship as the foundation for the resuscitation of sugar, while becoming an unwavering campaigner for settling time-expired Indians on empoldered lands, for the creation of a viable peasantry. However, they, unlike the planters, must expect no subsidy from the State.

> . . . the settlement of the coolies on the frontlands of the colony is deserving of our most careful attention, for upon the success or failure of the scheme for settling time-expired coolies upon their own lands under cultivable conditions, depends to a great extent the future welfare of the colony. The danger the coolies are in now of becoming disheartened through the flooding of their lands in heavy rainy weather is by no means imaginary, and if it is not regarded by the government in a serious manner, the coolie settlements will soon become as profitless as the bulk of the village lands along the coast. What every acre of land on the alluvial portion of the colony [the coastland] requires, if it is to be kept in a state of cultivation, is thorough drainage; and part of a thorough drainage scheme is thorough protection of dams against tides and 'bush' water [from the backlands]. It is very hard for a number of small settlers on a large block of land to combine satisfactorily amongst themselves to maintain a drainage scheme for the whole block; and unless the whole block is included the scheme is practically useless. *The government alone can render the working of such a scheme possible: but on no account should it be done at government expense* [emphasis added]. The settlers should be made clearly to understand what the cost of the scheme would be; and how much would fall to be paid towards it by every holder of say an acre of land, before the government should undertake the scheme. The coolies being by nature industrious and disposed to agriculture will be amenable to reason if the question is carefully laid before them; and the probability is that not one will decline to become responsible for his share of the work for the common good. With drainage secured, and where possible, a supply of water, these coolie settlements are likely to become rich and profitable estates, giving the settlers a good return for the labour they spend upon them. The fertility of the coastlands is not to be questioned . . .

Leader, *The Argosy*, 21 January 1899

The Argosy returns to the subject in May 1899, contending that the government's efforts at settling time-expired Indians are still tentative, lacking imagination, such as the settlements at Helena (Mahaica) and Nigg (Corentyne). These people, the paper argues, pay their dues by their reliability to sugar estates; they deserve "special consideration"; they could become "not only the peasantry but the strongest section of the middle class".

> . . It was accepted as a postulate that the coolie would insist on going back to his native India, and consequently earnest attention was not devoted to providing means of inducing him to settle down permanently in this land. Even now when the coolie seems more and more disposed every year to remain where he is, rather than return to risk unfriendly reception in his native village in India, the government is making only half-hearted efforts to foster that disposition and to confirm the coolie in the belief that he could do better for himself by remaining here than in going back to his native land. There are two government coolie settlements so-called [Helena and Nigg], neither of which shows the masterhand of statesmanship, and on neither of them are the settlers found to be comfortable and content as are the time-expired coolies who have settled on farms, such as Novar in Mahaicony, where the land is owned by an East Indian and the conditions of tenancy arranged by himself. It is to be regretted that the Helena settlement, the latest formed and the larger of the two settlements, is not redeeming that promise of success which was looked for when it was started, and which could be assured if proper attention were paid by the government to the needs of the coolies until such time as they shall have thoroughly settled down amidst their new surroundings.
>
> In the indentured coolie we have the reliable labourer, who can render the cultivation of our sugar estates possible, and without him, the colony would soon go to ruin. He, being of such value to us, is entitled to special consideration when he becomes a time-expired man, and as his desire is towards land of his own, the government of a colony in which land is plentiful, but men are few, ought to have land prepared in a suitable way against the settlement of a people who give promise of becoming not only the peasantry but the strongest section of the middle class, in the near future . . .

Leader, *The Argosy*, 27 May 1899

Bechu's enforced silence continues, but a tradition of writing to the press, to articulate their grievances, is now established among his compatriots. In July 1899, an Indian from Berbice, Joseph Ruhomon, expands on the shortcomings of government-sponsored, 'coolie' settlements, especially a flawed land-apportionment system militating against crop diversification and the security of settlers. (Ruhomon usually uses the pseudonym, 'East Indian Descendant', in his letters to *The Daily Chronicle*.)

'East Indian' [Joseph Ruhomon] to the Editor, *The Argosy*:

Sir, A great deal has been written lately about coolie settlements, and the giving of lands to my countrymen in lieu of back passages to India. No doubt everything that has been done in connection with this matter has been done for the best, but I am of the opinion that the advice of those capable of judging best on our side have not been asked. This is a matter that ought to be settled by unbiased minds. I know what goes on behind the scenes, and I write from intimate knowledge of the facts of the case.

The people who take the lands that are offered them are ignorant of a good many things until by bitter experience they find out their mistake. The lands as given out under the present system, are not at all suitable, Sir, for the purpose of creating a peasant proprietary. The quantity may be enough, but in being fit for the purpose of growing rice only, or ground provisions (not both), discontent, I am afraid, will follow. I think everyone who forfeits his right to a return passage to India ought to have land that can supply him with both rice and ground provisions, and where he will be able, should he so desire, to build his own house and have a suitable homestead for himself and family. This is, in my opinion, the only way whereby we can establish a contented family. A splendid beginning can be made with such land as is to be seen in some parts of Essequibo and the Upper Corentyne, where reefs and savannahs run alternately across the estates. Let our time-expired immigrants be accorded the advantages I have suggested, and I have no difficulty whatever in predicting that in a reasonable number of years, the offspring of these people will form the yeomanry of the colony – the happy possessors of their own lands.

I would, therefore, strongly insist upon the lands being given out in such a way as would permanently benefit the coolies. The lands that the people get under the present system enable them to grow rice mostly, with very little provisions, but in the majority of cases they can plant nothing else but rice. Now, it should be remembered that the time they spend in growing, watching and reaping the rice is six months. They are practically kept occupied for this period only, but the other six months must be spent in idleness or search for work, precious little or none of which can be had in these days. But let them have land on which they can grow ground provisions, as well as rice, and they have something to do all the year round, capable of regularly yielding the necessaries for the family living [off the estates] and those of our countrymen who are under indenture. Many would then take advantage of working on the estates, or anywhere else where work is to be had, whilst their wives and children could watch and attend to the growing crops. The rice crop is generally reaped at the end of the year along with the sugar crop. This no doubt was the cause of the planters applying for the 5,000 immigrants [for 1899–1900].

I am aware, Sir, that it is necessary for the sugar estates to have reliable resident labour while the crop is being made; but, surely, after five years' indenture, the coolies cannot be blamed for endeavouring to better their position elsewhere and live more independently. There is room in this colony and virgin lands for double the number of immigrants introduced yearly, and I am sure, provided they are settled under favourable circumstances, they will be able to make a better living here than they can in India. In a leading article in your paper [27 May 1899, pp. 200–01], you very wisely advocated land for the people – which shows that you are aware of the necessity that exists for the settling of these time-expired immigrants, on their own freehold instead of returning them to India, which policy would largely benefit the colony, the government and my countrymen. I trust, Sir, you will continue using your powerful influence in promoting so worthy an object, and in advocating the giving out of the land on the lines I have indicated. In my opinion and the opinion of all clear-headed thinkers, it would not only be a distinct saving to the government, but a most powerful means of inducing the time-expired people to remain in the colony and contribute towards the development of its vast resources . . .

The Argosy, 22 July 1899

The centrality of empoldering potential settlements, of providing both irrigation and drainage, is underlined in the latter half of 1899, when another infamous, prolonged drought on the Corentyne Coast devastates crops and stocks. Up to the end of July, only 29 inches of rainfall are recorded, compared with 45 inches in Demerara and 50 inches in Essequibo. Meanwhile, discussions on a water supply scheme never move beyond an avalanche of theoretical propositions.

> The farms of the coolies and creoles are dried into hard-bake, which allows of no work being done upon the land . . . the ground provisions have become so scarce that the starving people are being driven by hunger to help themselves wherever a remnant of crop is to be found. The coolies are crying out to be sent back to their native land . . . The present drought is a matter which the government could not have prevented; but it should be possible to provide the farmers with a scheme for the supply of water to their farms in dry weather; and if it be possible, the digging of the necessary trenches would form an appropriate relief work. The cost of the work would have to be placed upon the land to be benefited, and reasonable time given for its repayment.

The Argosy, 19 August 1899

In October 1899, as the drought on the Corentyne Coast reaches catastrophic proportions, a *Daily Chronicle* correspondent sends his impressions, extolling the virtues of this healthy district as well as its pitfalls as an area of settlement.

> . . . there is no more promising district from Skeldon to Playa Point [the northern extremity of the alluvial coastland] than the Corentyne. His Excellency Sir Walter Sendall remarked when on his recent visit to Berbice that the coast possessed capabilities for development greater than any part of the West Indies with which he was acquainted; and no one who visits the place can fail to come away impressed with the adaptability of the soil for general cultivation. The regeneration of this colony, according to such expert authority as the West India Commission, will depend not so much upon the rehabilitation of sugar as the development of alternative industries carried on in the main by a peasantry, African or East Indian, settled on their own homesteads. It has been objected that the alluvial

littoral where the population is at present concentrated . . . is ill-suited for the profitable cultivation of any . . . product other than sugar. That idea has, however, been fairly exploded; to quote *The Times* correspondent, we have confined ourselves to sugar rather by choice than by any natural necessity [*The Daily Chronicle*, 11 October 1899]. But whatever force there may be in the objection as applied to the counties of Demerara and Essequibo, it has absolutely no application in respect to Berbice. In the first place, the physical conformation of the coastlands of the latter county is entirely different from that of any other part of the colony. Instead of a uniform mud belt extending several miles inland, we have on the Corentyne a series of sand reefs running parallel with the foreshore and sandwiched by deep belts of alluvial soil. Every rood of this land is susceptible of profitable occupation. The reefs are admirably adapted to the raising of provisions – plantains, bananas, corn, cassava, and so on; while rice can be grown on the low-lying savannah lands that lie between . . . the Corentyne enjoys advantages as an agricultural district which are not shared by any other portion of the coastlands of the colony.

Negro and Coolie Settlements

. . . It is true that less than a fifth of the land held by the Negro inhabitants can be said to be utilized to any very great advantage. These people are content to devote their farms, which are invariably too large for their requirements, to cattle raising, a most unremunerative business on the Corentyne, and what little cultivation they put their hands to is only desultory and spasmodic, designed simply to supply their own immediate wants. But on the other hand, those parts of the coastland that have been purchased within the last few years by time-expired East Indians – there are some hundreds of such settlers – are models of what small farming might and should be in this country. The success of these settlements, heavily handicapped though the coolies have been by climatic and other circumstances, is a striking proof of advisability of securing our immigrant population as a permanent factor in our midst. The plots are small, but they are quite large enough to enable the East Indian and his family to live and thrive upon. One has but to see these farms in order to understand what 'beneficial occupation' really means and to form an idea of the possibilities of the Corentyne. The houses of the coolies are built on the reef behind instead of being huddled together, 'village' fashion, near the road, whilst the reef lands surrounding the houses are laid out for the raising of every variety of horticultural product. When I went over these lots a few days ago I was agreeably surprised to find every available rood of this reef land planted with provisions. It is true that cultivation is languishing on account of the prolonged drought, and that there is a danger, unless rain comes speedily, that the farmers will be totally deprived of the fruits of their industry. Already rice cultivation has entirely disappeared; the savannah lands which a couple of years ago gave an excellent crop of this cereal are now either arid wastes or are overgrown with bush and parasitical vegetation. This condition of things is due, however, to causes beyond the control of the settlers . . . It is perhaps necessary to state that my remarks above do not apply to the government settlement of the coolies at Whim, which so far shows very slight indications of permanency.

. . . The health-giving properties of the Corentyne sea breeze are pretty well known to colonists, but it requires to be experienced before it can be fully appreciated. The breeze too is sufficiently robust to reduce to comparative mildness the scorching sun rays in the hot season; and this also is one of the few places in the colony where one can sleep in comfort without the kindly offices of the mosquito netting . . .

The Drought and Distress

Unfortunately, with all these natural advantages in its favour there are certain influences at work on the Corentyne which until they are removed will give the country no industrial stability. Within a couple of years hundreds of acres that had been planted in rice have gone out of cultivation and are again given over to the wild growths which had been cleared away only by the expenditure of much patience and industry. The failure of the rice crop is so complete that with the exception of the small acreage provided with artificial means of irrigation, there is not a stalk to be reaped on the coast this year. The cause, it is hardly necessary to state, is due to the prolonged drought, which the inhabitants say is the most severe within living recollection. A capricious and uncertain rainfall is undoubtedly the greatest shortcoming of the Corentyne, and we cannot hope for much from the district until some provision is made to meet such contingencies as drought and inundation. The failure of the rice crop is a matter of serious moment to the small farmers at the very outset of their career as independent agriculturalists.

'Impressions of the Corentyne, I', *The Daily Chronicle*, 25 October 1899

It is noteworthy that these Indian settlements in which *The Daily Chronicle*'s correspondent sees so much prospect for development were all founded independently of the government. The sole government 'coolie' settlement on the Corentyne, Whim, inspires gloom among settlers and observers. The correspondent corroborates Joseph Ruhomon's observations (*The Argosy*, 22 July 1899, pp. 201–02):

> Brief reference has already been made to the evidence supplied by the Corentyne of the value of the East Indian as an agent in the formation of a peasantry in this colony. The testimony is so strong that the government would be justified in going to an expenditure far beyond the cost incurred in repatriation in order to secure the immigrant population as permanent residents. Thus far the measures that have been taken for this purpose have not been very great, and we have yet to find whether the means employed to settle the coolies will prove successful and to the satisfaction of the immigrants who accept the government's terms.

An Official Error at Whim

The government settlement at Whim on the Corentyne was one of the first undertaken in the colony, some 574 coolies agreeing to abandon their right to back passages in return for lots on this estate. At the outset the results were most encouraging, the settlers having applied themselves to the growing of rice with much success. The dry weather has however caused all that cultivation to disappear; at the same time it has brought out more clearly than would have been possible had the seasons recently been normal, the grave defect in the methods adopted by the authorities in laying out the lots. The land has been apportioned in sections running across the estate and parallel with the foreshore . . . the sand reefs which cross the alluvial soil of the coast run in the same direction; and it therefore follows that most of the coolies will have land consisting entirely of low-lying savannah which is suited only for rice cultivation, while other lots will consist chiefly of sand reefs, which stand too high for rice and are best adapted for the growing of provisions. It will be easily seen how this system of allotment works out for the coolie occupiers. If through drought or inundation the settler who holds alluvial lands finds himself unable to raise a rice crop, he will have no provision plot in reserve to tide him and his family over his difficulties. This is actually what has happened in the present year [1899], as for some time the coolies of the settlement have been dependent mainly on the opportunities that have offered for work in the neighbourhood, on the estates and elsewhere. Even in the most favourable seasons the same difficulty will present itself to the majority of the coolies, though of course in a lesser degree. It is impossible under existing conditions to raise more than one rice crop within the year, so that for six months or thereabouts the coolie will have little or nothing to do on his lot, and will be obliged to seek employment somewhere. Under such circumstances how can it be expected that the coolies of Whim will ever feel satisfied with their bargain with the government?

Most of them can never look forward to the prospect of a life of absolute independence; they will always have to rely more or less upon outside employment. What guarantee can there be, therefore, that the settlement at Whim will have any durability? Obviously the correct method would have been for the government to lay out the estate so that each lot should consist partly of reef and partly of savannah – in other words, instead of giving out the land in lots running approximately parallel with the coastline, the government should have arranged that the allotment run at right angles to the shore. If this course had been followed the settlers would not have have been left dependent upon a single crop; if the rice failed through any cause they would have their provisions on the reefs to save them from privation. These views, I might point out, are held by the coolies themselves as well as by every intelligent resident on the coast. The blunder is an extremely unfortunate one, since it is difficult to see how it can now be corrected. It might be practicable, perhaps, partially to solve the difficulty by digging a trench to intersect the lots and throwing up an embankment upon which those provisions in most general consumption could be grown. But this work would have to be undertaken by the government, as the coolies would never combine to do it on their own initiative . . .

'Impressions of the Corentyne, II', *The Daily Chronicle*, 26 October 1899

This astute observer concludes his article on the Corentyne with the assertion that irrigation *and* drainage are indispensable for the progress of the district; and that the people must be organized to maintain the complex hydraulic system. This is a paramount prerequisite, claiming precedence over the suggested railway. He also offers a clear option about funding, however demanding.

> . . . The exact form that government assistance should take at first is universally acknowledged now to be a more or less comprehensive scheme for irrigation and drainage. It is quite impossible to debate the wisdom of that view after one has seen for oneself the present state of cultivation on the coast. Even those who advocated the railway as the first consideration have receded from their position, and every person of intelligence recognizes what has been repeated in the columns of *The Daily Chronicle* – that no reliance can be placed on the permanency of cultivation on the coast until nature's forces are placed under some control. The idea is by no means of recent growth, it having been vigorously agitated as far back as the eighties, but it had to give place to other schemes of greater magnitude . . . The situation in this respect has materially changed since, and increased attention is being given to small cultivation. The only obstacles in the way are as regards the raising of capital and the possibility of the scheme proving a failure . . . the best source open to the government for procuring the money is through the Imperial Parliament; but it would be well for colonists to recollect that if a loan is granted under such conditions as the Colonial Loans Act . . . the colony stands in danger of parting with the supremacy that the elective members now hold in the Combined Court, it being the policy of Her Majesty's Government at the present time to exercise an effective control over the public finances of a dependency when the imperial credit is pledged for the repayment of a loan . . . It is recognized that the Canje Creek must be the source of [water] supply, and all agree further that something must be done to organize the people, by special Ordinance or otherwise, so as to secure that the back dams will be kept up, the drainage kept in order, and the 'kettings' [outlets to the sea] prevented from silting up. With precautions such as these, it is almost certain that the population would rapidly increase and in a few years there would be no danger of the project becoming a failure . . .

'Impressions of the Corentyne, III', *The Daily Chronicle*, 29 October 1899. [This three-part article obviously had some merit; it was forwarded to the Colonial Office. – See CO 111/514 Sendall to Chamberlain, no. 324, 25 October 1899, encl.]

Unmasking the Plantocracy: Bechu, Indentureship and 'King Sugar'

Bechu's ally and compatriot, 'East Indian Descendant' [Joseph Ruhomon], also, is impressed with the article on the Corentyne. He sees it as a corroboration of his own criticisms of the settlement at Whim, and proceeds, as Bechu would have done but for his imposed silence, to underline the wisdom of settling time-expired Indians on empoldered land.

'East Indian Descendant' (New Amsterdam) to the Editor, *The Daily Chronicle*:

> . . . I am especially pleased with his corroboration of my statement regarding the official blunder committed at Whim in the apportionment of the land which makes it impossible for the majority of coolies to engage in the planting of provisions, possessing as they do lots on the low-lying savannahs suitable for the cultivation of rice only [*The Argosy*, 22 July 1899, pp. 201–02]. I have already pointed out how injuriously this system would operate against the poor settlers in times of drought or inundation, and have strongly advocated the distribution of the land in lots consisting partly of reef and partly of savannah, so as to enable the people to plant both rice and provisions for the maintenance of themselves and their families all the year round. It is indeed greatly to be regretted that such an error was ever made, as the unfortunate people are still suffering considerably from it . . . It is extremely difficult now to remedy the mistake, but I think the best thing that could be done under the circumstances would be to adopt the suggestion of your representative, and that is, to dig a trench to intersect the lots and then to throw up an embankment upon which provisions could be grown. Of course, this is what the government should do. It is to be hoped, however, that the authorities will adopt the right course when they next come to give out new lands to the people; and I trust this will be done. I have often stated that there is sufficient land in this colony for thousands of my people who are willing to take it in lieu of the back passage to India; and that the government would do well to retain these time-expired immigrants instead of repatriating them. Your representative has also referred to the wisdom of this policy, and has properly called attention to those vast areas along the Corentyne which could be admirably utilized by the government for the formation of other settlements for the free coolies, instead of sending them back to their own country. It has been stated that over 3,000 time-expired immigrants are ready to accept land on the Corentyne if offered it. From my knowledge of

the coast I still maintain, as I have done in the past, that with its exuberant fertility of the soil and its reefs and savannahs running alternately along, it ought to present considerable facilities for the successful establishment of a large and contented peasantry. The government, therefore, should not neglect this opportunity of securing the time-expired people as permanent settlers. They should, without delay, parcel out the land among them, as this policy cannot but be advantageous to the colony, the government, and the immigrants themselves, who accept the government's stipulation. I was exceedingly pleased to hear that the necessary amount has been noted for the survey in connection with the proposed water scheme for the Corentyne. I now understand that operations have already commenced, and we all hope that our heart's desire will soon be satisfied in the possession of a perfect water supply and drainage system, closely followed up by the absolutely necessary and indispensable railway. This will assuredly make the Corentyne the busiest and most populous district in the colony, and contribute in a vast measure to the general well-being of the inhabitants.

The Daily Chronicle, 3 November 1899

As this debate on the settlement of Indians on land away from sugar estates continues, the plantocracy are eloquently silent on support for this promising venture, epitomized by the emergence of the cattle and rice industries; neither are they keen on reindenture, as advocated by Bechu and others. They are obsessed with Indian indentureship – cheap, bound labour partially subsidized by the colony. In late 1894, a prominent absentee planter with interests in British Guiana had pleaded, on behalf of his colleagues, with the Colonial Office that as everyone in the colony is "directly or indirectly" dependent on sugar, they should be grateful for their 'bound coolies' and bear the "whole cost of immigration for the next five years". The fledgling gold industry, he claims, is taking away labour from sugar estates.

Quintin Hogg (Deputy Chairman, the West India Committee) to Lord Ripon (Secretary of State for the Colonies), 6 October 1894:

... Your Lordship is aware that the colony – that is, its government, revenues, institutions and the general welfare of its people – is principally dependent upon the prosperity of the sugar industry. And this industry has been maintained, hitherto, mainly by means of the coolie immigration from India – an immigration which, it is admitted on all hands, has not only been of enormous benefit to the coolie, but has been an unmixed advantage to all classes of the colonial community. Hitherto, the cost of immigration has been borne to the extent of two-thirds by the sugar industry and one-third by the public revenue – a proportion which in view of the general benefits of this immigration, as shown by long experience, is manifestly unwise in the present condition of affairs. We therefore submit that we are justified in asking that the cost of immigration should be more equally shared by all who are benefited, directly or indirectly, by an industry the maintenance of which is essential to the general welfare, and is only possible by the continuance of coolie immigration from India.

One means of carrying out this object is already before Your Lordship in the Resolution passed at the Public Meeting held in Georgetown on 28 August last [1894]. That meeting was fully representative of the general interests of the colony and was practically unanimous. The meeting agreed to the specific proposal that the general revenue should bear the whole cost of immigration for the next five years (one important ground for this proposal being that the gold industry participated largely in the labour supply of the colony) – the limit of number to be introduced being fixed at 5,000 annually, and if necessary, that a loan of one million dollars or £200,000, should be raised to defray the necessary expenditure . . .

An alternative method is that the revenue should contribute one half of the cost of immigration together with the whole cost of the medical staff, the medical men being increasingly used for colonial as distinguished from immigration purposes, as a permanent measure of relief of the sugar industry . . .

CO 111/474 (West India Committee), 6 October 1894

Several years later, in March 1900, two other absentee planters with old links to British Guiana, write to the Colonial Office expressing grave fear of the consequences if the proposed reduction of 'coolies' to the colony were implemented. They call up the well-worn argument that the whole population benefits from the sugar industry, which is not sustainable without indentured labour. Both letters underline the plantocracy's apprehension of the spread of Indian settlements – inexorable claimants of labour away from the sugar plantations.

W. Middleton Campbell (Curtis, Campbell and Co) to Charles P. Lucas (Colonial Office), 9 March 1900:

Dear Sir, All connected with British Guiana are greatly alarmed and disappointed that the number of coolies to be imported for the coming year has been so much reduced . . .

Two other points I would lay before you, first, that as regards the interests in the colony other than those of the planters, I believe that every man, woman and child imported into the country is of direct benefit to those other interests. Instead, therefore, of discouraging immigration, they should encourage it. Secondly, it is the wish of the Colonial Government as well as the proprietors that everything should be done to encourage free coolies being located either on the estates in which they have worked or in the neighbourhood, and thus lead to their spending the rest of their lives in the colony rather than go back to India entailing as it does considerable expense to the colony. Now how can you expect the proprietors to encourage this settlement of the coolies on their own allotments if they find they cannot get new immigrants to take their place? . . .

CO 111/525 (Individuals), W. Middleton Campbell, 9 March 1900

Henry K. Davson (S. Davson and Co) to Charles P. Lucas (Colonial Office), 13 March 1900:

Dear Sir, You will not be surprised when you hear of the consternation of the Sugar Estates' Proprietors of British Guiana at the reduction by the government of the requisition of immigrants for 1900/01. So many of the time-expired coolies, who used to work on the estates, have left for their own independent occupations that the labour supply is growing every year more limited. It is true that during the past year, owing to the very severe drought, there was great distress among the labouring classes on account of their own lands being sterilized, and some calamity affecting the sugar estates and limiting agricultural work; but this distress was only temporary and under very abnormal circumstances, and, as I predicted at the time, would be rectified, as it has been, by the first fall of rain . . .

I am painfully aware of the present financial condition of the colony which calls for every effort towards the reduction in expenditure, but the improvement of that condition will depend as much on the increase of revenue as in the reduction of expenditure. The saving of the cost of the introduction of immigrants for the cultivation of the sugar estates, which constitute the backbone of the whole colony, means a curtailment of the circulation of capital which adds to the general revenue of the colony, and my contention is, that money spent on the introduction of immigrants more than repays that cost to the colony.

I would further urge on the Colonial Office the fact that the number of immigrants introduced into the colony over a series of years, are not, as a whole, available as labourers, as a great many of the time-expired men become absorbed into the general population.

If the existing cultivation is to be maintained the absorption must be filled up. The desire also is to increase the cultivation, as the larger the area under cultivation the more economical will be the production and, in consequence, the greater [the] power of the planter to contend against the unfair competition of the bounty-fed continental beet grower . . .

CO 111/525 (Individuals), Henry K. Davson, 13 March 1900

By January 1900, there are signs of recovery in the sugar industry and the planters accelerate their unrelenting demand for indentured labourers. *The Daily Chronicle*, it seems, has had enough of their carpings with their capacity to bend the government to their will. The paper's leaders increasingly vindicate Bechu's arguments about sugar monoculture. (After a prolonged absence, Bechu returns to the pages of *The Chronicle* in January 1900 with undiminished vigour.)

On every side we are confronted with the follies and extravagances of former administrations and legislatures which are now as scorpions applied to the backs of the unfortunate colonists. Our expenditure on government has almost doubled itself within the last 40 years, and on looking around we can see no practical good that has come of the increase. Our industrial position has receded; there has been little or no development in the interior; and we have no important public works of a remunerative character. It is clear . . . that the colony has got little or no return for this expenditure, and it is therefore without justification . . . A public debt of close on four million dollars has been accumulated within the past few decades, but little or no portion of the money thus raised has been devoted to remunerative purposes. The colony has thus to pay the interest on that sum at the rate of four percent. This expenditure . . . is sterile and unprofitable. Within the past 30 years the colony has also managed to build up at the public expense an extensive medical service costing annually one-ninth of the total administrative expenditure, or about $164,700 after deducting the one-third share borne by the employers of immigrants. The service was established chiefly for the benefit of the planting community, in order that a plentiful supply of cheap labour should be available. From the first the system was indefensible and has been permitted to continue only because the sugar industry has been so closely bound up with the well-being of British Guiana. It cannot be expected, however, that the public generally will continue to bear one-third of the cost of maintaining an institution which has its *raison d'etre* in the demands of the planters for a cheap and constant labour supply.

Leader, *The Daily Chronicle*, 24 February 1900

A few days later, *The Daily Chronicle* unleashes its most clinical critique of the plantocracy; it is no longer persuaded by some of the old arguments of 'King Sugar'.

. . . as sugar remains the principal prop of the colony's industrial stability it is perhaps but right that the community generally should contribute a share towards the support of the immigration system, although the practice is in violation of the accepted economic laws. At present the public contribution for this purpose amounts to about £162,300 per annum, besides the heavy outlay necessary to maintain an elaborate medical service . . . in looking back over the immigration records it is startling to find the immense inflow of East Indians that has taken place within the past half century and the inappreciable impress they have left on the general prosperity. Their presence has led to no new industrial development – the colony is worse off in that respect than it was 50 years ago – and would appear only to have heightened the impoverishment of the masses of the people. Altogether, the immigrants introduced from India have numbered 198,000, and the coolie population is computed at present to amount to about 114,500 souls. With such large numbers of an industrious people to reckon with, it is amazing to observe how largely the ebb and flow of emigration and immigration has been a thing apart from the industrial life of the community. The colony has had nothing approaching a commensurate return for the enormous expenditure represented by the figures we have quoted . . . The element of competition, it was suggested, should be eliminated as far as possible from the local market for immigrant labour. This, we fear, is the principle which underlies the calculations of the planters in preparing their applications from year to year; at least that seems to be the case judging from the crowds of coolies who prefer to work for a precarious subsistence in the city rather than submit to the low rate of wages on the sugar estates. The artificial conditions that have been established make the planters entirely independent of the ordinary laws which regulate the amount to be paid to the labourer. Improved prices for sugar have no effect upon the scale of remuneration allowed either to indentured or unindentured immigrants. At present well-equipped sugar estates under capable management are yielding handsome returns, in proof of which we need but point to the general tendency to increase the area of cultivation. But the lot of the labourer has not improved, by the smallest extent, in consequence of the increased profits that sugar is now earning. Indeed, it is one of the features of the time that, unless the condition of the planters has improved, the masses of the population are in a state of poverty unprecedented perhaps since the days of Emancipation . . . There is little doubt that a ready supply of labour would be forthcoming were the planters willing to offer competitive prices for it, and that many of the coolies whose term of indenture has expired and who have sought other means of gaining a livelihood would speedily return to the estates if the wages given afforded a sufficient inducement. If the limitation of the indents for the coming year will help to raise the present rate of wages on the estates, the colony generally will have little reason to regret the decision of the government.

Until some better provision is made for the retention of the coolie in the colony the introduction of immigrants in such quantities as demanded by the planters would be an imprudent and unprofitable undertaking. Outside the sugar industry there is scarcely another beneficial pursuit to which the immigrant can turn after his period of industrial residence is completed. He is usually thrown upon his own resources without encouragement or direction, and it is not unnatural that the public institutions of the colony should in the long run become the refuge for many of his class . . . The interests of the planters cannot be the sole consideration for the guidance of the government in the future [emphasis added]. *We should have thought that this fact was now universally accepted, but from the aggressive attitude of a member of the deputation [to the Governor] on Monday it would seem as if the changed conditions had still to be properly appreciated by some of the planting community. With several of the assertions advanced for the enlightenment of His Excellency and his advisers – the argument that the government were 'cutting their own throats' in reducing the number of immigrants, and that without sugar there would be no colony – the public are now tolerably familiar and will know exactly the value to attach to them. These antiquated weapons have grown rather rusty in the service of the local sugar industry, and something more original is needed to carry conviction. At any rate, the planters must get out of their minds the delusion that the colony should be administered for their particular benefit rather than that of the inhabitants generally* [emphasis added].

Leader, *The Daily Chronicle*, 28 February 1900

In response to *The Daily Chronicle*'s critique, a prominent planter, the Manager of Plantation La Bonne Intention (LBI), repeats a few of the old, "rusty" rationalizations:

E.C. Luard to the Editor, *The Daily Chronicle*:

. . . I assumed that in writing that article your objective was the well-being of the colony as a whole . . . [but] what would be the result of the colony if the sugar industry became extinct in a comparatively short space of time? What could or would take the place of the $30,000 to $40,000 now paid for wages per week on the sugar estates on behalf of the above industry?

... As regards your charge against the planters, which is that they pay too little for work done, it is only necessary to quote the names of various sugar estates which have gone under in the race for existence, to show how closely the line of profits approaches that of losses. You infer that because some estates made a fair profit last year they will always continue to do so, and you ignore entirely the fact that an estate which made money last year may have lost the previous one or may do so again next one. You remarked that some sugar estates are clearing large sums of money, and as proof of this you point to the general tendency to extend cane cultivation, but surely to an intelligent writer the thought must have occurred that the object of such extension was economy of production pure and simple.

May I ask what sum, in the form of addition to wages, would be sufficient to call further the latent energies of the people to whom you refer as able to supply all the necessary labour in lieu of the immigrants which the sugar estates wish to obtain, always bearing in mind the very narrow margin there is to draw upon to meet this end? It is absurd to suggest that a sugar estate should go on from year to year without making some profit ...

The Daily Chronicle, 3 March 1900

The Daily Chronicle's rejoinder to Luard shows no remorse. It restates the planters' obligations to local labour and questions the rationale for indentureship:

... We have never suggested that a sugar estate 'should go on from year to year without making some profit', but we do maintain that when the prices for sugar are good and the future of the planters fairly favourable some consideration should be given to the large body of impoverished labourers, creole and East Indian, and reasonable terms offered them as an inducement to work on the estates. There is something seriously wrong with the colony's economic condition when, notwithstanding that we have thousands of unemployed labourers in our midst, we still continue to introduce an indentured supply [sic] of cheap labour from outside sources.

Leader, *The Daily Chronicle*, 4 March 1900

A correspondent sees indentureship as an expensive system perpetuated to undermine the local labour market. It should be abolished, but he is in favour of "voluntary immigration", the attraction of settlers.

'X' to the Editor, *The Daily Chronicle*:

... The planters' sole object in bringing hordes of East Indians is to glut the labour market to such an extent that they can get men to work for a bare existence, not caring one iota for the burden thrown on the taxpayers by the hordes of loafers who spread themselves over the city and become a source of enormous expense to the colony generally. The time has really come when the present expensive immigration system should be abolished ... [and] a new system of voluntary immigration instituted, namely, the offering of lands to families and advances chargeable on the lands made to them to tide them over the first two or three years; followed by subsidized steamers to carry the fruits of their efforts to suitable markets. The present system is a terrible incubus and a terrible source of danger in very many ways. I am one who would like to see the population increased tenfold, but with a suitable population [settlers].

The Daily Chronicle, 4 March 1900

Another correspondent, an ex-planter, writing from Berbice, bemoans the government's short-sightedness on settling time-expired Indians on the land and their past subservience to the will of the plantocracy.

'D' to the Editor, *The Daily Chronicle*:

... Although not a sugar planter now, I went aback of one of those estates [on the Corentyne] with the Manager at the end of last year [1899], and saw for myself creoles and coolies working together, digging trenches in new land, the top crust being so hard that it had to be cut with axes. When the Manager told me the price he was paying, I was simply astonished, it was ... half what it could have been done for 30 years ago, and the people were glad to get it ... Hitherto the government had been guided by the plantocracy, and no doubt it is to the planters' interest to keep the labour subservient. So well have they done this that the taxpayer has to pay for it. Had the government a few years ago listened to other advice, lands would have been prepared for those who had served faithfully their five years' apprenticeship to enter into at their own expense, whereby they could make an independent living without having again to return to their own country or be subservient to any one. This has been neglected by Governor after Governor until the present Governor by sheer force of will is now taking the initiative, and if he is allowed to remain as Governor for some years, the planters and all others in the colony concerned will have no cause to regret it, but the plantocracy being so powerful, have been known before this to get a Governor removed who has gone against their grain . . .

The only remedy propounded years ago, is to prepare lands for the people to settle on. Offer it at reasonable rates to those who would prefer purchasing. Give it to those who would prefer it, in lieu of return passages, and few would willingly return to their native land.

The Daily Chronicle, 6 March 1900

Another correspondent joins the debate in a forthright manner: the government must provide time-expired Indians with empoldered land or repatriate them "at once".

'A Mason but Ready to Tackle Anything' to the Editor, *The Daily Chronicle*:

. . . To make the immigrant a good and valuable self-supporting inhabitant and contributor to the upkeep and welfare of the colony, there must be a change and a radical one. They are not, at the present time, satisfied with their lot, and the longer this goes on the more difficult the problem will be to settle.

It is utterly impossible for them to prepare their own drainage and irrigation. This must be done for them and under control, and, unless the government is prepared to provide in sufficient and workable communities, proper lands, before it is too late, better to repatriate at once all those whose term of ten years has expired. They are easily led, and are loyal when they see they are being fairly treated and an interest is taken in them;

but when indifference is shown to them and they are ordered to turn out and do the work required or clear out, dissatisfaction and insubordination must follow and, too often, they are incited by those who have already passed through the ordeal.

The late drought has had a demoralizing effect on thousands of those people and others in the colony. Irrigation, so easily obtainable in any part of British Guiana and which would be most willingly paid for, seems to me to be the only feasible plan whereby we can secure these people and make them content and happy. We have the land and water and, instead of saying there is no unity amongst creoles and immigrants, let the powers that be turn round and say 'let there be unity amongst ourselves', and give them that which is requisite for their well-being and ours afterwards.

Sugar must be propped up for years to come and this can be done by those immigrants in their initiation, but it can never succeed by expecting them to continue after their apprenticeship in a condition which they consider serfdom . . . Agricultural lectures will be of no benefit whatever unless the requisite lands are there for the people lectured to operate on and in no part of the colony can it be said that the land is to be found properly irrigated and drained, and this can never be done successfully in small sections on account of the cost. Districts must be taken in hand and laid out properly before any good can be done.

The Daily Chronicle, 30 March 1900

The Daily Chronicle restates the correspondent's case that if Indians were provided with empoldered land they would be prepared to pay for it. These people could constitute a "reliable peasantry" which British Guiana needs.

. . . In the course of a few years the condition recently introduced with regard to back passages will begin to operate . . . the immigrant before he can claim the right of repatriation must be prepared to defray one-half of the cost of his return passage. The sum will appear a large one to the mind of the average coolie, and if he is afforded any encouragement at all he will prefer to remain a permanent resident in British Guiana. There will be many besides who will not have the means sufficient to entitle them to repatriation. It is therefore evident that before long our free population will be materially added to year by year, and it would [be] near-sighted in the extreme were the authorities to make no arrangements to meet the contingency thus created.

That is the ambition of nearly all the East Indian immigrants, and to attain it they are quite ready to devote whatever little savings they may have accumulated before their contract with the estates expired. It is deeply to be regretted that the coolie is not taken in hand by the government at this stage and provided with the opportunity he needs . . . at the end of their indenture the coolies require no more than a suitable piece of well-drained land, within some polder area by preference. They are usually quite prepared to pay for the privilege of using the land, and might be reckoned upon as a remunerative and reliable peasantry . . . not only would it help to form an industrial class of which the colony stands much in need, but it would prevent the immigrants from squandering their earnings after leaving the plantations, and from drifting eventually to join the flotsam and jetsam of the city, becoming members of that superfluous 'jobber' element which could barely manage to keep body and soul together by honest means.

Leader, *The Daily Chronicle*, 31 March 1900

Bechu rejoins the debate, arguing that the indentured immigrant is "treated so like a slave", hence his repugnance to the plantation. He is ill-treated by drivers and overseers and deprived of the full statutory wage.

Bechu (Georgetown) to the Editor, *The Daily Chronicle*:

Sir, Your correspondent, 'A Mason But Ready to Tackle Anything', has, in my opinion solved our 'surplus labour' problem, and if our sugar estates can only be prevailed upon to act up to his suggestions, they will find that the breach between them and their coolie labourers is not such an extraordinary one to bridge over after all.

I have often said before, and I repeat it again, that during his term of indenture our immigrant is treated so like a slave that it is next to impossible to expect him to take kindly to sugar cultivation after the expiration of his five years.

Of all the people in the world there is none so loyal and easily led as the 'mild Hindu', and I am positive that estates' Managers could safely count on getting twice as much work out of his class of labourer if they insisted on their overseers and drivers treating them less harshly. In this respect a coolie is very much like a donkey – deal kindly with him and he will unmurmuringly do anything, but put undue pressure on him and he becomes stubborn.

Prior to his departure from India a coolie binds himself to work for seven hours, at the rate of a shilling a day, but I am confident that the majority of them would willingly give ten hours labour if they were certain of receiving the statutory wage.

In the event of the planters being no longer in a position to pay the statutory wage, the best thing for them to do is to get the Government of India to consent to the lowering of the wage to 6 pence [12 cents], but it is a shame to entice these men to leave their homes on the understanding that they will receive 6 shillings [$1.44] a week, and then pay them only 9 bits [72 cents] for six days.

The Daily Chronicle, 1 April 1900

The Daily Chronicle in a leader on the Report of the Emigration Agent in India for British Guiana, 1899-1900, corroborates some of Bechu's misgivings of the system of indentureship; but the paper still sees India as the source of settlers for the colony.

. . . The system of coolie immigration has been in vogue now for nearly a generation, and it cannot be said with any degree of truth that it is now what it ought to be. The coolies are imported like so many human machines to run the sugar estates, and the local government has smiled benignly on the system and fed and nourished it, leaving the coolies for the most part to shift for themselves. It is true they earn more money than they possibly can in their native land, but their social state is sadly neglected; and the prospect for intending emigrants far from inviting. It is probably due largely to those causes that the Emigration Agent in India finds his work growing more and more difficult . . . The report does not touch the question of opening up this colony as a field of emigration for Indians with the view of getting them to settle on the soil, and thus relieve some of the congested districts of India; but this question is pressing itself to the front, and if the difficulties of recruiting emigrants continue, and the social conditions of the East Indians in this colony are not improved, the present system may have to be either mended or ended, and sugar planters left to carry on their estates as any private business is carried on. As between India and this colony, and as between the people of India and the people of this colony, there is very little good in our present immigration system. It is but a make-shift between one period in our industrial life and another; but before it is cast aside it would be well, if out of it could be evolved a system for the peopling of this colony with some of the over-population of the great Indian Empire of the Queen.

Leader, *The Daily Chronicle*, 6 June 1900

Bechu deplores the repatriation of some of the best immigrants, while many of the "weakest and worthless" remain, derelicts in the capital. He again calls for the reintroduction of reindenture to encourage more to settle in the colony, while deprecating the offer of unirrigated plots at schemes such as Helena and Whim.

Bechu (Georgetown) to the Editor, *The Daily Chronicle*:

Sir, Notwithstanding the fuss that was made when our worthy Government Secretary [Sir Cavendish Boyle] fought like a Trojan to get this year's indent for immigrants cut down from 5,200 to 2,500, yet nobody – not even our *energetic* Immigration General – seems to take the slightest trouble to retain the strongest – both physically as well as pecuniarily – of the immigrants who year after year leave these shores *at the expense of the colony*. On the other hand special care appears to be taken to keep the weakest and worthless *always* with us. If you doubt me, just take a stroll down Water Street any Friday morning (on which day they turn out in full force) and you will have a *deckho* for yourself.

From enquiries made, I find that the cost of each man's return passage is $60. Instead therefore of chartering vessels to convey our thoroughly trained men back to India, don't you think that the money thus expended would be profitably spent if those entitled to back passages were offered that amount in hard cash on condition that they reindenture themselves for a further term of five years and after that period renounce their claim to return to India at the expense of government? To avoid a rush, the number required each year should be restricted to say, 3,000, and every one of the men wishing to reindenture should be subjected to a strict medical examination as to fitness, as was done when he sailed from Calcutta. In a letter which appeared in your issue of the 27 January 1897 – the day on which the West India Royal Commissioners landed in this colony – I made a special proposal, but no notice was taken of any suggestion, nevertheless *nil desperandum* is my motto, and sooner or later I feel certain that the authorities will have to resort to something of that sort.

Mr Mitchell, the Emigration Agent for this colony in India, is no greenhorn, and when an official of his standing after an experience of 20 long years, lifts up a warning finger and tells us in plain language (*vide* his report for 1899-1900) that despite the plague and famine he found it exceptionally difficult to get men to sever all their home ties and cross to a distant land and unknown work, it behoves our government to seriously consider this matter and devise some means to induce those who are on the spot to 'abide with us'.

It is all bosh and nonsense to offer unirrigated plots of land. Huis't Dieren, Helena and Whim, on which estates such a mint of money has been squandered, have turned out miserable failures, and no sane immigrant with any spunk in him would be so foolish as to forego his claim to a back passage for a solitary acre, as it would be tantamount to Esau's selling his birthright for a mass of pottage.

The Daily Chronicle, 12 June 1900

Bechu's faithful ally, Joseph Ruhomon, invariably agrees with him. He writes in support of reindenture, the need for irrigation on new settlements, and the flaws of the settlement at Whim, on the Corentyne Coast.

'East Indian Descendant' [Joseph Ruhomon] (New Amsterdam) to the Editor, *The Daily Chronicle*:

Unmasking the Plantocracy: Bechu, Indentureship and 'King Sugar'

Sir, The arguments of Mr Bechu, in your Tuesday's issue [12 June], in favour of the reindenture of time-expired immigrants, are very forcible and convincing. I have always thought of the desirability of inducing this class of people to remain in the colony, and have often advocated it through the press. Why, year after year, such large numbers should be allowed to leave these shores when they can be easily induced to remain, I do not know. I am sure a good many would be only too glad to be reindentured under the conditions so wisely suggested by Mr Bechu.

I quite agree with your correspondent as to the futility of offering lands to the people as an inducement for them to remain when these lands are not properly irrigated. A large number who have availed themselves of the government's offer have very good reasons now for regretting it, as it is utterly impossible for them, do what they will, to make their lands a source of profit, for not only are those lands devoid of proper irrigation, but in a good many cases they are most unsuitably laid out, especially at Whim, which makes it impossible for the owners to go in for both rice and provision cultivation combined, which is absolutely necessary if they are to have an independent and permanent living. What a pity that these people should suffer through the blunder of government officials!

Well may Mr Bechu draw our attention to the prospect of a considerable shrinkage in coolie immigration. It is also not unlikely that immigration will one day come to an end, so far as this colony is concerned. The government should, therefore, be quite prepared to meet the new condition of things whenever it comes, and to do so it behoves the government to hold out every possible inducement to the time-expired people to remain in the colony. There is no doubt that the free coolies have no desire to return to India if they can have a comfortable existence here; and we know that the government are decidely in a position to satisfy their wants and so keep them for good. And who can doubt the inestimable benefits to the colony that would follow the adoption of such a policy?

The Daily Chronicle, 16 June 1900

A correspondent responds to Bechu, explaining the limitations of the settlement at Helena. He also emphasizes the futility of allotting unempoldered lands to Indian settlers, but the government, as usual, is immovable.

'Time Flies' to the Editor, *The Daily Chronicle*:

Sir, Bechu comes very near the mark when he says, 'It is all bosh and nonsense to offer unirrigated plots of land. Huis t'Dieren, Helena and Whim on which such a mint of money has been squandered, have turned out miserable failures.' Only too true. What must now be the feelings of those who had the actual . . . [conception] of those settlements? Whoever it may have been, they had no idea whatever of the requirements of the special duties those lands were intended to be used for. Helena proper and the other estates attached to it are not on the same level. They are supplied [with water] from the Lamaha conservancy. Some of the lands must be specifically supplied from different sources and heights by motive power before a successful rice crop can be assured. I hear some of the coolies are renting out their lands for ground provisions, as they are too high for rice, and a great many more are ignoring the land altogether.

Whim has certainly turned out a whimsical freak, and an expensive one to boot.

Bechu's reindenture system for another five years, even at $60, will barely meet the requirements. Taking 365 days to the year this would be little over 3 cents per day. Would this satisfy Bechu's countrymen who may have young children to support, and who would like to be free and have their own homesteads? I am afraid not. Many would enter into it, but compulsion in present circumstances will scarcely stand the strain. How much less would it stand it now?

Had the government offered a prize for the best course to adopt in the laying out of the lands for those settlements, many varied and different opinions would undoubtedly have been given, but then there would have been a collection to select from.

I have thought over a plan that has been in my noddle for some time. Instead of squandering more money foolishly for coolie settlements let the government borrow the money for practicable water schemes, make a charge on the lands to pay the interest and so much of the capital yearly, give those coolies who are entitled to return passages a certain amount down, whatever may be agreed to in lieu of their return to India or anywhere else for five years, and allow them to choose their own lands, which they will readily do.

Irrigated districts must be an indispensable condition within a given time, and then the balance of the whole amount, whatever it may be, so long as they have not left the colony. Work would be provided for the unemployed, and there would be no cause for their leaving in search of work.

The Corentyne and West Coast Berbice can easily be irrigated, and those districts would readily be taken up by the immigrants and could be readily rented to them, especially the Corentyne. And Whim then would be a success. Unless something of this sort is done in the near future Whim may cost several times over what it should have done in the first instance.

Let us pause for a moment and think of the advantage of having irrigated lands, when two crops of rice would be assured. No East Indian would hesitate to pay $10 and $12 per acre per year rent for such lands. Without irrigation any rent is looked on suspiciously as it has been proved on trial. Where there is no regular water supply the crops in five years may be numbered at three and these not full ones – either too much water or a giving out of the supply before the cereal has come to maturity . . .

The Daily Chronicle, 17 June 1900

Bechu's incisive letters to *The Daily Chronicle* since late 1896 have stimulated a growing tendency for Indians to write to the press, to articulate one grievance or another. One such correspondent, a rice planter from the Corentyne, assesses the hazards of rice culture and its prospects, focusing on the necessity for irrigation *and* drainage; the two are inseparable – a crucial observation underlined by the devastating drought of 1899 and the equally destructive floods which followed in 1900.

Thomas Drepaul (Cromarty, Corentyne) to the Editor, *The Daily Chronicle*:

Sir, I have never written yet to the newspapers, and would not now if I did not want information. The coolies about here say now [that if] the water scheme is to be made we will get plenty of rice . . . What I wish to know is when will the work begin, and when will it likely end? I was born on this coast and always lived on it. I have a wife, six children, and an aged mother to support. The last two or three years we have suffered much: work not to be had sufficient for me to support such a family. I planted rice with others aback here at the beginning of the year. Last month and the month before we cut it, but there was so much water the heads of the rice fell in it, and I found it is sour and very little of it good to eat. Last year [1899] we did not get one grain [because of the drought]; the year before little – the water was too much. A good crop, however, may be got at the end of this year if the water in [the] savannah holds out. If it goes away before the rice is ripe it will be a loss again. We cannot grow rice here unless we are sure of water, and we cannot get work as we did before. If water is to be impounded for rice, I and others wish to bring our families out here. If we get water whenever we want it, we can get two crops of rice in one year, and live well and be able to pay for the water. I have been sending money for my family in India, but for two years now I have not been able; the times are too hard. I have had to sell nearly all of my stock to live for the last two years, and if we are to suffer again what are we to do?

I want to know how much it will cost everything landed in Demerara for a passage from India. The old people are not able to work on a sugar estate, and should be brought cheap. The able ones would have to go indentured to sugar estates. They now suffer much in India – far more than we have done here lately, although we have been bad enough for some time, but plenty of water will cure all this . . .

I saw by your paper of last Thursday the opening of the railway to Rosignol [on 1 August 1900] and how well the rice in that side was looking. I know all that part well. The rice cannot look better than on the Corentyne. This is a good year so far as it has gone for the second crop, but if the water fails before the ears of the rice are full there will be a heavy loss. If the water holds out, however, it will be the largest crop the colony has ever had, and I hope the water will hold out. We will be worse off than last year. My neighbouring friends tell me the land here grows more rice than in India, but what is the use of trying for more than one crop a year? . . .

I have been to Essequibo, and often to the East and West Coasts of Demerara. There they have water when we are dry here. The Corentyne is healthier than those parts. When we get the water here, there is not another part of the colony [which] can grow rice with the Corentyne. I have travelled the Corentyne savannah in wet weather and dry. The savannah of the Corentyne and West Coast Berbice will grow more rice than all the other parts of the colony. If the land from the line surveyed on the Corentyne down in [the] savannah to the sea were all left to be cultivated, it would be taken up in ten to 15 years; . . . the same would, I believe, happen on the West Coast Berbice, which is not nearly so healthy . . .

The Daily Chronicle, **10 August 1900**

Another Indian correspondent underlines the urgency of a reliable water supply to the success of rice. The government's scheme for the Corentyne, meanwhile, meanders its way through a conceptual maze, government's ambivalence, and the sugar planters' paranoia of minor industries.

'Fairplay' to the Editor, *The Daily Chronicle*:

> . . . I can only repeat that all that Whim wants is a regular water supply . . . Let all those who take an interest in us give us water and we will prove that rice can be profitably grown in this colony and especially on the coast . . . the matter is important not only to us East Indians but the colony generally . . .

The Daily Chronicle, 14 August 1900

Bechu is unwavering in his advocacy of reindenture as a means of retaining some time-expired Indians in the colony.

Bechu (Georgetown) to the Editor, *The Daily Chronicle*:

> *Sir*, The government has strong objections to giving our time-expired immigrants an opportunity of reindenturing in the colony; nevertheless it tells them in effect: 'Take advantage of your claim to a free return passage and, after you have gone through your little savings, ask our Agent in Calcutta to reindenture you there, and we shall be happy to receive you with open arms.' And this is exactly what the majority of the return immigrants who arrived last week in the *Avon* and *Forth* have been doing. But do you happen to know at what cost? According to my calculation it cannot be anything under $240 per head, ie: $90 for his first introduction, $60 for his back passage, and $90 for his reintroduction, or roughly speaking $100 per head more than it would have cost had the authorities taken my advice and offered them in lieu of their back passage $50 in hand cash, as an inducement to accept reindenture in the colony.
>
> Is not this economy with vengeance?

The Daily Chronicle, 18 October 1900

Bechu debunks the myth of cheap 'bound coolie' labour, again making his case for the reindenturing of some time-expired Indians, rather than importing costly indentured labour.

Bechu (Georgetown) to the Editor, *The Daily Chronicle*:

Sir, On running my eye over the Immigration Fund Account, I was thunderstruck to see that during the season 1899–1900 the exorbitant sum of $355,439.90 was expended to introduce 4,959 statute adults in the colony, and that a further sum of $100,079.74 was paid for back passages, making in all a total of $455,519.64. Now, Sir, if we are to accept these figures as correct, is it not a waste of public money, seeing that a like number of able-bodied and well-trained indentured labourers of the same class could easily have been obtained on the spot for less than half that amount?

I am aware that our acting Governor [Sir Cavendish Boyle] is not at all to blame in the matter because about two years ago, in his capacity as Government Secretary, he addressed a communication to the Immigration Agent General, requesting that officer to feel the pulse of the planters, and let him know whether they were in favour of the reindenture system, but the latter was treated so confidential that, much as I tried to do so, I could not learn the result. I found out, however, that one or two of the leading planters objected to it on the ground that only the weak and lazy ones would come forward, but how they ever came to that conclusion I for one fail to see. Indeed, in my humble opinion, that is the only way they could count on getting reliable men, for on a man's applying for reindenture, all that the Immigration Agent of the district would have to do is take his ticket of exemption and send it on to the Manager of the estate on which the immigrant served, asking him to write on it (as a captain does on a discharge certificate of a sailor) what character the man bore during his term of indentureship and, in the event of the immigrant being able to produce a good character and pass a strict medical examination, reindenture him at once.

In a meeting which was held in the Court of Policy on the 4th instant, the acting Government Secretary's motion fixing the number of indentured immigrants to be introduced during the next three sessions at not more than 4,000 adults, was carried by a mere fluke – only three on the elective side voting in its favour. It is, however, to be hoped that wiser counsel will prevail and that steps will be taken to indenture the 4,000 locally.

The Daily Chronicle, 25 October 1900

Bechu's letter (above) on reindenture and the cost of maintaining Indian indentureship evokes a positive response from *The Daily Chronicle*, which deems the system "extravagant and out-of-date".

> ... We receive in this colony a large number of coolies every year, most of whom, when their period of indenture is over, go back to India, and some of whom again come back here under similar conditions to those under which they came in the first instance ... As it is when every industry is burdened with taxation it behoves the government to consider if such an expensive feature in the life of the colony could not be changed in the direction of sounder economy. The immigration system requires two establishments, one here and one in India; and there are besides charges in connection with recruiting and transporting to the colony, as well as back passages, and some expenses in England, all of which have to be borne by this colony. The total cost is larger than is generally anticipated. For the year ending 31 March last, for instance, 4,959 adult East Indians were introduced into this colony, at a cost of $71.68 per head, including the passage money, the allowance being £10 per head. The expenses in connection with the system in India including the cost of the establishment at Calcutta, amounting to $13,913.40; charges in connection with recruiting throughout India, $55,765.43; charges connected with the voyage, such as clothing, etc, supplies to coolies on the voyage, $82,205.63. The cost of back passages and the incidentals connected during the same year amounted to $100,079.74; the cost of the medical service to $51,176.16; and the cost of the local establishment to $34,059.80, so that the establishment in the colony is about the least expensive item connected with the system. The total expenditure on immigration for the past year, therefore, amounted to $540,775.60. The sources of income which met this heavy account were indenture fees, acreage tax, and the colony's contribution, making a total of $563,277.71, which left a small balance at the credit of the fund. The chief item in which an economy could be effected is in respect of the return of coolies to India and the introduction of others from India. Thus in the year under review, while 4,959 coolies were introduced into the colony, 1,228 were sent back. They are, of course, entitled to be sent back, as it is one of the conditions under which they are recruited; but it would be no infringement of this condition to give them a certain sum of money down

as an option to a return passage. It has been pointed out that it would be no use to do this unless something was done to provide some means of livelihood for those who would prefer to accept the bonus but who would not reindenture. Many time-expired Indians would no doubt gladly reindenture themselves if they got a cash bonus at the expiration of their first term; and this would be a far better policy than the present so long as the bonus was less than the cost of introducing a fresh man. There may be difficulties in retaining our time-expired East Indians in this way; but we certainly do not think it is impossible. Nor do we think that, if suitable opportunities were offered, the coolies would refuse to take advantage of them. At any rate it is the duty of the government not only to render it possible for time-expired coolies to settle permanently in the colony, but to encourage such settlement.

Leader, *The Daily Chronicle*, 25 October 1900

The Daily Chronicle is now an ally of Bechu. It contends that indentureship is perpetuated because the poor wages paid to Indians undercut the level of wages for free labour. There are "sufficient coolie labourers" in the colony to meet the requirements of sugar; every effort, therefore, should be made to retain time-expired workers and stem the tide of expensive repatriation. The paper also sees merits in African workers.

... Every year about 4,000 East Indians are imported to work on the sugar estates of the colony under indenture, and about 2,000 are sent back, all at the cost of this colony. In other words the colony is, roughly speaking, spending £60,000 a year in taking people back to India and replacing them. The liability of the colony to repatriate Indians in this way is so great – being fully three quarters of a million sterling – that if the colony through any unforeseen occurrences were suddenly called upon to meet it, would find it an utter impossibility to do so. Our informant ['an old planter'] assures us that he has experimented with both coolies and Negroes by giving them small allotments of ground, and getting them to do estate's work for him, and that it proved entirely successful. The difficulty was in getting away from the red tape of the government. The scheme he proposes is to pay the coolies a small sum at the expiration of five years as an inducement to get them to settle on the soil, giving them suitable allotments, and opportunities to continue doing some estate labour. In this way the £60,000 spent on sending away time-expired labourers and introducing new ones could be utilized, and would far more than suffice to give each of the 2,000-odd East Indians who return to India annually a small bonus to help him start on the allotment given him. Indeed, if only £5 were given each at the end of the first five years as has been proposed, it would swallow only a fraction of this sum; and if it were found necessary, on account of failure of the first crop, a further contribution might be given to settlers, still leaving a big margin of the £60,000. As we have repeatedly pointed out, the *raison d'être* of the desire of the planters to continue the present expensive system, which is wholly out of proportion to the financial condition of the colony, is the fact that the imported labour is cheap. *The miserable pittance paid for the labour on the estate is so small that only those who adopt the habits of life of the coolies can possibly subsist on it. Labourers, for instance, dressing after the European fashion could not possibly do it. It is for this reason chiefly, we venture to say, that the Negroes as a race have all but abandoned work on the sugar estates. The evidence given before the Royal Commission was to the effect that the labour of the Negro is fitful and cannot always be obtained when wanted. Those who saw the splendid work done by the Negro labourers in laying down the tram lines will feel inclined to doubt this. Where the Negro has been tried with a respectable wage he has been found not only a willing but a capable workman; but he has been ousted slowly but so surely by imported coolies that the Royal Commissioners, in the face of the strong evidence of planters, reported that 'it seems unwise, having regard to the peculiar circumstances of British Guiana, to bring any more East Indians until there is some prospect of the revival of the sugar industry'* [emphasis added]. The dictum is constantly being disregarded from year to year, although there are sufficient coolie labourers in the colony to carry on the cane cultivation and the manufacture of sugar and rum, and no prospect of the revival of the sugar industry referred to by the Commissioners.

Leader, *The Daily Chronicle*, 30 October 1900

A proplanter correspondent calls up the exhausted notion that the whole colony benefits from indentured immigration; but one's credulity is stretched very thin when he asserts that African people, also, are beneficiaries of "cheap coolie labour" – as employers!

> Francis G. Harvey to the Editor, *The Daily Chronicle*:

... Now, sir, whilst every colony and all the countries of the New World are vying with each other to induce immigrants to enter their territory, you would close the door of this colony, merely trying to keep the few you have.

You state that 4,000 immigrants arrive and 2,000 leave annually, balance left in colony 2,000 ... I think you know what the population was ten years ago, and what it is today; you also know that practically the death rate exceeds the birth rate. Will you just figure out the result of ten years of your policy for the benefit of the people?

The paltry £60,000 that seems to cause you so much concern, and to increase in its overwhelming stupendity as the article goes on, is not a dollar per head of the population, and would hardly cover the cost of the machinery on some estates, but through the expenditure of which the estates alone are enabled to circulate pretty well £5,000,000 annually, to say nothing of all the other industries and callings in which coolies are employed; and the black man, it must be remembered, is not the smallest employer of that same coolie labour you would have us believe has ousted him out of his birthright.

The black man, sir, in spite of all his extravagances of youth, is fast becoming a proprietary body and employer of labour, and annually this class is largely on the increase, and that is the secret, coupled with the gold-digging, why many have withdrawn from estates' labour; not that the planters with malice aforethought ousted him; and instead of trying to help and stimulate this tendency by supplying what you recognize as cheap labour (and it is only by cheap labour, that is, cheaper than the black man's, that he can manage to rise), you would close the door and throw the Negro back again into serfdom. For [if] it is as dear as his own he perforce cannot employ his equal.

Throw open the door of immigration, I say, give everyone, black and white, a plentiful supply of cheap labour. Remember it is not only sugar estates and sugar planters that employ and monopolize the benefits of cheap coolie labour; the black man is fast running the planters a good second. With cheap labour and a steady policy of immigration to keep up the labour market, a graduated scale for the purchase of canes by the estates fixed by law, and made compulsory as a quid pro quo for free immigration, and the black man will immediately take his place in the community amongst the proprietary class as a sugar planter.

The Daily Chronicle, 6 November 1900

Bechu responds to Francis G. Harvey, arguing that although the wages of indentured labourers are paltry – the statutory minimum is a fiction – imported labour is not cheap for the colony. He observes that low wages have driven many Africans and Indians away from plantation work.

Bechu (Georgetown) to the Editor, *The Daily Chronicle*:

Sir, Your correspondent Francis G. Harvey who accused you the other day of wishing to close the door of immigration in this colony writes as if he were a Rothschild or a Vanderbilt! He speaks of £60,000 as a 'paltry' sum, and wonders why the expenditure of that *trifling* amount annually should cause you so much concern, when 'all the countries of the New World are vying with each other to induce immigrants to enter their territory'; but he carefully avoids mentioning the names of the countries that spend as much as this colony does year after year to bring 4,000 immigrants in by the front door and let 2,000 out by the back door!

One of Mr Harvey's reasons for advocating foreign labour is with a view to increase our population which is fast diminishing. If that be so, why go all the way to India to make up our deficiency when Barbados in a much shorter time could supply us all the agricultural labourers we need? With regard to Mr Harvey's other reason, I am at a loss to understand what that gentleman terms 'cheap labour'. Our imported labour may be viewed as cheap in one sense, seeing that the men on arrival are paid 6 pence *per diem* instead of the statutory wage [12 pence], but if Mr Harvey will just take the trouble to figure out the charges in connection with the recruiting and transporting of our immigrants, the cost of their clothing and supplies on the voyage, and the cost of medical services, he will find that it would be far cheaper in the long run to offer a higher wage and secure all our agricultural labour locally.

In an article which appeared in the *New Century Review* on the West Indian labour problem and which you reproduced in your issue of 16 March last, the writer very truly says:

> The cry that is raised against the laziness of the Negro is strangely one-sided. That the Negro does sometimes refuse to labour when work is offered to him is an undeniable fact. But what is largely the cause of his refusal? Simply that the wages offered him are not sufficient to induce him to devote his energy to arduous toil. Being in many cases peasant proprietors, the Negroes prefer to work for themselves when they can; and then they very often never obtain the money they earn. It is a common complaint of Negro labourers that if they bargain to work for one shilling and 6 pence a day they will scarcely get more than one shilling. Knowing this, they frequently scamp their work and thus endless disputes arise between employers and employed.

The same remarks, sir, are equally applicable to our East Indian labourers and account for the large number of vagrants in our city [Georgetown] and inmates in our gaols.

The Daily Chronicle, 9 November 1900

An established white pioneer of the rice industry on the Corentyne, a keen advocate of the settlement of Indians on the land, is unequivocal that drainage and irrigation are the foundation of agricultural security. He, like Bechu, sees no wisdom in importing more labour while "surplus" labour is "floating" around, with no work on the sugar estates and settlement rendered precarious by the unreclaimed state of the land.

W.T. Dalgety (Maida, Corentyne) to the Editor, The Daily Chronicle:

> ... There must be that which will give the time-expired immigrant the wherewithal to make his own living and in his own way. At the present time the facilities afforded him are not sufficiently attractive, and this explains why so many of them return ... to India or turn loafers and

become quite worthless – a burden to themselves and a disgrace to the colony.

The East and West Coast of Demerara are fairly well cultivated where water is accessible; the Essequibo cultivated only in some parts; the West Coast and Corentyne districts of Berbice, where there is room for many thousands of those time-expired immigrants, are but swamps in wet and burned up in dry weather. *No reliability can be placed on lands where there is no water supply* [emphasis added]. The local industry in the future will depend largely upon the existence of a rice industry.

We cannot expect immigration to continue indefinitely unless something is done to utilize the surplus imported labour that is floating about the colony; and the only industry for that labour is rice. There is not much work now on the sugar estates for all the surplus labour, neither are there attractive or useful lands to be got for them. The land is there but it is not in a condition to be cultivated.

The Daily Chronicle, 11 November 1900

Bechu's most consistent indictment of the indentureship system, "another form of slavery", rests on his allegation that indentured labourers do not get the basic statutory minimum wage – 24 cents (12 pence) per day for men; 16 cents (8 pence) per day for women – whether for time or piece work. Indeed, from his first letter to *The Daily Chronicle* (1 November 1896), he is insistent that this statutory wage is not negotiable, whatever the financial state of the sugar industry. By late 1900, Bechu gains a formidable ally, the charismatic Rev H.J. Shirley, an English Congregational minister in New Amsterdam, whose attention he draws to an "evil" on estates – the sexual exploitation of Indian women. (In the letter that follows, for the first time, Bechu gives no address.)

Bechu to the Editor, *The Daily Chronicle*:

Sir, The vexed subject of our immigration system has once again cropped up, and as on this occasion a prominent member of our Court of Policy and one of the leading planters in the colony [Hon R.G. Duncan] has aired his views in a newspaper owned and supported by the planting fraternity as well as by a few merchants who have planting interests [*The Argosy*], I earnestly solicit the favour of your kindly granting me a little space to have my say in your paper.

As an indentured immigrant, Sir, I have had extensive and exceptional opportunities of observing from behind the scenes the actual workings of our immigration system which led me long ago to apprehend its evils and impelled me to offer myself as a witness before the West India Royal Commissioners [1 February 1897], who it gives me much pleasure to see, have recorded my evidence in their voluminous report. What I said then with respect to indentured immigrants not getting their statutory wage, although they work long after hours, I still maintain, and I defy Mr Duncan – who I am sure, prides himself in being a truthful Briton – or any other God-fearing planter, to put his hand on his heart and give me the lie. Sir, leave a poor pilgarlic like me out of the question, but let the above-named honourable gentleman pay a surprise visit along with the Rev Mr Shirley to any estate on any Saturday and stand beside the pay tables while the indentured men and women are being paid and they shall have ocular and demonstrative proofs of what I have over and over again asserted. Should any attempts be made by interested parties to dub these people as lazy as a reason for their not earning their statutory wage, surely the law is open to the planters instead of their taking it, as they invariably do, into their own hands. And granted that those men are lazy and not up to the mark, what about the men and women who work in the factory from 4 am to 8 or 9 pm, when the grinding goes on? Are they not forced to work till a certain number of boxes of liquor have been extracted, and are they paid for the full number of hours they serve?

I doubt if Mr Duncan has ever seen India, yet he confidently asserts that the immigrant is in every way benefited by his removal from India to British Guiana. If this is so, why then is there necessity for *indentured labour*, – which is certainly another form of slavery, seeing that a large number of immigrants are today serving their time in gaol, because they refuse to be downtrodden.

At this moment the Indian government is feeding a large number of famine-stricken wretches who might as well have been fattened on board the ship, and sent here as *free* immigrants to increase our population; but no, *enforced* labour has to be resorted to, so as to keep down wages at starvation point. I cannot for the life of me see the wisdom of such a policy when the planters could do the business more economically by either reindenturing immigrants on the same terms here or raising the rates of wages. Mr Duncan quotes ancient history when he cites Surgeon Major Comins [who visited the colony in 1891] as his authority for saying that we immigrants are benefited by our removal from India to British Guiana.

The Rev Mr Shirley is perfectly right, Sir, in all that he has written to *The Birmingham Post*. Lest people should think that I am in communication with the reverend gentleman I am willing to make an affidavit to the effect that I have not the pleasure of his acquaintance nor have I seen him as yet. Long before I knew of the existence of Mr Shirley I wrote to Lord George Francis Hamilton, Secretary of State for India, and gave him my opinion of the immigration system [27 April 1899]. I even wrote to the Secretary to the Government of India in the Department of Revenue and Agriculture asking him to bring the matter to the notice of Lord Curzon, the present viceroy.

There indeed is one other thing Mr Shirley can do to save this colony from destruction, and that is to move both earth and heaven to put a period to the immorality that goes on on estates with East Indian women – unless all the ministers of the various denominations are prepared to help him to stamp out this evil which I firmly believe is the main cause of this colony's deplorable condition, they might as well take up their bags and baggages and clear out of our modern Babylon. I would do so tomorrow, only that I have not the means.

The Daily Chronicle, 29 December 1900

In November 1900, Rev H.J. Shirley writes to *The Birmingham Post*, contending that if an overseer "beats or kicks a coolie", the latter has no chance of getting justice, whereas if the 'coolies' threaten the authorities on plantations, armed policemen are quickly summoned. In December 1900, the ruling elite attacks Shirley for inciting the people. He responds that by failing to address the issue of poor wages on estates, by vacillating on the Corentyne water scheme, by footing the "unnecessary immigration expenditure", the government, not he, is inciting the people.

> . . . Incite the people forsooth! . . . The people have enough to incite them in actual occurrences. When men have to work for twelve hours at

throwing sugar as thick and heavy as clay for just over a penny an hour, and dig 3 rods of trench a foot deep for which sometimes they get nothing at all, if the overseer does not pass their work through a shower of rain washing into it, after its being dug for 4 shillings; is that not calculated to embitter man?

. . . the government play into . . . [the] hands [of the planters]. What need is there for the immigration system when letters written from the planters' standpoint admit that there is more labour than work . . . . Why is immigration continued? We hear again and again that nobody has suggested the ways and means for the Corentyne water scheme. That is a paltry subterfuge. If they wish they could find the means. The abolition of the unnecessary immigration expenditure would be one of the items towards it, and others could be the disestablishment of the churches and the reduction in the Civil Service vote. These three items would, in time, pay off a loan for the Corentyne water scheme . . . When these things are done is it I or the government who are inciting the people?

The Daily Chronicle, 16 December 1900

One can, therefore, appreciate Bechu's admiration for Shirley. For Joseph Ruhomon of New Amsterdam ['East Indian Descendant'], the radical minister becomes his mentor. On 4 December 1900, he writes to *The Birmingham Post*, endorsing Shirley's indictment of Indian indentureship in British Guiana, "that tyrannical system".

'East Indian Descendant' (British Guiana) [Joseph Ruhomon] to the Editor, *The Birmingham Post*:

Sir, It was with a good deal of interest and pleasure that I read in your issue of a few weeks ago the letter by the Rev H.J. Shirley on the situation in British Guiana. My object in now writing is to heartily support his statements in every single detail. The newspaper press of the colony, the planters, and other supporters of the government would make it appear that Mr Shirley has grossly falsified the existing condition of affairs and given the British people in England an erroneous impression of the situation that is calculated to do considerable harm to the colony and reflect seriously on the government. But those of us who are acquainted with things from personal knowledge and experience entertain a different opinion. Mr Shirley's allegations against the planters of this colony, for instance, as regards their treatment of the indentured East Indian immigrants in their employ, are absolutely and unquestionably true, despite what his opponents may say to the contrary.

The unfortunate immigrant is of no account in the eyes of the master, save that he represents so much labour. He is a mere machine, and in a good many cases all personal considerations for him must give way to the exigencies created by that tyrannical system at work on not a few of our sugar plantations that peremptorily insists upon the contribution of labour at any cost.

It is true that immigration authorities are supposed to look after and protect the interests of the indentured immigrants, but it is a regrettable fact that they are not as much alive as they should be to their obligations and responsibilities. The Rev Mr Shirley, therefore, so far from misrepresenting things has given a true and faithful picture of the real state of affairs . . . The spirit of disaffection is everywhere. Unutterable are our feelings of intense dissatisfaction with the policy of the powers that be – a policy whose effects are to be seen in the widespread depression of the colony and the neglected and despicable condition of the people . . .

Reproduced in *The Argosy*, 2 February 1901, from *The Birmingham Post*, 29 December 1900

Bechu's letter of 29 December 1900 (above) evokes varying responses from three correspondents. The first one, a person of "mixed race", agrees with Bechu that the statutory wage rate is not usually honoured on sugar estates. Moreover, unlike the planter/legislator, R.G. Duncan, who is already seeking to undermine the projected Corentyne water scheme, he sees it as potentially beneficial to rice and sugar, as the population increases in this healthy district.

'One of the Mixed Race' to the Editor, *The Daily Chronicle*:

Sir, Mr R.G. Duncan's utterances lately . . . [will] do sugar more harm than good . . . I am in a position to say if Bechu's surprise visit was made to a sugar estate on pay day, his assertion would be found pretty correct; that is, the indentured gangs do not generally receive the amount allotted by law. I have worked on sugar estates, but am unable to do so now on account of the small wages. I am neither a coolie, Chinaman, Negro, or white, but know what is going on around me.

If the water scheme for the Corentyne is not to be inaugurated the sugar estates must raise their wages for the people to live. Mr Duncan says:

> In the first place the colony could not probably borrow the money, and in the second place if borrowed the inhabitants of the Corentyne could never repay it, and the burden would fall to the taxpayers generally.

Mr Duncan knows very well [that] with water to grow rice the Corentyne would be the most thickly populated part of the colony; being the healthiest, it would attract, and be the means of raising population for the other parts, and reduce the mortality and immorality of the colony, for in no part of it will you find marriage amongst the lower orders more generally carried out than on the Corentyne.

The Daily Chronicle, 4 January 1901

Another critic of Bechu who, deceptively, bears an Indian name, shows no compassion for the Indian labourer. This letter and a few of his subsequent ones have a plantocratic feel; this and the fact that he uses three different addresses, between January and March 1901, cast a shadow on his Indian credentials suggested by the name, Ramsing [sic].

'Ramsing' (12 Croal St, Georgetown) to the Editor, *The Daily Chronicle*:

> . . . It is with pleasure . . . I take the pen to record my sentiments with respect to a letter which made its appearance in your issue of 29 December 1900, signed 'Bechu'.
>
> The flimsy foundations on which the better portion of his letter are [sic] built I will attack first. Mr Bechu has often alleged that the East Indian labourers of the estates do not get their good wages without referring to the circumstances that attend the sugar industry and the planters. What that gentleman calls good wages I am at a loss to know.

Does he expect them to get wages that will enable them to live like petty princes and rajahs? The gentleman never takes the trouble to find out what is the cause of such a reduction in wages compared with former times, but simply runs bigoted with the notion that the planters do not pay fair with the view of cheapening labour at starvation point. Surely, Sir, if this be so it is a most extravagant folly; but there are labourers now on estates, who are physically adapted for strong labour, earning their statutory wages, while those with inferior working capacity earn their fair little pay.

Apart from this, I take the pleasure of adducing a few facts, that will tend to convince Mr Bechu that the ordinary labourers are perfectly well paid in proportion to wages now received by men in other trades and professions at large.

A dispenser that used to get his $60 a month hardly gets $30 now; a bookkeeper who was getting his $50 a month is only too glad to base his time with $20 a month . . . I do not know if Mr Duncan has ever seen India, but I have not; yet I maintain his views in stating that the immigrant is in every way benefited by his removal from India to British Guiana; and its truth can easily be shown. Let the most backward schoolboy take a run to the Immigration Depot when the immigrant is landed and observe carefully his condition, action, and manners; then for a moment revert to those of the time-expired one and he will readily perceive the basis of the exclamation, 'Halloo babu! Is that you? You have improved first class in every way.'

The Daily Chronicle, 5 January 1901

A planter joins the debate to sing lavish praises of Indian indentureship, although he claims, erroneously, that planters would prefer to have "free immigrants" as labourers, as Bechu advocates.

'Creole Planter' to the Editor, *The Daily Chronicle*:

. . . In reply to the statements of Mr Bechu, let us see what are the facts of the case. The East Indian labour in this colony is well looked after. There is nothing approaching slavery in the system, and in spite of all Mr Bechu says I do not think there are any happier labourers in the world than our indentured ones. An indentured labourer is not a cheap labourer by any means – except so far as being a reliable one. The rates of wages paid them allow of all who have been agricultural labourers in India, earning more than the stipulated wage; but as Mr Bechu must know more than half the people who come to the colony are the scum of India . . . I draw my conclusions from the following facts. Allotments of new immigrants arrive – men and women; they are taken to the field; a glance from an experienced eye soon detects those who are field labourers, and results prove the correctness of the judgment thus formed. The following results I have seen myself – an allotment has arrived; the men are given a three-bit task [24 cents – the statutory wage], the woman a two-bit one [16 cents – the statutory wage]. Some of the men and women finish their task with ease, others do not; next day some of the women ask for and get a three-bit task instead of the two-bit one, and they finish it while some of the men who are new to fieldwork cannot finish more than a two-bit task. The Immigration Agent arrives and complains of some of the earnings; the people are called before him and admit they are new to some of the work and cannot earn more. Now, what should be done? Put the law in motion and make these earn their stipulated wage, cause them to think it a hardship, cause them to desert and become unhappy, or allow them to be happy in their own way earning not only enough to live on but also to save? I think I am correct in saying that all estates pay for all kinds of work by the task, and surely so long as the rate is one that allows the average man to make his day's pay, and the strong man more – no one can growl at the lazy or incompetent doing less . . .

If the Hon Mr Duncan cares to do so he can show Mr Bechu's error; and he can also take Mr Shirley or any other interested gentleman to the pay table of any well-conducted estate, and while he will find indentured labourers drawing less than the statutory wage, he will also find others drawing considerably over it; and if he goes a step further he will find that as a rule the labourers, whose earnings are low, will say they do not like fieldwork. Mr Bechu shows his ignorance of the subject when he says 'enforced labour has to be resorted to so as to keep down wages to starvation point.' On the estates I know, the highest rates are paid to the indentured labourer.

Again, I think every planter will agree with me that if the government will bring in free immigrants, as Mr Bechu suggests, not an estate will take indentured ones. I quite agree with Mr Bechu that if the planters study their own immediate interests they would go in for reindenturing, or like an estate I know, [for] having no indentured immigrants; but as any sensible person knows, this would mean trying to keep all the people on the sugar estates, and not encouraging them to settle in the villages, which I take it should be the duty of everyone who has the colony's interest at heart. I know of no good agricultural labourers who leave the estates unless it is to settle on lands of their own. The ones seen in the towns, picking up odd jobs, are, I presume the ones he has in his mind's eye, when he talks of their not being paid the statutory wage. If the planters could, without injury to themselves, increase the wages of their labourers and other employees, I have no hesitation in saying that rates would soon be back at the figures they were in the seventies – when an indentured labourer could earn 2 shillings a day with ease, and yet the estates cleared more money than they can now, though thousands of pounds have been spent on improving machinery, etc.

Do you think I am satisfied with my salary? I am not – it is very small – and I think in comparison I am worse off than any indentured labourer, but I thank God I have some intelligence and realize that half a loaf is better than no bread and, while I would gladly join any sensible movement to improve our position, I trust I shall not live to see the day when sugar estates will be extinct; for labourers' wages alone, not including the staff, it takes from $25 to $30 to make a ton of sugar – and without sugar estates in this colony we should be in a sad plight.

The Daily Chronicle, 6 January 1901

Bechu responds to 'Creole Planter'; apparently the would-be Indian, 'Ramsing', does not merit his attention. Bechu sees nothing redeeming in indentureship: it is corrupt to the core – the statutory wage is not honoured; the 'coolie' is a pawn in the hands of avaricious drivers. Indeed, he says that some indentured labourers consider jail "a paradise compared with an estate", and the system provides ample opportunity for their wishes to be granted. (It is noteworthy that this letter, dated 7 January 1901, comes from Tuschen, West Coast Demerara. He has left Georgetown. He is about to leave British Guiana.)

Bechu (Tuschen, West Coast Demerara) to the Editor, *The Daily Chronicle*:

Sir, Do all he may, 'Creole Planter' will never be able to justify himself or his brother planters for withholding from indentured immigrants their statutory wage. According to the law these men cannot be paid less than a shilling for seven hours' work, and even if a task is imposed it must not be so heavy that they cannot complete it within seven hours. We hear too much of 'vested rights' in this colony. The clergy, the immigration officials, and indeed every man-jack in the public service claims it; but the poor coolie who comes here under a strict contract which the government is bound to see enforced is robbed of his 'vested right'.

'Creole Planter' is perfectly right in saying that there are several indentured immigrants who earn the statutory wage and even more, but do you happen to know who those men are? Well, Sir, I will tell you. These men are the drivers' favourites who, in addition to doing a deal of foot kissing, cut grass for their drivers' cattle, till their farms on a Sunday, and occasionally fetch wood for them from aback. Woe be unto those who refuse to do as they are bidden!

I remember having on several occasions, not only shamed my own shipmates but other indentured immigrants for going to prison so often, and do you know, Sir, what they invariably gave as their reply?

> Bechu, the gaol is a paradise compared with an estate. We have not to rise so early in the morning as we are compelled to do on an estate. Our hot molasses tea is served out to us before we turn out to work. Our breakfast is not a movable feast as we eat it at stated hours. If the work given to us is in the open, we knock off when it rains. When the day's work is done, we have a jolly good bath and then take our dinner which is cooked and served to us steaming hot, and after that when it gets dark we turn in. But on an estate we have to rise before 4 am, cook our victual, tramp sometimes miles before we get to the field where our work has been allotted, work away in the scorching sun and pelting rain, breakfast whenever we can snatch the time, renew work after that till sunset, and then tramp back home which we reach so late that, after taking our baths, cooking our food, and partaking of our meals, it is about time for us to turn in to rest our weary bones.

In India, Sir, we look down with contempt on a man who has been to gaol; but here the best of us dare not do so for we can hardly tell when we shall have the misfortune to be sent there ourselves.

Apologizing for again taking up so much of your space and thanking you in anticipation.

The Daily Chronicle, 9 January 1901

Bechu's would-be Indian critic, 'Ramsing', responds swiftly, attributing to Bechu's friends who prefer jail to the rigours of plantation work, natural indolence. Greater vigilance should be exercised in India to weed out "these lazy fellows".

'Ramsing' (12 Croal St, Georgetown) to the Editor, *The Daily Chronicle*:

Sir, Your correspondent Mr Bechu in his letter in your issue of the 9th inst. states that on having tried to shame his shipmates for going to prison so often they replied 'that the jail is a paradise compared with estates' living'. I admit such an honest reply, which only gives the fair deduction of their being a naturally indolent set of labourers who would rather spend their time in the so-called 'paradise' than try to earn a respectable living. Scanty wages cannot be responsible for these fellows always being in jail, for there are hundreds of labourers on estates who are getting a fair living in view of the hard times; and since so many can obtain a living, we cannot rationally see the difficulty that is being put before the wretched fellows in sharing the same life.

If the Indian Agent would take a little more trouble in selecting the labourers for this colony, we could get rid of these lazy fellows who come here only to be a burden on our government after expending so much money on them, and would be able to effect the saving of a few hundred dollars in the prison department which would be reducing taxation.

The Daily Chronicle, 12 January 1901

'Creole Planter', another of Bechu's critics, counters that Bechu's allegation that only the pawns of the drivers are able to earn the statutory wage is untenable, for Managers and overseers would not condone it and those from authentic labouring castes would "scorn" any such obsequiousness. He also claims ignorance of a preference for jail among any labourers on sugar estates.

'Creole Planter' to the Editor, *The Daily Chronicle*:

... I beg to deny Mr Bechu's assertion that it is only the drivers' favourites 'who earn the statutory wage and even more'. The immigrant who has been an agricultural labourer in India would scorn to do what Mr Bechu says – in fact, they have no cause to court the drivers' favour; and I don't see how such a course can be carried on without the attention of the Manager and overseers being drawn to it. I know that a light or easy task is always given by orders of the Manager or overseer to those who deserve or need help, but not to those who can easily perform the average task and often ask for more work. I can say without the slightest fear of contradiction that the people who are known as Chamars, Khurmees, Choires, Bhars, Khawotes, Lodes, etc, who are labourers in India, find no difficulty in performing their tasks and more when they come here; but the Naws, Jalahas, Brahmins, Dobis, Sonars, Khoits, do find hardship in performing theirs... I can assure you, Sir, that no agricultural labourer from India has any cause of complaint, nor do we find these complaining. Whenever there is a strike or any discontent among our indentured labourers, you will find it is not a *workman* who leads it, but a *loafer*. With regard to their fondness for the gaol, I can only speak of the estates that I know, as I have not Mr Bechu's experience of the colony though I was born in it and have lived in it for over 40 years, and on these estates very few of the indentured immigrants go to jail...

The Daily Chronicle, 16 January 1901

What is most fascinating about Bechu's letters is their power to evoke a wide range of opinions, to draw out the passions of this colonial society. The following three letters, from creole (African) correspondents, on the "position of the Negro" at the end of the 1800s, reflect the diversity of responses even within specific ethnic sections.

Unmasking the Plantocracy: Bechu, Indentureship and 'King Sugar'

George Sobers (Albert Town) to the Editor, *The Daily Chronicle*:

... If I were asked to voice a remedy for the penurious state of the Negro, I would say: Let the Negro engrave the word – independence – in the true light of the word – on his mind, put the bundle of books, bible [sic] and all, on the uppermost shelf, consider the practical side of life, and remember that the Portuguese's and East Indians' hundreds were not made through the medium of books ... I admire the Negro's literary abilities, but the clink of coin is the voice of power. Get coin honestly, by commerce and agriculture, and the white man will soon recognize him and his son, and the sooner he gets coin the sooner he will realize his dream of lofty aspiration. Start commerce and agriculture on a small scale, and gradually creep up by observing economy ... Forget the millions earned in the goldfields and wasted in the taverns and shops of the city; start at once to deny yourself of the superfluous trappings of civilization and practise economy, for the good of the coming generations of Negroes ...

The Daily Chronicle, 9 September 1900

'Well-Wisher' to the Editor, *The Daily Chronicle*:

... About 12 years ago when ... [the colony] was in a flourishing state, young men had little or no difficulty to procure employment; in fact, employers were glad to obtain their services. But in these burdensome times, there are scores of people who would willingly labour for small salaries, but on account of the dullness of business in general, they are unable to get anything to do. This reverse is a grievous one. In my estimation the population is too much mixed up, there being too many Chinese, Portuguese, and coolies in the colony, whereas if one-half of each of them were shipped to their respective country, the poorer classes of creoles [Africans] here would suffer less. Most of these foreigners after they have acquired a certain sum of money retire to settle down on their income.

The Daily Chronicle, 22 November 1900

The final 'creole' correspondent's perspectives are the most comprehensive critique of indentureship ventilated at the time. Like Bechu he argues for the termination of a system which benefits the plantocracy, but which "native labour" practically subsidizes. However, he is receptive to a scheme for settlers provided some development is initiated to accommodate them, as in Canada. This letter is such a searing indictment of Indian indentureship that it is reproduced in its entirety.

'A Creole' to the Editor, *The Daily Chronicle*:

Sir,   The very argument put forward by the planters that the prosperity of this colony rests on a *single* industry – sugar – is, I think, a sufficient reason for every citizen to concern himself about the future of this colony.

It is common knowledge that as long as any country is dependent on any *one* industry for its prosperity and development the condition of such a country must always be precarious and unstable.

It is also well known that the development of young colonies has been usually effected by some well-designed system of immigration having for its *primary* and immediate object the general welfare of the immigrant settlers themselves and the benefit of the whole community; and for its *ultimate* or incidental purpose a supply of labour to foster *any* industry.

These facts granted, all must desire to see an influx of capital and of immigrant settlers.

But a distinction should be carefully drawn between our system of immigration, which is a hybrid one of immigration and *emigration,* and well-planned immigration, such, for instance, as obtains in Canada.

Our system of immigration viewed not from the planters' standpoint, but from that of the people or government, has *four fatal* defects:

(a) It involves an emigration system; inasmuch as it provides a periodic return of immigrants: thus depopulating the colony. In 1891, no less than 2,151 immigrants were repatriated.

(b) It tends to pauperize the country; inasmuch as the immigrants who thus return take with them every penny which they save by stinting themselves of the necessaries of life – food and clothing. In 1883, they took away $152,980 in cash and $30,858 in jewels and gold pieces. It is important to bear in mind that there is an annual return of immigrants.

Unmasking the Plantocracy: Bechu, Indentureship and 'King Sugar'

Mr Chamberlain [the Secretary of State for the Colonies] who, it must be supposed, is anxious to see a unit of the Empire develop, expressly sanctions a system involving principles destructive to the two fundamental factors, capital and population – which are so necessary for the development of any young colony.

(c) It sanctions the *exclusive* service of all the immigrants to *one* industry – sugar – while it compels every other industry, every taxpayer, to pay one-third of the cost of importing such immigrants and a costly medical service, chiefly for their benefit. The general taxpayer was until recently also compelled to pay the cost of return passages. This gives a bounty to sugar planters that is more detrimental to this colony generally and less excusable than the continental bounty. Owners of continental factories and growers of beetroot reside in the country which gives the bounty; whereas, in this colony, the profits of the sugar industry are spent abroad, in concerns unconnected with the colony.

(d) Lastly, *our immigration system compells the native labourer [the African worker] to pay part of the cost of importing foreign labour to work for wages on which the native labourer cannot live. The native labourer cannot live on a gallon of rice a week, nor can he clothe himself with a yard of cotton. Thus he is punished by being made to contribute one-third of the cost of introduction of his important competitor* [emphasis added].

Because the native labourer considers himself worthy of his hire and will not work for less than what he considers a fair wage, he is branded in the face of the world as lazy and incapable of continuous work. And this is done notwithstanding he undertakes long and arduous journeys into the far interior; ascends and descends dangerous falls where hundreds of his fellow native labourers have perished; notwithstanding he endures all this and more and works on placer claims where his daily task is harder by far than any to be found on a sugar estate, within reach of neither doctor nor hospital; where insanitation, dysentery, and fever are rife, and yet, after doing all these things, the planters continue to slander him and call him lazy.

It seems almost incredible that a class of men should be found within Her Majesty's Empire so wanting in common justice as to thus slander the labouring class of this colony.

What British labourer would allow himself to be taxed to bring in foreign labourers to compete against himself and benefit primarily one class of employers? What body of businessmen in Scotland or England would be so bold as to wait on the Home Secretary or Prime Minister to request that the British working man should be taxed to pay part of the labour bill of the British farmer? Yet some time ago a deputation waited on Sir Walter Sendall [the Governor] with such a request.

It would seem to be but common justice that the planter should now pay the whole cost of his labour bill. Surely, it is enough that the general taxpayer is burdened with the maintenance of the many pauper immigrants scattered throughout the colony?

It has been said that if the planter had to pay the entire cost of immigration he would abandon his estates. I do not believe that abandonment to any appreciable extent would follow. Businessmen do not relinquish paying concerns and my belief is that even under such circumstances sugar would pay.

Success in any line of business depends greatly on a knowledge of the practical details connected with it: the fact that sugar estates are paying concerns although owned by absentee proprietors, is, I think, fair proof that the profits are abnormal. One estate alone last year cleared over £30,000!

The energetic Secretary of the Institute of Mines and Forests can prove that the statement regarding the laziness of the native labourer is untrue. He says he is unable to find sufficient work for all willing to go into the interior, and that some 6,000 of them have been working steadily, continuously and for years in the goldfields of the colony.

A few months ago a leading planter, in order to show that our present system of immigration was a proper system, stated that sugar put into circulation over $6,000,000, in one year, compared with $2,000,000 by gold. He tried to prove that as sugar circulated three times more money in wages than gold, sugar was entitled to receive from the general taxpayer three times as much as gold receives. But gold receives nothing.

I am of opinion that there is at present in the colony more labour than employment, and that, consequently, immigration should be stopped. With the aid of the large sum now paid for immigration the colony might be developed to some extent, and after that a proper system of immigration might be considered for the purpose of bringing in *settlers*.

The present system might be continued for the benefit of the sugar planters provided the general taxpayer is not made to contribute to its cost.

Having exclusive use of the immigrants the planters should in my opinion pay for their introduction.

The Daily Chronicle, 25 January 1901

The fictive Indian, 'Ramsing', is not impressed by 'A Creole's' compelling arguments; he insists that everybody, including African people, benefits from sugar. He parades many of the familiar platitudes, including the tired dogma that the industry would be crippled without reliable, indentured labour, and that the consequent "evils" would redound on the whole of British Guiana: it was, therefore, in the "native" taxpayers' interest to contribute to Indian immigration.

'Ramsing' to the Editor, *The Daily Chronicle*:

Sir, 'A Creole' intimates that immigration should now be stopped, or if continued the planters should pay its whole cost, because the taxpayers have to pay for that which is of no benefit to them whatever. 'A Creole' must understand that the natives [Africans] are not the only class of people who contribute to make up the one-third spent towards immigration; that every immigrant thus introduced also shares its cost. But 'A Creole' asks why should the natives pay to bring these men to compete against them. It is evident that if the natives were of themselves sufficient to till and develop their own lands, and to give the planters their regular labour as required for the upkeep of the sugar industry, there would have been no just cause for our government to introduce outside labour. But the natives would not work on the sugar estates for the wages that the foreign man [Indian] is working for, notwithstanding the downfall in the price of sugar. Besides this, the natives would not under any circumstances work regularly for six days in the week, and at grinding seasons when the crop comes to maturity, to work in the fields from 4 am to 11 or 12 pm. And this, the sugar industry must of necessity require. But 'A Creole' says that some of them have been working steadily and continuously for years in the goldfields, which [is] so laborious; but this kind of alternate [periodic] labour would not do for the sugar industry. The number of cases that are tried by the Magistrate for breach of contract, can prove the reliability of some of the native labour. If, under these circumstances, foreign labour is not resorted to, the sugar industry, which has absorbed so many dollars, which circulates so much money, which employs so much labour, and which in an indirect manner benefits the government as well as the natives, is sure to be crippled; and the evils that would result therefrom would be great. For the above reasons, I am of opinion that the native taxpayers are justified in paying for immigration. But if the natives would all get back on the estates – give their labour as called upon, and work for the same money as their foreign brothers, until sugar comes up, then the planters should pay the whole cost of immigration.

The Daily Chronicle, 1 February 1901

In early 1901 Bechu writes from West Coast Demerara that he is "about to say farewell" to British Guiana, but his antagonism to indentured immigration does not wane. The following two letters underline his unwavering stance that priority must be given to the alleviation of the condition of despairing labourers in the colony. He dramatizes the absurdity of the colony's immigration policy when, provocatively, he provides information to local Africans on employment possibilities on Hawaiian sugar estates.

Bechu to the Editor, *The Daily Chronicle*:

Sir, Here is a splendid opportunity for the sturdy black labouring population of this colony and Barbados obtaining steady employment and liberal wages.

Thirty thousand men are needed immediately in Hawaii to work on the sugar plantations of the islands, and efforts to secure the men in New York do not appear to have met with success.

Mr George E. Baldwin, representative of the Hawaiian sugar men, has opened an office at No. 3, Pearl Street, New York. He is now at Vancouver sending 64 men to the islands. Mr Frank Alves who represents him during his absence, in an interview with a reporter of *The World*, said:

> When the United States took over Hawaii the planters knew they would have to let the Chinese and Japanese labourers go, and they were rather glad of it.

The men of Asia cannot work as well as the Europeans. One sturdy white man can do more work than three yellow men.

The planters expected that there would be a rush of men from the United States to the islands, and so they let most of their workmen go. But men did not go to the islands from the United States and the sugar planters are in a bad way for hands.

Fifteen thousand are needed immediately and 15,000 more will be needed inside of a year. We pay a man's fare out there and provide him with food and good accommodation while he is travelling. In Hawaii a man is required to work ten hours a day and we pay him $22 a month and provide him with good board, lodging and medical attendance. Overtime is paid for.

We especially want men with families, and any man who wants to take a wife with him may do so and we will pay her fare. We will also defray the travelling expenses of their children. Women may work if they wish and their pay will be $15 a month and board and lodging. Children who are able to work will get $10 a month. The planters hope to populate the island . . .

The Daily Chronicle, 6 January 1901

The following letter, Bechu's last before he leaves the colony, takes a final shot at Indian indentureship, and challenges a correspondent's assertion that the 'coolie's' life is better in British Guiana than in India (see below).

Bechu (Tuschen, West Coast Demerara) to the Editor, *The Daily Chronicle*:

Sir, *Although I am about to say farewell to this colony* [emphasis added], I am hopeful that at no distant date Mr Chamberlain will, in answer to Dr Rohlehr's suggestion in the English press, appoint a Commission to enquire into poor Guiana's affairs and devise some measures to rescue her from her present deplorable condition.

It is a matter much to be regretted that at this particular time Sir Cavendish Boyle who has this colony's interests so near to his heart is shortly to leave us, and that one who perhaps knows not Guiana may be sent here to take his place. Our departing Government Secretary and you too, sir, have done all that lay in your power to lighten the burden of the taxpayers by strongly protesting against the introduction of more immigrants so long as we have such a large unemployed labouring population in the colony, and I am anxiously awaiting to see whether our representatives in the Combined Court will knock the immigration vote on the head when it is brought up for discussion this week. I am no advocate for the stoppage of East Indian immigration, but what I earnestly desire to see before I leave these shores is that it be suspended for at least three years, by which time all our surplus labourers can be provided for and the colony's gate then thrown wide open to *all comers*. Those of my countrymen who are hankering to come to this land which is flowing with sugar and molasses, should be made to do so at their own cost.

How puerile of your correspondent, 'Observer', to jump to the conclusion that because 'most of the letters posted from India to this colony are sent postage unpaid' that in itself is 'a powerful argument proving the better condition of the coolie labourer in this colony'. The ways of the Postal Department are so wonderful that most of us, to ensure the safe delivery of our letters, prefer to receive them 'bearing', for when a fee is payable we may rely on their reaching us even if a 'registered' cover does not.

The Daily Chronicle, 6 February 1901

'Observer' to the Editor, *The Daily Chronicle*:

Sir, A powerful argument proving the better condition of the coolie labourer in this colony than his brother in India is the fact that most of the letters posted from India to this colony are sent postage unpaid, while no coolie thinks of sending an unpaid letter from this colony to his people in India.

The Daily Chronicle, 2 February 1901

CHAPTER FIVE

Bechu, the Salvation Army and Derelict 'Coolies' in Georgetown, with Special Reference to the Work of Ghurib Das

Bechu, an orphan, was brought up by a Scottish woman, a missionary in Calcutta, and was obviously shaped by basic Christian tenets with respect to the poor and the powerless. Bechu's Christianity was not tolerant of the rigidity and pretentiousness of the so-called established denominations. It is hardly surprising, therefore, that he defends the Salvation Army, in mid 1897, when some of its leaders, including Mrs Widgery, are tried and convicted for disturbing the peace with their tambourines and drumming. He sees the Salvation Army as the church of the underdog – reaching out, in a practical way, to give hope to those Indians who exist on the edge, in destitution in Georgetown.

Bechu (Georgetown) to the Editor, *The Daily Chronicle*:

Sir, The parsons of the established churches in this colony ought to feel deeply grateful to 'Impartial' for having taken up the cudgels on their behalf, because it certainly is news to the majority of us to be informed that they do 'watch for souls as they that must give account.' With the exception of

Rev A.M.B. Jemmott, however, I defy him to name another curate or rector who goes out to the 'hedges and highways' to reclaim souls.

Since scripture plainly tells us that 'All have sinned and come short of the glory of God' and again, that 'There is none righteous, *no not one*,' it would be absurd for any mortal to style himself or herself a saint, but my object in quoting the passage that Christ 'came not to call the righteous but sinners to repentance' was merely to show that our Saviour was not so much concerned about those who were within the 'fold' as He was for those who were straying far away from it. It is evident however that, in this colony, His so-called disciples can only reach respectable sinners and do not trouble themselves to go amongst those who will not come within the reach of salvation unless it is carried to them. Is it because they are supposed to be past redemption?

If 'Impartial' wishes me to do so, I will give him the name of a person in whose parish I resided over two years [Pln Enmore, East Coast Demerara] who never visited his flock – black, white or brown – once during all that time, but he regularly paid his weekly visits to the tennis parties given by the master of an estate.

The Daily Chronicle, 13 June 1897

A more conservative correspondent takes a different view of the Salvation Army. He sees nothing redeeming in their ministry: they are disturbers of the peace, potential subversives. Here one gets a feel for perceptions shaped by class and status: the official, plantocratic conception of the role of the church vs Bechu's rebellious Christian spirit. The Salvation Army is closer to the latter.

'Facts' to the Editor, *The Daily Chronicle*:

. . . Mrs Widgery, four young women and Dowridge, were on Saturday night holding a meeting 'in a public way'. They had five tambourines and a drum. The Sergeant Major went up to them while they were beating these noisy instruments and told them he had had orders to request them to cease beating. Mrs Widgery asked who gave him orders, and was told that the County Inspector did. She refused to obey and continued beating. Dowridge and the others went on also. She and Dowridge were prosecuted.

Dowridge pleaded guilty and said in extenuation that he acted in accordance with the orders of his superior officer. He was convicted and fined $10. Mrs Widgery pleaded not guilty but was found guilty. She was fined $25 . . .

Now, in all fairness, have these Salvationists shown themselves the Christians they are supposed to be? Is wilfully infringing the law of the land a Christian action?

I should have mentioned, Sir, that the Magistrate told Mrs Widgery and Dowridge that he would be willing to ask the Inspector to withdraw the charges against them if they would promise to keep the law in future. They did not deem it advisable to do so and therefore the case was proceeded with.

Now, Sir, in defying the police, are not these people paving the way to a general disregard to the 'protectors of the peace' . . . Are they not leading an erstwhile law-abiding people to become belligerent and insubordinate? Your correspondent . . . is guilty of gross misrepresentation. Mrs Widgery and her fellow soldiers have not been sent to prison because they are trying to prevent people from using bad language, but because they wilfully disregarded the law, and this after they were warned. Instead of being regarded as martyrs, they should certainly be branded as disobedient subjects of their Queen and Country, as would-be martyrs, and as probable riot makers. I hope the punishment they are now undergoing will teach them a salutory lesson, and that they may at the end of their terms of imprisonment be prepared to live as law-abiding citizens . . .

The Daily Chronicle, 11 June 1897

As a Christian, Bechu believes that Indians on the sugar estates, "heathen labourers", should be won over to Christ, but he sees a lack of will and resolve among Christian parsons, who prefer the beaten path. The underlying point, here, is the contrast in approach reflected in the work of the "persecuted" Salvation Army.

Bechu (Georgetown) to the Editor, *The Daily Chronicle*:

. . . Having scores of times, in the discharge of my duties in the field, been myself tortured by mosquitoes and sandflies, I should not have thought that a labourer in Christ's vineyard would consider that – [work among Indians] – a hardship worth mentioning. Do not our *heathen* labourers on the sugar plantations (who are, I presume, made of the same clay as our parsons) suffer quite as much and even so much more? Do not all that we enjoy, as returns of the soil, come from their patient and untiring labours, and shall we – trusting that our souls are safe – feel unconcerned and indifferent about theirs?

The office of a Christian parson is a most solemn and responsible one. He has souls committed to his charge, and if he wilfully neglects his duties, blood shall be required of his hands.

I know it is not an easy matter to convert the coolie to Christianity, but if our labourers in Christ's vineyard do not meet with much encouragement and success, let them remember that if they are the instruments in God's hand of saving a few souls, then shall our King and Redeemer say unto them: 'Well done good and faithful servant, enter thou into the joy of the Lord.' 'And they that be wise shall shine as the brightness of the firmament, and they that turn many to righteousness as the stars for ever.'

The Daily Chronicle, 17 June 1897

Alexander Alexander, an extraordinary Scotsman who had been an overseer on an Essequibo plantation for 18 years, joined the Salvation Army in 1886. In 1897, he decided to dedicate his life to help Indian paupers in Georgetown. He assumed the Indian name Ghurib Das, became a vegetarian, adopted Indian clothing, and walked barefooted. He opened his first home in July 1897; two more followed, providing cheap board and lodging for many destitute Indians – casualties of indentureship and the inflexible plantation regime. Ghurib Das was popularly known as 'Coolie' Alexander. He epitomizes the true rebellious spirit of Bechu, in addition to his gift for organizing. Even the conservative *Argosy* recognizes his wonderful contribution within the Salvation Army.

. . . [At the Salvation Army Coolie Shelter in Georgetown], many otherwise homeless coolies, waifs and strays about town find a cheap bed and a cheap supper, with a degree of order and cleanliness quite unobtainable for them in any other quarter. It is quite in accordance with the principles of the Army men to associate their evangelical work with practical efforts for the bettering of the condition of the poor; and we have no hesitation in saying that, whatever we may think of their religious views and their mode of expressing them, the local leaders of the Army have already done for the poor of the city what could not have been done otherwise . . .

The Argosy, 30 October 1897

By mid 1898, as Ghurib Das' work gains recognition, Bechu, also, praises him, but he begins to use the colony of Indian paupers and deserters in Georgetown as a weapon to condemn the whole indentureship system. In this letter, he advocates the setting up of an industrial farm, preferably under Ghurib Das or Adjutant Shaw of the Salvation Army, in order to salvage some of his compatriots from dereliction and despair.

Bechu (Georgetown) to the Editor, *The Daily Chronicle*:

The establishment of a 'Coolie Industrial Farm' on the lines suggested by your correspondent, 'Colonist', is a capital idea and deserves to receive the consideration of 'the powers that be'.

You are constantly telling us, Sir, that one of our sorest needs in this colony, which has such enormous natural resources, is free East Indian labour, and yet you seem to shut your eyes to the fact that there is at the present time in this city more than a shipload of unemployed labourers of that class who are knocking about the streets without the slightest effort being made to utilize their services. From enquiries made I find that almost all of them are under Section 199 of the British Guiana Immigration Ordinance entitled to be provided, at the expense of the colony, with a passage back to Calcutta. That being so and taking into consideration that they have saved the government such a nice round sum by not claiming their right, the least their 'Papa Crosby' [the Immigration Agent General] should do for them is to ask the Legislature to offer a grant of a couple hundred acres of Crown land to either Adjutant Shaw or Mr Alexander [Ghurib Das], together with a small loan, returnable in three years, if either of them agrees to take these people in hand and place them in a position to earn a living. The last-named gentleman is a well-known planter, and is so much liked by the coolies that he could get them to cheerfully work under him in any capacity . . .

The Daily Chronicle, 3 August 1898

Bechu's concern for the condition of Indian destitutes in Georgetown is echoed by a correspondent, who speaks of their scavenger-like existence.

'Charlestown' to the Editor, *The Daily Chronicle*:

Sir, A lot has been lately said about the good done among the poorer classes by the opening of soup kitchens, Salvation Army shelters, etc, but many are not aware of the very great amount of misery and want that still exists among the very poorer classes of people in the city, especially the coolies, many of whom have not the penny to buy the food, sold at the shelter and kitchens, and cannot earn it, being unable to do so from the very debilitated state and condition they are in. *They are known to eat the garbage off the streets*. In a community such as ours, ought this state of things to be allowed to exist? The Alms House is overcrowded it is said, but as these unfortunates are brought here by the government, are the government not bound to at least see they are fed, and not allowed to starve? . . .

The Daily Chronicle, 4 August 1898

Ghurib Das corroborates Bechu, arguing that many menial jobbers in Georgetown are, indeed, deserters from the sugar estates, where "harsh and inhuman" treatment often leads to flight.

Ghurib Das to the Editor, *The Daily Chronicle*:

. . . If an acting Inspector-General [of Police] would use his sultry remarks to the immigration authorities who in their turn would rebound them on estate Proprietors and Managers, so that some more care might be taken of their labourers in the slack season, there would then be fewer deserters and more labourers on the estates, and less of the half-starved element about town.

To imagine that these jobbers can earn two or three bits [16 cents or 24 cents] a day as jobbers is wide of the mark. I believe that 6 cents *per diem* is much nearer the mark. Why they prefer this half-starved life, in many cases, is the harsh and inhuman, unsympathetic way they are treated by many of their more fortunate brethren, the drivers [Indian foremen], hence the great percent of deserters from estates, indentured as well as free . . .

The Daily Chronicle, 23 August 1898

As the debate on Indian destitutes continues, a 'Salvationist' writes to *The Argosy* to refute the allegation that the Salvation Army's shelter, run by Ghurib Das, is a loafer's and deserter's retreat.

'Salvationist' to the Editor, *The Argosy*:

Sir, In *The Argosy* of the 20th inst, I read a statement to the effect that the Salvation Army Shelter is becoming the haunt of deserters, as well as a refuge for able-bodied loafers and vagrants.

Statements like the above . . . tend to make false impressions on the minds of the public.

I therefore beg to say that in the first place, there is no room in the Salvation Army shelter for loafers. A loafer, as I understand the term, is a person who won't work, an individual who will sponge on anybody rather than toil for his own livelihood.

It is a fact that the food sold at the Army shelter is at a small sum, yet, *there is a charge* made for everything that an individual desires to have. He pays what is required of him, is satisfied with his purchase and goes away, leaving the way clear for others of his rank to do likewise. This a loafer cannot do.

It is quite against the principles of the Salvation Army either to make or encourage hangers-on.

Secondly, how is the officer in charge of the Shelter to know who are and who are not indentured men, seeing that neither party bears a mark of distinction? Surely somebody can come to the rescue and so make a way out of the dilemma . . .

The Argosy, 27 August 1898

Norman Bascom, a planter from Plantation Cove and John, responds that the Salvation Army could detect deserters by demanding their certificates of exemption from labour, their "free tickets". He contends that an "ostensibly religious organization" should not continue to pave what amounts to a "royal road" to desertion, by providing cheap food and lodging. Three days after this letter appears, Bechu's most controversial letter is published in *The Daily Chronicle* – the subject of this correspondent's brother's charge of libel against him.

Norman Jas A. Bascom (Cove and John) to the Editor, *The Argosy*:

Sir, In your issue of the 27th ult, 'Salvationist' asked how those in charge of the Army shelter could possibly distinguish a deserter from a free coolie. As no one has answered him I would suggest the legal method of demanding free tickets. A free man who has lost his certificate can always obtain another 24 cents, and anyone unable to earn that amount, above his daily sustenance, in this country, must surely be a fit subject for either the Pauper Asylum or the Colonial Hospital.

'Salvationist' may argue that it is not the duty of the Army to recapture defaulters for the estates, but at any rate he will admit that it is at least unseemly for an ostensibly religious organization to aid and abet them in avoiding the fulfilment of their contract. Furthermore it may not be amiss to point out that the representatives of the Army bring themselves under the law in so doing.

The lazy coolie who remains on the estate can generally in time be induced to abandon his evil ways, but the deserter at once places himself beyond the reach of all corrective discipline, and his offence is one which no vigilance on the part of his superiors can prevent.

The long delay which ensues before he is recaptured and the slight deterrent effect of the punishment prescribed by law, too, all tend to make desertion the royal road to avoiding the obligations of the Immigration Contract; and this it will probably continue to be until some stringent measures be taken with old offenders, such as flogging for the third or fourth offence.

Why then should deserters receive assistance in their wrongdoing, in the shape of food and lodging supplied at a nominal rate?

The Argosy, 10 September 1898

The Daily Chronicle endorses Ghurib Das' suggestion to the sugar planters that they could reduce desertion and vagrancy in Georgetown by offering Indians small grants of land on the estates, to grow food. The paper adds that they make good farmers, and that many disillusioned Indians in the city would return to their estates, as "land seems to possess a special attraction" for them.

In a letter which appeared in our columns yesterday [issue missing from British Library], 'Ghurib Das' – the oriental name by which the well-known religious and philanthropic enthusiast, Mr Alexander, chooses to obscure his identity – draws pointed attention to a social question which requires urgent solution. It is the custom for a large number of coolie immigrants, when their terms of residence on the estates have expired, to drift away from the land and to live an unprofitable and not infrequently parasitical existence in the city. The tendency is increasing rather than diminishing, since the ranks of East Indians in Georgetown who earn a precarious hand-to-mouth subsistence are being daily added to by new arrivals from the country. To some extent, perhaps, it is but human that on the expiration of their indentures the coolies, in the first flush of freedom and unrestraint, should feel inclined to abandon the particular sphere of labour that their contracts obliged them to follow. Naturally, too, they gravitate towards the centres of population where the opportunites for less irksome and continuous employment are likely to be most numerous. In this fashion, hundreds of East Indians find themselves in Georgetown today, with no fixed and settled employment, without a shelter to cover their heads, and dependent largely upon charity for the food that sustains them. A protracted existence under such degenerate conditions must tend not only to deteriorate the physique of the coolie and to habituate him to idleness, but also to rob the colony and the planters of a fair return for the money expended on immigration. From every standpoint, therefore, it is desirable that this vast amount of 'waste labour' with which the city teems should be utilized in some profitable way, and in this respect Mr Alexander makes a suggestion which is deserving of some consideration. He urges, in effect, that the planters should encourage the unindentured coolies to take up their residence on the estates by giving them small grants of land – half an acre each would be sufficient – for the purpose of cultivating products for their own consumption. A gift of this description would give the coolie a certain home interest in his surroundings and would enable him to tide over 'the slack season', when his labour would not be in much request on the estate. That such terms would be readily accepted by the coolies themselves, there can be no doubt. The offer of land seems to possess a special attraction for the East Indian, who invariably makes an industrious farmer, and Mr Alexander testifies to the eagerness with which the grants volunteered by the planter who applied to him for labourers were availed of. We believe that if those estates' Managers who complain of the dearth of labour were to offer similar terms to the coolies, they would find a ready and generous response on the part of the unsettled East Indian population. There are many coolies now in the city who would only too willingly return to the estates if the inducements offered them were at all sufficient. Disillusion and disappointment quickly follow in the wake of their newly found independence, and once they have learnt the difficulties they have to encounter in earning a livelihood in Georgetown, they are the more likely to feel content to abide as labourers on the estates. It is a fact also, as Mr Alexander asserts, that such coolies are much more physically capable than those lately introduced, and they have the additional advantage of being familiar with the work they will be required to do. The area of land that would be needed to apportion amongst a hundred coolies or so would be comparatively insignificant in view of the extent of most plantations of the colony, and we feel assured that the planters would speedily find themselves compensated for their generosity and trouble.

Leader, *The Daily Chronicle*, 17 February 1899

A few days later *The Argosy* reports that another periodic "raid" has been made on "coolie jobbers and loafers" in Georgetown, in order to determine their status. (For most of 1899, Bechu is obligated to remain silent because of the protracted libel case brought against him by F.C.S. Bascom, the Manager of Plantation Cove and John.)

> On Saturday and Monday the police made a raid on the coolie jobbers and loafers about town, and conveyed 129 of them to the Immigration Depot. Thirty-eight of them were found to be deserters and were retained to be sent to the estates to which they were indentured. The 'free' people were released as soon as they were identified. These raids are made by the police at intervals and have been going on since about 1883. It will interest planters and others to learn that during last year [1898] 212 immigrants deserted.

The Argosy, 25 February 1899

Periodically, some deserters, usually newcomers, absconded from the sugar estates and fled to the forests, impelled by the notion that they could find a "short road" to Calcutta! A correspondent relates such a case from the East Bank Demerara in January 1900.

'J.B.' to the Editor, *The Daily Chronicle*:

Sir, There are a number of comparatively new indentured coolies straying in the forests within the vicinity of Coverdant, Lucy's Delight and Soesdyke, Demerara River, searching for a new and short road to Calcutta. On Thursday afternoon while loading my craft with wallaba wood brought down from the hill, one of these newcomers made his appearance. He gave his name as Rampholsing [sic], ship's name *Lena*, allotted to Pln Non Pareil two months ago. Himself and about four others left the estate about a week ago walking through the backlands, and the others strayed from him, or they lost each other. He had not eaten anything for several days. I invited Mr Ramphol [sic] down to my cultivation where my house is, and gave him a dinner or rather a bunch of plantains which he cooked and ate the greater part of. As I had to come to town on Friday night I intended to bring him down with me and hand him over to the police. Seeing an old free coolie, who came to me, he got scared, thinking no doubt, this man was one of the estate's sirdars, who had been sent for him, he quietly said he was going to drink water. This was about midday, and since then he has not been seen up to the time I left the farm at about 9 pm.

I was further told by this free coolieman that there are several of them at the back, and a constable had taken two or three of them to Hyde Park where they have been handed to the police 3 or 4 miles off.

This is not the first time these people have been found wandering in the district. Later on they find themselves in the city joining the very large number of jobbers. So that they earn sufficient to pay their board and lodging in the coolie shelter, they will desert any plantation for more remunerative employment.

The Daily Chronicle, 10 January 1900

After nearly a year's absence from the correspondence columns of *The Daily Chronicle*, Bechu returns in January 1900 to defend Hindus and Muslims against what he sees as the distinct partiality of the State towards the Christian denominations. The occasion is the debate in the Combined Court on the old clause exempting the latter from paying duty on imported materials and church furniture. Bechu's stance is entirely in keeping with his capacious Christian vision, his partiality for the underdog.

Bechu (Georgetown) to the Editor, *The Daily Chronicle*:

Sir, At the discussion which took place at yesterday's meeting of the Combined Court with regard to the item, 'Materials and church furniture specially imported for any place of worship of the Christian religion in the colony,' it was somewhat amusing to hear the financial member for Essequibo [Hon R.G. Duncan, a planter], argue that 'we should adhere to what has been the rule for many years.' Such old-fashioned ideas 'won't wash' nowadays, especially on this the eve of the twentieth century.

If Mr Duncan really believes that the government should tax the Hindus and Mahomedans [sic] in order to make proselytes of them he may wait till doomsday and he will never have his wishes gratified.

In conclusion, allow me to say that when Christian things are done in a Christian way there is nothing to fear, but it is when un-Christian things are done in the name of Christianity or when Christian things are done in an un-Christian way, that mischief and danger are occasioned. Rather let the planters by their lives, example, and conversation recommend to the '*Heathens*' around them the religion they profess.

The Daily Chronicle, 25 January 1900

A few days later, when the discriminatory clause is revoked by nine votes to eight, The Daily Chronicle lends its authority, even more forthrightly, to Bechu's principles with regard to the religious neutrality of the State and un-Christian conduct.

. . . We believe that not only in precept but in practice these churches should fight their own battles without being fed by the spoon of the State. If the population of the colony all professed the Christian religion, the case would be wholly different. But nearly half of their number are Mohammedans and Hindus. To bestow a favour on the Christian churches of the colony partly at the expense of those other religions is not creditable to the religion we profess; and conversely the other religions have claims upon us that have a right to be respected. The Hindu religion is much older than the Christian religion, and the Mohammedan religion is younger; and both have a large following in this colony, and have strong claims upon our toleration. Both these religions have much in common with the Christian religion, which if it ever supercedes them, will be not by proselytizing or intolerance, both of which all good Christians repudiate. The fact that the Christian churches of the colony in the past were favoured by the tariff schedule is no justification that this should continue, nor even that the same favour should be extended to all places of worship.

Leader, *The Daily Chronicle*, 28 January 1900

A planter from East Coast Demerara advocates the issuing of badges (licences) to "coolie porters and jobbers" in Georgetown, as a means of arresting the tide of desertion from sugar plantations.

'A Planter' to the Editor, *The Daily Chronicle*:

Sir, Some time ago a letter from the Manager of Pln Marionville [Mr Morison] on the subject of the army of coolie jobbers in Georgetown . . . [was] published in your columns, the point being aimed at by the writer being endorsed by the Hon Immigration Agent General, Mr Alexander. The letter pointed out that the coolie jobbers were largely recruited [from] deserters from the sugar estates, the loss of whose services meant so much money out of pocket of proprietors, and it was suggested that if the coolie porters and jobbers in Georgetown were obliged to wear a badge – a metal plate with a number on it on the left arm, as is commonly seen in England and elsewhere, which badge they could get from the Town Council on production of their Certificate of Exemption or vouchers from the Immigration Office, a very powerful preventive and deterrent to desertion from the sugar estates would be forthwith established to the benefit both of Georgetown and the estates.

Since Mr Morison called attention to it, the matter seems to have dropped, but it is one in which all connected with sugar should actively interest themselves, and if our worthy Mayor and Town Council will only take the matter up I am sure it will not be long before the present rate of desertion from sugar estates will be greatly reduced.

The Immigration Agent General has already publicly expressed his approval of such a measure as the one advocated, and it would be interesting to know what the Inspector General [of Police] thinks of it. He has constantly deprecated the members of his force having to take charge of coolie deserters. I should also like to have the benefit of Mr Garribdass' [sic] opinion on the subject . . .

The Daily Chronicle, 20 February 1900

Ghurib Das responds quickly, endorsing 'A Planter's' suggestion, but he also recommends a legal wage and police protection to ensure that jobbers are not defrauded. He observes that police raids have led to a drop in desertions, while deprecating them as "inhuman".

Ghurib Das (2 Lombard Street [Georgetown]) to the Editor, *The Daily Chronicle*:

>Sir, To issue licences for coolie jobbers from the Immigration Office would, I believe, benefit jobbers, planters and revenue. Then establish a legal tariff and let police protection be given in the many cases which occur daily (of the jobber not getting paid) about the railway station and steamer stellings as well as instances all over the city.
>
>The percentage of deserters is, I believe, much decreased since Mr Morison wrote on this subject which has been brought about through several very inhuman raids among the jobbers at night by the police, viz, dragging all the jobbers they could lay their hands on, not even giving them a chance to take their free tickets from their box, and giving all a free night's lodging in Brickdam [Police Station] until they are released next day at the Immigration Office.
>
>By issuing licences the percentage of deserters would have a greater decrease than the police raids have made, as the smaller lodging houses at present still offer more protection than the shelters do.

The Daily Chronicle, 21 February 1900

'A Planter's' rejoinder to Ghurib Das speaks of repeated absconding by the same people on his estate. It suggests a tradition of desertion – a form of resistance, even if it is a pyrrhic, self-destructive kind.

'A Planter' to the Editor, *The Daily Chronicle*:

>... I cannot ... agree with Mr Ghurib Das that the percentage of deserters is much decreased since Mr Morison wrote on this subject. No doubt the raids of the police had some effect at the time, but many deserters having served their punishment for absence from the estate immediately desert

again as soon as they return to it. I have some deserters on the estate who periodically are arrested in town, taken before the District Magistrate, convicted of desertion, and who then serve out their punishment, return to the estate in charge of the police, and then immediately run away again. I wait a short time, have my deserters identified and arrested in town, and the same comedy is re-enacted. Passing by the market [Stabroek] on the way to the Ferry or Suddie Stelling I often see one or other of my deserters.

I quite agree with Mr Ghurib Das that by insisting upon the coolie jobbers being licensed the percentage of deserters from the estates will be more largely reduced than can be effected by the raids of the police. I trust that Mr Ghurib Das' letter, as well as this and my former one, will catch the attention of the Inspector General of Police.

The Daily Chronicle, 23 February 1900

The Georgetown Town Council imposes a by-law requiring "coolie jobbers" to be licensed and begins to prosecute defaulters. Bechu, however, opposes imprisonment and "unproductive" labour in jail as a deterrent to desertion. He believes deserters should be returned to the sugar estate and made to work in the field, "under police supervision", for the duration of their sentence.

Bechu (Georgetown) to the Editor, *The Daily Chronicle*:

Sir, Will you kindly allow me to make a suggestion with regard to the disposal of unlicensed coolie jobbers? I see our worthy Police Magistrate, Mr P.H.R. Hill, inflicted a nominal fine, or in default one week's imprisonment on the eight men who were placed before him yesterday, but what good will that punishment do? If such men are to be forced to do the work His Worship said they were brought to this colony to perform, the best course to adopt is to detain them in the lock-up in charge of a police officer and direct them to take them to the nearest sugar estate and there under police supervision be directed to do nothing but field labour, the estates' authorities to pay the Inspector General of Police a shilling *per diem* [the statutory wage for male indentured labourers] for each labourer so supplied, the proceeds going towards the maintenance of the prisoners and the salary of the police officers thus employed. When these jobbers see that they will either way be compelled to do field labour, they will soon get reconciled to estate work and earn a living, rather than getting nothing for their pains while in police custody.

It seems to me a great pity to consign these men to gaol to do unprofitable labour, when their services can be utilized more beneficially to the colony as well as by the planters. To send them to prison to mix indiscriminately among a lot of hardened criminals only tends to make them, in a very short time, shameless, and convert them into graduated criminals.

The Daily Chronicle, 2 March 1900

In the campaign to detect deserters, all 'coolie' jobbers are under scrutiny. Some are so impecunious, they cannot afford the licence fee of one shilling. The Magistrate responds to Bechu, noting that he does not have the authority to send defaulters to the sugar estates.

At the Police Magistrate's Court yesterday, 12 jobbers were charged by the Town Clerk, before Mr P.H.R. Hill, with acting as public porters without being licensed. They pleaded guilty, and said that they were sick and too poor to pay a shilling for a licence, but that if they were given time and allowed to pay a cent at a time, they would try to do so. They were fined $1 each, or seven days' imprisonment. His Worship said he had noticed that Mr Bechu had recommended that men like the defendants should be sent to the sugar estates instead of to prison, but he had no authority to do that.

The Daily Chronicle, 3 March 1900

Bechu deplores the imposition of a licence fee of one shilling on jobbers seeking to make "an honest living". He adds, ironically, that had they joined the ranks of the "professional beggars", they would not have been prosecuted: their reward for industry is jail.

Bechu (Georgetown) to the Editor, *The Daily Chronicle*:

Sir, As you are aware, no less than 20 peaceful jobbers have, during the past week, been provided with accommodation within the precincts of the Georgetown prison, simply because they were too poor to take out licences, so as to enable themselves to earn an honest living! Did you ever, sir, come across anything more absurd? Had these men joined our army of professional beggars, and been a pest to the community at large, the police would never have dreamt of making a raid on them, but because they scorned the idea of being a nuisance to the public they have been tapped on their shoulders and told, well done good and faithful citizens as you have been trying hard to keep yourselves on only one meal a day, enter now into the house of many mansions a paternal government has prepared for you at Werk-en-Rust, and where you will be provided with grub *ad lib*!!

The Daily Chronicle, 6 March 1900

Bechu again seeks to defend the jobbers, arguing that the by-law with regard to licence fees applies only to "porters"; by arresting jobbers the police are acting without authority.

Bechu (Georgetown) to the Editor, *The Daily Chronicle*:

Sir, I was pleased to see an elective member of the Court of Policy who I least expected to have done so taking up the cudgels on behalf of our poor downtrodden jobbers. If, as the government Secretary informed Mr Luard yesterday, the police had no power to arrest such men, since the existing Town Council by-laws apply *only to porters*, it is surprising how a Magistrate of Mr Hill's experience, instead of taking our overzealous guardians of the peace to task for acting without authority, should have perpetuated the blunder of sending the men to prison.

The Daily Chronicle, 9 March 1900

Another correspondent strongly deprecates the practice of jailing 'coolie' jobbers for defaulting on licence fees – a measure designed purely to apprehend a few Indian deserters from the sugar plantations.

'One Interested' to the Editor, *The Daily Chronicle*:

Sir, I am wholly at a loss to conceive what beneficial effect can be obtained by imprisoning these innocent jobbers . . . [who] had not provided themselves with licences. If these men had the means, no doubt, they would have willingly done so; but it would be the height of absurdity to expect from such men a fee for a licence, men who have to walk every corner of the city in order to get a job for a cent or a penny, which only serves for a meal or half-a-meal. How can men like these be able to produce the money required for a licence? Sir, . . . [I] think this practice of jailing the jobbers is a highly improper practice, and it will surely be abandoned if our respected Mayor and the police authority will give the matter their consideration.

The main object of the planters in having recourse to this measure and molesting the lives of the jobbers is that indentured immigrants abscond from the estates. Is it judicious to punish all the coolie jobbers for the sake of one or two indentured immigrants? . . .

The Daily Chronicle, 10 March 1900

Ghurib Das sees the imposition of the licence fee as an act of racial discrimination against "Sammy", the Indian, and asks:

Sir, . . . Why is the difference observed in nationality re a jobber's licence? Why is poor 'Sammy' always hauled before the Magistrate while others can be seen picking many of the choice jobs about sales, railway station, and the steamer stellings? . . .

The Daily Chronicle, 30 March 1900

Meanwhile, maltreatment on some estates continues to feed the culture of desertion. In May 1900, a report from Leguan Island (Essequibo) speaks of desperate, absconded, new indentured 'coolies' in quest of the elusive track back to Calcutta.

> On Sunday morning last week, a coolie lad, a cow minder at Uniform [Leguan], whilst walking through the high grass in search of cattle, was surprised by two cooliemen hiding under a clump of paragrass. He was frightened, as the men scarcely had any clothes on, and reported the fact to the man in charge of the estate. Several other coolies with dogs turned out and found the men to be two of 14 newly indentured coolies who, four days previously, ran away from Plantation Success. Later in the day five more were seen walking along the drift mud in the Clonbrook koker trench. Seven more were found aback of Enterprise under a huge oronoque tree, where they had camped with their blankets, etc. They presented a wretched appearance and were all desperately hungry. Several constables conveyed them back to the estate. The men said they were in search of a way to Calcutta, and alleged that the cause of their running away was that the driver beat them in the field and the Sahib (Manager) would not believe their complaints.

The Daily Chronicle, 29 May 1900

In July 1900, a report from Berbice speaks of the culture of desertion being prompted and perverted by a fraudulent Indian, a rice farmer from the Corentyne. He promises four of his compatriots to show them "the road to India overland" – for a fee.

> At the New Amsterdam Police Court on Monday, before Mr Gall, Ramdeen was charged by Captain De Rinzy with having obtained $9 from Gopaul, Dammoor, Nardam, and Ramlall, with intent to defraud.
> The parties are immigrants on Plantation Adelphi [East Canje], and it was represented in the charge that the accused got the money on the pretence of showing his victims 'the road to India overland'. Defendant went to the men and asked them why they were punishing themselves in

this colony when he could take them to India. The men agreed to go to India and advanced the defendent $9 [$2.25 each, equivalent to nine and a half days' wages, at the statutory wage, per man]. Instead of taking them to India, defendant took them to his place at Massiah, Corentyne, where they planted rice for him for two weeks, at the end of which time, the men asked the defendant to return the money. Then one evening he disappeared.

After commenting on the serious nature of the offence, His Worship fined the defendant $126, or three month's imprisonment.

The Daily Chronicle, 19 July 1900

Ghurib Das, the champion of the Indian underdog, always tries to do something practical: he seeks aid in Essequibo for famine relief in India as well as for local destitutes. He believes that his adoption of some crucial symbols of Indianness is central to his mission.

During the week, Mr Ghurib Das, known in Essequibo as Mr Alexander, who some years ago was known as a planter on Pln Aurora, visited several villages and plantations. Attired in East Indian costume, the erstwhile planter cycled throughout his journeys, and attracted much attention on the part of those who knew him when . . . [he] dress[ed] differently. His object was to solicit aid from the inhabitants for the poor, famine-stricken people in India and on behalf of the Salvation Army; he urged on many the necessity of self-denial and pity.

The Daily Chronicle, 4 August 1900

In October 1900, the second issue of *War Cry*, the organ of the Salvation Army in British Guiana, reports that Ghurib Das of the East Indian Social Work is visiting Jamaica to assist with the opening of the Kingston Social Institution. The paper elaborates on the work of Ghurib Das and the Army on behalf of destitute Indians in Georgetown.

Our work amongst the East Indians also has been attended with a wonderful measure of success. A striking evidence of this is afforded by the fact that previous to the commencement of our work amongst them four years ago, there were on an average 400 East Indian paupers in the Alms House. This number has gradually declined until at the present time there are only about 110 inmates. Our three institutions provide accommodation for 250 men every night, and the average receipts for cheap food supplied is $240 (£50) per week. Many good converts have been made and have become real blood-and-fire Salvationists. Three East Indian corps will be at work in a few weeks in connection with the institutions.

The Daily Chronicle, 10 October 1900

The same issue of *The Daily Chronicle* reproduces an article on Ghurib Das from the *Jamaica Times*. It stresses the practicality of the man on behalf of Indians, including waifs and orphans, but also recognizes his purity of motives and magnanimity of spirit.

A Scotsman, Mr Alexander [Ghurib Das] worked 18 years in Demerara [British Guiana] in charge of sugar factories there . . . It was when paying a visit to Scotland on furlough in 1886, that he joined the Army . . .

Back in Demerara, Captain Alexander was for some time at his old sugar-making work, but wearing, as Manager, the Army's uniform, and doing Army work also. The colony abounds with East Indians, and it was especially to work for these that he at length entered the field of battle in out and out Salvation Army fashion. To give them cheap and good food and shelter was among their great needs. And to meet this he started his first home with only $50 in hand. Georgetown now contains three homes, and their large usefulness will be seen when it is stated that in a single day something like 90 gallons of coffee are served out; this goes at a cent (1/2 pence) per pint; and besides supplying it at the homes, it is sent out in neat carts and sold at other parts of the city. Bread and other food suitable to the East Indians are also served. The work is paying its way and developments are projected, and to this, the funds subscribed there are to go. It has already been extended to include children, for whom there are two free schools. The pupils are mostly waifs and orphans, and besides instruction and moral training, efforts are made to aid them with clothes.

Bechu, The Salvation Army and Derelict 'Coolies' in Georgetown

Like Mr Booth Tucker, the Captain has not hesitated to enter fully into the East Indian life, and to get in touch with their lives by adopting their costume, and like themselves going barefooted. A man thoroughly in earnest in his aim at sacrificing self in the service of man, and a shrewd man he is, as emphatic as General Booth himself against any form of charity that tends to pauperize or demoralize the recipients, he thoroughly shares the General's view that all that is done to better a man's body must aim at a change in that man's nature.

The Daily Chronicle, 10 October 1900

Shortly after Ghurib Das returns from Jamaica, he refutes Bechu's allegation that often on sugar estates, the wages bargained for are not honoured at the completion of the task. He suggests that Bechu should do something to lift the morale of the masses.

Ghurib Das to the Editor, *The Daily Chronicle*:

Sir, Your correspondent Bechu in this morning's issue [*DC*, 9 November] quotes *The New Centenary Review*'s authority for saying that 'It is a common complaint of Negro labourers that if they bargain to work for one shilling and 6 pence [a day] they will scarcely get more than one shilling," and concludes that this is equally applicable to the East Indians here.

If Mr Bechu will state a case I will again assist him in bringing the individual to bear the indignation he deserves, while such statements I consider are a gross misrepresentation of facts, and a libel on the whole colony.

In my 12 years' experience on sugar estates I have not one recollection of ever offering one wage so as to induce the labourer to start, and when the task was complete to pay different; neither have I any knowledge of anything being done like this on estates.

If Mr Bechu would indulge in fewer imaginations and try a little practice in elevating and encouraging the masses, he would find the advantage of saving the honour of our colony; but not by tarring the flock because he had one black sheep in it.

The Daily Chronicle, 10 November 1900

Bechu is incensed and turns his pen against Ghurib Das, hitherto his ally. He claims that he is "sticking up for the planters" because they gave financial help to the Salvation Army.

Sir, Your correspondent 'Ghurib Das', who is better known as 'Coolie Alexander', must have an eye to business when he jumps on me for maintaining what I have all along said about the East Indian immigrants not receiving the statutory wage, but if he, or any one else who still doubts what I say, will only accompany me to any estate on a Saturday and stand beside the pay tables while the labourers are being paid, I am ready to prove the truth of my assertion. However, I can quite account for Mr Alexander sticking up for the planters. Shortly before he went to Jamaica he succeeded in collecting a pretty decent sum from them for the Salvation Army.

The Daily Chronicle, 11 November 1900

The following article on Ghurib Das by a staff writer of *The Argosy*, in early 1901, is a detailed, sympathetic assessment of a remarkable Scotsman. His commitment and sacrifice, in order to give some meaning to the lives of the "lowest of the low", the "coolie jobber" in Georgetown, are an epic of heroic dimensions. Ghurib Das [Captain Alexander] deserves a place in the social history of Indians in British Guiana; yet, hitherto, no recognition has ever been accorded his labours in the vineyard of the damned. The piece is reproduced almost in its entirety – a tribute to his energy and imagination.

REGENERATING THE COOLIES: GHURIB DAS AND HIS WORK
BY J.R.B.

...Walking with a friend in Water Street [Georgetown] one day, my attention was attracted by a curious object passing along on wheels. It was a bicyclist – a man tall, gaunt, and of serious aspect. He wore the most original attire for a cyclist that it had been my lot to see in my travels. On his head he had a most elaborate white turban, and in place of a jacket he sported a brilliant, scarlet blouse with letters in gold across the breast, while his trousers were blue and of the description and fashion common to Europeans. His feet were innocent of all covering in the shape of shoe and stockings. Rude though it was, I could not help standing and staring after the unique figure. 'Who in all the earth let that lunatic loose?' I exclaimed. 'Why', replied my friend, 'that is "coolie Alexander".' I thought everyone in Georgetown knew him . . .'

'Coolie Alexander' [Ghurib Das]

Some 18 years ago [c 1883], there arrived in Demerara a young Scotsman bent like many a youth before him, and even still, upon seeking his fortune as a worker upon the sugar estates. This was Alexander Alexander, a native of Aberdeenshire, who had come out to an appointment as an overseer on one of the Essequibo plantations [Aurora]. A raw youth, innocent of the ways of the world – and especially that world represented upon sugar estates in the eighties, when money was fairly plentiful and life gay, and not unfrequently fast – young Alexander was not long in adapting himself to his surroundings . . . But although he participated in the rough and ready life in which he was thrown, the conditions under which the coolies lived after leaving the estates was not unobserved by him; and thus it was, when he realized the responsibilities of his position, he began to think what he could do on their behalf. Having occasion frequently to pass through the outskirts of Georgetown, he was much impressed by the fact that hundreds of coolies slept out all night in the rainy season without shelter or cover of any kind.

About five years ago Mr Alexander went home on vacation, and when away from the scenes of his labours the desire to do something for the coolies took such a hold of him that he resolved to give up all his prospects as a planter and to devote himself entirely to rescue work among the outcasts of the class over whom he had ruled heretofore. With this purpose he returned to the colony, and in July 1897, he opened his first shelter at Kingston [Georgetown]. He found that to work successfully he must have some strong organization behind him, and so connected himself with the Salvation Army. This was a happy choice both for the Army and Mr Alexander, and he soon rose to the rank of captain.

Many people have carried on missions among the East Indians, but Captain Alexander set about the work in a way new to British Guiana – on lines which are adopted by the Salvation Army all over the world. He thought the best means of getting at the Orientals would be to live among them and identify himself with them. With this object in view he adopted their method of dress, and having learned Hindustani through associating with the coolies, he soon became as one of themselves. He even went the length of changing his name, and he is now known as Ghurib Das – 'the poor servant' – the idea being that as most men were seeking to be something great, he should be known to them as one whose aspirations in this world were lowly, his desire being only to secure their interests. He early learned that coolies had no respect for one who pretended to be a teacher and who did not exercise a considerable amount of self-denial. No consecrated man with the Hindus may eat flesh, so Captain Alexander has been a vegetarian for years. Naturally at first those among whom he worked looked on him with doubtful approval as an intruder, but they soon began to see that he was solely seeking their good, and came round about him.

It may be remarked that Captain Alexander, shortly after adopting the coolie dress . . . sent a copy of the photograph home. The only comment his sister made upon it, in acknowledging it, was 'I hope you did not send one to any other body.'

His Work

Captain Alexander's labours, until recently, had been almost entirely among the lowest of the low – the type of people that are not touched by any of the denominations – the immigrant 'jobber'. The vicinity of the [railway] station was the great camping ground of the jobber, and it was this fact which prompted Mr Alexander to make a beginning in this district in July 1897. He soon found, however, that more good might be done by opening a home in the centre of the coolie population, and so, in November of that year, he started the central home in Lombard Street, now known as 'The Metropole'. This proved almost an immediate success and has even been the most profitable and best patronized of the ventures he has entered upon. Captain Alexander almost at the outset of his work, discovered that to make a large impression upon the East Indian population, he must get at the children. Those of the grown-up men whom he came in contact with, were so hardened in their way of living that it was difficult to do much for them morally or spiritually. He felt convinced that the children must be reached, and accordingly he launched forth in November 1898, into his most important venture of all – the leasing of La Penitence old manager's house as a rescue home and school.

The success which has since attended his efforts in this direction have justified the steps which he then took.

The Metropole

The premises in Lombard Street consist of a building of five apartments, comprising a front store or sale room with kitchen, eating room and two other rooms behind. This is the place from which the Kingston and La Penitence homes get their food supplies, and it is the best paying of these enterprises. In addition to clearing all its own expenses, it is able to contribute to the support of the other two establishments. Coolie food is a speciality, and is supplied at the cheapest rate possible. Although the East Indians are the people catered for, the eating house is popular with the poor of all races. The menu may not be so varied as that of a first-class restaurant, but it is more than sufficient for the needs of the people. In the early morning, coffee with bread or broken biscuits is served, and for breakfast [lunch] 'rootties' [rotis] with fish and vegetable curry, or curried rice may be had. Dinner is a repetition of breakfast. Of these dishes, the most popular is the coffee with bread or biscuits. At the outset the coolies fought shy of it, but now they prefer it even to their much-loved rice curry. It will be some indication of the demand if it be mentioned that . . . more than 80 lbs of ground coffee is consumed in the week. A travelling coffee stall is sent out in the morning and is largely patronized, especially by the dock labourers. The cost of the three meals is only 8 cents a day and a man or woman may live comfortably, if not luxuriously, on 2 shillings [48 cents] per week. The charge for a night's shelter is one cent, so that the board and lodgings combined only reaches 2 shillings 3 pence [54 cents] a week, Sunday not being charged for. Kingston House is conducted on similar lines.

La Penitence Home

La Penitence Home, as becomes the old house of an estate Manager, is large and roomy. On the ground floor there is a shelter and cellarage; on the first floor the school room and dining room, with the kitchen and sleeping accommodation behind; and on the second floor, quite separate from the others, are the overseers' apartments, and Captain Alexander's own room. This is quite a recent development of the work. As has been stated, the Captain found that to benefit the coolies he must 'catch 'em young', and this he is endeavouring to do by carrying on a school. The school is conducted by a young creole, Lieutenant Belgrave, and although there are 30 on the roll, the attendance is not such as would warrant him applying for government grant. At first the parents were against allowing their children to go to school, but their scruples in this connection have been overcome, and now not only are they willing to have their children educated, but they send them clean and tidy, if not well clothed.

Overseers' Home

The feature of La Penitence House is the accommodation for overseers out of work [usually young Scotsmen from the sugar estates]. This idea occurred to Captain Alexander some time ago, and by putting it into form he has met a long felt want. It is well known that when an overseer lost his situation there was nothing for him but to come to Georgetown. Young men thus thrown on their own resources do not take long to go through the little money they may have saved, as the cost of living in a hotel or elsewhere is by no means cheap. After they have spent all their savings it is only another step for them to become shabby in appearance, and we all know it is more difficult for a man to obtain a situation if he is 'out at elbow', than if he is spruce, neat and tidy. Captain Alexander's idea is to get hold of such young men before they get 'out at elbow', and by boarding them cheaply – he only charges 3 shillings 6 pence [84 cents] per week – he enables them to live a longer time on their small capital, and at the same time he assists them on the outlook for a vacancy. When a man's money is done he is not turned out. He is fed, housed, and even clothed . . . and if 'his ship does come in', he may make recompense to the Salvation Army . . .

A Paying Concern

The eating houses are conducted on purely business lines. Although everything is sold at the cheapest possible rate, sufficient is made to keep them going without loss, and even with some profit. The system of book-keeping is not elaborate, but it is clear and effective enough to show at a glance how things stand. The houses are under the personal supervision of Captain Alexander, his superior being Brigadier Gale of Barbados, to whom a monthly statement of affairs is submitted.

J.R.B. Interviews Captain Alexander (Ghurib Das)

J.R.B.: Among what class is it that your work is principally carried on?
Capt Alexander – hereafter G.D.: Those among whom I have been working during

the past four or five years are what may be called immigrant jobbers, such as you may meet at all corners of the street. These are men whom nobody seems to care for, and to whom practically no attention is paid. I have ... walk[ed] around the outskirts of the town on a rainy night and counted as many as 150 such outcasts of society lying sleeping in the wet. These may now have a comfortable night's shelter in any one of the Salvation Army homes, for one cent, while they may be fed for 8 cents per day.

J.R.B.: What is it that brings those men about town; is there not work for them on the estates?

G.D.: There are various reasons, but I think the Town Council are in a large measure to blame for the loafing which is prevalent. There is an Ordinance which provides that a strict jobber must obtain a licence, and in proof of their being licensed each must wear a badge. Some attempts were made to put this Ordinance into force, but it was found there was some flaw in its construction and there was an uncertainty as to who should prosecute the offenders. The result is that immigrants whose time has expired come into town to see their friends off or to meet new arrivals, and here they see their city brethren knocking about the streets apparently having a good time of it, and at any rate existing with no signs of labour. With that natural inclination to laziness which is characteristic of the Oriental, they drift into the same method of life, and swell the ranks of the unemployed. I think if the Town Council were to do their duty and have the Ordinance put into force, there would be a considerable reduction in the number of idle coolies frequenting the streets of Georgetown.

J.R.B.: What do you think is the greatest cause of poverty among the coolie population?

G.D.: (*emphatically*): Ganje [ganja] and laziness are the greatest curse of the coolies. Ganje has a very soothing effect and does not seem to bring about the results which rum drinking does. It seems to make the man who indulges in it sleepy, happy, and quite oblivious of his surroundings. Those addicted to it have no desire to exert themselves, and no ambition to do anything but lounge. It appears to be a great deal more enticing than rum or any other intoxicant.

J.R.B.: In the course of your rescue work have you ever endeavoured to send men back to work on the plantations?

G.D.: I have done so, but it was not successful. Men, when they quarrel with the drivers of the estates, leave and begin to wander about. When once they start roaming they do not care to settle down to work. I have sent them to work with the farmers, but they will not stay, preferring to chance their luck in the city.

J.R.B.: What about your home for overseers? Is it much taken advantage of?

G.D.:	Yes, I have always about half-a-dozen overseers in the home. They come here when their circumstances will not permit their going elsewhere. I try to get situation for them, and am pleased to say that as a rule I have been very successful. They are at liberty, however, to stay here as long as they like, and it only costs them a sixpence for lodging and 3 shillings for board [84 cents per week]. The planters appreciate this part of my work, as I found when I recently made a tour of my old friends on the estates, for subscribing towards the maintenance of our school and overseer home, the revenue from which does not cover expenses. They invariably made inquiries regarding it, and in addition made me handsome donations, and wished success to the venture.
J.R.B.:	Do you think your work is having a good effect morally and spiritually on the coolies?
G.D.:	It is difficult to answer such a question. I hope for the best, but it is not for one in the heat of the conflict to judge of the progress we are making. This much I must say – our influence among the coolies is being felt, and there seems to be a growing tendency towards Christianity, but it is of the youth and children that we have the greatest hope. I may add that the Superintendent of the Alms House gave me an unsought testimonial, as to the good results of our work. Before we opened our refuges there were about 400 people in the Alms House; now there are about 130, and the Superintendent has been kind enough to say that this reduction is due to the work which we are carrying on.
J.R.B.:	What sort of religious services do you hold?
G.D.:	We hold on an average five services at each home in the week. I address the people in the schoolroom at La Penitence, and in the dining room in the other places. I don't speak to them until after their appetites have been satisfied, and then I preach in Hindustani. I learned the language from among themselves, and it might be more aptly termed 'Creole Hindustani'. Indeed, I sometimes see a smile pass over the countenance of newly arrived immigrants when they hear the expressions which I use and am afraid my Hindustani is not very pure, but it serves its purpose.
J.R.B.:	How is your attendance at night?
G.D.:	The homes in the city are well patronized, but I am sorry to say there has been a falling off at La Penitence. This is accounted for by the fact that a lot of gambling, ill-conditioned fellows hang about the grounds and roughly handle and rob any coolie who they think is possessed of a few cents. These homeless ruffians consider themselves fairly safe here. I myself have tackled them and driven them off, but they do not seem to care for any other one. Our home at La Penitence is just outside the city boundary, and therefore is without that police protection

	which it otherwise might have.
J.R.B.:	(In conclusion I asked Captain Alexander how his work was being recognized by the colonists as a whole.)
G.D.:	People are beginning to realize the true nature of my work. The planters at first looked askance at it, but they soon found that it was not my intention to ignore them, but the reverse. Now they are favourable to me. Indeed, the late Mr Luard [Manager of Pln LBI] gave me La Penitence house for $24 a year less than its real rental, in order that I might carry on my work. Some people wonder how I can go about bare footed, but like the vegetarianism which I practise, it seems to agree with me. Of late I have readopted the custom of wearing shoes occasionally; and here I may mention how some of the people look upon me and watch my every action. Since I reappeared with shoes I have frequently heard women call out to their neighbours – 'Look he, he has got shoes on, he will be off with the money next!' The reason why I have recently again taken to shoes may be explained. I was sent over to Jamaica to open a new home there which a gentleman had given, and which is of the value of £650. This home required a considerable amount of money to fit it out for our purpose. When I arrived in Jamaica I had to set about raising funds in order to open the home free of debt if possible. In my coolie dress and barefeet I would not have looked so presentable as I might have, and this might have affected my object adversely. I found that to get subscriptions I would have to call upon business people and I preferred to do so in a garb more suitable than the one I have adopted in Demerara. The result exceeded my expectations for in about four weeks I raised £70, and we opened the home free of debt. When I returned here I continued to wear my shoes occasionally . . .

The Argosy, 2 March 1901

CHAPTER SIX

Bechu and his Challenge to Colonial Authorities

Bechu was fearless in challenging various authorities in the colony – on and off the plantations. It is noteworthy that he did not have a wife or children in British Guiana; this gave him space for his rebellious spirit to grow. This, however, should not detract from his continuity of purpose, a real gadfly of the Immigration Agent General and his Agents in the various districts, as well as Managers, overseers, and drivers on the sugar estates. The following excerpts from his memorandum to the West India Royal Commission of 1897 are reproduced again, as they demonstrate that even when he was still an indentured immigrant, he was prepared to challenge the Manager and the Immigration Agent.

> . . . Although it is *optional* for indentured immigrants to *take task work* they are forced to accept it, and the terms fixed by the employers are so hard that it is often the case that a task cannot be completed in less than two days, thus making it *impossible* for an indentured coolie from earning a shilling *per diem*. I should feel deeply grateful if the *Order Book*, which is kept up in all estates, is referred to; it will only *then* be seen how during the past five years the rate, for the same nature of work, for which a man was paid one shilling [24 cents] when the Immigration Act came into force, has now to be performed for 6 pence [12 cents].
>
> . . . gross immorality exists in [sic] most of the estates . . . I am in a

position to state that a fellow shipmate of mine, a Punjabi, was at one time making overtures to a woman with a view to matrimony, but he was deterred from doing so, as he came to hear that she had got in tow with an overseer, who eventually gave her the money to purchase her freedom. I don't recollect the name of the overseer, but the name of the woman is Leloo, and she is at present residing at Pln Lusignan, East Coast [Demerara]. This is another ground for discontent and sometimes leads to riots, yet Immigration agents close their eyes to the matter.

... Under article 18 of the Immigration Ordinance it is the duty of the Immigration Agent to give advice to coolies, conduct investigations, institute prosecutions, and to assist the Magistrate in the estimate of wages; but the officer in charge of the district to which I belong, beyond visiting the estate once a month for a little over an hour, taking down a few 'averages' of the earnings of the stronger men, and listing a few family quarrels, does little else. Only a couple months back I had occasion to deny a statement which was made in *The Argosy*, to the effect that this officer most religiously explains to all newly arrived immigrants the terms of their contract, and that denial had the effect of bringing him to a sense of his duty when the last three shipments arrived. He seldom visits the hospital, and, as long as I have been on Pln Enmore, has never on one occasion been to the 'nigger yards' or inspected any of the coolie dwellings. Besides taking no interest in the coolies, whose protector he is supposed to be, he is on such friendly terms with the Manager as to have succeeded in getting his daughter employment in his house as governess. How is it possible, under the circumstances, to receive justice at his hands? . . .

Memorandum by Bechu to the West India Royal Commission, 1897 (Appendix C. – Part II, British Guiana, section 158)

In early May 1897, Bechu writes to *The Daily Chronicle* (this issue, unfortunately, is missing from the British Library files), on behalf of an indentured immigrant, Surjudass, who, he claims, could get no assistance from the Immigration Agent of his District, Henry Taylor, on a sensitive matter – his wife's relationship with an overseer. Taylor is so infuriated by Bechu's "monotonous" allegation that he writes to *The Argosy* to defend himself against that "dangerous demagogue".

Henry W. Taylor (Immigration Agent, No. 5 District, Essequibo)
to the Editor, *The Argosy*:

Dear Sir, Permit me in your widely circulated columns to protest publicly against the attacks against myself and others in authority lately so frequent in the daily press, and signed 'Bechu'.

When it is realized that these effusions are entirely unsupported by direct evidence or any personal knowledge possessed by the writer, but merely hearsay from interested and prejudiced sources, it is a matter for surprise that they should be admitted to publication by the editor. In no single instance, however, has 'Bechu' even pretended to possess any knowledge of the facts, but he has contented himself with accepting any story supplied to him by correspondents as absolute facts on which to form an indictment against the authorities.

I was always under the impression that all communications addressed to the newspapers, especially those of a personal character, were carefully considered and weighed by the editors who usually rejected any that were unsupported by some sort of evidence. It would seem I am wrong.

In my case 'Bechu' has thought fit, with the approval of the editor of *The Daily Chronicle*, to make a personal attack on me in my official capacity. I quote from his last letter (Sunday's) as follows:

> Surjudass *like most coolies* has apparently learnt from dear bought experience that it is useless seeking the assistance of his protector, *for such officials are virtually the protectors of the planters.*

The italics are mine, and the latter sentence is a direct assertion by 'Bechu', and of so monstrous a character that I can only suppose the editor was unable to realize and appreciate its gravity.

As such attacks are calculated to interfere with me in my official capacity and hamper me in the discharge of my duties, I must claim some sort of protection. Already some harm has been done here. In the case of the 'Injured Husband', as it has been made the subject of public discussion, it is only fair to mention that after very searching inquiry it was proved on the *most unquestionable* evidence that the complaint of Surjudass was utterly without foundation. It may surprise the public to know that Surjudass and myself are on excellent terms. Only on Saturday last he came to see me on some business, and I told him about Bechu's letters, but Surjudass denied stoutly that he had written to him saying that

I had given him 'a severe telling-off' in any way. Surjudass likewise expressed himself satisfied with the enquiry and that his original suspicions were unfounded.

As it is possible I may have to bring 'Bechu' to account for this unprovoked attack, I now warn him that any such interference with the people in my district will only result adversely to [sic] them, so that if he really has the interests of his fellow countrymen at heart, he will leave me to protect their interests against all oppressors and mischief makers including such dangerous demagogues as 'Bechu' himself.

Trusting that a spirit of fair play will admit this letter to publication . . . .

(As Mr Taylor signs his letter and seems anxious to have it published, we insert it; but in our opinion he is only breaking a fly upon the wheel. – Ed *Argosy*)

The Argosy, 15 May 1897

In November 1897, Bechu initiates correspondence with the Immigration Agent General to procure a passport to travel to England to study. This, however, is refused although his indentureship had been commuted since February 1897: he must complete five years' residence in British Guiana (he had arrived in December 1894), or he must repay the full cost of his introduction to the colony before his request could be granted. Bechu is enraged. He asserts that the framer of the law was "evidently under the thumb of the planters", and that the "objectionable" section was "tantamount to slavery". He sends the whole correspondence to *The Daily Chronicle*.

Bechu to the Editor, *The Daily Chronicle*:

Sir, The Immigration Law of British Guiana has always seemed to me to be the most objectionable piece of legislation that ever saw the light of day. Anybody who runs his eyes over its pages will see at a glance that the framer was evidently under the thumb of the planters who were all powerful in the Court of Policy at the time it was drafted. The law – such law! – practically treats us East Indians as a race apart from all other British subjects in the colony, and places us under most irksome and oppressive restrictions. Take Section 196 for instance. It seemingly gives no power to

His Excellency the Governor – Her Majesty's representative in this land – to allow an immigrant who has resided in this colony for under five years, to leave these shores, although *he has obtained and is in possession of a certificate of exemption.* Should such an [sic] one apply to go away, he is told point blank that in accordance with the Ordinance, the colony has a claim against him for the entire cost of his introduction. When the authorities reminded me of such a claim, I felt inclined to retort in these words of Henry Lord Brougham:

> In vain you tell me of the laws that sanction such a claim. There is a law above all the enactments of human codes the same throughout the world, the same in all times . . . It is the law written by the finger of God on the heart of man; and by that law, unchangeable and eternal, while men despise fraud and loathe rapine, and hate blood, they shall reject with indignation the wild and guilty phantasy, that man can hold property in man!

To elucidate what I mean I beg to submit for the perusal of your readers the following correspondence which has passed between me and authorities on the subject:

====================

To the Honourable
Sir Cavendish Boyle, KCMG
Government Secretary
British Guiana
Dated Georgetown, the 8th Nov., 1897

Honoured Sir, The *Sheila*, the vessel on which I came to this colony, is I see expected to arrive in this port about the middle of January next, and as I am known to most of her officers, I am wishful of making arrangements to go on her to England, but owing to the restrictions placed on people of my nationality by the Indian Immigration Ordinance of 1891, I find that although His Excellency the Governor has been graciously pleased to commute the remaining term of my indenture, I cannot leave British Guiana without a passport, and furthermore, no passport can be granted me by the immigration authorities without the special permission of the Governor, until I shall have resided in this colony for at least five years.

As I feel that my time is being wasted in Demerara, I humbly and respectfully beg your Honour to be so kind as to obtain for me the required document to enable me to quit these shores, it being my great desire to visit London, so as to have an opportunity of acquiring a course of instruction, such as the times demand. Some of my late employers who were anxious to take me home with them, will, I am positive, give me all the help I shall need to attain that object.

I have the honour to be,
Honoured Sir,
Your most obedient Servant,
BECHU

===================

British Guiana
Immigration Department
Georgetown, 24th Nov, 1897

Sir, Referring to your application to be granted a passport to enable you to leave the colony, I am directed by the Governor to ascertain from you for His Excellency's information, whether you are prepared to repay the entire cost of your introduction in accordance with the Immigration Ordinance.

I have the honour to be, Sir,
Your Obedient Servant,
(Sgd) C.B. KING
Acting Immigration Agent General

To Bechu

===================

To the Honourable C.B. King
Acting Immigration Agent General
Dated Georgetown, the 25th Nov, 1897

Honoured Sir, In reply to your letter No. 2687/3483, dated 24th instant, I beg to express my surprise at being asked whether I am prepared to repay the entire cost of my introduction. I offered to make good the amount in February last, but under instructions from His Excellency Sir Augustus W.L. Hemming and the Honourable A.H. Alexander, Mr H.J. Gladwin granted me my 'certificate of exemption' without any charge whatsoever. How it comes to be asked for now is therefore a mystery to me. If, as you say, the Ordinance demands it, I must take steps to have that objectionable section of the Ordinance repealed, as it is in my humble opinion tantamount to slavery.

I can[not] but view with disregard the style in which I have been addressed. Common courtesy demands that when addressing the humblest individual it is necessary to prefix 'Mr', but when I remember that there are two kinds of gentlemen in this world – gentlemen by birth and gentlemen by position, I am not surprised.

I have the honour to be,
Honoured Sir,
Your most obedient Servant,
BECHU

===================

British Guiana
Immigration Department
Georgetown, 25th Nov, 1897

Sir, With reference to your letter of this day's date, I have to point out that what you offered to do in February, 1894 [sic], was to 'commute' for the remaining term of your indenture, but as no indenture fee had been charged in your case, the estate was not entitled to any payment for you. This is quite distinct from the claim which the colony has against you for the cost of your introduction, and as I was directed by the Governor to ascertain from you whether you are prepared to pay this amount, I shall be obliged if you will furnish me with a reply for the information of His Excellency.

I have the honour to be, Sir,
Your obedient Servant,
(Sgd) C. B. KING
Acting Immigration Agent General

Mr Bechu

===================

To the Honourable C.B. King
Acting Immigration Agent General
British Guiana
Dated Georgetown, the 26th Nov, 1897

Honoured Sir, In answer to your letter No. 2698/3483 of yesterday's date, I humbly and respectfully beg to state for His Excellency's information that I only landed in this colony on the 20th December, 1894, so that it is impossible for me to have offered to 'commute' in February of that year.

I regret exceedingly to say that I have no further reply to give with regard to the claim which you inform me that the colony has against me, beyond what is contained in my letter of 25th instant. If there happens to be a claim, I am ignorant of it, and you should therefore seek to recover it in a court of law.

I have the honour to be,
Honoured Sir,
Your most obedient Servant
BECHU

===================

British Guiana
Immigration Department
Georgetown, 27th Nov, 1897

Sir, Referring to your first paragraph of your letter of yesterday's date, I have to inform you that your petition was dated 16th February 1894, a mistake of course, for 1897, and this error in date was inadvertently copied in my letter to you of the 25th instant.

I shall submit your replies to my letters to His Excellency the Governor.

I have the honour to be, Sir,
Your obedient Servant,
(Sgd) C. B. KING
Acting Immigration Agent General

Mr Bechu

===================

I have documentary evidence, Sir, to prove that prior to leaving Enmore, a countryman of mine offered to pay into the Immigration Fund whatever commutation money the Hon the Immigration Agent General might have demanded in my case, but His Excellency Sir Augustus W.L. Hemming very generously exempted me from paying a cent towards the cost of my introduction, and Mr H.J. Gladwin under instructions from the Honourable A.H. Alexander, accordingly granted me my certificate of exemption on the 26th February, 1897.

Such being the case, and holding as I do at this present moment, the certificate referred to, it would be very foolish of me to stump up 90 dollars *now*. The authorities must fancy I have gone daft to expect me to do so!

As this question of withholding passports is of importance not only to me but to every free East Indian immigrant and his descendant, I beg you will be so kind as to give publicity to the whole correspondence, so that it may catch the eyes of our present lawgivers, the majority of whom being gentlemen of the legal profession, will see at once how the tendency has been to treat us British-born subjects in this British colony as common slaves.

The Daily Chronicle, 30 November 1897

The same issue of *The Daily Chronicle* responds condescendingly to Bechu's "amusing correspondence" with the Immigration Department, noting that his intelligence could not earn him special treatment; it would set a "dangerous precedent". It concludes that his "heroic fulminations" against the restrictions and his insistence on being addressed as "Mr", "the peculiarly English prefix", could not be taken seriously; it regrets that Bechu could not treat this with the "Englishman's sense of the ridiculous". The paper is unable to summon the generosity to address him as "Mr" Bechu, as he requests.

We publish elsewhere an interesting and rather amusing correspondence between Bechu and the acting Immigration Agent General. It appears that the well-known spokesman of coolie grievances, is anxious to take advantage of the departure of the ship *Sheila*, early next year [1898], to go to England, there to take 'a course of instruction such as the times demand'. The project is a most commendable one, but unfortunately Bechu has obligations to the Colonial government which the latter cannot very well allow to be disregarded. Accordingly Bechu was informed by the acting Immigration Agent General that he might leave the colony on payment of the cost of his importation from Calcutta. Bechu seems to consider this a great injustice, contending that the certificate of exemption from labour generously granted to him by His Excellency [Sir Augustus Hemming] in February last cancels any claim the government may have upon him in the event of his leaving the colony before the expiration of his term of indenture. We fear Bechu expects a little too much consideration, and he does not seem to realize that to allow him to depart after being in the colony only three years, without recouping the government for the cost of his introduction, would be to create a dangerous precedent. The position of the government is perfectly reasonable. We are sorry for Bechu, who seems to have ambitions which are entirely creditable to him. At the same time the fact that an immigrant is capable of carrying on his own correspondence with the Immigration Department, is not sufficient reason for treating him with special favour. Bechu's heroic fulminations against what he calls 'irksome and oppressive restrictions' of the immigration law, and his insistence upon being addressed with the peculiarly English prefix of 'Mr' are more calculated to raise a smile than seriously to impress anyone who reads them. It is a pity that Bechu, Anglicized as he is, has not yet acquired the Englishman's sense of the ridiculous. It would save him from many a bad *faux pas* in his little controversies.

Leader, *The Daily Chronicle*, 30 November 1897

Whatever the size of the guns mustered against him, nothing daunts Bechu. He indicts the immigration authorities for serving poor food to departing 'coolies', while the contractor makes "enormous profit". He commends the "superior" cheaper meals served in the homes run by Ghurib Das, and expresses fear that the authorities are trying to silence him for "inciting my countrymen to rebel".

Bechu (Lot 14, Water St, Georgetown) to the Editor, *The Daily Chronicle*:

Sir, Last Friday afternoon it would appear I committed a huge mistake by asking Mr J.H. de Jonge, in his capacity as Financial Representative for this city, to kindly pay a surprise visit to the Immigration Depot and compare the food that the present contractor serves out to the coolies returning to Calcutta, by the ship *Erne,* for 16 cents per head, *per diem,* with the superior stuff that is daily issued at the Salvation Army shelter and Mr Alex Alexander's [Ghurib Das'] 'Home' for only 6 cents per head, *per diem,* as the immigration authorities here have somehow got scent of the letter and have not only sworn vengeance against me for bringing to notice the enormous profit the contractor makes by the transaction but have actually threatened to run me in for inciting my countrymen to rebel.

In any other country where the Union Jack floats I would treat such menace with silent contempt, but as in a colony like this, it is not difficult to trump up a charge of the nature contemplated, one cannot be *too* careful, and as 'fore-warned is to be fore-armed', I beg the favour of your kindly giving publicity to this letter in your widely circulated paper so that in the event of my, one of these days, having occasion to appear before the Beak I shall be in a position to substantiate what I now assert.

(Our correspondent is probably under some misapprehension. We cannot see why the Immigration Department should threaten him, as he alleges, for taking steps which may possibly result in a future saving of money to that department. – Ed, *DC*)

The Daily Chronicle, 1 July 1898

Bechu's vigilance enables him to apprehend, quickly, circumstances of potential compromise, if not collusion, between colonial officials, with the power to adjudicate on Indian affairs, and the plantocracy. *The Daily Chronicle* (7 July 1898) reports tersely: "Mr Magistrate Gall has removed from Haslington House to Pln Enmore." Bechu grasps the implications immediately.

Bechu (Lot 14, Water St, Georgetown) to the Editor, *The Daily Chronicle*:

Sir, In your this morning's issue, under the head 'Victoria Notes', I see that Mr F.A. Gall, who is at present acting Stipendiary Magistrate of the Mahaica

Judicial District, has removed from Haslington to a house adjoining the residence of the Manager of Plantation Enmore.

However high-minded that official may be, is it right, sir, that he should be living in close proximity to the manager of the estate, when he is constantly required to take cognizance of the complaints of immigrants and to determine their wages? When a Magistrate can live on a plantation and be on friendly terms with the Manager and exchange his hospitalities who, permit me to ask, is to protect the *indentured* men? As matters stand . . . their lot is not as happy as you would have us believe.

The Daily Chronicle, 8 July 1898

Bechu says that the arbitrary stopping of wages by overseers on the estates is "indefensible". He contends that this and a general perception that channels for the ventilation of grievances are not available, lead to frustration and violence. He does not have much confidence in the so-called protectors of the Indians, the Immigration Agents.

Bechu (Lot 14, Water St, Georgetown) to the Editor, *The Daily Chronicle*:

Sir, My attention has been drawn to a case in which Purdaree, an East Indian immigrant, belonging to Plantation Ogle, was on Monday last placed before Mr R.A. Swan, the presiding Magistrate in the Sparendaam Court, charged with having attempted to assault an overseer of that estate for having stopped his wages.

My file of cuttings from *The Daily Chronicle* does not date very far back, but if my memory serves me as well as it usually does, it was, I think, on or about 19 January 1897, when an almost similar case was tried by His Honour Sir E.L. O'Malley, our late respected Chief Justice who, prior to passing a lenient sentence on the prisoner (a man named Simondarsa) drew the attention of Mr Moir, the Manager of Plantation Vergenoegen, to Sections 103 and 104 of the British Guiana Immigration Ordinance of 1891, and severely rebuked him for illegally tampering with an immigrant's wages and characterized such action as a 'mean, cowardly, dishonest fraud'.

Happily in the present instance there were so many present to prevent Purdaree from doing any bodily harm, else the result might have been serious. According to the strict interpretation of the law the practice of stopping an immigrant's wages is indefensible, and leads one to suspect that those who have been appointed to protect the immigrants do not take the slightest trouble to see to their interests. The result is that the unfortunate wretches foolishly take the law into their own hands.

By the way, isn't it extremely significant that so many coolie chopping cases have occurred of late? This is a matter which calls for strict investigation by the authorities! If a coolie has a grievance, it may be said that he can complain to the Magistrate, but it is not easy for any coolie to prove his case. It is a matter altogether for the Immigration Agent to enquire into and remedy, if not to transfer him to another master, and if he again neglects his work it can readily be seen that he does not want to work. *The Immigration Agent should be easily approachable to the meanest coolie; but he should be unapproachable to the lordliest employer* [emphasis added].

The Daily Chronicle, 23 July 1898

Bechu and Joseph Ruhomon ('East Indian Descendant' from New Amsterdam) had, by 1898, virtually established a tradition of Indian writing to the press to articulate their grievances. In July 1898, Joshua Ramphul, an Indian businessman from New Amsterdam, writes to *The Daily Chronicle* explaining that the services of Madras (Tamil) interpreters at the Magistrate's Court are superfluous: most Madras people can speak English; besides they are a small minority of the Indians in the colony.

Joshua Ramphul (New Amsterdam) to the Editor, *The Daily Chronicle*:

Sir, As I have often read in your columns that economy should be exercised in the various government departments in this colony, I beg to show where a saving of £100 per annum could be effected.

If the Hon the Immigration Agent General would look carefully into the matter, he would find that the services of the Madras interpreter attached to the New Amsterdam Magisterial Courts here could be dispensed with entirely. Formerly there was no Madras interpreter attached to the courts here as there was no need for one. I have learnt that the

Magistrate of the Corentyne District has reported to the Immigration Department that he has no need of a Madras interpreter, as the old heads are fast dying out and the community of young ones speak fair English to satisfy him or anyone else. If the Magistrate of the above-mentioned district, where there are hundreds of Madras coolies, can say that, one can safely say that the town of New Amsterdam and other districts attached to this town, where there are only a few Madras inhabitants, do not need one; and if in case of special need, the Immigration Office here has a Madras interpreter who can act on occasion.

I trust that the Hon the Immigration Agent General will see where economy in his department can be used.

The Daily Chronicle, 22 July 1898

Ramphul's observations are corroborated by a correspondent, 'Perseus', who argues that apart from the economic case in favour of the termination of use of many Madras interpreters, it is common sense for the Immigration Department to use Hindi interpreters, since the overwhelming majority of its complainants are Hindi-speakers.

'Perseus' to the Editor, *The Daily Chronicle*:

Sir, In your last Friday's issue I noticed a letter signed 'Joshua Ramphul' in which the writer very sensibly pointed out how a saving of £100 per annum could be effected upon the abolition of the office of Madras interpreter in connection with the New Amsterdam Magistrate's Courts. Your correspondent's suggestion is decidedly practical, and has every claim upon the consideration of the proper authorities. It is indeed very surprising to see the Immigration Department here still maintaining so many Madras interpreters whose services could very well be dispensed with, without any detriment to the service, taking into consideration the fact that we have such a comparatively insignificant number of Madras people in our midst who do not understand English, Madras immigration having been discontinued as far back as 15 years ago . . . A considerable amount of money, therefore, could be saved annually if the practically useless Madras interpreters should be struck off the service, as far as it is consistent with the proper working of the service, as well as the judicious application of economy.

I should also like to point out . . . the serious anomaly existing in the [Immigration] Office [in Georgetown] . . . where not a few of the so-called interpreters, who know comparatively little of the Hindustani language, are supposed to attend to the coolies, who not unfrequently [sic] have important statements to make, and serious complaints to lodge in which their vital interests are involved. Surely there is a considerable amount of slackness and want of efficiency in the Immigration Service of this colony that call for a good deal of attention on the part of the government.

The Daily Chronicle, 26 July 1898

Bechu is impressed with 'Perseus' objection to Madras interpreters servicing a predominantly Hindi-speaking workforce. He makes the prescient recommendation that it should be compulsory for Immigration Agents and overseers "to pass an examination in colloquial Hindustani" in 12 months after they are appointed, thus bringing the 'coolie' and the authorities in direct contact, without intermediaries and potential misunderstanding.

Bechu (Georgetown) to the Editor, *The Daily Chronicle*:

Sir, I was very much pleased to read 'Perseus' letter in your impression of today's date because he has touched upon a matter I have long wished to write about. Ever since I obtained my freedom I have striven hard to find out how the Immigration Agent General's Office came to be so full of the Madras element.

It may not, perhaps, be out of place for me to suggest that if East Indian immigration is to be continued the government should make it compulsory for every Immigration Agent and overseer, within 12 months of their first appointment to pass an examination in colloquial Hindustani. The advantage of this plan would be to bring the overseer and the coolie into closer contact. They would then understand each other perfectly, and many causes of dissatisfaction and disagreement would be avoided which now often occur simply from the intervention of an interpreter or driver. It seems passing strange that the ignorant *uneducated* coolie should be required to learn a foreign language, and that the *educated* European should save himself a little trouble to acquire the language of the people with whom he has so much to do. Civil as well as military officers in India and Burma are required to learn the language of the people serving under them.

The Daily Chronicle, 28 July 1898

The following is Bechu's most controversial letter, which was published in *The Daily Chronicle* on 13 September 1898. He alleges that the Manager of an estate "not 20 miles away" from Georgetown, refused a sick 'bound coolie', Bhagri, medical attention – indeed, turned him out of the hospital "without the permission of the doctor" who had admitted him. Bhagri died or as Bechu puts it, he was "released from the grip of his oppressors". The Manager of Plantation Cove and John, F.C.S. Bascom, brought a charge of libel against Bechu for defaming his character.

Bechu (Georgetown) to the Editor, *The Daily Chronicle*:

Sir, So few instances of man's inhumanity to man on our sugar estates find their way to your columns, that I beg you will in the interests [sic] of justice give publicity to the case I am about to relate, which occurred recently on a plantation on the East Coast, not 20 miles away from this centre of civilization.

The facts briefly stated are as follows:

About a fortnight ago an indentured immigrant named Bhagri, who came to this colony in the *Avoca*, of 1894, reported himself sick, and presented himself at the estate's hospital for treatment, but the sicknurse hunted him out with the remark that there was nothing at all the matter with him. The following day, however, being the doctor's day, the man presented himself before the government Medical Officer, who after examining the man admitted him as an in-patient. He remained in hospital that night but, strange to say, the next morning the sicknurse, under orders from the Manager and without the permission of the doctor, discharged him and he was accordingly sent back to work. That, however, was the last occasion the estate authorities could prosecute the poor fellow, for happily death came to his rescue and released him from the grip of his oppressors.

The wrong is so serious that I am sure it has only to be known to be remedied. It is hoped that the Immigration Agent of the district will keep a sharp lookout on this estate.

The Daily Chronicle, 13 September 1898

The Daily Chronicle which, for over four years, had shown admirable courage by giving Bechu a forum to challenge colonial assumptions, had itself vacillated on the question of indentured labour and the role of sugar in British Guiana. Bechu, however, was consistent in his belief that bonded labour was an anachronism serving a pampered, irresponsible and greedy plantocracy. By late 1901, after Bechu had left the colony, the paper had arrived at essentially the same position on the sugar industry as him.

> . . . Apparently, in the eyes of our contemporary [*The Argosy*] it is something approaching sacrilege to suggest that the immigration system has any shortcomings at all, that it is being conducted on a basis not quite satisfactory, and that it would be better for the masses of the inhabitants if the indent introduced annually for East India was materially reduced. Immigration is, seemingly, a sacred institution to maintain which in its integrity ought to be the great objective of all good citizens . . . [so] when our contemporary urged that immigration was an inviolate institution which no profane finger might touch, we regarded it as our duty to counsel a more sensible policy . . .
>
> This view we are not only compelled to dissent from; we hold it mainly responsible for the present industrial backwardness of the colony. Our idea of prosperity in British Guiana is not limited by the well-being of the sugar industry alone. How can any honest colonist maintain that the welfare of the colony is entirely dependent on the prosperity of the sugar industry after the lesson of the last few years? The planters had fairly favourable seasons and very good prices, and made in some instances even handsome profits. But has a corresponding measure of prosperity visited . . . the labouring population and the other classes of the country? The steadily decreasing value of imports introduced during the last few years

supplies the answer. While the planters were making money the imports continued to decline, indicating beyond a doubt that the purchasing capacity of the masses had not improved but had rather decreased. The explanation is obvious. It is not into the pockets of revenue-producing inhabitants that a substantial share of the profits go. Even the immigrants on the estates have not benefited in their wages. The truth is, the money goes to pay the dividends of gentlemen who for the most part reside in Great Britain and contribute nothing to the revenues of the colony. A fraction of it, of course, must perforce get into circulation in the colony. When there is an unusual demand for labour on the estates, as during the grinding season, outside labour has a chance of earning something, and business in the colony proportionately benefits . . . The sugar industry at present is to a great extent what economists would call 'alien' to the colony. The labour by which it is carried on comes from outside; the labourers' savings are as a rule taken back to India; and the profits earned by the estates for the most part go abroad to be spent in London or elsewhere. Our objective is to secure that this purely artificial status of the local sugar industry shall be placed upon a sounder and more natural footing. The profits accruing from the cultivation of the soil should not be allowed to drain so copiously into other countries. In effect, the resident population ought to benefit more from the sugar industry than it does at present. The question as to whether the prosperity of sugar in the colony benefits all classes requires to be put beyond dispute. To this end it is necessary, first, that immigration be conducted on more statesmanlike lines, involving not only its judicious limitation and if possible its ultimate abolition, but also a settlement of immigrants in the colony as their terms expire; secondly, that cane farming among all classes of the peasantry be encouraged so as eventually to supply the estates' factories with canes in such quantities as to make it practicable for the proprietors to do with considerably less labour.

Leader, *The Daily Chronicle*, 3 November 1901

BIBLIOGRAPHY

A. Primary Sources

1. Colonial Office Records
CO 111/395 Scott to Kimberley, no. 27, 26 February 1873.
CO 111/474 West India Committee, 6 October 1894.
CO 111/488 Boyle to Chamberlain, no. 353, 11 November 1896.
CO 111/489 Hemming to Chamberlain, 26 November 1896.
CO 111/489 Hemming to Chamberlain, no. 389, 8 December 1896.
CO 111/492 Hemming to Chamberlain, no. 3, 2 January 1897.
CO 111/492 Hemming to Chamberlain, confidential, 6 January 1897.
CO 111/498 (Offices – Miscellaneous [Quintin Hogg]), 9 January 1897.
CO 111/498 (Offices – Miscellaneous [Charles S. Parker]), 15 December 1897.
CO 111/500 (Individuals – Quintin Hogg), 1 February 1897.
CO 111/504 Sendall to Chamberlain, no. 206, 23 June 1898.
CO 111/509 (Individuals – Henry K. Davson), 15 February 1898.
CO 111/513 Sendall to Chamberlain, no. 182, 6 July 1899.
CO 111/513 Sendall to Chamberlain, confidential, 19 July 1899.
CO 111/513 Sendall to Chamberlain, no. 205, 19 July 1899 (Minute, 4 August 1899).
CO 111/513 Sendall to Chamberlain, confidential, 19 July 1899 (Minute, 4 August 1899).
CO 111/514 Sendall to Chamberlain, no. 324, 25 October 1899.
CO 111/516 Offices (India), 7 June 1899.
CO 111/516 Colonial Office (Minute), 7 June 1899.
CO 111/525 (Individuals – W. Middleton Campbell), 9 March 1900.
CO 111/525 (Individuals – Henry K. Davson), 13 March 1900.
CO 114/64 Report of the Immigration Agent General, 1894–95.
CO 114/68 Report of the Immigration Agent General, 1895–96.
CO 114/74 Report of the Immigration Agent General, 1896–97.
CO 114/78 Report of the Immigration Agent General, 1897–98.
CO 114/172 Report of the Immigration Agent General, 1919.

2. Newspapers

The Argosy (Georgetown, British Guiana), 1896–1901.
The Daily Chronicle (Georgetown, British Guiana), 1896–1901.

3. Report

Report of the West India Royal Commission, 1897. H.W. Norman, chairman. London: HMSO 1897.

B. Secondary Sources

Adamson, Alan. *Sugar Without Slaves: the Political Economy of British Guiana, 1838–1904*. New Haven: Yale University Press 1972.

Beaumont, Joseph. *The New Slavery: an Account of the Chinese and Indian Immigrants in British Guiana*. London: W. Ridgway 1871.

Gordon, Leonard A. *Bengal: the Nationalist Movement, 1876–1940*. New York: Columbia University Press 1974.

Kirke, Henry. *Twenty-Five years in British Guiana*. London: Sampson Low, Marston and Co. 1898.

Kopf, David. *British Orientalism and the Bengal Renaissance: the Dynamics of Indian Modernization, 1773–1835*. Berkeley: University of California Press 1969.

Laurence, K.O. *A Question of Labour: Indentured Immigration into Trinidad and British Guiana, 1875–1917*. Kingston, Jamaica: Ian Randle Publishers 1994.

Look Lai, Walton. *Indentured Labour, Caribbean Sugar: Chinese and Indian Migrants to the British West Indies, 1838–1918*. Baltimore: The John Hopkins University Press 1993.

Mangru, Basdeo. *Benevolent Neutrality: Indian Government Policy and Labour Migration to British Guiana, 1854–1884*. London: Hansib 1987.

———. 'The Hincks-Beaumont imbroglio: partisan politics in British Guiana in the 1860s', *Boletin de Estudios Latinoamericanos y del Caribe*, no. 43 (1987).

———. *Indenture and Abolition: Sacrifice and Survival on the Guyanese Sugar Plantations*. Toronto: TSAR 1993

———. 'James Crosby: hero, protector, friend of Indians in Guyana', *Indo-Caribbean Review*, 1, no. 1 (1994).

———. *A History of East Indian Resistance on the Guyana Sugar Estates, 1869–1948*. Lewiston, NY: The Edwin Mellen Press 1996.

Moohr, Michael, 'Patterns of change in an export economy: British Guiana, 1830–1914'. PhD thesis, University of Cambridge 1970.

———. 'The discovery of gold and development of peasant industries in Guyana, 1884–1914: a study in the political economy of change', *Caribbean Studies* 15, no. 2 (1975).

Moore, Brian. *Race, Power and Social Segmentation in Colonial Society: Guyana, 1838–1891*. New York: Gordon and Breach 1987.

Nath, Dwarka. *A History of Indians in Guyana*. London: The Author 1970 (1950).

Potter, Lesley M. 'Internal migration and resettlement of East Indians in Guyana, 1870–1920'. PhD thesis, McGill University 1975.

———. 'The post-indenture experience of East Indians in Guyana, 1873–1921'. In *East Indians in the Caribbean: Colonialism and the Struggle for Identity*. Bridget Brereton &

Bibliography

Winston Dookeran (eds). Millwood, NY: Kraus International Publications 1982.

Ramnarine, Tyran. 'The growth of the East Indian community in British Guiana, 1880–1920'. DPhil dissertation, University of Sussex 1977.

——. 'Over a hundred years of East Indian disturbances on the sugar estates of Guyana, 1869–1978: an historical overview'. In *India in the Caribbean*. David Dabydeen & Brinsley Samaroo (eds). London: Hansib 1987.

Raychaudhuri, Tapan. *Europe Reconsidered: Perceptions of the West in Nineteenth Century Bengal*. Delhi: Oxford University Press 1988.

Rodney, Walter (ed). *Guyanese Sugar Plantations in the Late Nineteenth Century: a Contemporary Description from the 'Argosy'*. Georgetown, Guyana: Release Publishers 1979.

——. *A History of the Guyanese Working People, 1881–1905*. Baltimore: The Johns Hopkins University Press 1981.

Ruhomon, Joseph. *India; the Progress of her People at Home and Abroad, and how Those in British Guiana may Improve Themselves*. Georgetown: C.K. Jardine 1894.

Ruhomon, Peter. *Centenary History of the East Indians in British Guiana, 1838–1938*. Georgetown: The East Indians 150th Anniversary Committee 1988 (1947).

Seecharan, Clem. *India and the Shaping of the Indo-Guyanese Imagination, 1890s–1920s*. Leeds: Peepal Tree Press 1993.

——. *'Tiger in the Stars': the Anatomy of Indian Achievement in British Guiana, 1919–29*. London: Macmillan 1997.

——. *Joseph Ruhomon's India: the Progress of her People at Home and Abroad – the Centenary Edition* (forthcoming).

——. 'The making of the Indo-Caribbean People: Guyana and Trinidad to the 1940s', *Journal of Caribbean Studies* (forthcoming).

Singhal, D.P. *India and World Civilisation, Vol. II*. London: Sidgwick and Jackson 1972 (1969).

Tikasingh, Gerad. 'The establishment of the Indians in Trinidad, 1870–1900'. PhD thesis, University of the West Indies, St Augustine, Trinidad, 1976.

Tinker, Hugh. *A New System of Slavery: the Export of Indian Labour Overseas, 1830–1920*. London: Oxford University Press 1974.

INDEX

Achibar, 74, 75
Adamson, Alan, 13, 30, 81n.1
Addison, Joseph, 155
Adelphi Plantation, 276
Africans: Alexander Alexander on, 279; *Argosy* on, 57-58; aspirations of, 249; compared to Indian workers, 4, 15, 30, 57-59, 163, 179-180, 185, 204-205; and Creole gang, 42-43, 45, 130-131; *Daily Chronicle* on, 181-182, 233; and emancipation in British Guiana, 32; and gold industry, 253-254; Guyanese, 52; in Hawaii, 254; as immigrants, 249-253; Langton on, 128; leaders in British Guiana, 8; and Norman Commission, 233; peasantry of, 55; racism toward, 253-254; "Ramsing" on, 253; Ruhomon on, 26; and Salvation Army, 65-66; as settlers in British Guiana, 195-196, 203-204, 234-235, 247-248; on sugar plantations, 51, 57, 115-117, 128, 179-180, 233, 250, 253; treatment of, 57, 87n.83, 89n.103, 236.
Agriculture: alternatives to sugar, 167-168, 185; cattle, 190-191; cocoa, 198; coffee, 116, 198; and coolie settlements, 201, 203-204; irrigation and drainage, 191-193, 199, 203, 205, 207-208, 219-220, 225, 227; resistance to alternatives to sugar, 194-198, 208. *See also* Rice industry; Sugar industry; and specific plantations
Alexander, A. H., 34-36, 77-79, 88-89n.102, 144-145, 148-150, 293, 296
Alexander, Alexander (Ghurib Das): and African workers, 65-66, 279; *Argosy* on, 260-262, 280-287; attitudes of, 278-281; and Aurora Plantation, 277, 281; background of, 281; colonists on, 287; and Norman Bascom, 94-95n.204; compared to Bechu, 61-66; compared to Tucker, 279; and coolies, 260, 271, 281-286; *Daily Chronicle* on, 265-266, 277-278, 279; on donations from plantation owners, 66; and fund raising, 287; as Ghurib Das, 62-66, 70, 260-262, 271, 279, 281-282, 297; and Hindu practices, 282; and immigrant workers, 261-263, 278-279; and India, 277; and Indian children, 282-284; and Indian workers, 65-66, 92n.160; in Jamaica, 65, 277, 280, 287; *Jamaica Times* on, 65, 278-279; and jobbers, 282, 284-286; and La Penitence Home, 282-285; as plantation driver, 281; plantation owners on, 287; on plantocracy, 62, 92n.153, 278, 286-287; on racial discrimination, 275; and religion, 286; and Salvation Army, 61-62, 176, 260-262, 277-278, 280, 281; on wages, 94-95n.204, 279; *War Cry* by, 65
Alms House, 278, 286
Anandamath (Chatterjee), 21
Arab confederacies, 117
Argosy: on Africans, 57-58; on agricultural alternatives in British Guiana, 190-192; on Alexander Alexander, 62, 260-261, 280-287 ; and *Birmingham Post*, 241; Bechu letters, 40-44; on case of plantation driver, 78; on coolies, 186-187, 199-200, 266, 267; on drought, 203; on indentureship, 186-187, 199, 289; on irrigation and drainage, 203; on land reclamation, 91n.128; and Langton, 40, 126-127; on plantocracy, 54-55; on repatriation, 200; on rice industry, 54, 190-191; on Ruhomon, 27; and Russell, 46-47; on Salvation Army, 61, 263-264; on sugar industry, 90-91n.127, 186-187, 199; and Taylor, 93n.184, and Thompson, 42-43, 129
Asiatic Society of Bengal, 20, 82n.13
Aurora Plantation, 61, 277, 281

Baldwin, George E., 254
Bande Mataram (Chatterjee), 20
Banerjea, Surendranath, 23, 84n.24
Barbados, 116, 117, 254
Barbour, Sir David, 18, 79, 89n.102, 129-130
Barrett, C. R., 78
Bascom. F. C .S., 73-74, 76-77, 153-154, 267, 303
Bascom, Norman, 63, 74, 76-77, 94-95n.204, 264-265
Beaumont, Joseph, 72
Bechu: arrival in British Guiana, 3, 18, 27, 123, 126, 148; as bachelor, 288; as Bengali, 3, 13, 18-21, 45; as British subject, 70, 83-84n.19, 296; as Christian, 19, 23, 25, 60, 257, 259, 268-269; departure from British Guiana, 30, 71, 79, 254; education of, 3, 4, 18, 19, 82n.7, 122, 147, 257; employers of, 24-25; home in Georgetown, 24; Indian influences on,

309

Index

17-23, 82n.8; jobs held by, 4, 18, 19, 33, 122-123; and missionaries, 18; origins of, 3, 17-18, 82n.8, 122; as orphan, 257; passport request of, denied, 291-297; shipmates of, 68; signature of, 40, 42, 85n.30; travels of, 126; upbringing of, 125-126
—adversaries and critics: F. C. S. Bascom, 73-74, 153-154; Norman Bascom, 76-77; Bethune, 14, 43-44, 130-131, 149; Boyle, 223, 292; Canon, 45; "Civis Mundi," 45, 137-40; Africans, 247-248; de Jonge, 298; Harvey, 235-236; Langton, 40-41, 106, 111, 112, 126-127; letter of "Well-Wisher," 49-50; letter of "West Coast," 132-133; "Ramsing," 242, 247; Russell, 46-47, 141-145; Taylor, 290-291; Thompson, 42-43, 129; Van Nooten, 34, 36, 107, 144; vilification generally, 10, 69-70, 76, 79
—indentureship: Enmore Plantation, 3, 6-7, 14, 32-47, 67, 127, 148, 289; status, 122, 291; termination, 15, 47, 145, 149, 293-294, 296-298; worker, 3, 18, 24, 33-47, 59, 67, 98-100, 120
—inspirers and supporters: Adamson, 81n.1; "Admirer of Bechu's talent" to *Daily Chronicle,* 156; Bhagri, 73, 75-76; Brougham, 292; *Daily Chronicle,* 232-233; friendships generally, 25, 84-85n.29; Gladwin, 14, 120; Hemming, 15; McTurk, 177-178; Olivier, 15, 79, 150-151; "One of Mixed Race," 241-242; Ramsawmy, 45; Ruhomon, 16-17, 27, 43-46, 57, 70-71, 134-136, 224-225, 240-241; Shirley, 16, 240-241; J. R. Wharton, 38, 109
—letters: to *Argosy,* 40-44, 54-55, 57-58; to Boyle, 293-294; to *Daily Chronicle,* 14, 15, 33-38, 47-54, 58-60, 98-100, 106-110, 112-118, 129, 132-133, 143-145, 174-178, 237-239, 254-258, 261-262, 272-273; to Hamilton, 152-154; to Immigration Agent General, 292-296; to legislature, 71; response by readers, 33-47, 101-106, 110-111, 179, 182, 216; to Secretary of State of India, 79-80
—Norman Commission: commentary on, 3, 4, 6, 13-14, 18, 31, 41, 118-132, 176-177; memorandums, 37, 67-68, 119-121, 288-289; and Norman, 19; testimony, 33, 48, 78, 81n.1, 87n.83, 122-126, 131, 153-154, 238
—as political leader: as activist, 143-145, 150, 177, 300; compared to Alexander Alexander, 61-66, 260- 262, 279- 280, 297; compared to Rohlehr, 60; compared to Ruhomon, 179; compared to Vivekananda, 23; influences on, 17-23, 227-228, 248-253; libel charges against Bechu, 9, 15, 53, 63, 72-81, 81n.1, 303; mystique of, 17; radicalism of, 15, 72, 129; as symbol, 14, 79; wit of, 13, 146-148
—political views on: Africans, 52, 59-60, 115-118, 155, 164, 179, 254; agricultural alternatives in British Guiana, 116; Arab confederacies, 117; Bengal, 169; British rule, 23, 116-118; Burma, 169; Church and scripture, 258-260, 268; Colonial Office, 10; commutation of indentureship, 69; coolies, 40, 70-71, 90n.118, 115-118, 164, 176-177, 245, 261, 300, 302-304; Cove and John Plantation, 67, 77, 153-154; desertion of workers, 61, 272; economic reform, 50, 118; Hamilton, 152-154; heathenism, 259; Hindus, 268; Immigrant Agent General, 6-7,

14, 47, 52, 70, 76, 109, 112, 124, 170, 230, 288; immigrant rights, 5, 9-10, 16, 54, 68, 70-71, 79-80, 221, 246, 288-289; immigration increase, 49, 125, 159, 170, 175-176, 236, 256; immigration system, 59, 68-69, 118, 152-154, 157, 176, 235-236, 238-239, 297-298; indentured workers, 15, 38, 42, 49, 79-80, 155-156, 237, 245, 254, 280; indentureship agreements, 98-100, 108; jobbers, 273-274; land allocation to coolies, 48, 170; Madras interpreters, 71, 302; Muslims, 268; Non Pareil Plantation, 5, 34-35, 36, 112, 113, 143-145; plantation operations, 145-146, 156-157; plantation owners treatment of workers, 9, 14, 107, 280; Planters' Association, 52; plantocracy, 38, 42, 48-60, 72, 76, 155, 176-177, 178, 298; prison, 272-274; reindentureship, 50, 52, 159-160, 164-165, 170, 223-224, 226, 229, 230, 238-239; repatriation to India, 48, 50, 125, 177, 223-224; request to leave British Guiana, 291-293; rice industry, 52, 159-160, 165, 169-170; Rohomon (A.) and Company, 24-25, 47 175; Salvation Army, 60, 61, 176, 257, 280; Sealy, 154; Secretary of State for India, 78, 79; Sendall, 79; sexual exploitation of Indian women, 7, 67-69, 121, 125, 239, 289; silence of, 201; Spencer, 154; sugar industry, 8, 13, 116, 117, 155, 157-158, 159-160, 169-171, 221-222; task work, 120, 124; Trinidad, 3, 122; tyranny of plantation drivers, 9, 14, 52, 67, 177, 222, 246, 288; Uganda, 117; unemployment, 91-92n.151, 261; union of West Indies with United States, 84n.19; wages paid to indentured workers, 38, 40, 100, 106-107, 113, 117, 164-165, 170, 176-177, 221-222, 235, 237, 245, 279, 280, 289, 299; working conditions on plantations, 4, 5, 8-10, 13-14, 123
Bengal, 19-22, 83n.17, 169
Bengalis, 137-138, 140
Berbice, 54, 190, 227, 228, 237, 276. *See also* Corentyne Coast
Berbice Gazette, 189
Bethune, G. W., 14, 43-44, 79, 82n.10, 87n.83, 130-131
Bhagri, 9, 73-76, 78, 303-304
Birmingham Post, 239-241
Bisnauth, Dale, ix
Blacks. *See* Africans
Blairmont Plantation, 89-90n.113, 94n.195
Bovell, H. A., 35
Boyle, Cavendish, 89n.104, 223, 230, 292-293
British Guiana. *See* Coolies; Economy; Immigration and immigrants; Indenture system; Indians; Plantocracy; Sugar industry; Rice industry
Brougham, Henry, 292
Burma, 169, 303

Calcutta, 18, 19
Cameron, E. D., 78
Campbell, W. Middleton, 90n.115, 212
Canon, Josa, 45
Caribbean historiography, ix-x
Caste system, 3

310

Index

Census of British Guiana 1841, 185
Chamberlain, 115, 151, 166, 176, 251
Chatterjee, Bankim Chandra, 20, 21, 83n.17
Children's Protection Society, 45
"Civis Mundi," 45, 137-140
Cocoa industry, 198
Coffee industry, 116, 198
College of Fort William, 20, 82n.13
Colonial Government Office, 212-213
Colonial Loans Act, 208
Coolies: and Alexander Alexander, 271- 272, 282-284; *Argosy* on, 182-183, 199-200, 267; British Guiana's dependence on, 160, 161, 185-187, 210-212; classes of, 164-165, 187, 200-201, 220-221, 249, 285; complaints of, 28, 117-120, 285; Curzon on, 182-183; *Daily Chronicle* on, 90n.118, 94n.193, 181-186, 189-190, 206-207, 265-266; desertion of, 92n.162, 270, 272-274, 276; diet of, 283; drought effect on, 203; freedom of, 90n.118, 160-161, 201, 215-216, 225, 232, 265; as jobbers, 271-275, 282, 285; Langton on, 103-106, 111; *Morning Post* on, 182-183; need for more coolies, 89-90nn.113-115; press portrait of, 113; in prison, 246, 247, 274; and rice industry, 89-90n.113, 201-202, 206-207; and Ruhomon, 201-202, 206; settlement incentives, 232-233; settlements for, 190, 199-202, 206, 226-227, 261; as settlers, 184-186, 196-197, 212-213, 219-220, 225, 227-228, 266; and Shirley, 239; treatment of, 15, 34-35, 101-102, 106, 177, 179-180, 196-197, 303-304; violence against drivers by, 94n.195; wages paid to, 94-95n.204, 176, 183-184, 218-219; and Whim Settlement, 206. *See also* Immigration and immigrants; Indentured workers system; Indians; Sugar industry
Corentyne Coast, 54, 86n.48, 190, 203-206, 227-228, 236, 242, 276
Corentyne Settlement, 210-211, 229, 237, 239-240
Cove and John Plantation, 9, 15, 63, 73-78, 153-154, 264, 267, 303
Creoles. *See* Africans
Crosby, James, 4, 5, 10, 72, 144, 261
Crown Land Ordinance, 25, 30-31, 102
Crown Land Regulations, 48
Curzon, Lord, 182-183, 239

Daily Chronicle: on Africans, 181-182, 233; on agricultural diversification, 203-204; on Alexander Alexander, 265-266, 277-279; on F. C. S. Bascom. 73;, on Norman Bascom. 63; Bechu's letters to, 14, 15, 33-38, 47-54, 56-60, 98-100,106-110,112-118, 129, 132-133, 143-145, 174-178, 237-239, 254-258, 261-262, 272-273; and Bhagri case, 9; on British born subjects, 70; and "Civis Mundi," 45; on communication of indentureship, 70; on coolies, 90n.118, 94n.193, 181-183, 189-190, 206-207; on Crown Land Ordinance, 31-32; on desertion of workers, 93n.163, 276-277; on drought, 203-204, 205; on economy, 214; on Immigration Agent General, 10, 17-18; on immigration system, 56, 181-182, 184-186, 296-297; on indentured workers, 174-175, 184-188, 217, 222-223, 231-233; on Indian immigration, 53, 56, 71-72, 80, 183-183; on inquiry of Bechu, 17-18; on irrigation and drainage, 208; and Jardine, 26; on Luard, 217; and Non Pareil Plantation shootings, 34; on Planters' Association, 53; on plantocracy, 53-56, 92n.153, 92n.160, 174-175, 214-216, 304-305; and Ramsawmy, 45; on reindentureship, 52, 231-232; on religion, 269; on repatriation, 232-233; on rice industry, 56, 190, 205; and Rohler, 58; and Ruhomon, 45, 134-136; on Salvation Army, 92n.153, 278-279; and Sendall, 150-151; on settlements for immigrants, 265-266; and Shirley, 81-82n.6; on sugar industry, 51-52, 80, 167, 174-175, 184-188, 203-204, 213-216, 304-305; on Thompson, 130; on wages, 38, 94-95n.204, 185-186
Dalgety, W. T., 236-237
Dargan, Patrick, 37-38
Davis, Darnell N., 30-31
Davson, Henry K., 89-90n.113, 212-213
De Jonge, J. H., 298
De Rinzy, Captain, 34-36, 144-145, 276
Demerariana: Essays, Historical, Critical and Descriptive (Langton), 127
Des Voeux, G. W., 72
Des Voeux, William, 9
Desertion of indentured workers, 61-62, 64, 92n.162, 93n.163, 267-268, 270-274, 276-277
Diamond industry, 25
Drepaul, Thomas, 57, 227-228
Drought in British Guiana, 203-206, 209, 220, 227-228
Duncan, R. G.: on immigration, 237-239, 243-244; as legislator, 51; as planter, 51; and Planters' Association, 171-173; on rice industry, 192-194, 242; on sugar industry, 166, 192-194, 241; on taxation, 268

East Indian Institute, 26, 38, 85n.32
East Indians. *See* Indians
Economy: of British Guiana, 2, 31, 50, 56, 172, 189-190, 196-198, 214, 231-232; and cost of immigration system, 215-216; and indentured workers, 213; of sugar industry, 28, 29, 42, 114-115, 157-159, 217, 305; and unemployment, 91-92n.151, 102, 261; and wages, 34. *See also* Rice industry; Sugar industry
Emancipation, 31-32
Enmore Plantation: Bechu at, 3-7, 14, 32-47, 67, 127, 148, 289; and Bethune, 43, 79, 130; and Creoles, 87n.83, 130; and deputy manager Nicholson, 33; and Hogg, Curtis and Campbell firm, 33; and indentured workers, 32, 131; and Jackson, 78, 79; and labour strikes, 28; management at, 14, 15, 19, 78, 289, 298-299; rice planting on, 168; and sexual abuse of women, 78; working conditions on, 68, 87n.83, 123, 124, 130-131
Evans, George, 74, 75

Flood, Thomas, 26, 84n.29

311

Index

Gall, F. A., 68, 298
Garnett, Harry, 35, 36
Georgetown: city council in, 63-64, 272, 285; Salvation Army in, 60, 265-266, 278, 281
Ghurib Das. *See* Alexander, Alexander (Ghurib Das)
Girmitiyas: The Origins of the Fiji Indians (Lal), x
Gladwin, H. J., 14, 34-35, 41, 120, 144, 293, 296
Gold industry, 25, 195, 198, 210-211, 234, 252
Goldsmith, Oliver, 137
Gordon, Leonard A., 83n.17, 84n.24

Hamilton, George, 77-78, 152-154, 239
Harvey, Francis G., 59, 234-236
Hastings, Warren, 140
Hawaii, 254-255
Helena Settlement, 54, 56, 200, 223, 225-226
Hemming, Sir Augustus, 15, 35, 293, 296-297
Hill, P. H. R., 272-274
Hinduism, 19-22, 221, 268, 269
Hindustani, 71, 286, 302, 303
Hogg, Curtis and Campbell firm, 33
Hogg, Quintin, 36, 90n.115, 164, 210-211
Huis't Dieren estate, 54, 56
Huller, Engelburg, 171

Immigration Agent General: A. H. Alexander as, 78, 145, 148-150; annual reports of, 104-105, 109, 112; and Bechu's work status, 47, 291; and commutation of indentureship, 69; and coolies' complaints, 26, 28-29, 34-35; and Cove and John Plantation investigation, 76; Crosby as, 4, 5, 10, 72, 144, 261; on desertion of workers, 270; inquiry of Bechu, 17-18; King as acting, 293-295; and Madras interpreters, 300-301; on Non Pariel Plantation uprising, 35; and plantocracy, 13-14, 29; and protection for immigrants, 68, 302; and reindenture of immigrants, 223, 230; on repayment for early termination, 293, 296; role of, 4-7, 10, 124; on wages paid by plantations, 38, 119, 170
Immigration and immigrants: and Africans, 250, 251; and Alexander Alexander, 278-279; continuation of, 120-121, 156, 158-159, 163, 193, 234-236; convictions of employers and immigrants under Immigration Ordinance, 1874-1875; cost of, 175, 215-216, 231-232, 235-236, 251-255; Davson on need for, 89-90n.113; and emigration, 250; Fund of British Guiana, 296; increase in, 49, 125, 159, 170, 175-176, 236, 256; law in British Guiana generally, 70, 120; of Madras, 301; ordinance of 1891, 261, 289, 291-292, 299; population in British Guiana, 118, 120, 170, 197, 215, 249-251; rights of, 5, 9-10, 16, 54, 68-71, 79-80, 221, 246, 288-289; as settlers in British Guiana, 245; surplus of, 237; system of, 58, 86n.48, 184-185, 210-211, 214-216, 250, 253, 256, 304-305. *See also* Africans; Coolies; Indenture system; Indentured workers system; Indians; Reindentureship; Repatriation
Immigration Fund Account, 230
Indenture system: *Argosy* on, 186-187, 199; and commutation, 69-70, 196-197; cost of, 234, 251; *Daily Chronicle* on, 174-175, 222-223; development of, 118, 173-174, 176, 235-236; investigation of, 9, 10; Rohler on, 58-59; Russell on, 46-47, 141-142; Sendall on, 173-174; and sugar industry, 1, 2, 9, 24, 69, 152-154, 156-157, 167-168, 251; terms of indentureship, 38, 80, 99-100, 105, 155, 172-173, 197, 209-210, 223, 238-239, 266, 297-298. *See also* Africans; Coolies; Immigration and immigrants; Indentured workers system
Indentured Worker Contract, 99-101, 105, 110-111, 122
Indentured workers system: and Alexander Alexander, 61-62; compared to open labour market, 218; *Daily Chronicle* on, 174-175, 184-190, 213-214; demand for, 56, 218, 233; desertion of, 61-62, 64, 92n.162, 93n.163, 267-268, 270, 272-274, 276-277; on Enmore Plantation, 32; freedom of, 244-245; health of, 89n.103; Indians as, 39, 48, 49, 52, 56; Langton on, 103-104, 110-111; last to arrive in British Guiana, 80; legal protection for, 68; plight of, 15, 61-66, 120-121, 155-156; poverty of, 1, 2; protection for, 68; reduction in, 174, 212; release of, 99; Ruhomon on, 134-135, 241; as slaves, 60, 237, 238; and sugar industry, 56, 171-172, 234-235, 243-245; terms of indentureship, 38, 80, 99-100, 105, 155, 172-173, 197, 209-210, 223, 238-239, 266, 297-298; treatment of, 6, 77, 221-222, 275, 304-305; wages of, 4, 36, 37, 38, 40, 99, 100, 221-222, 233, 235-237, 243-245, 279, 280, 289, 299. *See also* Africans; Coolies; Immigration and immigrants; Indians; Indenture system; Reindentureship; Repatriation; Sugar industry
India: and acceptance of immigration system in British Guiana, 176; and Alexander Alexander, 277; emigration from, 175-176, 182, 186, 223, 235; famine in, 238, 277; religions in, 25; Secretary of State for, 77-79, 152-154, 239. *See also* Indians; Immigration and immigrants; Repatriation
India; The Progress of Her People at Home and Abroad (Ruhomon), 26, 27
Indian Association of Calcutta, 23
Indian National Congress, 22-23
Indians: activists at Non Pareil Plantation, 36-37; and Alexander Alexander, 282-284; born in British Guiana, 170-171; caste system of, 3; and Christianity, 259-260; compared to Africans, 4, 15, 30, 57-59, 163, 179-180, 185, 204-205; contributions to British Guiana, 174, 248; exploitation of immigrants, 5, 6, 15, 101-102; and famine in India, 238, 239; immigration to British Guiana, 52-53, 102, 156, 163, 183-184, 193, 195-196; as indentured workers, 1, 2-3, 44, 48-49, 52, 60, 218; languages of, 71, 303; leaders in British Guiana, 3, 26; peasantry of, 55, 220; and press in British Guiana, 71; racism toward, 136-138; and rice industry, 54-57, 158-160; and Ruhomon, 70-71, 139-40; and Salvation Army, 65; settlements for, 219-220, 226; as settlers in British Guiana, 80, 161, 182-183, 195-196, 203-206, 218, 220-221, 224-225, 229, 236; women exploited sexually, 7, 67-69, 121, 125, 190,

312

Index

239, 289. *See also* Immigration and immigrants; Indenture system; Indentured workers system; India; Repatriation
Interpreters. *See* Hindustani; Madras Interpreters
Ireland, W. Alleyne. *See* "Langton" (W. Alleyne Ireland)
Irrigation and drainage, 191-193, 199, 203, 205, 207-208, 219-220, 225, 227

Jackson, J. F., 78, 79
Jamaica, 65, 116, 185, 277, 287
Jamaica Times, 65, 278-279
Jardine, C. K., 26
Jaundoo, F. E., 84n.29
Jemmott, A. M. B., 258
Jobbers, 273, 274, 282, 285

Kayashtas (literary castes), 3
King, C. B., 293-295
Kingston Social Institution, 277
Kirke, Henry, 27-29, 89n.103
Khan, Gool Mohumad, 84n.29
Kopf, David, 82n.13, 88n.93

La Bonne Intention Plantation, 56, 216
La Penitence home, 282-287
Labour strikes, 28-29, 86n.43, 94n.195, 193
Lal, Brij, x
Land reform, 26
"Langton" (W. Alleyne Ireland): on Africans, 128; Bechu on, 86n.46, on convictions of employers and immigrants under Immigration Ordinance, 1874-1875; on Creoles, 128; *Demerariana* by, 127; on indentured workers, 40-41, 127-128; on Non Pareil Plantation shootings, 103-106; on Norman Commission, 127-128; and Russell, 143; on sugar industry, 128; on wages paid to immigrants, 110-111, 128
Laurence, K. O., 28, 85n.38
Look Lai, W. 28
Luard, E. C., 56, 216-217, 274, 287
Lucas, Charles P., 212-213
Lusignan Plantation, 68, 289

Macaulay, Thomas, 45, 46, 88n.93, 137-140
Madras interpreters, 26, 71, 94n.93, 300-301, 302
Mangru, 15
Marionville Plantation, 270
McTurk, Sir Michael, 178
Missionaries, 16, 18, 19
Mitchell, Robert, 18
Morison, Mr., 270
Morning Post (London), 182-184
Morris, Dr., 185, 193, 197-198
Mudaliar, Veerasawmy, 26, 84n.29
Murray, H. E., 90n.114
Muslims, 268, 269

Naoroji, Dadabhai, 26, 85n.32
Nath, Dwarka, 13, 90n.122
Negroes. *See* Africans

Nehru, Jawaharlal, 22, 83n.16, 84n.25
New Amsterdam, 300-301
New Century Review, 236, 279
Newspapers. *See Argosy*; *Berbice Gazette*; *Birmingham Post*; *Daily Chronicle*; *Jamaica Times*; *Morning Post* (London); *New Century Review*
Non Pareil Plantation: deserters from, 267; and Hogg, 36; indentured workers on, 28, 108-109; and Indian activists, 36-37; influence of, on other plantations, 119, 123-124; Langton on, 103-104; shootings at, 14, 34, 35, 37, 98, 103-104, 129, 143-145; uprising on, 5, 8, 28, 36-37, 68, 112-113, 144-145; wages paid at, 38, 41, 87n.64, 107; and J. R. Wharton, 101
Norman, Sir Henry, 18, 19, 30-31, 79, 88-89nn.102-103, 170
Norman Commission: on Africans, 233; on agricultural diversification, 49, 194-196; and A. H. Alexander, 88n.102; and Barbour, 79; and Bethune, 130-131; on coolies, 37; on Crown Land Regulations, 49; and Davis, 30-31; findings of, 6, 70, 194-198; and Indian workers' grievances, x, 197-198; and Langton, 6, 127-128; memorandums to, 37, 67-68, 191-121, 288-289; and Sir Henry Norman 18, 19, 30-31, 79; and Olivier, 43, 79; on peasant land holdings, 194-196; on plantocracy, 55, 194-196; proposal of, 115; recommendations to, 193, 224; on reindentureship, 50; report of, 176-177, 194-198; on rice industry, 198; and Rohlehr, 58, 179-180; Ruhomon on, 134; and Russell, 46; on sexual exploitation of women, 7; 18-19, 30-31, 79; and sugar industry investigation, 1, 3-4, 14, 18, 48-49, 194, 196-197; and sugar industry subsidy, 48; testimony to, 33, 38, 48, 78, 81n.1, 87n.83, 88-89nn.102-104, 122-126, 131, 153-154, 238; and Thompson, 42, 130; on wages, 28, 89n.104, 119-120; as West Indian Royal Commission, 28, 30-31, 70, 193, 224

Ogle Plantation, 68, 299
Olivier, Sydney, 15, 43, 79, 81n.5, 130-131, 150-151
O'Malley, E. L., 299
Orientalism, 88n.93
Overseers. *See* Plantation drivers
Ozzard, A. T., 74, 75

Panama, 114, 116
Parker, Charles, 90n.115
Peasant land holdings, 194-196
"Perseus," 301-302
Plantation drivers: *Argosy* on, 177-178; coolies' violence against, 94n.195; role of, 5, 6, 67, 119, 131, 180, 247-248; tyranny of, 9, 14, 52, 67, 222, 246, 288
Plantation owners: on Alexander Alexander, 287; donations to Salvation Army, 66; financial burdens of, 183-184, 252-253, 254; operations of farms, 145-148, 156-157, 173-174, 179-180; and peasant land holding, 194-196; on reindentureship, 50-51, 238-239; treatment of workers, 65, 178, 182-183, 215, 275

313

Index

Plantations. *See* specific plantations
Planters' Association, 52, 90n.114, 171-173, 175-176
Plantocracy: and African workers, 250; Alexander on, 62, 278; *Argosy* on, 55; in British Guiana, 2, 10, 32, 72; criticism of, 51; *Daily Chronicle* on, 53-56, 174-175, 214-216, 304-305; and Davis, 30; and Immigration Agent General, 13; and indentureship, 171-173, 210; Norman Commission on, 55, 194-196; Ruhomon on, 57; standard of, 218-219; and sugar industry depression, 170, 212; system of, 38, 48-60, 76, 155, 167, 170, 194, 210-212; Thompson on, 129; and worker desertion, 64, 93n.163. *See also* Indenture system; Indentured workers system; Plantation owners; Sugar industry
Portuguese, 25, 249
Postal system, 256
Potter, Lesley M., ix
Prisons, 246-248, 274

Racial diversity, 27-28, 30. *See also* Africans; Coolies; Indentured workers system; Indians
Racism, 30, 43-44, 46, 59, 65, 132, 136-138, 275
Ramnarine, Tyran, x, 13
Ramphul, Joshua, 71, 300, 301
Ramsawmy, 45
"Ramsing," 242, 247, 253
Raychaudhuri, Tapan, 21-22
Reindentureship: cost of, 26, 229; critics of, 163; plantation owners on, 50-51, 238-239; support for, 158, 160, 164, 223-225, 230. *See also* Indenture system; Repatriation
Repatriation: *Argosy* on, 200; Bechu on, 48, 50, 125, 159-160, 164-165, 170, 223-224, 226, 229, 230, 238-239; cost of, 90n.122, 220, 223-224, 232-233; *Daily Chronicle* on, 52, 232-233; Duncan on, 172; fraudulent offer of, 276-277; government refusals of requests for, 125, 177; Indians' settlement in British Guiana versus, 182, 201, 212, 225, 236; statistics on, 53, 125. *See also* Indenture system; Reindentureship
Rice industry: as alternative to sugar industry, 159-160, 168, 169, 188, 193, 198; *Argosy* on, 190-191; in Bengal, 169; in Burma, 169; and coolies, 89-90n.113, 198, 201-202, 206-207; on Corentyne Coast, 228, 236, 242; *Daily Chronicle* on, 205; and drought, 205-207, 227-228; on Enmore Plantation, 168; establishment of, 50-51, 61, 163, 165; failure of, 205; and global demand, 169-170; in India, 192; and Indian immigration, 54-57, 158, 169, 192; Norman Commission on, 198; threats to, 191
Rodney, Walter, 59, 67
Rohlehr, J. M., 58-59, 179-180, 184
Rohomon, A., 47, 175
Rohomon (A.) and Company, 24-25
Roy, Ram Mohan, 20, 82-83n.14
Royal Agricultural and Commercial Society, 28, 166, 188
Ruhomon, Joseph: as advocate, 15-16, 43-46, 134-135, 179 300; on Africans, 26; on agricultural diversification, 201-202; *Argosy* on, 27, 85n 35; Aryanism of, 85n.35; and Bechu, 84n.29; on "Civis Mundi," 136-137, 139-140; on coolies, 201-202, 206, 209; on Corentyne Settlement, 206, 210-211; on drought, 209; on indentured workers, 134-136, 241; *India; The Progress of Her People at Home and Abroad* by, 26-27; and Indians, 70-71, 139-140; on land distribution to freed workers, 201-202; and Macaulay, 46, 140; on Norman Commission, 134, 224-225; on plantocracy, 57; on racism, 136-137; on reindentureship, 224-225; on Shirley, 240-241; and Thompson, 134, 135; on Whim Settlement, 210-211, 224-225
Ruhomon, Peter, 13
Russell, John, 46-47, 141-145

Salvation Army: and Alexander Alexander, 61-62, 176, 262-263, 278, 284; *Argosy* on, 61, 263-264; and Norman Bascom, 63, 264-265; and Christianity, 259; *Daily Chronicle* on, 92n.153; in Georgetown, 60, 260-262, 285; and indentured workers, 62, 262; and poverty of immigrants, 65; role of, 263-264; shelter provided by, 176; and *War Cry*, 277; and Widgery, 258
Sealy, F. D., 73-75, 77-78, 154
Secretary of State for India, 77-79, 152-154, 239
Secretary of State for the Colonies, 79, 251
Secretary of the Institute of Mines and Forests, 252
Secretary to the Government of India in the Department of Revenue and Agriculture, 239
Sen, Keshab Chandra, 83n.16
Sendall, Sir Walter, 17, 52, 79, 90n.114, 148, 150-151, 171-173, 203, 252
Settlements. *See* Corentyne Settlement; Helena Settlement; Whim Settlement
Sexual exploitation of women, 7, 67-69, 121, 125, 239, 289
Shirley, H. J., 16, 81-82n.6, 86n.48, 237-241, 244
Singhal, D. P., 20, 82-83n.14
Sobers, George, 249
Spencer, Daniel, 77, 154
Standard, 113
Stead, Mr., 174-175
Strikes. *See* Labour strikes
Success Plantation, 29, 92n.162, 169, 276
Sugar industry: and African workers, 233; aid to, 8, 48, 211, 216; *Argosy* on, 90-91n.127, 186-187, 199; compared to gold industry, 252; and coolies, 176, 187-188, 200, 210-212, 303-304; on crop diversification, 49; *Daily Chronicle* on, 183-190, 203-204, 213-214, 304-305; depression in, 165- 170, 193; and desertion of workers, 62, 270; economy of, 28, 29, 42, 114-115, 157-159, 166-167, 217, 305; financial recovery of, 213-215, 218; in Hawaii, 254-255; indenture system in, 1, 2, 9, 24, 69, 152-154, 156, 167-168, 251; indentured worker demand in, 56, 158, 172-174, 192, 213-214, 251, 253; Indian workers in, 1, 2, 56, 156, 176, 183-184, 193, 212-213, 234; and labour availability, 218-219, 233; and labour strikes, 28, 29, 86.43, 193; and Norman Commission, 1, 3-4, 14, 18, 233; Ruhomon on,

Index

201-202; Russell on, 142; stability of, 171-173, 216, 220-221, 250, 251; and Venn Commission, 6; and wages paid, 29, 86n.43, 87n.64, 172, 215, 216-219, 237, 242, 305. *See also* Indenture system; Indentured workers system; Plantation owners; Plantocracy; and specific plantations
Sugar Planters Association, 28
Surjudass, 289, 290-291
Swan, R. A., 299

Tagore, Rabindranath, 21
Taxation, 268
Taylor, Henry W., 69, 93n.184, 289-291
Thompson, James, 42-43, 86n.46, 129-130, 134-135
Thorne, J. P., 37
Tikasingh, Gerad, ix
Trevelyan, Sir George, 88n.93
Trinidad, 3, 85n.38, 107, 115-116, 118, 122, 174, 185
Tucker, Booth, 279

Uganda, 117
Unemployment, 91-92n.151, 102, 261
University of Guyana, ix
University of Warwick, ix

Van Nooten, Gerard, 8, 34, 36-37, 40, 107, 144
Venn Commission, 6
Vergenoegen Plantation, 299
Vivekananda, Swami, 21-22, 23, 84n.25

Wages: Alexander Alexander on, 94-95n.204, 279; *Daily Chronicle* on, 38, 94-95n.204, 185-186; Immigration Agent General on, 38, 119, 170; increase in, 90n.114; in indentured worker contract, 99-100; of indentured workers, 36, 37, 38, 99-100, 221-222, 233, 235-236, 237, 243, 244, 245; Langton on, 103-104, 110-111, 128; at Non Pareil plantation, 40-41, 87n.64; Norman Commission on, 119-120; paid by plantations, 29, 34-35, 40, 89n.104, 101, 107, 164, 216-217, 241, 289; "Ramsing" on, 242-243; reduction of, 85n.38, 86n.43, 87n.64, 89n.104, 98, 117; Russell on, 142; Shirley on, 239-240; stoppage of, 299-300; Van Nooten on, 40, 144
War Cry (A. Alexander), 65, 277
West India Royal Commission. *See* Norman Commission
West Indies, 84n.19, 116
Wharton, J. R., 38, 44, 84n.29, 101-102, 105-106, 109
Wharton, James, 26
Wharton, W. Hewley, 26, 84-85n.29
Whim Settlement, 54, 56, 206-207, 210-211, 224-227, 229
Widgery, Mrs., 257-259
Wingfield, Edward, 90n.113
World Parliament of Religion, 21

315

www.ingramcontent.com/pod-product-compliance
Lightning Source LLC
Chambersburg PA
CBHW050838230426
43667CB00012B/2048